W9-BEW-349

Trauma Services for Women in Substance Abuse Treatment

Trauma Services for Women in Substance Abuse Treatment

AN INTEGRATED APPROACH

Denise Hien
Lisa Caren Litt
Lisa R. Cohen
Gloria M. Miele
Aimee Campbell

AMERICAN PSYCHOLOGICAL ASSOCIATION
WASHINGTON, DC

Published by
American Psychological Association
750 First Street, NE
Washington, DC 20002
www.apa.org

To order
APA Order Department
P.O. Box 92984
Washington, DC 20090-2984
Tel: (800) 374-2721; Direct: (202) 336-5510
Fax: (202) 336-5502; TDD/TTY: (202) 336-6123
Online: www.apa.org/books/
E-mail: order@apa.org

In the U.K., Europe, Africa, and the Middle East, copies may be ordered from
American Psychological Association
3 Henrietta Street
Covent Garden, London
WC2E 8LU England

Typeset in Goudy by Circle Graphics, Inc., Columbia, MD

Printer: Maple-Vail Book Manufacturing Group, Binghamton, NY
Cover Designer: Berg Design, Albany, NY
Technical/Production Editor: Devon Bourexis

The opinions and statements published are the responsibility of the authors, and such opinions and statements do not necessarily represent the policies of the American Psychological Association.

Library of Congress Cataloging-in-Publication Data

Trauma services for women in substance abuse treatment : an integrated approach / Denise Hien . . . [et al.].—1st ed.
    p. ; cm.
  Includes bibliographical references and index.
  ISBN-13: 978-1-4338-0410-6
  ISBN-10: 1-4338-0410-7
  1. Dual diagnosis. 2. Post-traumatic stress disorder. 3. Substance abuse. 4. Psychic trauma.
I. Hien, Denise. II. American Psychological Association.
  [DNLM: 1. Stress Disorders, Post-Traumatic—complications. 2. Stress Disorders, Post-Traumatic—therapy. 3. Substance Abuse Treatment Centers. 4. Substance-Related Disorders—complications. 5. Substance-Related Disorders—therapy. 6. Women.
WM 170 T777455 2009]
  RC564.68.T73 2009
  362.29—dc22
                                                                                              2008025624

British Library Cataloguing-in-Publication Data

A CIP record is available from the British Library.

Printed in the United States of America
First Edition

In Greek mythology, Pandora, the first woman,
created by the God of Fire and endowed by the gods with many gifts,
was treacherously presented with a box containing all the evils that
could trouble mankind. When a naturally curious
Pandora opened the box, all of the evils flew out and spread
over the earth. Realizing what had happened,
Pandora struggled to close the box and was able to do so
in time to keep Hope from escaping. This book is dedicated to the
women we work with and provide treatment for, whose hope
and endurance serve as our inspiration.

CONTENTS

PREFACE

Many substance abuse treatment providers believe that trauma treatment is not possible until sobriety has been achieved, for fear that combined treatments will open a Pandora's box of troubles that will overwhelm both clients and clinicians. Yet emerging research reveals that many women want to and are able to successfully receive trauma-related services in the context of their work in addictions recovery. The field has produced a growing body of manualized treatment approaches that attempt to tackle these problems in a safe and manageable format, promoting psychological growth and recovery and minimizing risk of relapse. Many of these approaches, however, have yet to be widely adopted in community treatment settings because of a number of barriers, including staff and client attitudes, limited training and supervision, staffing challenges, and financial considerations.

This book is our effort to help reclaim Pandora's virtues—to offer hope and guidance to client survivors of trauma and the clinicians and programs helping them with their recovery. We wrote it for program directors and other decision makers who are interested in designing programs based on the specific approaches and treatments described herein. This book is also relevant for clinicians working in substance abuse treatment settings who are interested in making adaptations to their programs and practices in order to offer the women they treat interventions that are attentive to trauma. Finally, we wrote this book for the many clinicians and researchers who are invested in improving the quality of substance abuse treatment and seek to deepen their understanding of the interrelated nature of trauma and substance addictions. In the service of these goals, our book brings together work being done in the fields of trauma and addiction using a blended clinical and research approach to address the challenges inherent in integrating and tailoring trauma services within addictions treatment settings.

We, the authors, are a team of providers and treatment research scientists (i.e., psychologists and social workers) who have worked together for more than 10 years in community addictions treatment in New York City, integrating the science and practice of treating women with co-occurring disorders. The material presented is an outgrowth of our work during this time that has consisted of developing, testing, and implementing interventions for substance-abusing women with comorbid posttraumatic stress disorder and complex trauma histories. Our work enables us to bring a unique perspective to this material. Collectively, we founded and developed The Women's Health Project Treatment and Research Center, a specialty program for women with trauma and addictions in a community hospital setting, St. Luke's–Roosevelt Hospital Center. We also bring our experience leading numerous clinical studies on trauma and addiction funded by the National Institute on Alcohol Abuse and Alcoholism and the National Institute on Drug Abuse (NIDA), including leading a multi-site national effectiveness trial for this population of women with the NIDA Clinical Trials Network (CTN). The CTN is a partnership between NIDA, clinical researchers, and community-based treatment providers with the fundamental goal of improving the quality of treatment for patients with drug dependence by conducting rigorous research on the effectiveness of promising new treatment innovations and promoting the widespread adoption of treatments that have been shown to be effective. The CTN grew in part out of a landmark study by the Institute of Medicine (1998), which concluded that there existed a serious gap between the research enterprise and community-based treatment. Considerable advances were being made through research on both behavioral and pharmacological treatments for substance use disorders, conducted mainly at tertiary care and research centers, yet the evidence supporting these advances was little known outside of research circles. Dissemination activities were limited, new treatments were slow to be adopted by the majority of treatment providers throughout the United States, and evidence was often lacking to support the effectiveness of these new treatments when transported into community-based treatment settings.

As a result of these endeavors, we have gained a comprehensive picture of current practices in substance abuse treatment programs across the country. In our view, many problems of substance-abusing clients who are also in recovery from trauma are not being adequately addressed by standard treatments. Therefore, we provide important background material and practical information on how to minimize the gap between what is needed and what is typically offered to more effectively serve this complex, chronic, and in-need group.

The women we work with and provide treatment for, whose lives at times seem overwhelming and filled with hopelessness, have been our inspiration. As our treatment has helped open new possibilities for them, we hope to do the same for providers who may feel that there is little possibility for these women to transcend their pasts and move forward. Our clients come to us with multiple challenges that include a range of mental health, medical, family, and financial problems, which further complicate their efforts to obtain and sustain recovery and often contribute to a sense of mistrust and avoidance. As a result, these clients are typically seen as difficult and resistant, leading providers to feel ill-equipped and at times resentful. Viewing our clients in the context of their trauma histories allows us to connect the seemingly disparate fragments of their addictive and often self-destructive behavior by understanding these behaviors as efforts to manage the aftermath of events that were frightening and outside of their own control. One of the principles of our work, and one that we hope to convey throughout this book, is a strengths-based approach in which we view symptoms and what has often been considered "pathology" as efforts to adapt to incredibly stressful life circumstances.

In addition to the many women we have worked with over our collective decades in the field, we would like to acknowledge the NIDA CTN, the Long Island Regional Node of the CTN, the seven community treatment programs and six Regional Research and Training Centers that participated in the CTN Women and Trauma Study, the staff of The Women's Health Project Treatment and Research Center, the staff of the Addiction Institute of New York and the Department of Psychiatry, St. Luke's–Roosevelt Hospital Center, and the Social Intervention Group in the Columbia University School of Social Work, for their support and commitment.

Trauma Services for Women in Substance Abuse Treatment

INTRODUCTION

Substance use disorders plague millions of women nationwide. Research has shown that for the majority of women seeking help for substance use disorders, interpersonal violence is a backdrop of life experience interwoven in their efforts to achieve abstinence. The women's movement in the late 1970s focused national consciousness on the escalating rates of interpersonal violence in the lives of women. Nearly 3 decades later, advances in clinical research have underscored the continuing urgent need for women's services that can address interpersonal violence and related psychological consequences. For women, substance abuse is one of the most significant factors associated with a history of victimization. Yet still, in community treatment programs for addictions, trauma-related services are few, and many addictions clinicians continue to fear that raising these issues will bring further harm to women, placing them at risk of continuing violence or chronic relapse to addictive behavior.

With this discrepancy in mind, the aims of this book are threefold:

1. Describe the key concepts necessary for understanding the trauma-related issues facing women in substance abuse treatment.

2. Identify the specific, yet multifaceted needs of our clients in order to advance a problem-oriented approach to treatment and program planning.
3. Anticipate and address the real-world challenges of implementing trauma-focused therapeutic approaches in community-based substance abuse treatment.

In Part I of the book, The Relationship Between Trauma and Substance Abuse, we present the current knowledge base on trauma exposure, posttraumatic stress disorder (PTSD), complex PTSD, and related psychiatric comorbidity among women in addictions treatment. The aim of Part I is to present the empirical literature gathered over more than 20 years of study that serves to characterize women in recovery and their unique challenges as well as the most effective treatments available for substance abuse and trauma comorbidity.

In Part II, The Impact of Trauma on Functioning, we cover four major functional areas (i.e., emotion regulation, interpersonal functioning, parenting, and physical consequences) that are directly affected by trauma exposure, and we provide critical information for understanding the ways that living with trauma and addiction can affect and be affected by these important areas of functioning.

Finally, in Part III, Strategies for Implementation, we present essential elements for considering implementation of trauma services into addictions treatment settings, including how to train and supervise clinicians to provide these services in addictions treatment programs and how to address many of the clinical challenges that arise, with special consideration given to ethnocultural influences in many of our clients' backgrounds. Throughout the book, case examples and clinical insights are offered to highlight particular client symptoms and experiences related to implementing trauma services in substance abuse settings.

We recognize that women with trauma histories and addiction are not a homogeneous group. They may be women who were traumatized as children or women whose first traumatic exposure occurred in adulthood. They may have severe and persistent psychiatric problems or they may have very circumscribed addictions problems. Primarily, the women described in this book experienced victimization in childhood and have also been revictimized in their adult lives. In our experience, this is the most common background for women presenting for addictions treatment. In reviewing the literature, we also highlight PTSD, which informs much of our knowledge on survivors of trauma, as well as the broader literature on other trauma-related symptoms and presentations.

One of the primary purposes of this book is to provide a framework for considering multimodal treatment approaches that can address all levels and types of problems associated with traumatic stress exposure. With this volume, we hope to encourage clinic directors and other stakeholders in addiction settings to use the multimodal treatment framework that we present to inform decisions regarding how or even whether to integrate trauma services into their programs. We recognize that external program factors will influence these decisions about what services to provide women with trauma—whether care includes availability of trauma treatment; psychopharmacology; or medical, dental, educational, occupational, and other relevant services, for example. Alternatively, a program may be sensitive to and aware that many of their clients have trauma exposures (i.e., the program may be *trauma informed*; e.g., see Harris & Fallot, 2001; Jahn Moses, Reed, Mazelis, & D'Ambrosio, 2003) but will choose to send clients to other programs for additional services. In this book we try to honor the range of ways that a program or clinician might either consider providing services directly or think with an eye toward locating services for a traumatized client, given available resources.

In this volume, we also identify several specific treatment models to illustrate the kinds of approaches that we know can be helpful and that currently have an evidence base to accompany a manualized treatment approach. We recognize that the examples of specific treatments that we name, and thus highlight, do not compose a comprehensive list of treatment models, and we do not want to suggest that only these treatments can or should be used. Rather, we provide them as examples.

Finally, we include three appendixes to refer to specific approaches, assessments, and training methods that we can recommend on the basis of our own direct experience. As attention to this important area increases, the list continues to broaden with new and helpful additions.

I

THE RELATIONSHIP
BETWEEN TRAUMA
AND SUBSTANCE ABUSE

1

PERSPECTIVES ON TRAUMATIC STRESS, POSTTRAUMATIC STRESS DISORDER, AND COMPLEX POSTTRAUMATIC STRESS DISORDER

The field of trauma has grown tremendously over the past 2 decades. Contributors to the field include an interdisciplinary group of international researchers, clinicians, neuroscientists, psychobiologists, nurse practitioners, primary care physicians, and social scientists. In this chapter we present a current understanding of modern traumatology and a review of the most salient issues and debates in the field. We provide a framework that substance abuse providers and supervisors can use when considering treatment options for their trauma-exposed clients. We lay the groundwork for program directors to begin considering alteration of their treatment programs to address trauma and trauma-related problems. To do this, we review the literature regarding the long-term effects of trauma in women, which may often take the form of posttraumatic stress disorder (PTSD) or complex PTSD. Next, we discuss the integral connection between trauma, trauma-related psychological conditions such as PTSD, and substance use disorders. Finally, we examine models and hypotheses about the pathways between trauma and addictions.

Over the past 2 decades, the significant co-occurrence of trauma exposure and substance use disorders among women has become increasingly apparent. Although men are, overall, more likely to be exposed to trauma in their lives, women are more often exposed to chronic high-impact trauma such as childhood sexual violence, physical abuse, and neglect (S. H. Stewart, Ouimette, & Brown, 2002). In addition, once exposed to trauma, women are more vulnerable to developing PTSD than men (Breslau, Davis, Andreski, Peterson, & Schultz, 1997; Cottler, Nishith, & Compton, 2001). Findings from a large-scale epidemiological survey highlight these gender differences, showing that in the U.S. population, approximately 61% of men and 51% of women are exposed to trauma, yet 5% of men meet criteria for PTSD compared with 10% of women (Kessler, Sonnega, Bromet, Hughes, & Nelson, 1995). Exhibit 1.1 summarizes what is known about PTSD and substance abuse disorders.

The relevance of trauma and trauma-related disorders to understanding the clinical presentation of women with addictions has also become more evident with studies documenting the frequent co-occurrence of PTSD and substance use disorders, particularly among female clients. For example, rates of PTSD among substance abusers range from 14% to 60% (Brady, Dansky, Back, Foa, & Carroll, 2001; Donovan, Padin-Rivera, & Kowaliw, 2001; Najavits, Weiss, & Shaw, 1997; Triffleman, 2003). Substance-dependent women who have been exposed to interpersonal trauma and violence represent a particularly high-risk group. The majority of women dually diagnosed with PTSD and substance use disorders are not only victims of childhood abuse (P. J. Brown & Wolfe, 1994; Polusny & Follete, 1995) but also more vulnerable to repeated interpersonal traumas throughout their lives (Dansky, Saladin, Brady, Kilpatrick, & Resnick, 1995; Fullilove et al., 1993). These women tend to present to treatment with high rates of other comorbid disorders and marked interpersonal, behavioral, and affect regulation deficits that significantly complicate treatment and prognosis (Brady, Dansky, Sonne, & Saladin, 1998).

PTSD is one of the most significant and common psychiatric consequences of traumatic exposure, a syndrome marked by symptoms of intense horror or fear following a psychologically distressing event involving a real or perceived threat to physical integrity. This disorder typically results from an extreme, catastrophic, or overwhelming experience and is accompanied by the following symptoms: reexperiencing the event through flashbacks, nightmares, and intrusive memories; avoidance of stimuli associated with the event; and increased physiological arousal (Amdur, Larsen, & Liberzon, 2000; American Psychiatric Association, 2000).

In the *Diagnostic and Statistical Manual of Mental Disorders* (*DSM–IV–TR*; 4th ed., text rev.; American Psychiatric Association, 2000) an event is considered traumatic if the person experienced, witnessed, or was confronted with an event or series of events that involved actual or threatened death or serious injury, or threat to the physical integrity of self or others, and if the person's response to the traumatic event involved fear, helplessness, or horror. Traumatic events may be categorized into three general types: (a) intentional human causes (e.g., terrorist attacks, combat, sexual or physical abuse),

EXHIBIT 1.1
Important Facts Substance Abuse Treatment Clinicians Should Know About Posttraumatic Stress Disorder and Substance Use Disorders

Gender differences
- Posttraumatic stress disorder (PTSD) is 2 to 3 times more common in women than in men.
- Among clients in substance abuse treatment, 55% to 99% of women with substance abuse problems report a lifetime history of physical, sexual, or both physical and sexual abuse.
- Most women with this co-occurring disorder experienced childhood physical, sexual, or both physical and sexual abuse; men with both disorders typically experienced crime victimization or war trauma.

Profile severity
- Women with PTSD tend to abuse the most serious substances (i.e., cocaine and opioids); however, abuse of prescription medications, marijuana, and alcohol are also common.
- Women with PTSD and substance abuse have a more severe clinical profile than those with just one of these disorders.
- Women with both disorders also suffer a variety of life problems, including interpersonal and medical problems, maltreatment of their children, custody battles, homelessness, HIV risk, and domestic violence.

Risk of continued cycle of violence
- Women with PTSD and substance abuse are more likely to experience further trauma than women with substance abuse alone.
- Repeated trauma is common in domestic violence, child abuse, and some substance-using lifestyles (e.g., the drug trade).
- While under the influence of substances, a person may be more vulnerable to trauma (e.g., a woman drinking at a bar may go home with a stranger and be assaulted).
- Perpetrators of violent assault often use substances at the time of the assault.
- Helping the client protect against future trauma is likely to be an important part of work in treatment.

Treatment complications
- Counselors should recognize and help clients understand that becoming abstinent from substances does not resolve PTSD; in fact, some PTSD symptoms become worse with abstinence. Both disorders must be addressed in treatment.
- Treatment outcomes for clients with PTSD and substance abuse are worse than for other dual-diagnosis clients, or for clients with substance abuse alone.
- From the client's perspective, PTSD symptoms are a common trigger of substance use.

Note. Portions of this exhibit are taken from *Seeking Safety: A Treatment Manual for PTSD and Substance Abuse* (pp. 1–2), by L. M. Najavits, 2002, New York: Guilford Press. Adapted with permission.

(b) unintentional human causes (e.g., industrial accidents, motor vehicle accidents), and (c) nonhuman causes (e.g., acts of nature such as floods or earthquakes, being diagnosed with a life-threatening illness). When the stressor is of human design (i.e., an intentional human cause), the disorder may be especially severe or long lasting. This is significant to those working with women in substance abuse treatment, because the majority of women enter treatment with histories of child maltreatment and adult interpersonal violence (i.e., intentional human causes).

Symptoms that characterize PTSD usually begin within 3 months after the trauma, although symptom development may be delayed for weeks and even years. To meet the diagnosis, symptoms must be present for more than 1 month and must cause significant distress or impairment in social or occupational functioning. Kessler et al. (1995) estimated that a person with PTSD might endure 20 years of active symptoms and will experience almost 1 day per week of work impairment, which speaks to the huge toll that PTSD has on the individual and on society.

The characteristic symptoms of PTSD occur in three clusters, as follows:

1. Reexperiencing (e.g., intrusive and recurrent thoughts, vivid images, perceptions, flashbacks of the traumatic experience, nightmares).
2. Avoidance and numbing (e.g., feelings of detachment, persistent avoidance of memories, feelings, people, places, or situations that arouse recollection of the trauma).
3. Increased arousal (e.g., difficulty sleeping or concentrating, irritability or anger, exaggerated startle response, hyperalertness not present prior to traumatic exposure).

Individuals with PTSD also often report associated features such as intense guilt about surviving when others did not survive, decreased awareness of their surroundings, forgetfulness or amnesia, feeling that things are unreal or strange, and feeling detached from their bodies.

Although patterns of psychological distress following traumatic events have been described in professional and popular literature since World War II and even earlier, PTSD was not included as an official psychiatric diagnosis until 1980 and has been slow to gain general acceptance (Davidson, 2001). National awareness of trauma and its effect on psychological functioning has been heightened since the attacks of September 11, 2001.

Estimates indicate that 40% of Americans have experienced at least one major trauma, and 8% to 12% will develop PTSD at some point in their lives (Kessler et al., 1995). Rates of the disorder vary depending on degree of exposure to traumatic events, showing that multiple exposures pose more than twice the risk of developing PTSD than exposure to a single event (Foy, Resnick, Sipprelle, & Carroll, 1987). Certain communities and subgroups are also at higher risk for developing PTSD—for example, individuals living in high crime rate areas and those who work as emergency medical personnel or firefighters. There are significant gender differences in PTSD: Women are affected twice as often as men (Najavits et al., 1997; Triffleman, 2003). Also, whereas for men PTSD typically stems from combat or crime trauma, for women it most commonly derives from a history of repetitive childhood physical or sexual assault, sometimes both.

PTSD can occur at any age, but children and adults may express PTSD symptoms in different ways. For example, children may express their fear by disorganized and agitated behavior and through repetitive play or reenactments of the trauma. Trauma that occurs in childhood years can be particularly damaging because it may disrupt critical emotional and social development and lead to long-term difficulties in these areas, especially when trauma exposure is chronic. Childhood sexual abuse, in particular, is also a risk factor for subsequent victimization in various forms, including sexual assault, physical assault, and domestic violence (Courtois, 1979).

The course of the disorder is variable with approximately one half of the cases recovering in 3 months (termed *acute PTSD*) and other cases experiencing *chronic PTSD* (i.e., symptoms persist for more than 3 months and often much longer). Depression, substance abuse, and other anxiety disorders commonly co-occur in individuals with PTSD. It is not known to what extent these disorders typically precede or follow the onset of PTSD. There is evidence that development of substance abuse often occurs after PTSD and that, in many cases, substances are used to manage or avoid the distressing PTSD symptoms. The presence of additional psychiatric disorders often exacerbates symptoms and complicates treatment.

The range, type, and level of PTSD-related impairment will differ among individuals depending on the degree of impact that the traumatic event has had on one's life. For example, individuals displaying risk factors such as exposure to extremely severe and sudden trauma, prior trauma history, preexisting psychiatric conditions, and lack of adequate social support are more likely to need further intervention. Treatment is clearly indicated when PTSD symptoms make it difficult for an individual to function at his or her normal capacity. This may be evidenced in a variety of ways such as major depression (e.g., hopelessness, suicidal thoughts or feelings), chronic grief, intense fear, persistent avoidance of trauma-related stimuli that interferes with daily activities, social withdrawal, and immobility.

COMPLEX POSTTRAUMATIC STRESS DISORDER

Complex PTSD is another common outcome of past trauma found among women in substance abuse treatment. *DSM–IV–TR* field trials (Roth, Newman, Pelcovitz, van der Kolk, & Mandel, 1997) demonstrated that it was not the prevalence of PTSD symptoms themselves, but depression, outbursts of anger, self-destructive behaviors (e.g., substance abuse, eating disorders, self-mutilation), feelings of shame, self-blame, and distrust that differentiated a treatment-seeking sample with PTSD from a non-treatment-seeking community sample with PTSD. These and other similar findings prompted members of the PTSD task force of the *DSM–IV–TR* to identify a syndrome of psychological problems called *complex PTSD* or *disorders of extreme stress not otherwise specified* (DESNOS), shown to be frequently associated with histories of prolonged and severe interpersonal abuse (Pelcovitz et al., 1997; van der Kolk, Roth, Pelcovitz, & Mandel, 1993).

The constellation of symptoms making up complex PTSD include alterations in the following:

- regulation of affective impulses, including difficulty modulating anger;
- attention and consciousness leading to dissociative episodes;
- self-perception such as chronic feelings of guilt and shame;
- relationship to others, such as problems with intimacy and trust;
- somatization; and
- systems of meaning.

The earlier the onset of trauma and the longer the duration, the more likely people are to experience high degrees of all symptoms categorized as complex PTSD. Studies also show that interpersonal trauma, especially childhood abuse, puts individuals at higher risk for developing complex PTSD than accidents and natural disasters (Roth et al., 1997). Further complicating the picture is evidence that childhood sexual abuse is a risk factor for subsequent victimization in various forms, including sexual assault, physical assault, and domestic violence (Polusny & Follette, 1995).

Early abuse has substantial negative effects for women in a number of areas. In a survey of 1,931 women who were being treated in primary care settings, 22% reported experiencing childhood or adolescent physical or sexual abuse (McCauley et al., 1997). Compared with those who only reported adult abuse histories, respondents reporting childhood abuse had significantly more physical, psychological, and behavioral problems. Women who were victimized as children had more physical and psychiatric symptoms, including nearly 4 times the history of attempted suicide and more than 3 times as many psychiatric hospitalizations. These women also had almost 5 times greater drug abuse and twice the alcohol abuse as those who were abused as adults only. In another large-scale survey study, women with childhood sexual abuse had higher numbers of sexual partners, higher rates of sexually transmitted diseases, and higher affiliation with aggressive and sexually risky partners (Testa, VanZile-Tamsen, & Livingston, 2005).

The majority of women in addictions treatment settings report at least one, if not multiple, lifetime exposures to trauma. Thus, many of the psychological problems encountered by providers treating women in community-based substance abuse programs are long standing and the result of what is usually early onset, chronic, and repetitive physical or sexual trauma, including family violence, incest, and severe childhood neglect. Substance misuse and abuse is often an integral component of complex PTSD; it may be seen as an attempt to manage emotions, impulses, and bodily experiences in individuals with limited coping strategies. Although few studies have directly addressed the comorbidity of addiction and complex PTSD, it is easy to see how the dysregulation, impulsivity, and self-harm, which are associated with complex PTSD, can be manifested through substance abuse. Difficulties in emotion regulation leave women with few adaptive coping resources, and substance use and abuse can become a coping method of choice. Standard PTSD treatments, and even those particularly developed for co-occurring disorders of addiction and trauma, typically do not address the variety of symptoms that arise in individuals with complex PTSD and substance abuse. These complex symptoms necessitate more comprehensive treatment models and approaches (Courtois, 2004).

We should clarify that to date these syndromes, complex PTSD and DESNOS, although widely adhered to in the field of trauma, do not yet constitute official *DSM–IV–TR* diagnoses. Nevertheless, these constellations of symptoms often provide the most useful descriptors of the experiences of our clients with histories of chronic early abuse and best encapsulate their presenting issues.

PATHWAYS TO ADDICTION

The co-occurrence of PTSD and substance use disorders is well documented, with lifetime rates of PTSD ranging from 14% to 60% among substance abusers (Brady, Dansky, Back, Foa, & Carroll, 2001; Donovan et al., 2001; Najavits et al., 1997; Triffleman, 2003). Among PTSD populations, co-occurring substance use disorders may occur in 60% to 80% of individuals (Donovan et al., 2001).

SELF-MEDICATION HYPOTHESIS

Despite the abundant information now available regarding the strong link between PTSD and substance use disorders, the exact nature of this association remains unclear. There are three major causal pathways that have been hypothesized. The most well-known causal explanation, based on clinical as well as empirical observation and evidence, is the self-medication hypothesis (e.g., see Khantzian, 1997). This theory posits that some individuals with PTSD use substances as a way to manage or avoid the distressing PTSD symptoms (e.g., intrusive memories, physical arousal). Substances such as alcohol, cocaine, barbiturates, opiates, amphetamines, or other drugs are frequently abused in attempts to relieve emotional pain.

The self-medication model is consistent with the developmental findings suggesting that exposure to childhood trauma disrupts emotion regulation processes, leading to long-term difficulties. Self-regulation deficits have also been implicated in the initiation and maintenance of substance use disorders (Horowitz, Overton, Rosenstein, & Steidl, 1992; Khantzian & Schneider, 1986; Krystal, 1997) and, thus, may play an important mediating role between trauma exposure and substance use dependence. For example, findings from the addictions literature show that difficulty in emotional regulation and intolerance of painful feelings, inability to self-soothe, and instability of behavioral control is typical of adolescent and adult substance abusers (Horowitz et al., 1992; Khantzian & Schneider, 1986; Krystal, 1997). Self-medicating with alcohol and drugs can lessen the effects of hyperarousal and numbing symptoms in individuals with posttraumatic stress. Hyperarousal symptoms may be diminished or masked by alcohol or other depressants, whereas numbing symptoms may be temporarily relieved by stimulant use, thereby providing temporary relief from dysregulated feeling states that accompany PTSD.

Such self-medication provides only temporary relief from symptoms, and a state of withdrawal in which PTSD symptoms are exaggerated often follows. Some evidence indicates important gender differences in this regard. Women's reasons for substance use tend to be to soothe uncomfortable emotions such as anxiety and depression. Men, however, tend to use drugs or alcohol in a more social or celebratory way and in response to positive events as opposed to negative events. This suggests that the self-medication model may be more applicable for women than for men. Indeed recent research has identified that women most commonly present with "primary" PTSD, whereby the PTSD develops first, followed by the substance use disorders; some studies have found this to be the reverse in men (Back, Brady, Sonne, & Verduin, 2006), although clearly many men report using substances to manage overwhelming feelings or memories related to trauma.

Two other pathways between PTSD and substance use disorders have been proposed, including the high-risk and susceptibility hypotheses (e.g., see Chilcoat & Breslau, 1998a, 1998b). The high-risk hypothesis suggests that substance use and associated high-risk activities increase the risk for traumatic exposure thereby indirectly increasing the likelihood of PTSD. The susceptibility hypothesis posits that substance use may play a causal role, in that substance users may be more susceptible to PTSD following a traumatic event because of impaired psychological or neurochemical systems as a result of substance use.

The self-medication model is the only model with empirical support. Chilcoat and Breslau (1998a, 1998b) conducted a study testing causal pathways between PTSD and substance use disorders in a random sample of 1,007 young adults (ages 21–30) who were members of a large HMO. Participants completed baseline interviews and two follow-up interviews over a 5-year period.

Researchers found support for the plausibility of the self-medication hypothe-sis but not for the other two alternative causal models. As Chilcoat and Breslau noted, these results are an important step in understanding the causal relation-ship between PTSD and substance use disorders, but further research testing specific pathways is needed.

CONCLUSION

In this chapter, we reviewed highlights of the modern trauma field as it relates to our special population of women in substance abuse treatment. We emphasized two of the most commonly found clinical presentations, PTSD and complex PTSD, that women with trauma exposure struggle with in the context of their addictive disorders. Furthermore, as we presented the known linkages between symptoms of PTSD and complex PTSD and addictive behavior, we hope to have established the unique and multifaceted set of problems that may challenge the ability of a woman who is also a survivor of trauma to stay in recovery. Likewise, it is critical for service providers and clinicians to recognize the many faces of these trauma-related disorders to adapt addictions treatment for such clients. Our review provided important background for our subse-quent in-depth exploration of the multimodal and comprehensive treatment needs of this population and for ways to address these needs in high-quality addictions care.

2

PSYCHOTHERAPY MODELS
AND TREATMENT CONSIDERATIONS

The past 20 years of empirical study on the epidemiology of traumatic exposure has resulted in an increased understanding of how to treat women with comorbid posttraumatic stress disorder (PTSD) and substance use disorders. In this chapter, we examine treatments that have traditionally been used for PTSD alone, as well as various substance abuse treatment models, informed by abstinence and harm reduction philosophies. Next, we present the relatively new but growing research on trauma and addiction comorbidity. Finally, we present the kinds of treatment approaches that currently exist for addressing comorbid PTSD and substance abuse, highlighting similarities and differences in the approaches.

In this context, we also introduce the contribution of the Women, Co-Occurring Disorders and Violence Study (WCDVS), a national project that has significantly helped move the field forward in integrating trauma treatment into addiction settings. We recognize that the evidence base continues to grow and expand, and we present the treatments we discuss as representative examples of the clinical approaches available to service providers when considering the types of trauma services to implement in their settings. We underscore a multimodal, problem-oriented approach that encourages attention to individualized needs in the timing and sequencing of treatment services for trauma and the application of relevant treatment models.

The field of psychology has taken a prominent role in the treatment of addiction and comorbid trauma-related syndromes. Beginning with work informed by combat veterans, psychologists began to examine the interaction of substance use disorders in clients with trauma histories. Several early studies (Boudewyns, Albrecht, Talbert, & Hyer, 1991; McFall, Veith, & Murburg, 1992) noted the comorbid characteristics and more severe treatment implications of veterans with PTSD and substance dependence. This interest moved into other client populations, including women with traumatic histories seeking substance abuse treatment. The Epidemiologic Catchment Area study (Reider & Cicchetti, 1989) provided definitive documentation of the high comorbidity rates for trauma-related disorders among substance-using women in a landmark national survey. In the early 1990s, a number of clinical researchers began systematically examining the comorbidity of PTSD and substance use disorders, including patient characteristics, severity, treatment outcomes, and the essential components of combined treatment for PTSD and substance use disorders (Dansky, Saladin, Brady, Kilpatrick, & Resnick, 1995; Najavits et al., 1997; Ouimette, Ahrens, Moss, & Finney, 1997; Triffleman, Carroll, & Kellogg, 1999).

Given the convergence of epidemiological findings, clinicians and researchers began to turn their attention to questions of treatment and how best to provide care for individuals facing dual psychiatric and substance use problems in the face of trauma exposure. Some of the most significant clinical decisions regarding treatment have involved how and when to treat co-occurring problems. Historically, substance abuse and psychiatric treatment providers believed that a client must first address substance abuse before focusing on PTSD symptoms, even after identifying the client as a trauma survivor. Clinical wisdom held that trauma-related symptoms and a traumatic past could not be dealt with unless the client was sober and substance free. Recently, research and clinical experience have challenged this position; trauma can and often should be addressed even in early recovery from substance abuse.

The onset sequence of PTSD and substance use disorder offers guidance for determining the timing and targeting of symptom treatment. For example, when PTSD is determined to have developed before the onset of substance abuse and is consistent with the concept of self-medication (Khantzian, 1997), it is clinically appropriate to address the root symptoms of PTSD directly as a way to also address substance abuse. Alternately, if a traumatic event and subsequent PTSD occur after the onset of a substance use disorder, a clinician might choose to focus on the substance abuse first. Finally, causality is difficult to untangle in some situations, including cases in which someone experiences a childhood trauma but does not start using substances until much later in life. Compounding the ambiguity of causal associations, clients with PTSD and substance use disorders often have more severe clinical profiles, including abusing more serious substances such as cocaine and opiates (Najavits et al., 1997) and experiencing interpersonal and medical problems (Becker et al., 2005; Brady, Dansky, Sonne, & Saladin, 1998). Thus, it is important to develop treatments that will be able to address the specific patterns and concerns of each client and her overall clinical picture. In line with these needs, addressing trauma and substance abuse in rapid sequence or simultaneously has become a more common and accepted course as opposed to postponing treatment of one set of problems until the other has been resolved.

Even when treating both disorders simultaneously, the sequencing of how to go about developing a treatment plan will vary, depending on substance use severity. General rules suggest the wisdom of attempting to achieve a level of stabilization in active substance users that may require detoxification. As in psychiatric crisis, no therapy work can occur until the acute crisis has been resolved. Conducting a diagnostic assessment involving trauma screening and making appropriate trauma-related recommendations can be a helpful first step in containing the traumatic symptoms and providing a more stable context in which to achieve some stability in a client's substance use.

TREATMENTS FOR TRAUMA-RELATED DISORDERS

Treatments for survivors of trauma who are also in recovery from substances continue to evolve, especially as experts in the fields of addiction and trauma join forces to create comprehensive treatment models. Most treatments designed to address comorbid addiction and trauma disorders evolved out of and in reaction to the models that have been shown to be efficacious for trauma only. We present a description of those empirically supported treatments geared specifically to PTSD alone, as well as the emerging treatment models for comorbid disorders. Appendix A at the end of this volume offers descriptions and information on many of the treatment models currently in use.

Clinical Interventions for Posttraumatic Stress Disorder

A number of psychological treatments are specifically designed to target PTSD and other trauma-related symptoms. Treatment for symptom alleviation related to PTSD dates back to work with military veterans in the 1970s. PTSD treatment for women accelerated at the end of the 1980s through pioneering work done by Edna Foa and others. Some treatments for PTSD include stress inoculation training (Foa, Rothbaum, Riggs, & Murdock, 1991), prolonged exposure (Foa & Rothbaum, 1998), skills training in affective and interpersonal regulation (STAIR; Cloitre, Koenen, Cohen, & Han, 2002), trauma recovery and empowerment (TREM; Harris & Community Connections Trauma Work Group, 1998), sensorimotor psychotherapy (Ogden, Minton, & Pain, 2006), and eye movement desensitization and reprocessing (Shapiro, 1989). These treatments have varying levels of research and empirical data to support their efficacy in treating clients with PTSD and allow for only preliminary conclusions (Foa & Meadows, 1997). Continued research will provide more answers.

Generally, cognitive–behavioral treatments have the best support, demonstrating effectiveness in several clinical research studies. This type of treatment typically involves two key components, skills training and exposure, in combination or alone.

Skills Training

Skills training focuses on building coping strategies to manage overwhelming emotions, to increase daily life structure, and enhance self-care. Clients are taught behavioral techniques to decrease distress and physiological arousal (e.g., breathing retraining, relaxation exercises). They are also provided with education about PTSD and strategies to identify and change maladaptive thinking patterns that have helped perpetuate the disorder. Relationship issues specific to this population (e.g., difficulty trusting others, problems in managing conflict) are typically addressed to help clients develop communication skills and a healthy support network.

Exposure Therapy

Exposure therapy involves emotional processing of the trauma and can take one of two forms: in vivo exposure and imaginal exposure. *In vivo exposure* asks clients to actively experience and confront places or objects related to the trauma in their real lives. In *imaginal exposure*, processing occurs by asking clients to repeatedly recount the memories of their traumatic experience in detail and with increased elaboration. Exposure therapy seeks to help clients assimilate and integrate their overwhelming experiences in a way that is controlled and tolerable. This process of habituation involves helping individuals confront the painful aspects of their traumatic experience that they have avoided and reexamine the traumatic experience in a safe, supportive atmosphere with the guidance of a skilled therapist.

Treatment of PTSD with exposure therapy has shown promising results (Foa & Rothbaum, 1998) but remains controversial because of the potential distress in asking clients to confront past traumas. Preliminarily, in vivo exposure has been shown to produce better outcomes than imaginal exposure

(Richards, Lovell, & Marks, 1994), although not all traumatic experiences lend themselves to that technique. In a review by Foa and Meadows (1997), exposure therapy is described as highly effective with an average of 60% to 78% reduction in PTSD symptom severity. Foa and Meadows and Foa, Rothbaum, and Furr (2003) offered a comprehensive review of psychosocial treatments for PTSD.

Treatments for Substance Use Disorders

When considering which trauma treatments to use, it is important to consider how a model will mesh with the treatment philosophy of the substance abuse program. Specifically, introducing trauma-focused interventions into a substance abuse treatment context may highlight differences between models of abstinence and harm reduction. It is important for programs and providers to be aware of the strengths and limitations of each perspective, how each might affect women with trauma histories, and the implications of integrating trauma treatment into a program that leans heavily toward abstinence or harm reduction principles.

Abstinence-Based Models

The disease model (Jellinek, 1962) helped move the perception of addiction from the realm of morally reprehensible behavior to a problem deserving attention from the treatment community. Diagnoses were established and abuse and dependence criteria were set. The disease model has specific assumptions about how a disorder should be treated, specifically that abstinence is the primary focus of treatment. It is presumed that a client must give up the problematic substance to manage the disease and that the disease is always present with the possibility of reoccurrence if abstinence is not maintained. This philosophy is at the heart of the 12-step model, now well accepted as among the most powerful vehicles of recovery for many substance-dependent adults and, thus, a prominent component in addictions treatment. The main treatment goal in these programs is abstinence; clients are directed to choose abstinence as their treatment goal and achieve and maintain abstinence in order to remain in good stead at what is often called a *drug-free program*.[1] This philosophy is long-standing and deeply engrained in many treatment agencies and providers. Moreover, abstinence-based programs often have providers who are in recovery themselves and have participated in 12-step programs to achieve and maintain their own sobriety, often predisposing them to support this model.

---

[1]In abstinence-only programs, abstinence is set as a goal. If a patient relapses, she may not necessarily have to leave treatment if she is committed to pursuing abstinence as a treatment outcome.

Harm Reduction Models

In the mid-1980s, differing opinions about substance use emerged in the treatment literature. The self-medication hypothesis (Khantzian, 1985), for example, highlighted substance use as a way of coping with painful negative emotions, as we discussed in chapter 1. This model suggested that drug use was a method of managing an underlying disorder or disease, not necessarily a disease unto itself. Around the same time, relapse prevention therapy was introduced. In their groundbreaking work, Marlatt and Gordon (1985) described relapse, or the return to substance use after a period of abstinence, as a normal part of recovery from alcohol and drug addiction. This approach made "slips" an expected occurrence on the road to recovery and further helped to destigmatize relapse. Relapse prevention also made it possible to address addiction outside the disease model. By learning relapse prevention skills, clients could learn to discontinue their substance use and maintain their sobriety without committing to the idea of having a disease. Relapse prevention assumes that substance use has a significant learned component that can be modified through skill development. Relapse prevention models are now widely used in many treatment programs and include cognitive–behavioral techniques, such as coping skills training to manage cravings and urges to use, thoughts about drinking and drug use, drinking and drug refusal skills, and planning for high-risk drinking and drug use situations (Dayton & Rogers, 2002). With specific treatment guides and manuals, providers have become more comfortable using these skills and approaches to help their clients.

Another treatment approach that has become widely adopted is based on research on stages of change (Prochaska & DiClemente, 1992). The transtheoretical stages of change model describes the process a person may traverse in thinking about and making changes to problematic behavior and includes precontemplation (i.e., before one is thinking about change or thinking a behavior is particularly problematic), contemplation (i.e., thinking about making a change, but feeling ambivalent about doing so), preparation (i.e., committing to and making a plan to change), action (i.e., implementing change), and maintenance (i.e., sustaining the change). A therapeutic style called motivational interviewing (W. R. Miller & Rollnick, 2002; Rollnick & Miller, 1995) emerged that was consistent with this concept. Motivational interviewing is a nonconfrontational approach that attempts to help clients with behavior change; it seeks to assist people in the identification of their desire to change and their preparation and planning to change behaviors that have become problematic. For example, for a drinker at a precontemplation level, a therapist might help the client identify possible pros and cons of substance use so that he or she can make a more informed decision about whether change is desirable. For an individual in the preparation stage, the therapist would help the client develop a reasonable and appropriate plan for behavior change. An important element of motivational interviewing is the collaborative relationship of therapist and client; the therapist addresses the client's issues from the client's perspective, especially in relation to his or her readiness to change, highlighting ambivalence and promoting statements affiliated with changing problem behavior.

These successful cognitive–behavioral and motivational therapies have helped to make the concept of harm reduction more acceptable in many addictions settings (Denning, 2000; Marlatt, 1998; Tatarsky, 2002). The harm reduction philosophy recognizes that abstinence is not always an immediate or preferable goal for every client. Although abstinence is most often the desired outcome, even within a harm reduction perspective, treatment proceeds by establishing incremental changes to reduce the harm associated with substance use. Needle exchange programs are another example of the harm reduction model in action. Many people are not ready to make changes in their injection drug use. By providing clean needles and collecting used ones, the potentially harmful health effects of needle sharing can be mitigated and engagement and connection to service providers can be increased.

For substance use, a harm reduction approach may begin with the goal of decreasing the amount or frequency with which people use substances. For example, a person who reports drinking too much may be asked to try to cut down the number of days drinking or the amount consumed each day, such as having three drinks instead of five. If such a goal is accomplished, perhaps a client will build self-efficacy and become inclined to try a more abstinence-oriented experiment—not drinking at all for a week, for example. If an individual is unable to make that change, there might be a reevaluation of goals. This can also help people see that their drinking might be more of a problem than anticipated. When an individual is unable to meet a goal, the behavior is analyzed and a new goal is set or the extent of the problem is explored and may result in greater understanding. Like motivational interviewing, harm reduction is client centered (Tatarsky, 2002), whereby the client is viewed as the expert on her own life. Cognitive–behavioral techniques, such as relapse prevention, are used to help a client set and achieve goals. Whereas abstinence-based models are high threshold, usually entailing a certain amount of clean time, a limited number of relapses, and negative drug test results, harm reduction sets a lower threshold for treatment entry and retention.

Integrating Trauma Treatment

Understanding the implications of abstinence-based and harm reduction models is particularly important in working with women who are survivors of trauma in recovery from substance use. An abstinence approach often assumes that a woman must be clean and sober before any work can be accomplished on mental health issues because there is heightened concern that delving into details of abuse and symptoms of trauma will lead to increased substance use and undermine her treatment. In a similar way, some abstinence-oriented clinicians believe that active substance users are unable to make effective use of psychotherapy or psychiatric medications while continuing to use substances. As a result, many programs and clinicians have been reluctant to address trauma-related problems until a woman has achieved stable sobriety.

Women who have experienced trauma, particularly those with complex PTSD, however, often have few resources or coping mechanisms other than substance use or other maladaptive behaviors for dealing with painful emotions. Removing the one effective, available coping mechanism by insisting on abstinence can lead to a significant increase in trauma symptoms (Brady, Killeen, Saladin, Dansky, & Becker, 1994), which, if not addressed, can lead to difficulty engaging and retaining clients in treatment. In abstinence-based programs, these women often have the experience of not being understood and failing because of their intense urges to use to manage their feelings and symptoms. By starting to work with a client who is actively using, in a collaborative way, clinicians can begin educating clients about tools to reduce their substance use and cope with distressing symptoms related to interpersonal trauma. Clients often are able to work effectively in treatment and develop coping skills, even in the context of continued use.

Combined Treatments for Trauma and Substance Use Disorders

Intervention models that can address both trauma and addiction have involved selecting best practices in each respective treatment field on the basis of empirical and clinical findings. Further consideration on how to combine approaches involves examining how treatment models for single disorders can be adapted to the special needs of individuals struggling with both sets of symptoms and consequences. Notably, most of the combined treatment models have incorporated methods to help clients develop some stability with substance use and the ability to regulate affect before embarking on potentially more overwhelming material related to their trauma.

As an emerging field, treatment development for comorbid PTSD and substance use disorders has had the benefit of drawing from previously established efficacious therapies for each individual disorder, including cognitive–behavioral therapy and skills training for PTSD and relapse prevention for substance dependence. Overall, these new treatment approaches have been tested either alone or in integrative or sequential combinations. They are typically designed for individual therapy but are often modified for use in groups, a more common modality in drug treatment program settings. Treatments for comorbid PTSD and substance use disorders typically differ from

PTSD-only treatments by adding components specifically designed to provide clients with skills training and cognitive restructuring related to substance abuse, such as cravings and relapse triggers and skills to address emotion regulation. We address clinical issues related to emotion regulation in detail in chapter 4.

Integrated models address trauma and substance use symptoms concurrently. Within a psychoeducational framework, regardless of the session focus, integrated treatments underscore and emphasize the links between trauma and addiction. Sequential models refer to some staging of treatment. Typically addictive problems are addressed first; coping skills and other relapse prevention (Marlatt & Gordon, 1985) techniques are taught in preparation for working on trauma-related symptoms later in treatment.

Evidence-Based Integrated Models

The most widely known evidence-based integrated model for treatment of comorbid PTSD and substance use is seeking safety (SS; Najavits, 2002).[2] SS is a structured and manualized integrated treatment and is cognitive–behavioral in orientation. Drawing from feminist theory and using a psychoeducational framework, with influences from many other clinical models, it focuses on the recognized need to establish safety in the process of recovering from both trauma (Herman, 1992b) and substance use.

The premise of the SS model draws on the work of Judith Herman (1992b), whose book, *Trauma and Recovery*, has been one of the most significant clinical contributions to the field of trauma treatment. Herman proposed three stages of recovery from trauma (i.e., safety, mourning, and reconnection) and underscores the importance of helping clients achieve a certain level of safety and stability early in treatment before working through their traumatic pasts and its impact in their lives. It is this first stage of recovery, safety, which informs the bulk of trauma treatment done by those in the addictions field, as clients most often come to substance abuse treatment with profound deficits manifested in their substance involvement, in addition to many other dangerous or self-destructive personal or interpersonal problems.

Toward the goal of achieving safety, the SS model offers a strong self-care message, accentuating the development and rehearsal of safe-coping skills, focusing on "healing" language and encouraging clients to "take back their power" (Najavits, 2002, p. 110) in their recovery. The treatment is divided into four content areas thought to address salient therapeutic issues for clients with comorbid PTSD and substance abuse: cognitive, behavioral, interpersonal, and

---

[2]Other integrated treatment models exist (see chap. 11, this volume, for a more detailed description of the Women, Co-Occurring Disorders and Violence Study; see also Appendix A, this volume), but we do not list them here because none has been tested in a randomized clinical trial.

case management. SS offers significant flexibility regarding order, number of sessions, and integration with other treatments.

The evidence base of 15 published studies represents a broad range of investigators and populations; it includes seven pilot studies, four randomized controlled trials, two multisite controlled trials, one controlled nonrandomized trial (a site from one of the multisite trials), and one dissemination study. The study samples were clients who were typically severe and chronic in both trauma/PTSD and substance use disorder. Overall, the model has (a) consistently shown positive outcomes on trauma symptoms and substance abuse as well as other domains (e.g., suicidality, HIV risk, social functioning, problem solving, sense of meaning); (b) generally outperformed treatment-as-usual; (c) shown comparable results to the gold-standard treatment, relapse prevention; and (d) consistently obtained high satisfaction by both clients and clinicians. In our own work (Hien, Cohen, Miele, Litt, & Capstick, 2004) that compared SS with substance use relapse prevention treatment (Carroll, 1998), women in both treatments showed improvement in PTSD symptoms, substance use, and other psychological domains at 6-month follow-up when compared with a community control group. These findings indicate that treatment addressing PTSD symptoms in a population of substance-dependent women did not escalate symptoms, as traditionally has been feared, but reduced symptoms related to PTSD and substance use. When provided with treatment adapted to their specific needs, women with co-occurring trauma and addiction were highly responsive to treatment and show marked improvements. In chapter 11 we describe two recent studies examining SS in community settings.

Evidence-Based Sequential Approaches

In sequential models, initial sessions tend to focus on substance abuse–related symptoms and emotion regulation skills before addressing trauma symptoms using trauma-processing methods, such as exposure therapy. Up until the past few years, however, the clinical application and empirical investigation of exposure therapy for PTSD had been limited to individuals without comorbid substance use disorders. As discussed earlier in this chapter, exposure work has generally been considered contraindicated for substance-using clients on the basis of concerns that reliving aspects of traumatic events through in vivo or imaginal exposure is too emotionally distressing, flooding clients with feelings they are not prepared to manage safely and making them susceptible to relapse (Zayfert & Black, 2000). Given the few effective treatments available for clients with comorbid trauma and substance use disorders and exposure therapy's promising impact, even among individuals with chronic PTSD, substance use disorder experts have recently begun to systematically study the use of imaginal exposure in comorbid populations. In contrast with the lack of empirical study of existing integrated treatment models other than SS, there are a number of sequential treatments that have been tested.

Substance Dependence–Posttraumatic Stress Disorder Therapy. Substance dependence–posttraumatic stress disorder therapy (SDPT; Triffleman et al., 1999) is a two-phase, individual cognitive–behavioral therapy using coping skills, stress inoculation, and in vivo exposure. Phase I, occurring over 12 weeks, focuses on developing and maintaining abstinence from substance use. Phase II, implemented over 8 weeks, addresses PTSD symptoms. Triffleman et al. (1999) conducted a small, randomized control trial with 19 men and women in outpatient methadone and cocaine treatment programs comparing SDPT with standard 12-step facilitation therapy (Nowinski, Baker, & Carroll, 1995). Data from the experimental and comparison conditions were combined because of a lack of outcome differences between them, and results for the combined data indicated improvement in PTSD, substance use, and other psychological symptoms.

Concurrent Treatment of Posttraumatic Stress Disorder and Cocaine Dependence. Concurrent treatment of PTSD and cocaine dependence (CTPCD; Brady, Dansky, Back, Foa, & Carroll, 2001; see also Back, Dansky, Carroll, Foa, & Brady, 2001) incorporates exposure techniques and cognitive–behavioral relapse prevention. Adapted from Foa's trauma work (Foa & Rothbaum, 1998), the treatment protocol included 16 individual 90-minute psychotherapy sessions, 6 to 9 of which included imaginal exposure. The researchers examined a sample of 39 (i.e., 32 women and 7 men) patients with cocaine dependence and comorbid PTSD recruited from substance abuse treatment programs. Fifteen (39%) attended at least 10 sessions and were considered treatment completers. Completers demonstrated significant reductions in PTSD symptoms and cocaine use as well as depression and other psychiatric symptoms at the end of treatment. Improvements in PTSD symptoms and cocaine use were maintained over a 6-month follow-up period. Baseline comparisons between completers and noncompleters showed that noncompleters had higher avoidance symptoms and fewer years of education.

These studies provide preliminary evidence that exposure therapy can be used safely and that it may be effective in the treatment of PTSD in some individuals with cocaine dependence. As the investigators note, their results show that exposure does not necessarily increase the risk of relapse. Although drop-out rates were quite high (e.g., 62% were considered noncompleters in the CTPCD study), they were lower than rates seen in other studies of psychotherapy for cocaine dependence (Crits-Christoph et al., 1999). Also, the results of the CTPCD study are not consistent with the notion that exposure treatment was the precipitant of relapse; no increases in positive urine tests during or after the exposure components of the intervention were observed and most treatment drop-outs did so prior to the exposure phase. Conclusions drawn from this study are limited, however, because of the uncontrolled nature of the design, small sample size, and high drop-out rate.

Transcend. Transcend (Donovan, Padin-Rivera, & Kowaliw, 2001) is another manualized, phase-based approach to treating PTSD and substance abuse problems. The 12-week protocol was tested with men in a partial hospitalization treatment program (Donovan, Padin-Rivera, & Kowaliw, 2001). After first completing a substance abuse rehabilitation program, individuals entered treatment in groups of eight. The first 6 weeks consisted of skill development (e.g., problem solving, anger management, emotional awareness), and the second 6 weeks were devoted to trauma processing (i.e., presentations of traumatic events with group feedback and nightmare resolution techniques). Substance abuse education, relapse prevention techniques, peer support, and 12-step attendance were encouraged throughout. Outcomes at 6- and 12-months posttreatment showed decreases in PTSD symptoms and substance use.

Seeking Safety and Prolonged Exposure. In a small pilot study of five men with PTSD and substance use disorders, Najavits, Schmitz, Gotthardt, and Weiss (2005) used a combination of SS and a revised form of prolonged exposure treatment over a 5-month period. All five men attended each of the 30 sessions offered, with a mean of 9 imaginal exposure sessions. Men in this sample had experienced a variety of traumas, with a mean age of onset of 8 years. Results showed significant improvements in drug use, trauma symptoms, dissociation, and social functioning. Treatment attendance, satisfaction, and alliance were high, although the sample size and uncontrolled design limit the ability to generalize findings.

Summary of Combined Treatments for Trauma and Substance Use Disorders

In sum, both integrated and sequential models of cognitive–behavioral therapy, including those incorporating exposure therapy, show promise in treating comorbid trauma and substance use disorders (see Table 2.1). More research is needed to examine the length of treatment and timing and combination of components, especially with larger sample sizes and randomized controlled research designs. Preliminary findings from these studies support the safety of addressing trauma simultaneously within substance abuse treatment without high risk of relapse. In these studies, PTSD treatments did not appear to make participants worse and, in fact, improved their trauma symptoms, as well as substance use and general psychiatric symptoms. These positive results provide justification to continue this line of research in controlled treatment trials with a range of drug-abusing populations to further demonstrate the feasibility of these approaches and identify the optimal integrated model of comorbid trauma and substance abuse treatment.

Other Relevant Treatment Models

Two additional evidence-based treatments have been found to be clinically useful with this population, particularly for clients with complex PTSD,

TABLE 2.1

Comparison of Treatments for Substance Use Disorders and Posttraumatic Stress Disorder

Study information	Najavits, Weiss, Shaw, and Muenz (1998)[a]	Triffleman, Carroll, and Kellogg (1999)	Donovan, Padin-Rivera, and Kowaliw (2001)	Brady, Dansky, Back, Foa, and Carroll (2001)	Hien, Cohen, Miele, Litt, and Capstick (2004)
Treatment name	SS	SDPT	Transcend	CTPCD	SS (RPT)
Sample size	27	19	46	39	107
Sex	Female	Mixed (53% female)	Male	Mixed (82% female)	Female
Mean age	36 years	35 years	—	34 years	38 years (SS) 33 years (RPT)
RCT	No	Yes	No	No	Yes
No. of sessions	24	40	60	16	24
Modality	Group	Individual	Group	Individual	Individual
Posttreatment follow-up	3 months	1 month	6/12 months	6 months	6/9 months
Results	Improvement in SU, PTSD, depression; increase in somatization.	Improvement in SU, PTSD, psychiatric; no gender difference.	Improvement in SU, PTSD.	Improvement in SU, PTSD, and depression.	Improvement in SU, PTSD at 6 months; no difference SS vs. RPT.

Note. SS = seeking safety; SDPT = substance dependence–posttraumatic stress disorder therapy; CTPCD = concurrent treatment of posttraumatic stress disorder and cocaine dependence; RPT = relapse prevention treatment; RCT = randomized controlled trial; SU = substance use; PTSD = posttraumatic stress disorder.
[a]References for other published studies on the seeking safety model with varying sample sizes, modalities, and age and sex of participants may be found at http://www.seekingsafety.org.

although they have yet to be empirically tested with clients diagnosed with comorbid PTSD and substance use disorders.

Dialectical behavior therapy (DBT; Linehan, 1993a) is a cognitive–behavioral therapy originally developed for borderline personality disorder (BPD). Notably, BPD is a disorder with frequent comorbidity in individuals with substance abuse and trauma-related disorders. BPD is often considered a disorder of self-regulation (Grotstein, 1987), with one of the hallmark features being emotion dysregulation. Symptoms associated with BPD, such as affect instability, marked reactivity of mood, inappropriate intense anger with lack of control, and unstable relationships are sequelae of fundamental and pervasive deficits in emotion regulation. Impulsive and self-damaging behaviors, such as suicidal gestures, self-mutilation, substance abuse, and binge eating, are viewed as efforts to manage overwhelming emotions.

DBT is based on the premise that dysfunctions of emotion regulation can result from biological vulnerabilities as well as invalidating environments. These invalidating environments during childhood fail to teach a child how to label and regulate arousal, how to tolerate emotional distress, and how to trust emotional reactions. The treatment offers a broad range of cognitive and behavioral strategies to help with these problems. Specific DBT emotion regulation skills include (a) identifying and labeling feelings, (b) identifying obstacles to changing emotions, (c) reducing vulnerability to emotional states, (d) increasing positive emotional events and mindfulness to current emotions, (e) taking the opposite action, and (f) applying distress tolerance techniques. Interpersonal effectiveness and self-management skills are also taught. Because so many of the women presenting to treatment have histories of complex PTSD, it is clear why DBT techniques have a direct relevance to this population and offers popular and useful tools.

As we discussed earlier in this chapter, STAIR (Cloitre, Koenan, et al., 2002) is a treatment developed specifically for women with PTSD related to childhood abuse. STAIR is actually the first module of a phase-based treatment that focuses on three core disturbances associated with childhood abuse: problems in emotion management, interpersonal functioning, and PTSD symptoms. During the second phase of this treatment, prolonged exposure therapy techniques are used to process traumatic experiences related to PTSD symptoms.

Imaginal exposure therapy, which requires the client to relate detailed memories of her abuse, may be difficult for many clients to tolerate, as we have discussed. Low levels of tolerance appear especially true for childhood abuse survivors who have not had the opportunity to develop emotion regulation skills necessary to deal with the fear, anger, and sadness that often arise in the context of this kind of narrative work. Studies confirm that childhood abuse survivors are consistently more troubled in areas of affect modulation, anger management, and interpersonal relationships (Cloitre, 1997) as compared with those with adult traumas, placing them at high risk for dropping out of exposure treatment. Rather than forgo the use of a potentially effective intervention for PTSD, Cloitre, Koenan, et al. (2002) modified the exposure treatment, most notably by adding skills training sessions (i.e., STAIR) before beginning trauma-related emotional processing work. STAIR is designed to address emotion regulation and relational difficulties on the basis of the idea that these are some of the most troubling symptoms to clients in their daily lives and that these problems are likely to interfere with future efforts to process traumatic experiences.

WOMEN, CO-OCCURRING DISORDERS AND VIOLENCE STUDY

The development of new treatments for trauma and addiction reflects the growing national recognition of the need for trauma services for women with co-occurring trauma-related symptoms and addictions. Also in response to this growing awareness, the Substance Abuse and Mental Health Services Administration (SAMHSA) initiated the WCDVS (see the Women, Co-Occurring Disorders and Violence Coordinating Center Policy Research Associates Web site for more information: http://www.prainc.com/wcdvs) as a demonstration project to examine multisite implementation of comprehensive trauma services in a variety of community mental health and substance abuse treatment programs across the country. The WCDVS evaluated the practicality, challenges, and effects of offering integrated treatment for substance use, interpersonal violence, and PTSD and other comorbid conditions in treatment programs that served women. We highlight several aspects of the WCDVS pertaining to the integration of PTSD and substance use disorder treatment in this chapter. In chapter 11 we provide more detail on WCDVS outcomes and implementation procedures.

The WCDVS helped lay the groundwork for addictions treatment centers to reconceptualize how to help women who are survivors of abuse or trauma in their programs, with encouragement to consider not only the direct clinical needs of women but the broad backdrop of factors relevant to a woman's recovery. The SAMHSA program stipulated the need to consider ways to provide both trauma-informed treatment and trauma-specific treatments. Trauma-informed treatment incorporates the larger clinical, agency, community, and state structures that influence a woman's access to treatment and her care. Trauma-specific treatments help women address their histories of trauma and its impact on their lives. The WCDVS defined trauma-informed services as the "services that might be offered, modified to consider and be responsive to the impacts of violence" (Jahn Moses, Reed, Mazelis, & D'Ambrosio, 2003, p. 1), and distinguished these services from trauma-specific services "designed to directly address the effects of trauma, with the goal of healing and recovery" (Jahn Moses et al., 2003, p. 1). Accordingly, we use the term *trauma-informed treatment* to reflect the broader backdrop of understanding that enables clinicians and programs to adapt their methods to the needs of women who are survivors of trauma, whereas we use the term *trauma-specific treatments* when we talk about particular treatment models that target symptoms of trauma. The WCDVS suggested that it is often not enough to introduce only trauma-specific treatment; survivors of trauma have observed how their treatments are often compartmentalized and rarely integrated or even coordinated. One of the four core principles of treating women with co-occurring disorders identified by the WCDVS steering committee was to provide comprehensive services, including but not limited to trauma-specific treatment (Huntington, Jahn Moses, & Veysey, 2005).

The WCDVS demonstration allowed individual sites to choose trauma-specific group interventions to implement, and as a result of this study, the models selected have become promising treatments for treating women recovering from addiction and trauma. Four sites selected SS (Najavits, 2002); three sites selected TREM (Harris & Community Connections Trauma Work Group, 1998); one site selected the addiction and trauma recovery integrated model (D. Miller & Guidry, 2001); and a final site developed a new intervention, the triad women's group model, with similar cognitive–behavioral, skills building, and empowerment components (Jahn Moses et al., 2003). Appendix A of this volume provides details on each of these interventions.

Qualitative data from the WCDVS highlight some of the struggles women face in achieving and maintaining abstinence from drugs and alcohol. Harris, Fallot, and Berley (2005) interviewed 27 women to determine key factors, both positive and negative, which affected a woman's substance abuse recovery. Seven themes emerged from these interviews. The four themes identified as "supporting recovery" were (a) connection, (b) self-awareness, (c) a sense of purpose and meaning, and (d) spirituality. The three factors identified as "obstacles to recovery" included (a) battles with depression and despair, (b) destructive habits and patterns, and (c) lack of personal control. These obstacles are the very types of symptoms that are commonly associated with complex PTSD. The sample had very high rates of chronic interpersonal violence, much of it starting in childhood. These qualitative findings highlight the need for treatments that extend beyond those typically provided in substance abuse treatment programs.

Overall, the results from the WCDVS are promising. At 6- and 12-month follow-up there was overall improvement in PTSD symptoms, with mixed findings for substance use and mental health outcomes. Sites with more integrated treatment had better outcomes in general (Cocozza et al., 2005; Morrissey, Ellis, et al., 2005). Given the quasi-experimental design and the comprehensive implementation of the study, it is difficult to determine the most important predictive elements of symptom outcomes.

CONCLUSION

Researchers have systematically examined the relationship between trauma exposure, mental health disorders, and substance use disorders. As a result, there are a good number of combined treatments and curricula for PTSD and other trauma-related symptoms and substance abuse, and many show promise in empirical studies as well. Additional resources, research, and practice–research collaboration are needed to enhance and build the therapeutic offerings available to women with co-occurring trauma and substance use disorders. In addition, community-based substance abuse treatment programs should continue to be cognizant and raise awareness of the limitations and impact of traditional addictions treatment on women who are survivors of trauma.

3

OTHER CO-OCCURRING
PSYCHIATRIC DISORDERS

Trauma has many psychological consequences. As mentioned earlier, posttraumatic stress disorder (PTSD) and complex PTSD are common outcomes of trauma but are not the only forms of trauma response. In many cases there are multiple consequences that could be diagnosed as distinct clinical disorders. These other comorbid psychiatric and behavioral problems cause impairment and distress and, like PTSD, may be sequelae of early and repeated trauma. The symptoms include mood and anxiety disorders, dissociation, compulsive behaviors, and features of various personality disorders. As a result of having many overlapping symptoms, diagnosing these conditions, especially in the context of substance abuse, can be complex. Women often enter addictions treatment with long lists of previously diagnosed psychiatric disorders, which can be experienced as stigmatizing and degrading as well as confusing.

The focus of this chapter is on reviewing some of the most commonly occurring comorbid conditions that present clinical challenges to the substance abuse treatment process and need to be addressed with psychotherapeutic and, in some cases, psychopharmacologic techniques. We present the most frequently co-occurring psychiatric conditions, along with some of their overlapping symptoms. In addition, we pay special attention to the interrelationships among these symptoms, PTSD, and substance use disorders. Our aim is to provide an overview of how to treat potentially complex diagnostic issues that may arise when working with a person who has experienced severe trauma, going beyond the diagnostic labels and addressing the functional impairments that face women with co-occurring problems.

We use the *Diagnostic and Statistical Manual of Mental Disorders* (4th ed., text rev.; *DSM–IV–TR*; American Psychiatric Association, 2000) as a reference point for our discussion of each co-occurring disorder. We recommend that interested addictions specialists read the *DSM–IV–TR* for specific disorders if they think their clients might be experiencing a comorbid condition requiring further assessment. It is important to underscore that diagnostic decisions should be made by individuals specifically trained in psychiatric assessment (usually psychiatrists and clinical psychologists); these are complicated cases and many symptoms may be present, regardless of whether full diagnostic criteria are met. Appendix B at the end of this volume contains a list of standardized assessments that are useful in diagnostic decision making, especially in the context of multiple comorbidities. Some of these scales and diagnostic interviews require specialized training, which can be arranged typically through the scale developer or others who are certified to provide training in these procedures.

Although specific and careful diagnoses are important, given the range of symptoms, syndromes, and other emotional problems experienced by women with addictions, we recommend that substance abuse practitioners develop treatment plans that focus on symptoms or behaviors, rather than on unitary specific disorders. This framework can provide a manageable way to prioritize the types of treatment needed for the most severe problem areas. Interventions such as psychopharmacology, individual counseling, cognitive–behavioral therapy, dialectical behavior therapy (DBT), and psychoeducation can each be useful in addressing these symptoms clusters.

EPIDEMIOLOGY OF PTSD AND CO-OCCURRING DISORDERS

PTSD frequently co-occurs with other psychiatric disorders. In fact, data from both community and clinical samples consistently indicate that the presence of additional disorders in those diagnosed with PTSD is the rule rather than the exception (e.g., see Brady, 1997). A recent epidemiological survey estimates that approximately 80% of individuals with PTSD meet criteria for at least one other psychiatric diagnosis, with 16% having one other diagnosis, 17% having two other diagnoses, and nearly 50% having three or more additional diagnoses (Kessler, Sonnega, Bromet, Hughes, & Nelson, 1995). Table 3.1 presents comorbid diagnoses for men and women who met criteria for PTSD in the National Comorbidity Survey (Kessler et al., 1995). The most common comorbid conditions are substance use disorders, affective disorders

TABLE 3.1

Percentage of Comorbid Diagnoses in Men and Women With Lifetime Posttraumatic Stress Disorder From the National Comorbidity Survey

Comorbid diagnoses	Men (%)	Women (%)
Affective disorders		
Major depressive disorder	47.9	48.5
Dysthymia	21.4	23.3
Mania	11.7	5.7
Anxiety disorders		
Generalized anxiety disorder	16.8	15.0
Panic disorder	7.3	12.6
Simple phobia	31.4	29.0
Social phobia	27.6	28.4
Agoraphobia	16.1	22.4
Substance use disorders		
Alcohol abuse or dependence	51.9	27.9
Drug abuse or dependence	34.5	26.9
Other disorders		
Conduct disorder	43.3	15.4
Any disorder		
No other diagnosis	11.7	21.0
1 diagnosis	14.9	17.2
2 diagnoses	14.4	18.2
≥ 3 diagnoses	59.0	43.6

Note. From "Posttraumatic Stress Disorder in the National Comorbidity Survey," by R. Kessler, A. Sonnega, E. Bromet, M. Hughes, and C. Nelson, 1995, *Archives of General Psychiatry, 52,* p. 1056. Copyright 1995 by the American Medical Association. Reprinted with permission.

(particularly depression), and other anxiety disorders. As we have noted, clients with chronic trauma beginning in childhood are also likely to have a variety of additional psychiatric problems including dissociation, poor impulse control, and interpersonal deficits.

The presence of additional psychiatric disorders also can exacerbate PTSD symptoms and prolong the course of the disorder. For example, individuals with chronic PTSD are more likely to have additional affective or anxiety disorder diagnoses than are individuals with nonchronic PTSD. The fact that PTSD is correlated with such a wide range of other problems makes its presentation quite variable and can complicate clinical assessment and diagnosis.

The extent to which associated disorders typically follow the onset of PTSD remains unclear. There appear to be multiple pathways resulting in several different subtypes of PTSD clients, rather than generalizable patterns of cause and effect. For example, whereas some individuals presenting with PTSD had preexisting psychological problems prior to trauma exposure, others developed additional disorders secondary to the onset of PTSD. There are also those for whom PTSD and related psychiatric conditions developed simultaneously at the time of trauma exposure. Clearly, more research is needed to further understand the variety of sequences and pathways involved in the development of PTSD and related disorders.

There are a number of possible explanations for the frequency with which PTSD occurs in the context of other disorders. Prior histories of other psychiatric disorders are actually risk factors for the development of PTSD, which may contribute to the high levels of comorbidity observed in this population. In addition, individuals with PTSD may have a tendency to report higher levels of symptoms than do those with other psychiatric disorders (Hyler, Fallon, Harrison, & Boudewyns, 1987). Substantial levels of comorbidity may be in part explained by the experience of high levels of global distress perceived by individuals with PTSD.

The substantial degree of overlap between PTSD and many other psychiatric disorders—most notably depression (i.e., sleep disturbance and social withdrawal) and other anxiety disorders (i.e., panic attacks and avoidance)— has led some experts to believe that the PTSD diagnosis is flawed in its failure to take into account the complexity of trauma adaptations. This argument has led to the proposal that many conditions classified as comorbid disorders should instead be recognized as part of a complex range of trauma-related problems, rather than conceptualized as separate and discrete disorders (van der Kolk, Pelcovitz, et al., 1996).

MOOD SYMPTOMS AND DISORDERS

Major depressive disorder (MDD) and dysthymia are the psychiatric disorders most likely to co-occur with PTSD (see Exhibit 3.1). In the National Comorbidity Survey (Kessler et al., 1995), those with PTSD were 2 to 3 times more likely to have an affective disorder than those without PTSD. The relationship between PTSD and MDD is complex as a result of the substantial overlap of symptoms, as illustrated in the Exhibit 3.1.

The main way to differentiate PTSD from major depression is to determine whether the PTSD symptoms were present before the traumatic stressor or began following exposure to trauma. In certain cases this sequence is easily determined. In individuals who have experienced childhood abuse,

EXHIBIT 3.1
Key Features of Both Posttraumatic Stress Disorder
and Major Depressive Disorder

- Sleep disturbance
- Difficulty concentrating
- Avoidance and withdrawal
- Lack of interest and pleasure in activities
- Sense of isolation and distance from others

multiple traumas, or both, the timing of symptom onset in relation to trauma exposure can be extremely difficult to assess.

In those who do meet criteria for both disorders, depression is often secondary to prolonged PTSD. In this scenario, the development of depression can be viewed as a response to years of struggling with chronic, painful, and disruptive PTSD symptoms. The reverse sequence is also common. A history of MDD has been identified as a risk factor for the development of PTSD following exposure to a traumatic event. Clinicians should also be aware that although PTSD and depression are related, they are frequently independent responses to the experience of trauma. As might be expected, those who meet criteria for both disorders are typically more distressed and have more chronic symptoms and a higher degree of impairment than those who have only one of the disorders.

PTSD, with or without major depression, is also a significant risk factor for suicidal behavior. Studies have shown that suicidality in those exposed to trauma is more frequent in individuals with a primary diagnosis of PTSD than in individuals with other diagnoses (Ferrada-Noli, Asberg, Ormstad, Lundin, & Sundbom, 1998).

Finally, another significant mood disorder that may co-occur with PTSD and substance use disorders is bipolar disorder. Bipolar disorder (frequently referred to as manic depression) is characterized by uncontrollable and significant mood swings. Of all Axis I disorders, bipolar disorder is most likely to co-occur with substance use disorders (Regier et al., 1990). Bipolar disorder has a number of different subtypes, but the presence of some form of manic or hypomanic episodes is the hallmark of the disorder. Mania and hypomania are both characterized by elevated mood or significant irritability, as well as by symptoms such as decreased need for sleep, increased activity and talkativeness, inflated self-esteem, racing thoughts, and distractibility. Mania and hypomania are distinguished by (a) the length of mood disturbance (at least 1 week for mania; 4 days for hypomania) and (b) the level of impairment caused by the episode (mania typically results in marked impairment and oftentimes psychosis and hospitalization, whereas hypomania does not). The symptom overlap of mania and hypomania with PTSD is mainly in the realm of PTSD hyperarousal symptoms (*DSM–IV–TR* Criterion D). These include irritability, sleep disturbance, and difficulty concentrating.

Anxiety Symptoms and Disorders

It is also common for individuals with PTSD to have at least one other anxiety disorder diagnosis, with prevalence rates estimated at about 50% (see Exhibit 3.2). This is not unexpected, because PTSD is also classified as a *DSM–IV–TR* anxiety disorder. Simple and social phobias are the most common anxiety conditions that are comorbid with PTSD, although panic disorder also frequently co-occurs. There is less systematic information available

EXHIBIT 3.2
Key Features of Both Posttraumatic Stress Disorder and Other Anxiety Disorders

- Phobic avoidance of certain places, situations, and/or people
- Persistent fear that is out of proportion to the situation
- Hyperarousal (e.g., accelerated heart rate)
- Derealization (i.e., feelings of unreality)
- Depersonalization (i.e., being detached from oneself)
- Fear of losing control
- Disturbed sleep
- Poor concentration
- Restlessness or feeling on edge
- Irritability

on the relationship between PTSD and generalized anxiety disorder or between PTSD and obsessive compulsive disorder.

As previously discussed with MDD, PTSD also has many symptoms in common with other anxiety disorders, which can make the diagnostic process challenging. For example, symptoms of avoidance are characteristic of social phobia, specific phobia, agoraphobia, and PTSD. Hyperarousal, derealization, depersonalization, and fear of losing control are physiological features of both panic disorder and PTSD. Symptoms of disturbed sleep, concentration, and restlessness are associated with all anxiety disorders. See Exhibit 3.3 for a clinical example of a client with comorbid anxiety and substance use disorder.

Dissociative Symptoms and Disorders

Dissociative disorders are characterized by disruptions in functions of consciousness, memory, identity, or perception of the environment (American Psychiatric Association, 2000). With the exception of PTSD, dissociative disorder diagnoses are the most closely associated with histories of severe childhood trauma. The degree of dissociation—the failure to integrate emotions, thoughts, and perceptions about specific events—is related to greater and earlier trauma and PTSD severity. Dissociation should be regarded on a continuum. Most drivers can relate to the experience of covering many miles and not really remembering the details of that part of the journey. This is a mild form of dissociation. In more clinically significant terms, individuals who lose track of time, space, self, or aspects of self may be at the more severe end of the continuum. In the DSM–IV (American Psychiatric Association, 1994) field trial (van der Kolk, Roth, Pelcovitz, & Mandel, 1993), dissociation was the most frequent symptom of PTSD, present in 82% of individuals with current PTSD and 52% of individuals with lifetime PTSD. Also of note are findings that those who experience dissociative symptoms at the time of the trauma exposure (e.g., "It was like I was watching him rape me from the corner of the room") are at

EXHIBIT 3.3
Clinical Case Example: Overlapping Axis I Mood, Anxiety, and Substance Use Disorder in a Woman With Multiple Childhood Traumatic Exposures

Sue was a 50-year-old, single Caucasian woman who presented for outpatient substance abuse treatment for drinking and depression. Sue reported drinking at least a pint of vodka every day and had not worked for months. She was in jeopardy of losing her apartment. Sue was also severely depressed. Her depression and drinking had increased after the break up of a long-term relationship with another woman. She had visited a neighborhood medical clinic for an evaluation and had received a prescription for Prozac. She was unsure how much it was helping, had run out of the prescription, and had not made it back to the clinic to get a refill. In general, she was withdrawn and was spending more and more time alone in her apartment. She was estranged from much of her family and had no social supports. She reported passive suicidal ideation ("I wish I were dead") but did not have a specific plan or intent to harm herself. She also had a history of self-harm, including burning herself with cigarettes (she was a heavy smoker). She had a family history of alcoholism, with her father and two brothers being heavy drinkers. Her mother died of cancer when she was 11 years old. After that time, her father physically and sexually abused her. She was very clear that she did not want to discuss her trauma history in any detail but acknowledged that it was something that had bothered her throughout her life. She was also very ambivalent about stopping her drinking.

Sue had many treatment needs. Her treatment plan addressed drinking, depression, trauma history, psychosocial functioning, and medical care. The treatment team worked with Sue to prioritize her goals and treatment. Sue agreed to try to decrease her drinking—she would not commit to stopping entirely until her depression was less severe. She was evaluated by the staff psychiatrist and was put on a combination of antidepressants and mood stabilizers as well as referred for a consultation for naltrexone treatment to help with her alcohol cravings and use. Her psychosocial treatments included weekly individual psychotherapy and an early recovery group. Her therapist began working with her on relapse prevention and coping skills training to address her drinking and began gradually introducing the potential effect that her trauma history could have on her continued drinking and depression. Given Sue's family history of cancer and her lack of medical care, she was also referred for general physical and gynecological exams. Her therapist also worked with her on her fears about addressing her medical needs.

higher risk for developing subsequent PTSD. Although a correlation has been shown between the severity and duration of the trauma and later severity of dissociative symptoms, current research does not allow for conclusions about causality.

Formerly known as multiple personality disorder, dissociative identity disorder (DID) is a dissociative disorder in which two or more distinct identities or personality states take control of a person's behavior, resulting in the person's inability to recall important personal information (American Psychiatric Association, 2000). Individuals with DID often report severe histories of childhood sexual abuse, physical abuse, or both. The different identities or dissociated self-states (Bromberg, 1993; Howell, 2005) may be seen as ways of coping with extremely stressful experiences. Given the high reports of trauma in individuals with DID, traumatic stress symptoms and PTSD often co-occur with the diagnosis, as do substance use disorders, self-mutilation, and suicidal behavior.

Eating Disorders

There is an ongoing debate regarding the role of childhood sexual abuse, and to a lesser extent childhood physical abuse, in the development of eating disorders. The central question is whether childhood sexual abuse represents a specific factor for development of an eating disorder or whether childhood abuse is a general risk factor for the development of any psychiatric disorder.

In eating disorder populations, an early trauma history seems most related to bulimia as well as comorbid mood disorders, borderline personality disorder (BPD), and problems with impulsivity. In nonclinical samples, bulimic respondents report significantly higher prevalence rates of current and lifetime PTSD than do nonbulimic respondents. Many clinicians have observed that for a subset of their clients, eating disorder symptoms have developed as an attempt to manage overwhelming negative emotions and psychic pain related to childhood trauma. For these individuals, disordered eating behavior may function as a maladaptive method for dealing with disruptive trauma-related symptoms, in the same way that substances are used to self-medicate when faced with symptoms. This model is consistent with clinical descriptions of binge eating as an escape from intrusive negative thoughts or distress. There has also been much discussion in the eating disorder literature about how childhood abuse, and particularly sexual abuse, may negatively affect body image and body esteem, leading to long-term difficulties in these areas. Issues of control are also central for those who struggle with eating disorders and are likely to have particular relevance for those who present with a history of interpersonal violation and abuse.

Personality Disorders

By definition, personality disorders are long-standing, maladaptive patterns of seeing and dealing with the world. The two most common personality disorders that co-occur with substance use and trauma are BPD and antisocial personality disorder (APD). BPD is a pattern of instability in relationships, self-image, and emotions (American Psychiatric Association, 2000). Another essential feature of the disorder is marked impulsivity. Early childhood histories of abuse and multiple childhood abuse experiences are also often reported in individuals with BPD, as well as in other syndromes involving impaired impulse control, such as eating disorders and self-mutilation. BPD, in turn, is associated with high levels of dissociation. It has frequently been hypothesized that early disruptions in relationships with primary caregivers, including parental abuse, neglect, or both, are central to the development of BPD and its characteristic unstable moods, behaviors, and relationships. Of BPD clients, 40% to 71% report histories of sexual abuse (Zanarini, 2000).

Although the retrospective nature of most investigations limits their conclusiveness, the theory that childhood abuse plays a formative role in BPD is supported, especially in those who are temperamentally vulnerable. This has led some experts to view BPD as a maladaptive behavioral response, which could be also classified as a complicated posttraumatic syndrome (Herman, 1992a, 1992b). Conceptualizing childhood abuse as an important factor in the development of BPD could lend some insight into the higher prevalence of this disorder among women. Because girls are 2 to 3 times more likely to be sexually victimized during childhood than boys, they are more frequently exposed to conditions that may put them at risk for developing BPD.

APD is characterized by a chronic disregard for and violation of the rights of others that begins in childhood (American Psychiatric Association, 2000). By age 15, individuals with APD demonstrate characteristics of conduct disorder, such as aggression or violence toward people or animals, destruction of property, truancy, and substance abuse. In adulthood, APD is manifest in behaviors such as repeated lying, breaking the law, irresponsibility, and lack of remorse for wrongdoing. Preliminary information about the association between APD and PTSD came from clinical studies with male veterans (Kulka et al., 1990). In this population the most prevalent disorders co-occurring with PTSD appear to be substance abuse, major depression, and APD. More recently, large epidemiological studies with civilians have also found high rates of co-occurring APD among individuals with PTSD (Kessler et al., 1995). Consistent with previous research on non-PTSD samples, men (43%) have been found to have higher rates of APD than women (15%).

The interconnections among childhood behavior problems, trauma, and adult antisocial behavior are complex. Much has been written in the clinical literature about how childhood victimization, and parental physical abuse in particular, can often lead to aggressive and antisocial behavior. Behavioral and object-relational models provide frameworks for understanding intergenerational cycles of trauma and violence. For example, the *cycle of violence theory* suggests that individuals with a history of abuse will be more likely to engage in physically violent behavior in adulthood. This theory has been supported by studies that have found higher rates of violence perpetration among individuals with a history of childhood abuse than among those with no history of abuse (e.g., see Kling, 2000). Consistent reports that criminal offenders with APD often have severe childhood abuse histories are also compelling.

There is evidence that a diagnosis of childhood conduct disorder is a risk factor for developing PTSD in response to trauma exposure in adulthood. APD also increases the risk for PTSD because it is correlated with the likelihood of being exposed to traumatic experiences. Data also indicate that PTSD is a risk factor for the development of adult antisocial behavior, even after childhood behavior problems and trauma exposure are taken into account. Thus, as with the disorders previously discussed, the relationship between PTSD and APD appears to be multifaceted and mutually influential.

Although there certainly are clients in substance abuse treatment who also present with personality disorders, clinicians should be aware of a tendency to overdiagnose these conditions, especially in the context of chronic trauma and substance abuse. As previously mentioned, BPD is diagnosed primarily in women, thereby leaving women clients more apt to receive the diagnosis just by virtue of their gender. BPD symptoms overlap with experiences common in PTSD, such as numbing (i.e., emptiness), impulsivity, difficulties in affect regulation, and dissociation. In addition, the diagnostic criteria for both BPD and APD include behaviors that can be attributed to chronic substance abuse. The differential diagnosis of Axis I and Axis II conditions can be complex and should be approached thoughtfully and with understanding of order of onset and other issues in evaluating patients with multiple diagnoses.

Furthermore, in our clinical experience, we have found it preferable to err on the side of underdiagnosing personality disorders in our clients. As we have been describing, women present to treatment with a number of different symptoms and conditions that need clinical attention and can be addressed in the context of an Axis I disorder. Axis II pathology has many negative implications for both patients and clinicians. Unless there is a compelling reason to do so, we refrain from labeling a woman *borderline*, a designation that can follow her through every treatment system she enters. Although we are not advocating misdiagnosis, we are advocating for the best treatment possible for women with oftentimes difficult-to-treat problems that can be off-putting and intimidating to treatment providers. See Exhibit 3.4 for a continuing case example highlighting overlap with Axis II psychopathology.

TREATMENTS FOR COMORBID DISORDERS

Although specific treatments are available for many of the comorbid disorders previously described, the approaches used to treat them have considerable overlap. We now present different treatments and models that can be used in the treatment of PTSD, substance abuse, and their comorbid disorders.

Treatments for Depression and Anxiety

In a meta-analysis of antidepressant treatment for depression and substance use disorders, Nunes and Levin (2004) recommended combined treatments including psychotherapy and medication. Guided by data from more than 40 clinical trials, Nunes and Levin concluded that antidepressant medica-

EXHIBIT 3.4
Clinical Case Example: Overlap With Axis II Psychopathology

Sue started treatment and began to follow through on the various aspects of her treatment plan. She began to meet with her individual therapist, who was a woman. Sue expressed difficulty in trusting her therapist, as well as with other providers she had met at the clinic and in the past. She had gone to the medical clinic for her physical but felt that the doctor talked down to her. She also had met with the clinic psychiatrist, with whom she also did not feel comfortable. She had attended one early recovery group that was led by another member of the clinical staff. Sue was quiet in group and did not participate. Various providers who had contact with her experienced her as defensive and irritable.

Sue appeared to be most connected to her individual therapist. They worked on issues of trust and how her lack of trust affected other relationships, including those with other treatment providers who were trying to help her. The therapist also focused their individual work on self-care and developing better coping skills in dealing with conflict or painful emotional states. In the early phase of treatment, Sue had significant difficulty cutting down on her drinking. The therapist's suggestion of the possible need for inpatient treatment was met with Sue's anger and accusations that the therapist, like others in her life, could not be trusted. Sue left the clinic and did not return for 2 weeks. When she did return, she was intoxicated, tearful, and reported suicidal ideation. The therapist took Sue to the emergency room, where she was evaluated and admitted for detoxification.

Note. This case study is continued from Exhibit 3.3.

tions exert a modest beneficial effect for clients with combined depressive and substance use disorders and that concurrent psychotherapy directly targeting the addiction is also indicated. This recommendation for combined treatments is in line with the clinical decisions we have encountered in working with substance-abusing women with trauma and depression.

Cognitive–behavioral therapy, in particular, has been used to treat depression for many years. Developed by Aaron T. Beck in the early 1960s as a short-term psychotherapy for depression (Beck, 1964, 1967), the cognitive–behavioral model focuses on the distorted or dysfunctional thoughts that influence mood and behavior and are common in all psychological disturbances. Cognitive–behavioral therapy is goal oriented and problem focused. It requires active client participation and educates a client about symptoms so that she can ultimately become her own therapist. The therapy is typically time limited and uses a variety of techniques to accomplish change.

Many treatments for PTSD and substance use disorders are also based on cognitive–behavioral principles. Relapse prevention (Carroll, 1996; Marlatt & Gordon, 1985), one of the most commonly used approaches for treating substance use disorders, is a cognitive–behavioral treatment. Seeking safety (Najavits, 2002) is also grounded in cognitive–behavioral principles. In any cognitive–behavioral model, whether dealing with symptoms of depression, PTSD, or substance use, therapy focuses on helping the client identify the underlying thoughts and assumptions in situations that contribute to the feelings and then behaviors related to the problems. For example, an individual with PTSD may assume that she will never be able to overcome her symptoms or that every situation is unsafe and has the potential for harm. These assumptions may lead to feelings of helplessness, which frequently contribute to depression. These assumptions might also lead to increased substance use. One of the first steps of any cognitive–behavioral approach is to help clients to identify these types of thinking patterns, assumptions, and beliefs; generate alternative perspectives; and determine useful actions and coping mechanisms to support them.

Because trauma exposure and PTSD have such significant effects on interpersonal functioning and development over the lifespan and a substantial overlap with depression, interpersonal psychotherapy (IPT) may help to address interpersonal problems in a more targeted fashion. IPT (Klerman & Weissman, 1993; Klerman, Weissman, Rounsaville, & Chevron, 1984) was developed to address the interpersonal dimensions of depression using a psychodynamic framework, but focusing on a more current here-and-now approach to addressing symptoms and social dysfunction so common to this major mental illness. Over the past decades, IPT has been applied more broadly and found to be effective in treating a number of other severe and persistent mental illnesses that affect interpersonal functioning (e.g., bulimia, anxiety disorders). Recently, efforts to apply IPT to trauma populations have also shown promise (Bleiberg & Markowitz, 2005). Typically, IPT is administered as a brief psychotherapy over the course of 16 sessions. In the first phase (1–3 sessions) an assessment of symptoms and diagnoses is made, as well as an assessment of social supports and social functioning. In the second phase, specific areas of interpersonal functioning improvements are targeted and strategies are developed to address these goals. In the final phase (usually the last month of treatment), improvements are reviewed and the treatment focuses on consolidating gains (de Mello, Mari, Bacatchuk, Verdeli, & Neugebauer, 2005). See http://www.interpersonalpsychotherapy.org for more information about IPT and its applications.

In addressing significant comorbid symptoms and syndromes, pharmacotherapy is often an essential component of treatment. If possible, a treatment team should include a psychopharmacologist who is familiar with the special needs of trauma survivors and who is comfortable with the flexibility needed in treating women with trauma and substance use disorders. Many different types of medications exist for all types of symptoms and disorders. As a result, clients may need to try more than one type of medication before finding one that is effective. Selective serotonin reuptake inhibitor (SSRI) antidepressant medications, such as fluoxetine (i.e., Prozac), paroxetine (i.e., Paxil), and sertraline (i.e., Zoloft), decrease problematic symptoms and help regulate sleeping and eating patterns, energy levels, and overall mood and may be appropriate for women with significant depressive symptoms. Bipolar disorder symptoms are almost always treated with psychotropic medications called *mood stabilizers*. The most commonly used and most effective for long-term stabilization is lithium; however, anticonvulsants, such as valproic acid, are good alternatives. These medications require monitoring to determine the appropriate blood levels for maximum efficacy. If psychotic features are present in any mood disorder, an antipsychotic medication, such as risperidone (i.e., Risperdal), aripiprazole (i.e., Abilify), quetiapine (i.e., Seroquel), and olanzapine (i.e., Zyprexa), might be used along with other antidepressants or mood stabilizers. In our clinical experience working with trauma survivors who have a number of other active mental health problems, including substance abuse and anxiety, these "new generation" antipsychotic medications can be particularly useful in treating the hyperarousal symptoms of PTSD that overlap with other disorders. Although many of the anxiolytic drugs have high abuse potential, these antipsychotic medications can exert a nonaddictive tranquilizing effect that clients report help with sleeplessness, anxiety, and other symptoms. These medications should be prescribed only for short-term use or they should be carefully monitored because long-term side effects are unknown.

SSRI antidepressants have also been approved for use with various anxiety disorders. In fact, sertraline and paroxetine are approved specifically for the treatment of PTSD. Although benzodiazepines, such as clonazepam (i.e., Klonopin), alprazolam (i.e., Xanax), diazepam (i.e., Valium), and lorazepam (i.e., Ativan), are also used to treat anxiety, they also have significant addiction potential and should be used cautiously with substance abusers. Of the benzodiazepines, clonazepam has the lowest abuse liability because of its long half-life; however, all of these medications have some abuse potential. Tolerance and withdrawal symptoms can occur with any of these medications, and therefore they should be used sparingly and under the careful guidance of a psychiatrist. Sleeping problems are hallmark symptoms for those with trauma histories and PTSD. A variety of nonaddictive sleeping medications to treat insomnia may be considered carefully for short-term use.

Treatment for Dissociative Disorders

The treatment for dissociative disorders has typically consisted of long-term, individual psychotherapy as well as medications that might decrease anxiety or mood symptoms. Psychotherapy has consisted of approaches that work toward recovering, reclaiming, and integrating the dissociated parts of one's life or experience. The most common approach is to work toward stability and integration over time. Clients with severe dissociative symptoms will most likely work in treatment for an extensive period. Movement toward integration and decreased dissociation typically requires persistence, patience, and continuity by client and clinician to enable a client to develop the necessary trust to engage in this difficult process.

Treatments for Personality Disorders

Because personality disorders are long-standing patterns of maladaptive behavior, psychotherapy for personality disorders tends to be long term and intensive, often lasting a year or more. DBT is the most researched and successful approach to treating personality disorders, especially BPD. DBT is used to improve the management of emotional states and affect regulation. Although DBT has not been used specifically for PTSD, many of its characteristics overlap with those related to complex trauma. As a result, the techniques of DBT can be quite useful for women experiencing problems with emotional regulation. Results from a trial of DBT in female opioid users (Linehan et al., 2002) also suggest its effectiveness in women who are known to have high rates of co-occurring trauma.

APD is largely considered one of the most difficult disorders to treat. Limited information exists on effective treatments for this disorder. Individuals rarely seek treatment on their own and do not acknowledge that they have a problem. Individuals with APD typically enter treatment through the legal system or drug abuse treatment. If open and willing to trust, these individuals may be able to make headway in group therapy with some pressure from peers. *Offender groups* are often used to treat individuals who have committed crimes, usually violent in nature. Many include cognitive–behavioral approaches. Few systematic studies of the efficacy of these groups exist, however. In clinical practice, antisocial behavior must be addressed in a straightforward way, being mindful of the interplay between antisocial behavior, substance abuse, and increased risk for being a victim or perpetrator of trauma.

Regardless of the treatment approach, the most important component of personality disorder treatment tends to be the therapeutic relationship. Therapists who treat individuals with personality disorders must provide a safe and stable therapeutic environment in a context of trust. Clients with personality disorders often are unable to see the negative consequences of their attitudes and behaviors. Therefore, therapists must be willing and able to point out, often repeatedly, the undesirable consequences of the client's behaviors. Setting ground rules, or boundaries, can also be important. In the case of Sue (see Exhibit 3.3), the initial work focused on developing trust, but when Sue's behavior became dangerous, the therapist had to set firm limits and provide a higher level of care and intervention in the form of evaluation in an emergency department and admission to inpatient care.

CONCLUSION

In this chapter, we presented a basic understanding of many of the psychological consequences of trauma exposure. We detailed how PTSD—the most common disorder associated with experiences of trauma—often co-occurs with a variety of other psychiatric disorders. We also presented information about how the relationship between PTSD and other associated disorders is often complex and defies simple cause-and-effect models. A growing area of research involves examining the multiple potential pathways between PTSD and other disorders and how various sequences may affect clinical presentation. Although additional investigation is needed to further clarify these issues, we do know that more often than not, women with PTSD have at least one additional psychiatric diagnosis and in many cases have more than one other disorder. The presence of other psychiatric disorders typically worsens and prolongs the course of PTSD and complicates clinical assessment and diagnosis. The most common comorbid disorders include substance use disorders, MDD, and other anxiety disorders.

We reviewed a number of suggested treatment modalities that encompass behavioral psychotherapy approaches in combination with medication for symptom reductions. In treating the comorbid client with PTSD and substance abuse disorders, clinicians must be vigilant in identifying and providing treatment for any additional symptoms that may arise. Above all, therapists must take into consideration the full scope of problems faced by such clients by using a multimodal approach, with clear symptom and syndrome targets, and goals.

II

THE IMPACT OF TRAUMA
ON FUNCTIONING

4
EMOTION REGULATION

Mental health and substance abuse treatment providers are all familiar with clients for whom managing emotion is a primary treatment focus. In particular, intense negative emotions, such as anger, sadness, and abandonment, can quickly become overwhelming for substance-using clients. Often, these are individuals who cannot identify specific feelings, are easily consumed by the intensity of their feelings, and are at a loss to bring them under control. These clients have adopted strategies to help manage moments of distress in ways that seem helpful in the short run but have proved to be ineffective at best and often outright dangerous or self-destructive in the long run. Especially for those with traumatic pasts, difficulties with emotion regulation significantly define their day-to-day functioning.

In this chapter, we provide an overview of the concept of emotion regulation and the developmental impact of trauma on emotion regulatory functions. We draw on converging empirical research in developmental psychology, addictions, and neuroscience to present material to better help practitioners understand emotion regulation deficits they are sure to encounter in settings of trauma and addiction. Finally, we present treatment approaches and models that can be applied by practitioners to help substance-using clients with emotion regulation deficits to cope in more adaptive ways.

EMOTION REGULATION

The complexity of the emotion regulation system makes it difficult to define; nevertheless, the concepts of *emotion regulation* and *emotion dysregulation* are critical to understanding both normal development and the development of psychopathology and substance use. Emotion regulation entails the processes by which individuals influence which emotions arise and when, and how they experience and express these emotions (Gross, 1999). Specifically, these processes involve monitoring, evaluating, and modifying internal feeling states and emotion-related physiological processes, often in the service of accomplishing one's goals (Eisenberg, Fabes, Guthrie, & Reiser, 2000; R. A. Thompson, 1994).

In this way, successful emotion regulation means having the ability to manage and to tolerate stressful emotional experience as well as related physiological arousal. For people with adequate emotional regulation skills, the experience of anger, for example, does not threaten to overtake them but rather can be absorbed and responded to effectively. Being able to respond in flexible and situationally appropriate ways is a critical component of good emotion regulation and provides an essential foundation for a range of subsequent capacities (Eisenberg, Cumberland, & Spinrad, 1998). For example, the ability to control and modulate emotional stimulation is thought to enable the development of social relationships (Calkins, 1994; Cicchetti, Ganiban, & Barnett, 1991; Snyder, Schrepferman, & St. Peter, 1997). It has also been suggested that core self-concepts are significantly defined by the capacity to regulate internal states and by behavioral responses to stress (Cole & Putnam, 1992). Accordingly, emotion regulation skills can influence not just an individual's ability to handle strong feeling states but also a number of related experiences, including how she knows herself and how she interacts with those around her.

In contrast, individuals with deficits in emotion regulation are typically unable to tolerate stressful emotional experiences and are easily derailed by the physiological states that accompany these feelings. This can jeopardize self-concept and interpersonal efficacy and increases the likelihood that an individual will seek out alternative ways to manage these experiences. Drug and alcohol use often become an attractive way to compensate for these deficits (Khantzian, 1997; Krystal, 1997).

DEVELOPMENTAL INFLUENCES ON EMOTION REGULATION

During infancy and early childhood, a child's caregivers play a significant role in regulating the child's emotions and behaviors. An infant's knowledge of her internal states is thought to be diffuse and undefined, and it is only through interactions with others around her that feelings are modulated, elaborated, and eventually become known and understood (e.g., see Bion, 1962). In this way a child starts to develop an understanding of what it means to be upset and soothed or hungry and fed, and with increasing complexity the child learns to differentiate her feelings as she grows. A caregiver's capacity to help her child absorb and comprehend varying emotions forms the basis for understanding and integrating affective experiences throughout her life.

With age, children become more active in this process and begin relying more on their own internal resources to manage and express their emotion (Eisenberg & Morris, 2002). Although preschool children are beginning to use some basic emotion regulation strategies, they still seek adults to help them regulate more arousing events (Cole, Michel, & Teti, 1994). Caregivers manage children's emotions by paying attention to their distress, by choosing appropriate situations for the child, and by providing information such as facial cues and narratives to help the child process and interpret experiences (Eisenberg, 1998). The absence of responsive caregivers who can help a child make sense of her internal world and her interactions with the outside world may set the stage for a child's emotional experiences to feel disorganized and ultimately unmanageable.

Given appropriate opportunities and environments, however, by age 8 children show advances in their ability to use a range of coping strategies to regulate emotional reactions to stressful situations (Eisenberg, 1998). Some strategies include thinking pleasant thoughts, reappraising the situation, shifting and refocusing attention, and cognitive avoidance (Eisenberg & Morris, 2002). At this point, children have begun to know and differentiate some of their feeling states and have begun to incorporate the emotion regulation skills and strategies they have learned through interactions with those around them. The success with which children learn to apply and implement these skills has implications for their ability to negotiate emotionally stressful situations, particularly traumatic stressors, as they grow into adulthood. This may influence their choice of alternative means of "coping," such as the use of substances to help manage overwhelming feeling states.

IMPACT OF CHILDHOOD VICTIMIZATION ON EMOTION REGULATION

The potentially serious short-term and long-term consequences of childhood exposure to interpersonal trauma have come into sharper focus because of the recent work of developmental researchers. There is now intriguing empirical support in developmental research suggesting that childhood victimization and associated traumatic stress may influence maturing self-regulatory systems, including emotion regulation.

As discussed earlier, appropriate emotion regulation is critical to successful family, peer, and social functioning (Pynoos, Steinberg, & Goenjian, 1996). Childhood trauma, however, can seriously disrupt the development of emotion regulation skills and the capacity for interpersonal relatedness, leading to long-term difficulties in these areas (van der Kolk, 1996). When physical or sexual abuse, family violence, or severe neglect or abandonment begin early in childhood, the child's psychological and biological development may be profoundly compromised. Some have argued that the problems of emotion regulation and interpersonal functioning are a distinct feature of childhood trauma and result from trauma's disruptive impact on the achievement of the developmental goals of affect regulation and interpersonal relatedness (van der Kolk, 1996).

Childhood victimization affects emotional regulation in multiple ways. Most childhood abuse occurs at the hands of someone known to the child, often a close friend of the family or a family member (e.g., see Molnar, Buka, & Kessler, 2001), contrary to alarmist notions perpetuated by the media, or among the general public, of children being abducted and harmed by strangers. By itself, this violation of a child's physical integrity and emotional trust is enough to send a child into a confusing and overwhelming emotional tailspin. She is asked to make sense of the bewildering experience of being violated by someone who is supposed to love and protect her. Her own development and ability to know and respond to her own feelings requires the consistent reflective feedback of those close to her, but how can this possibly occur when one of those people is turning her world upside down? This person not only fails to offer consistency and guidance in the development of emotional regulation but also introduces malevolence and violence in the guise of caring and affection, destroying any sense of what the child can rely on. She cannot possibly make sense of the conflicting feelings and roles thrust upon her. Davies and Frawley (1994) wrote of this impossible dilemma and how it often leads the survivor of childhood sexual abuse to feel crazy and out of control: "Theirs is a world that is dangerous and invasive; there is no order and predictability; people are either betrayers or abusers" (p. 113).

In addition, the abused child is often met with a lack of validation on the part of other family members, who cement her confusion through their ignorance of the abuse (or, in some cases, unwillingness to acknowledge its reality), disbelief as to its existence when reported, and even direct blame of the child as an instigator of the abuse. Thus, for children who have experienced early trauma, there is often the staggering effect of not only the traumatic events but also the inattentive and unresponsive family environment in which the abuse occurs or in which it is revealed. Children must grapple with the feelings created by the abuse as well as the reaction to the abuse, or the inaction, of those around her.

In families in which an abused child is able to report abuse and the report is met with an appropriate protective response, the impact of the abuse is frequently mitigated (Flannery, 1990). In the absence of such parental validation, however, the overwhelming experience of the physical violation overpowers the child's ability to regulate her distress adaptively. In the typical abusive family system, fear and distress are denied and minimized. Moreover, in families in which there is physical violence, either perpetrated on a child or between adults, emotion regulation skills are further undermined by the lessons of aggression. Although the pathways by which parental aggression is passed on to future generations are still being elucidated (e.g., see Hien, Cohen, Caldeira, Batchelder, & Wasserman, 2008), violence demonstrates that rage is acceptable, and even desirable. From a social learning perspective, when an adult in the house erupts violently, and no one is able to intervene, rage is modeled as a path to control, dominance, and intimidation, which a survivor may later adopt when faced with intense uncomfortable feelings, particularly those of shame, humiliation, and powerlessness. She has had no alternative models from which to learn the benefits or ways of modulating anger.

NEUROBIOLOGICAL CORRELATES OF EMOTION REGULATION DEFICITS

Advances in neurobiology have expanded our understanding of emotion regulation and the impact of trauma. Developmental neurobiological studies provide preliminary information as to how early childhood trauma may profoundly affect the developing brain structures responsible for basic self-regulatory functions such as emotion regulation mechanisms (De Bellis, 2002; Liu, Diorio, Day, Francis, & Meaney, 2000; Siegal, 1999; Teicher, 2002). Early trauma may be associated with an increase in the release of stress hormones, as well as with abnormal rhythms of hormone release, which may, in turn, negatively affect critical cellular growth during specific critical periods of childhood development (see De Bellis, 2002, and Teicher, 2002, for a full review of this literature). Repeated patterns of intense emotional experiences characteristic of early trauma exposure may also lead to chronic changes in emotional sensitivity levels (Siegal, 1999), leaving abuse survivors more vulnerable to emotional challenges as the threshold for becoming dysregulated is lowered.

Although it is not yet clear how complex brain structures are affected, excessive stress hormones may lead to impairments in the *limbic system*. Generally considered to be the emotional center of the brain, the limbic system is involved with the identification, processing, regulation, and memory of feeling states. At the center of the limbic system is a core set of three structures—the *amygdala*, the *hippocampus*, and the *hypothalamus*. Each of these structures has its own function with direct or indirect connections to other regions of the brain. When an emotion is triggered, the brain must determine whether the stimulus that provokes a feeling is real (e.g., a sensory input from the natural world) or imagined (i.e., a thought). The steps between perception of a stimulus and production of a feeling (i.e., the amygdala) involve the brain systems using recognition and memory (i.e., the hippocampus). Expression of feelings may take the form of automatic physiological responses (i.e., physical sensations generated by hormonal changes) such as sweating or blushing (initiated by the hypothalamus) or actions such as motoric changes in facial expressions or body language. It appears to be in the overlapping connections of the amygdala, hippocampus, hypothalamus, and their related brain areas that the basis for emotion is formed.

Neurobiological research on trauma and the stress response (e.g., see Pitman, van der Kolk, Orr, & Greenberg, 1990; Yehuda, 2000) has documented that adults with chronic posttraumatic stress disorder (PTSD) demonstrate neurobiological changes in the volume and activity levels of major structures in the limbic system, including the amygdala and hippocampus (Sapolsky, 2000; Teicher, 2002), hypersensitivity of the *hypothalamic-pituitary-adrenal axis* to *cortisol*, which is a hormone involved in the stress response (Yehuda, 2000), and release of neurotransmitters leading to the dysregulation of arousal systems (Friedman, 1993; Pitman et al., 1990; Southwick et al., 1999). The main symptoms of PTSD correspond to these documented neurobiological changes; all involve self-regulatory functions.

This research has highlighted the neurobiological underpinnings of the impact of traumatic stress on the body's ability to regulate emotion. Knowing how the brain and body are structurally and biochemically altered by trauma enables us also to consider a neurobiological perspective of a traumatized individual's vulnerability to substance use. Traumatic stress appears to be a vulnerability factor for substance use disorders in a variety of ways (see Hien, Cohen, & Campbell, 2005, for a full review); however, one specific pathway may involve the use of alcohol and other drugs to dampen the biological effects of dysregulated stress response systems (Higley, Hasert, Suomi, & Linnoila, 1991), increasing the probability of alcoholism and substance dependence.

DEVELOPMENTAL CONSEQUENCES OF EMOTION REGULATION DEFICITS

Research confirms that exposure to interpersonal trauma places a person at risk for lifelong problems with regulating emotions. Findings demonstrate that exposure to that childhood trauma disrupts many emotion regulation functions and is associated with cognitive and behavioral dysregulation (Shields, Ryan, & Cicchetti, 1994), hypervigilance (Reider & Cicchetti, 1989), biased information processing and cognitive problem solving (Crick & Dodge, 1994; Dodge, 1989), deficits of affect lability, poor emotional tolerance and expression, and maladaptive emotion-focused coping (Hien & Miele, 2003).

Exposure to childhood traumatic stress challenges maturing emotional regulation mechanisms at multiple developmental points. Trauma may interfere with the preschool tasks of naming and differentiating emotional states, with the school-age child's developing capacity to elaborate on emotional expression, and with the adolescent's task of achieving an understanding of the origin and consequences of emotions (Parens, 1991). The developmental achievement of emotion regulation rests on successful acquisition of these skills and has consequences for social self-development, as previously described.

Studies indicate that problems with emotion regulation in trauma-exposed children are already apparent in pre- and early teen years. For example, a study comparing the emotion management skills of abused girls with those of nonabused control participants, ages 6 to 12, found that the abused girls were more likely to hide their feelings and to have extreme emotional reactions (Shipman, Zeman, Penza, & Champion, 2000). The abused girls had fewer adaptive coping strategies and expected less support and more conflict in situations in which anger was expressed. Thus, even at an early age, childhood abuse is associated with insufficient coping skills, problems in handling strong emotions (particularly anger), and limited expectations of others as resources in emotionally difficult situations. Studies examining the specific role of emotional dysregulation in reactive aggression among children provide further support for the link between a child's inability to self-soothe and to modulate negative feelings during social interactions and aggressive behavior (Shields & Cicchetti, 1998; Snyder et al., 1997). The evidence of these deficits during the preteen and teen years is particularly noteworthy as we think about the use of substances to manage dysregulated emotional states. Adolescent years are a critical time period for the development of substance use disorders.

LONG-TERM CONSEQUENCES OF EMOTION REGULATION DEFICITS

We have seen how traumatized individuals as children and then as adults often experience severe ongoing problems as a result of inadequate emotion regulation skills. Studies confirm that the younger the victims are at the time of the trauma exposure and the longer the duration of the trauma, the more likely they are to have a range of problems in a variety of areas in addition to PTSD symptoms. These additional symptoms appear to represent various forms of emotional dysregulation and include affective lability, behavioral impulsivity, and aggression (Roth, Newman, Pelcovitz, van der Kolk, & Mandel, 1997). Furthermore, studies comparing individuals with childhood trauma only and individuals with childhood trauma and subsequent victimization in adulthood show that the revictimized individuals consistently have more trouble in affect modulation, anger management, and interpersonal relationships

(Cloitre, Scarvalone, & Difede, 1997; van der Kolk, Roth, Pelcovitz, & Mandel 1993; Zlotnick et al., 1996).

For many individuals, the long-term impact of deficits in emotion regulation on interpersonal functioning is particularly salient, spanning friendships, intimate relationships, relationships with family, and relationships with children. Survivors of childhood abuse frequently report the erratic nature of their relationships as they struggle to contain their own emotional intensity and lability. For survivors who remain in a constant state of hyperarousal following trauma, as if on permanent alert (Herman, 1992b), even minor interpersonal conflicts or small provocations can induce a seemingly intolerable internal experience. More significant interpersonal dilemmas can feel unbearable if the individual lacks the resources to manage her extreme distress. These failures in emotion regulation may lead the individual to react with unmodulated anxiety or withdrawal (van der Kolk, 1988), further confounding interpersonal struggles.

For many survivors, being unable to tolerate strong emotions may have devastating behavioral consequences that jeopardize the safety of the individual. Impulsive and self-damaging behaviors such as suicidal gestures, parasuicidal acts of self-mutilation, binge eating, and, of course, substance use can be seen as efforts to manage overwhelming emotions. The motivation behind self-harming behaviors is extremely complex, with multivariate determinations (see Davies & Frawley, 1994), but has frequently been cited as a response to intense and painful emotion. Among other contributing factors, self-destructive and violently dangerous acting-out behaviors may include a desire to use pain and the body as a way to relieve distress (Pattison & Kahan, 1983) or as a way to escape or avoid negative emotional experiences (Naugle & Follette, 1998). These behaviors offer a compelling but ultimately maladaptive solution to help manage emotion dysregulation.

Similarly, many survivors use dissociation as an effort to grapple with the fundamentally irreconcilable and unbearable feelings engendered by abusive situations. Dissociation, we mentioned earlier, is an identifying feature of the constellation of symptoms of complex PTSD. Dissociation can occur on a continuum from day-to-day dissociative experiences, such as daydreaming, to severe pathological dissociation (Bernstein & Putnam, 1986), including dissociative identity disorder. Throughout this range, dissociation has been understood to reflect a "disruption of normal integrative functions" (Putnam, 1989, p. 6) and represents a defensive function in the emotional world of an individual. As a response to trauma, dissociation represents a split in consciousness that enables part of the individual to be unaware of the traumatic events and intense feelings associated with it (Davies & Frawley, 1994; Herman, 1992b; Rothschild, 2000). By these means, the individual is able to package and put aside some of the intolerable aspects of her experience and carry on a semblance of her life. Rather than make sense of conflicting perspectives, such as the loving yet incestuous father, or tolerating the pain of his betrayal, those irreconcilable and contradictory features of the experience are tucked away, largely out of awareness.

Initiated as a means for the individual to manage inner conflict caused by trauma exposure, dissociation frequently becomes an enduring strategy used in overwhelming situations long after the original trauma has ceased (Putnam, 1989). Unfortunately, what proved valuable and effective during the original traumatic situation, in which a survivor may have had few or no alternatives, turns out to be a maladaptive strategy in the long run and leaves the adult survivor without other mechanisms with which to handle intense affective experience.

For dissociative clients, emotions that threaten to become overwhelming often trigger a dissociative state in which the distress, as in the traumatic past, is split off from the individual's experience. Depending on the intensity of the dissociative experience, the client's emotional experience may become even more out of control as a result, with the cut-off feelings sometimes rising unexpectedly and with even greater intensity. Individuals with significant dissociative episodes report the pervasive nature of the splitting off of the distressing emotional experience and the accompanying loss of connection to the present environment and to a sense of who she is. In more severe examples, clients report losing time because of the profound secondary confusion and functional impact dissociation. Like some alcohol-induced black-outs, these periods can involve the client in a variety of behaviors for which she has no recollection but the traces of which she may confront after the fact: people she doesn't recognize but who appear to know her, missing items, or new items for which she cannot account.

EMOTION REGULATION AND PSYCHIATRIC DIAGNOSIS

Rather than being characteristic of any one disorder, emotion regulation difficulties cut across multiple diagnostic domains and reflect broad classes of maladaptive psychosocial and behavioral functioning. Many psychiatric disturbances in addition to PTSD can be viewed as disorders of self-regulation (Schore, 1997). Mood disorders, for example, involve dysregulated emotional states that may lead to episodes of depression or mania. Borderline personality disorder is often viewed as a disorder of self-regulation (Grotstein, 1987) given its hallmark features of affect instability, marked reactivity of mood, inappropriate intense anger with lack of control, and unstable relationships.

As a result, numerous clinicians and researchers have suggested that relying on existing diagnoses may not be the best way to capture the range of problems and symptoms, including emotion regulation deficits, often associated with cumulative interpersonal trauma (Herman, 1992; van der Kolk, 1996).

As we discussed in chapter 1 of this volume, diagnoses such as complex PTSD or disorders of extreme stress not otherwise specified (DESNOS) have been proposed as alternative and more representative ways of delineating adaptations to chronic trauma, including pervasive affect regulation problems (van der Kolk et al., 1993). The DESNOS diagnosis includes symptoms of chronic emotion dysregulation and affective impulses, such as difficulty modulating anger and negative emotional states, aggression against self and others, and dissociative symptoms (Pelcovitz et al., 1997).

ASSESSMENT OF EMOTION REGULATION CAPACITIES

As discussed throughout the chapter, the construct of emotion regulation entails a range of domains including cognitive, behavioral, and physiological processes. For purposes of clinical assessment and intervention, it is important to get a picture of the fundamental ways in which the client experiences and manages emotion. Since many clients struggle with describing and differentiating their feelings, it is important for the clinician to ask specific questions to help articulate problematic emotional states and associated thoughts and behaviors. Specific questions should also be asked about the level and type of disruption that emotional difficulties are causing in the client's daily functioning and about any factors, including use of substances, that may make the client more vulnerable to experiencing intense emotion. It is also helpful to get a sense of the range of coping strategies, both unsafe and adaptive, that a client may use in the face of emotional distress and how these strategies are used to shift intolerable states. Maladaptive strategies can become an important focus of treatment, and when substances are involved can be critical in helping a client to establish a solid foundation for recovery. Finally, knowing whether the client is able to access positive emotions and how these are tolerated is also useful in terms of getting a comprehensive picture of a client's emotional life. See Exhibit 4.1 for examples of useful emotion regulation assessment domains and questions.

MANAGING EMOTION IN THE THERAPEUTIC CONTEXT

Regardless of treatment modality or focus, it is critical for clinicians working with traumatized clients to consistently monitor the level of affect in session. If a client's emotional level gets too high, she will likely experience symptoms of hyperarousal or dissociation, neither of which are conducive to therapeutic work. At the extreme end, they may set the stage for a client to be inadvertently retraumatized. If a clinician senses that a client is becoming emotionally overwhelmed, then the focus of the session should be shifted to

EXHIBIT 4.1
Helpful Questions in Assessing Difficulties With Emotion Regulation

Identification of problematic emotional states
- Which emotions or emotional states are most difficult or distressing for the client?
- Do these emotional states tend to flood the client suddenly or are there any precursors she can identify before they become full blown?
- What happens psychologically or internally during these states (e.g., feeling overwhelmed, frightened)?
- Are there any specific thoughts that go along with these states (e.g., "I cannot manage," "These feelings will never stop")?
- What happens physically during these states (e.g., increased arousal, breathing changes, tightness in chest, headaches, feeling dizzy or spacey)?

Associated behaviors
- What behaviors (e.g., aggression, violence, withdrawal, crying) tend to go along with distressing or overwhelming feeling states?
- How are drugs or alcohol used in relation to feeling states?
- Does the client engage in other addictive behaviors in relation to these feeling states?
- At these times how in control of her impulses does the client feel? Is she typically able to contain or delay impulses to act, or does she feel unable to keep them in check?
- Have there been any negative consequences for associated behaviors, such as arrest, being fired from a job, or being cut off by family or friends?

Level of intensity and disruption
- Does the client feel out of control or become disoriented (e.g., confusion as to surroundings or time frame, difficulty remembering what happened later)?
- In what specific ways do emotional states interfere or disrupt functioning? For example, does the client have to stop what she is doing to manage, or can she continue performing regular tasks and activities?
- How long do these states typically last? How long does it take to calm down after an emotional episode? For example, is the client distressed only briefly or does it continue for the rest of the day?
- Have these emotional states created problems in her relationships with others? Have other people told the client what she is typically like in these states or how it feels to be around her?

Contextual factors
- Are there specific situations or triggers that make certain emotional states more likely to occur (e.g., dealing with a specific person, feeling abandoned)?
- Is the client aware of actively trying to avoid specific feeling states or situations that might trigger certain feelings? If so, how? What is the extent of avoidance?
- How does use of alcohol or drugs affect the client's emotional states and associated thoughts and behaviors?
- Are there any other factors that make the client more vulnerable to reacting (e.g., feeling tired or hungry)?

Management strategies
- What does the client typically do when experiencing distressing emotional states (e.g., turn to others, withdraw, try to distract herself by engaging in another activity, use drugs or alcohol, eat, engage in cutting behaviors)?
- How well do these strategies typically work? How do they change the client's emotional state?
- How confident or competent does the client feel about her ability to soothe herself during these times?
- When the client turns to others, what reactions does she usually get? If she does not confide in others, what reactions does she assume or fear she will get?

Access to emotional range
- Are there any emotions that the client has difficulty feeling?
- Does the client often feel numb or unable to feel anything?
- How does the client tend to experience and manage positive emotions?

help the client reduce her emotional arousal to a more manageable level (Ogden, Minton, & Pain, 2006). An important clinical concept in this regard is the *therapeutic window* (e.g., see Briere & Scott, 2006), or the "window of tolerance" (Ogden et al., 2006). Awareness of these concepts helps clinicians monitor whether their clients seem to be working in therapy within a safe emotional window. These concepts grew out of the observation that there is a constructive affective range for working with survivors of trauma. Optimally, clients are neither overactivated nor triggered by working outside the therapeutic window in the upper and intolerable range or emotion, nor are they so emotionally uninvolved or detached from their experience that they are working outside of the therapeutic window in the lower range of emotional involvement. The width of this active range varies by client. Using appropriate interventions to keep a client within this window can help keep client and clinician in sync and on track.

Working outside the upper range of the therapeutic window seems to occur when a client is exposed to too much traumatic memory relative to her ability to manage the distress it causes. These may be explicit memories or they may be bits of memory, felt recollections, or any other kind of remembering or reexperiencing of a traumatic past. If not attended to by the therapist, clients who are triggered in this way will often resort to their typical modes of handling affect through "avoidance maneuvers" (Briere & Scott, 2006, p. 125) such as dissociation, distracting therapy behaviors, nonattendance, or substance use. If clinicians suspect that clients are becoming too activated by their memories, they may need to help the client use grounding or relaxation techniques (described later), redirect the client's attention to less distressing topics or aspects of their recollections, or focus on more concrete aspects of treatment at those moments. More structured therapies can sometimes be helpful in titrating the client's emotional reactions by returning to written material or exercises when more open exploration has proved too difficult for a client to tolerate.

Alternatively, clinicians may seek to increase a client's level of emotional activation when it seems that counseling or therapy is not engaging a client affectively enough. If it seems that a client could tolerate a little more activation to make more progress in her treatment, clinicians may cautiously try to increase attention to feeling states in what clients are describing, or they may direct attention to experiences that clients have avoided talking about (see Briere & Scott, 2006, and Ogden et al., 2006, for an elaboration of techniques).

Clinicians should be mindful that some clients when triggered may appear quite calm, though internally they are highly aroused. This underscores the need to develop a way of communicating about emotional levels with the client so the clinician can quickly check in and get a read of where the client is in her emotional response. For example, the clinician and client may be able to use a basic scale ranging from 1 to 10, with 1 being the least emotionally aroused or in distress and 10 being the most emotionally aroused or the most distressed she can imagine. At a time when the client is not emotionally triggered, the client and therapist can collaboratively identify specific anchor points for these ratings because during times of heightened arousal a client is often unable to access such descriptors.

Some of the difficulties that clients have in regularly attending treatment relate to the ongoing challenge of working within the therapeutic window. Often clients engage or disengage from treatment as a way to titrate the intensity of their clinical experience, related to both the interpersonal relationship(s) with the clinician or, in group, with other members and the potential for emotional triggering of traumatic material. Although it is tempting to judge a client's absence from treatment as an indication of her poor attachment to treatment (and, of course, sometimes clients are not motivated to attend treatment at a particular time), sometimes clients are in fact motivated and attached but are unable to sustain the intensity of regular attendance. Careful attention to the emotional pace of treatment can help prevent clients from modulating their affective involvement through their attendance.

INTERVENTIONS FOR EMOTION REGULATION DEFICITS

Over the past 10 years, several empirically based treatments addressing issues of emotion regulation have been developed. In some interventions, such as skills training in affective and interpersonal regulation (Cloitre, Koenan, Cohen, & Han, 2002) and dialectical behavior therapy (DBT; Linehan, 1993a, 1993b), work on affect dysregulation is a central focus of treatment, whereas in other treatments, specific modules on affect regulation skills are included along with other content areas. Most of the techniques being used are grounded in cognitive–behavioral principles, although some are also drawn from Eastern philosophies (e.g., mindfulness) and, more recently, somatic processing models. Some examples follow.

Providing Psychoeducation

Before presenting specific skill-building activities, it can be valuable to provide clients with some psychoeducation on emotion regulation and common problems trauma survivors often have in this area. Discussing with clients ways in which current difficulties in managing their fear, anger, and sadness may be linked to their abuse histories can go a long way in reducing a client's shame and self-blame. For example, a client may find it helpful to understand how she was forced to confront intense feelings at an early age without direction or appropriate role models. Explaining that as human beings we are not born with skills to manage our emotions and that traumatic exposure and chaotic family environments interfere with opportunities to learn these essential life skills provides an empathic and nonjudgmental framework. Communicating that these skills can still be learned in the context of treatment often inspires hope and motivation.

Increasing Emotional Awareness

The first step typically involves helping clients increase awareness of their feelings by learning how to label, identify, and differentiate emotional states. Although these skills may seem elementary, for many trauma survivors whose feelings were often ignored or minimized, it is novel to focus on their emotional experiences in such a systematic way. Labeling and naming emotional experiences can often make those experiences feel more manageable and organized rather than diffuse, overwhelming, and confusing.

To facilitate this kind of learning, self-monitoring strategies are often used. Through the clinical process clients may learn how better to identify their feeling states with the help of their clinicians during session, verbally as well as through the use of written exercises, lists of feeling states, or diagrammatic depictions of feelings. Because many clients have little emotional awareness or have been invested in avoiding their feelings for so long, they may need these additional tools to help them learn to describe their feelings rather than struggling to identify them spontaneously.

Clients may also be taught how to better self-monitor their experiences. Cognitive–behavioral methods use self-monitoring forms that are given to clients and can prompt them to identify and record emotions they may have between sessions. In addition to writing about what is happening emotionally, clients can try to identify associated thoughts and reactions and behaviors as well as the context in which feelings emerged. Clinicians need to communicate to clients that this work requires practice and that especially in the beginning they may not know what emotions they are experiencing, though this is still useful to record. Clients should also be encouraged to record any physical sensations they may notice at these times, which they may find easier to identify. If clients are unwilling, unable, or uncomfortable creating written recordings of their emotions, encouraging clients to take notice of difficult emotional situations that can be explored further in counseling sessions can still provide the basis for skill building in this area.

In addition to increasing feeling vocabulary and linking feelings to cognitive, behavioral, and physical experiences, self-monitoring can provide a way for clients to slow things down when they feel emotionally distressed. Going through the steps of thinking about what is happening internally and identifying associated triggers, thoughts, and reactions can interrupt the cycle of impulsive action as a response to certain emotional states. In the process clients can also begin to recognize their feelings more quickly at a lower threshold. Clients are then better able to identify precursors to escalating feelings, giving them more options for early response rather than waiting until they are overtaken by heightened emotional states.

Encouraging Emotional Acceptance

Helping clients begin to accept and trust their own feelings is another integral part of emotion regulation work. Many clients have been actively discouraged from having their feelings, especially negative feelings, and have internalized criticism and invalidation, making them intolerant and unsympathetic toward their own emotional experiences. This sense of shame tends to exacerbate emotional avoidance and increases fear of having strong emotions, let alone expressing them. Negative reactions to their feelings further complicate the picture and make it less likely that clients will communicate their emotions in a direct and productive way. For example, many trauma survivors fear that they will be rejected or that they will elicit anger from others if they disclose what they are feeling, so they do not take the risk. Some trauma survivors, because of their negative expectations of others, may express feelings in an aggressive or hostile way, inadvertently provoking the negative reaction from others that they predicted.

As a way to combat ongoing self-criticism and invalidation clients are often taught the importance of just noticing feelings without judging, questioning, or trying to squelch them. Mindfulness techniques, described later, are helpful in this process as well, as clients learn to apply nonjudgmental attention to themselves. Treatment models that encourage approaching oneself more compassionately also help clients to better accept their emotional experience without the harsh internal dialogue to which they are accustomed. This approach enables clients to understand how their traumatic past may have contributed to their emotional state and encourages them to move forward without blaming themselves for their feelings.

Learning Distress Management Techniques

Much work with trauma survivors involves helping them make changes to decrease levels of distress and to recognize and get out of distressing situations. To benefit from these approaches, clients must be willing to engage in the exercises even when they are upset. Clinicians can offer clients an opportunity to learn and practice something new, or to try an experiment if they are skeptical. Many clients report that learning and applying skills like these are extremely helpful in their recovery from abuse and addiction. When these skills are introduced, it is critical to point out that they require learning and practice. Clients may dismiss an exercise that does not bring immediate relief or that feels awkward or uncomfortable at first. They need to know that they are not expected to be able to instantly grasp the new skills, but that with practice (i.e., by practicing a few minutes periodically at home), they can become adept and comfortable at using these new skills when they need them. Sometimes clients appreciate the analogy of trying on a new coat; at first the coat may feel stiff and alien, but as it is broken in, it will come to fit more comfortably. New skills sometimes need time and practice to "fit." Clients familiar with 12-step axioms may connect with the notion of "fake it till you make it."

One of the most valuable things a client who is easily dysregulated can carry is a small note card of some kind on which she has written quick reminders of her new tools. If she can remember to pull out her note card for reference, that can be enough to remind her of the techniques that work for her. More recently, clients have found that programming these techniques into their cell phones, where they can easily access them, is also a good strategy. A tenet of DBT skills training, which specifically teaches clients how to tolerate and manage their overwhelming or negative emotions, is that clients are likely to need periodic training and reinforcement of new methods. DBT therapists fully expect clients to reach out to them for assistance with their new skills (Linehan, 1993a).

The sections that follow outline some helpful approaches to managing distress.

Meditation and Mindfulness

Techniques that promote mindfulness (Kabat-Zinn, 1990, 1994; Linehan, 1993b) help clients to disengage themselves from their internal distress. Instead, clients learn to develop mindful attention to the present, purposefully and nonjudgmentally. Clients attend to aspects of the world around them through the use of their senses (e.g., feeling their surroundings, noticing smells and sounds, observing visual details) or to internal experiences such as cognitions, feelings, or physical sensations. Mindfulness evolved from traditional practices of meditation.

Self-Hypnosis

Like hypnosis, self-hypnosis has a wide range of definitions. A common perspective is that clients can learn skills to bypass their normal, observing state of mind to make themselves more receptive to suggestions for relaxation, pain management, and, in some cases, behavior change. Some clients find that self-hypnosis is an important part of their recovery from engaging in addictive behaviors.

Grounding

Grounding provides clients with a similar set of present-focused skills to manage overwhelming affects. Clients learn to focus their attention on neutral or safe facts or images, intentionally directing their attention away from distressing internal experiences to focus on external and concrete experiences and thoughts. Mental and physical and grounding techniques help clients deescalate their distress (e.g., see Najavits, 2002).

Breathing Relaxation

Other helpful skills include breathing retraining and relaxation (e.g., see Craske & Barlow, 2007a, 2007b). Breathing relaxation recognizes the soothing potential of helping clients to learn to focus and deepen their breathing, especially for clients who tend toward shallow, rapid breathing when they become anxious or dysregulated. This exercise can be performed with eyes open or closed. Many trauma survivors are better able to lower their distress with any of these exercises by keeping their eyes open. Closing their eyes often reengages them with the upsetting internal imagery from which they are trying to extricate themselves (see Exhibit 4.2 for a demonstration script for a breathing relaxation exercise).

Progressive Muscle Relaxation

Muscle relaxation (e.g., see Craske & Barlow, 2007a, 2007b; Jacobsen, 1938; Schiraldi, 2000) helps clients learn to identify places in which stress and distress are manifest in the body in physical tension. Clients learn to become better aware of stress in their body and, through a series of tensing and relaxing exercises throughout the body, learn how to reduce that tension. These exercises are readily available online.

Safe Place Exercises

Establishing an image of a safe place is another valuable exercise that can be a useful tool for clients in distress. In preparation for times when they may feel unsafe or overwhelmed, clients identify a space or a place, either real or imagined, that offers solace. In writing or verbally, preferably with a clinician, the client thinks about this place in detail, and what specifically about it that is soothing, and once identified, keeps the safe place inside her mind to "pull out" in times of stress. In this way, once dysregulated, a client can be directed to think about her safe place in all of its details, quietly to herself or out loud. It is important that clinicians be sure that the space is truly safe. Occasionally, when a client starts to reflect on a place she has identified as safe, she realizes

EXHIBIT 4.2
Breathing Relaxation Exercise

Getting started—find a quiet comfortable place
- When you are first learning the technique, practice in a place where you will not be disrupted.
- You can either sit up straight in a chair or lie down on your back.
- If you are lying on your back, rest your arms comfortably by your sides with your legs fully extended in front of you.
- You can put your hands gently on your stomach and follow the natural rise and fall of your breath before you begin.
- You can close your eyes or keep them open, whichever is more comfortable, and allow yourself a few seconds to calm down.

Slow down your breathing
- Take a slow deep breath in.
- You should feel your stomach expand as you breathe in.
- Be aware of your breath as it flows into your body—as it passes through your neck and your chest and down into your stomach, filling it up like a balloon.
- Then begin to let out the air slowly.
- Be mindful of the air moving out of your stomach, back up through your chest, through your neck, and then out through your nose until your lungs feel empty.
- Pause briefly and then repeat.
- Continue to breathe in slowly and deeply; your stomach should rise and fall with each breath, and your shoulders and chest should barely move at all.

Add counting to make your breath more rhythmic
- Try counting silently to four slowly as you inhale (1-2-3-4) and count to 4 silently as you exhale (1-2-3-4).
- Focus your mind on your breathing. If thoughts or worries come into your mind, gently put them aside and refocus on your breathing. It is natural for thoughts and worries to come to mind; just let them pass and bring your attention back to your breath. Do not give up.

Continue to breathe slowly and deeply for up to 20 minutes
- When you are ready to stop, slowly open your eyes and remain still for a moment before resuming activities.
- Practice regularly—the more you use the focused breathing the better it will work for you.

aspects of the place that evoke unpleasant emotions or associations. Clinicians may want to redirect a client to another place that is not associated with anything unpleasant. Clients who are able to use this skill successfully find that they become calmer and more centered. It is important that a client be able to choose her safe place, rather than be asked to imagine a generic safe place, such as a beach. The idiosyncratic nature of triggering can mean that what is safe to one person may represent horror to another.

Developing Distress Tolerance

There is also recognition, of course, that some distress cannot be avoided. It is therefore important for clients to cultivate skills to help them manage and accept inescapable emotional pain when it arises and to understand ways that distress can be adaptive, for example, as a warning signal that something is wrong or as an important catalyst for change.

Identifying Unsafe Coping Strategies and Generating Alternatives

A central aspect of emotion regulation work is to help clients understand how certain strategies they use to cope with overwhelming emotions, though perhaps helpful in the short term, are ultimately creating more problems and actually increasing the likelihood of emotional distress. Women with trauma histories may resort to a range of unsafe behaviors in addition to using substances, such as binge eating, self-injury, or compulsive sexual behavior to help them avoid or manage negative emotional states. Many clients who end up relying on these behaviors do so not because they are inherently self-destructive but because these behaviors represent the only ways they have learned to relieve emotional pain and because they do not have faith or the skills to soothe themselves otherwise.

The goal of treatment is to teach clients more adaptive alternative strategies and to build confidence in their ability to use them. There are a range of methods, including the distress management techniques previously described, which generally fall into three categories—physiological, cognitive, and behavioral. Breathing retraining, muscle relaxation, tracking physical symptoms, and meditation are examples of *physiological strategies*. *Cognitive strategies* include grounding as well as attention shifting, distracting techniques to turn attention to the outside world and away from internal states, positive imagery, affirmations, and other helpful or compassionate self-statements. *Behavioral strategies* include taking a time out and leaving the environment strategically rather than as avoidance, generating specific replacement behaviors, or engaging in a behavior that is the opposite of or in opposition to the emotion being experienced.

Increasing Positive Emotional Experiences

Although much emotion regulation work is focused on helping clients manage their negative emotions, it is also important to help clients enhance positive feeling states. Many trauma survivors report having difficulty experiencing pleasurable feelings, and this can be for a variety of reasons. Some clients may not know how to access positive states, whereas others may find themselves actively cutting off positive feelings, which creates anxiety. Identifying obstacles and helping clients incorporate more pleasurable activities are ways to help clients attend to and cultivate positive feelings that allow for more emotionally engaged living. Helping clients to brainstorm activities that may be pleasant for them or using lists of pleasant activities (e.g., see Pleasant Events Scale; Schiraldi, 2000), can help jump-start a client in this direction.

CONCLUSION

Helping substance-abusing women with histories of trauma learn to manage their strong emotions in safe ways is often a central part of treatment. Emotion regulation interventions can provide both the client and the clinician with a means to address affective states in a way that is sensitive to how trauma may have interfered with the client's development in this area. Clinicians report greater confidence in working with clients after they have developed their own tool box of emotion regulation techniques to help clients through difficult moments. Just as clients need reassurance that learning and applying these skills take time, clinicians should not lose heart that clients may not immediately embrace the skills. Clinicians may repeatedly have to remind clients to use their skills and may even have to remind clients they do have skills from which to choose.

5

INTERPERSONAL FUNCTIONING

For women whose trauma has involved an experience of interpersonal violation, the ability to form healthy interpersonal relationships is often compromised, sometimes severely. This is particularly true for women whose abuse occurred at the hands of someone close to them, as is typical of early childhood abuse. Childhood abuse derails the development of important life skills, particularly the emotional and social competencies that form the basis of effective and satisfying relationships. Substance abuse treatment clinicians are often familiar with the interpersonal chaos in the lives of their clients and the ways in which interpersonal issues can interfere with their recovery.

Women with histories of trauma often report how difficult it is to establish safe and trusting relationships. They are unable to see danger or respond to cues that may signify danger and, at the same time, have a tendency to see danger around every corner and an inability to establish trust in anyone. These competing pulls contribute to difficulties in forming balanced relationships and increase the likelihood of continued abuser–victim relationship dynamics in adulthood. These problems can negatively affect many areas of a survivor's life, including intimate partner relationships and friendships, and can interfere with a woman's ability to negotiate work life effectively, manage parenting responsibilities, or make use of treatment resources. Understanding the range of interpersonal difficulties in their survivor clients' lives and the challenges they pose for recovery and the therapeutic relationship can help clinicians reframe their perspective and adjust their interactions and interventions.

In this chapter, we focus on the impact of childhood trauma on interpersonal development. We describe the interpersonal functioning of abused children and the functioning of adult survivors. We also cover related issues such as revictimization. We then discuss the impact of these interpersonal problems on the therapeutic relationship as well as other issues that may arise in therapy. Finally, we present relevant interventions and treatments.

IMPACT OF CHILDHOOD MALTREATMENT
ON SOCIAL AND INTERPERSONAL DEVELOPMENT

Child maltreatment interferes with the normal processes involved in developing and sustaining meaningful interpersonal relationships. Although trauma at any point can dramatically affect a girl's interpersonal skills and comfort with others, early maltreatment in particular can broadly affect this area of functioning. Childhood abuse often derails the formation of a healthy self-concept and compromises feelings of trust, safety, and control in relation to significant others (Cole & Putnam, 1992; Trickett & Putnam, 1993).

Traumatized children typically confront a life fraught with unpredictability and emotional distress, fear, and confusion. Especially when their caregivers are the perpetrators of chronic physical, emotional, or sexual abuse, they are asked to manage seemingly impossible tasks: holding themselves together at a time when their physical integrity is regularly violated and making sense of an environment in which they need to trust others for their own personal security and growth but in which those around them are untrustworthy and unsafe. When her "protectors" are also her assailants, an abused child is forced to adapt in a way that allows her to maintain her connection to her abusers, including using "doublethink" (Herman, 1992b, p. 101). In this way, a child is able to absolve the abuser of blame rather than risk the despair of embracing the truth of his cruelty; however, the child often absorbs the "badness" into herself, making sense of the maltreatment by blaming herself. The maltreated child learns to identify herself as the cause of the abuse and thus may fail to learn how to protect herself. This pattern often continues into adulthood, as observed with clients who present to treatment after having been in multiple abusive relationships. In many cases, the client minimizes the abusive behavior and culpability of a partner, believing that she can somehow ward off the abuse or that she is responsible for preventing it by altering her behavior. This is just one of a number of adaptive strategies that an abused child develops to survive her traumatic environment but that in the long term prove interpersonally maladaptive when they become the template for later relationships. Some more severe psychological adaptations that can be developed, discussed in the previous chapter, are dissociation and, at its most extreme, a self fragmented by dissociation into different identities (i.e., dissociative identity disorder).

In many families of victimized children, a number of factors are already at work prior to the abuse to predispose parents to maltreat their children or each other, to prevent identification and cessation of abusive behavior, and to contribute to disturbed attachment in their children. Abused and neglected children must deal not only with experiences of victimization but also with the general familial context in which the mistreatment takes place. There are often multiple stressors, including inadequate resources and finances. Parents are often struggling with mental illness and substance abuse issues as well as unstable and chaotic relationships. Such maladaptive caretaking environments do not provide children with adequate role models from whom they can learn critical emotional and interpersonal skills. Missed opportunities for social and emotional development and expectations for relationships that were developed in the context of abuse experiences can set the stage for ongoing difficulties in developing and sustaining healthy relationships.

DISRUPTED ATTACHMENT IN INFANTS AND CHILDREN

Abused children are traumatized during the most critical period of their lives, when beliefs about themselves and others are being formed and relationship skills are first being learned (Briere, 1992). At this time children are organizing templates and identifying effective contingencies for relating to others (Cloitre, 1998). A particularly useful framework for understanding how early interactions with important others help mold a child's developing understanding of relationships that she carries with her into adulthood is attachment theory (see Exhibit 5.1 for a summary of infant attachment classifications).

Attachment theory proposes that the infant–caregiver relationship provides the prototype for later relationships through a set of "internal working models" (Bowlby, 1973). These mental representations formed from interactions with attachment figures become the basis for subsequent interactions with others. The quality of a child's early attachment relationships is believed to stem from the extent to which a child can rely on caregivers to help regulate her emotional experience and provide a sense of "felt security" (Sroufe & Waters, 1977). The degree to which caregivers are sensitive and responsive to their children's needs forms the basis for a child's developing expectations about interacting with others.

Over time, interpersonal experience becomes internalized as "cognitive structures that guide expectations about relationships and interpretations

EXHIBIT 5.1
Infant Attachment Classifications
and Corresponding Infant–Parent Interaction

Securely attached infants display distress when a caregiver leaves but are easily consoled upon her return and quickly return to play, using the caregiver as a secure base through which to explore the environment. These children typically seek and use their caregivers for comfort. Ainsworth (Ainsworth, 1982; Ainsworth, Blehar, Waters, & Wall, 1978) found that parents of secure infants tend to respond to their infants in a reliable and consistent manner.

Ambivalently attached infants appear clingy and become distraught upon separation. When the caregiver returns, the infant simultaneously seeks her out and angrily rejects her attempts to comfort him or her. Caregivers of these children often demonstrate variability and incompetence in parenting.

Avoidantly attached infants tend not to fret when the caregiver leaves, nor do they attend to her return, seemingly avoiding the caregiver. These infants explore the environment on their own, without checking back in with their caregivers for comfort. According to Ainsworth's research (Ainsworth, 1982; Ainsworth, Blehar, Waters, & Wall, 1978), parents of these children tend to be cold and rejecting.

Disorganized/disoriented attachment (Main, Kaplan, & Cassidy, 1985) is characterized by an apparent *lack* of strategy for responding to separation. Infants with this type of attachment display confusion when reunited with a caregiver, including contradictory movement and seemingly random directed affect and have difficulty using caregivers to soothe their distress.

of experiences in relationships" (Bartholomew, 1993, p. 34), with particularly detrimental consequences for children with a history of abuse and maltreatment. Observational studies of maltreated preschool and school-age children have demonstrated this connection between abuse and maladaptive internal models of attachment (Carlson, Cicchetti, Barnett, & Braunwald, 1989; Main, Kaplan, & Cassidy, 1985; Solomon, George, & DeJong, 1995).

Attachment theory evolved further as a result of studies on children's reactions to separation from their caregivers (Ainsworth, Blehar, Waters, & Wall, 1978) and was later elaborated on to describe adult styles of relating. It provides a classification system that enables individual attachment styles to be described as either secure or insecure/anxious. Insecure attachment is further categorized as ambivalent, avoidant or disorganized/disoriented. Research on caregiver–child interaction has shown patterns of caregiver responsiveness that correspond to each classification of insecure attachment (Ainsworth, 1982; Ainsworth et al., 1978; see also Exhibit 5.1).

Numerous studies have demonstrated that insecure attachment is associated with childhood maltreatment (see Feerick, 1999, for a review). The disorganized attachment pattern, in particular, is common in high-risk samples (Fonagy, 1998), with research showing that as many as 80% of abused infants and children develop it. Disorganized attachment has frequently been associated with children of caregivers who may be abusive to or neglectful of their children and are also presumed to have unresolved loss or trauma in their own childhood histories (Alexander, 1992). This attachment pattern has also been associated with impaired self-regulatory behaviors (van der Kolk, McFarlane, & Weisaeth, 1996).

Insecure attachment is also associated with more problematic behavior. Children who are insecurely attached at 1 year are later less competent in preschool than their securely attached peers on empathy, aggression, popularity, and expression of positive feelings in relationships (Sroufe, 1988). Children who are avoidant evidence more hostile and antisocial behavior in preschool. Children who are ambivalent are more tense, needy, impulsive, easily frustrated, passive, and helpless in preschool and more likely to be victimized (see Alexander, 1992). In one study, bullying dyads involved insecurely attached children as either victim or perpetrator (Troy & Sroufe, 1987).

Even in the presence of healthy attachment, when a previously trusted caregiver becomes assaultive, the betrayal undermines the child's developing experience of relationships (Carlson et al., 1989). Similarly, poor responsiveness by the family to disclosure of abuse, either within or outside of the family, can destroy a child's trust, as does the failure of a caretaker to notice or respond to an abusive situation. These experiences of betrayal often have lasting impact on a child's beliefs about people and relationships.

ONGOING ATTACHMENT DIFFICULTIES IN ADULTHOOD

Attachment styles developed in early childhood generally remain stable throughout life (Main et al., 1985), and adult attachment research has provided counterparts to Ainsworth's infant attachment classification system to describe adult relatedness (Bartholomew & Horowitz, 1991). Research on adult attachment indicates that insecure attachment continues to predominate among survivors of childhood maltreatment (see Exhibit 5.2 for a summary of adult attachment classifications).

In our own findings (Hien, Cohen, Litt, & Miele, 2001), the majority of women dually diagnosed with substance use disorders and PTSD related to interpersonal trauma indicated an insecure, fearful/avoidant attachment style, with features such as being less likely to make self-disclosures or to turn to others when in distress, experiencing lower levels of intimacy in close relationships, and being hypersensitive to rejection and uncomfortable with closeness. In addition to compromised social functioning, these women acknowledged considerable problems with depression, mood instability, and impulsivity, including difficulties controlling anger and self-destructive behavior.

These results are consistent with other findings indicating that fearful attachment in adults is strongly associated with *intimacy anger*. Intimacy anger

EXHIBIT 5.2
Characteristics of Adult Attachment Classifications

Securely attached adults demonstrate trusting, close relationships, and are confident that relationships can endure and be gratifying. Relationships are highly valued by securely attached adults.

Ambivalent/preoccupied attachment in adults is marked by feelings of deprivation and exaggerated concern with the availability of an attachment figure. Ambivalent adults may be clingy, jealous. and anxious about relationships.

Avoidant/dismissing attachment in adults is characterized by difficulty trusting others in adulthood and a tendency to distance oneself from others and social situations. Avoidant adults tend to deny distressing aspects of interpersonal relationships, often rejecting others' assistance and strongly asserting their independence or counterdependence.

Fearful/disorganized attachment in adults has sometimes been seen as a parallel classification to disorganized/disoriented attachment in children (Main & Solomon, 1990). Fearful adults appear confused about relationships, are distrustful and socially inhibited, and demonstrate both avoidant and ambivalent–preoccupied traits.

describes a reaction of extreme anger that some individuals experience when faced with threats, such as separation or abandonment, to their attachment needs (Dutton, Saunders, Starzomski, & Bartholomew, 1994). Women with this attachment style often face a painful and confusing dilemma, unable to trust, yet desperate to be with someone who can reliably meet their needs. These patterns of relating characteristic of ambivalent/preoccupied or fearful/ disorganized attachment styles (e.g., instability of relationships, mood and affective lability, poor impulse control, questionable reality testing) are also consistent with many criteria of borderline personality disorder, which is frequently diagnosed in adult survivors of abuse (Briere & Runtz, 1987). High rates of fearful attachment (Patrick, Hobson, Castle, Howard, & Maughan, 1994) and malevolent expectations in interpersonal relationships (Westen, Lohr, Silk, Gold, & Kerber, 1990) have been found in samples with borderline personality disorder (Patrick et al., 1994).

INTERPERSONAL FUNCTIONING OF ABUSED CHILDREN

It has been established that children and adolescents with abuse histories often demonstrate interpersonal and social impairments. Early and prolonged trauma in childhood has been shown to affect the capacity to regulate emotion, including the intensity of emotional responses. Emotional dysregulation, in turn, interferes with successful family, peer, and social functioning (Pynoos, Steinberg, & Goenjian, 1996) and is associated with a host of problems from learning disabilities to aggression against self and others (van der Kolk, Perry, & Herman, 1991). The link between childhood abuse and aggressive behavior, in particular, has been well studied (see McCann, Sakheim, & Abrahamson, 1988).

Very young children are limited in their ability to understand and reframe aggressive behavior that they may have learned from experience or from witnessing in others. When abused children express their anger or aggression inappropriately, it reinforces their sense of shame and lack of control. These children often become socially marginalized and have limited opportunities to develop appropriate social skills. In addition, child victims of sexual abuse often relate to peers with precocious sexualized behavior, which can appear frightening and intrusive to other children and interfere with the development of healthy friendships.

Moreover, poor behavior at school may have academic consequences as well, leading abused children to further marginalization and less opportunity to develop a more mature understanding of interpersonal relationships and fewer chances to interact more effectively with peers. It is often in this context that children begin to experiment with substances, setting them on a path in which they socialize with other children who are using drugs or alcohol and endure the consequences of adopting the habits of this social circle.

In contrast, some children learn to present themselves normally to the world outside of their abusive home. They may have developed social skills that enable them to function well interpersonally, but at the expense of feeling isolated or fraudulent. Particularly in dominating families in which secrecy about the abuse was imposed, a child carries the burden of holding these secrets yet presenting herself to her peers as if nothing has happened. These children are frequently left with a hollow feeling that is sometimes later associated with depression, and they may report being troubled by an experience of inauthenticity (Herman, 1992b). The process of guarding her secret makes it impossible for the child to allow herself to be fully known to other people, and she often carries this experience into adulthood.

Self-disclosure is an important part of increasing intimacy between friends and between romantic partners in adulthood, and the inability to share information about oneself may limit the depth of connection with someone else. This can create a barrier to developing close relationships. Feelings of shame and guilt among survivors, as well as the common defensive belief that somehow they deserved or brought on their abuse, limits their ability to enter into an honest and open relationship. Girls and women may fear that they will once again not be believed or that they will be mocked or demeaned. As Herman (1992b) pointed out, a "false self" becomes harder to maintain over time as interpersonal challenges become greater. She wrote that a sign of recovery is that the survivor can "seek mutual friendships that are not based on performance, image or maintenance of a false self" (p. 205).

Briere (1992) described pervasive interpersonal effects of childhood abuse as stemming from two sources: (a) conditioned responses to victimization that extend into the long term (including distrust of others, feelings of being damaged, self-blame, and guilt) and (b) accommodations to ongoing abuse-related distress such as avoidance, passivity, or a tendency to sexualize interactions. Although adaptive in original early abusive circumstances, these habitual responses make it difficult to engage with others and to negotiate challenges in ways that are necessary for stable relationships.

Research supports clinical impressions that individuals with childhood abuse histories may be more likely to experience unsettled and unfulfilling relationships. For example, childhood abuse survivors, especially those with sexual abuse histories, tend to report more discord and lower satisfaction in their committed relationships than do nonabused women (DiLillo & Long, 1999; Jehu, 1988) and also show elevated rates of separation and divorce (Finkelhor, 1990; Mullen, Martin, Anderson, Romans, & Herbison, 1994). Difficulties are not limited to romantic involvements but also emerge in friendships and in work environments. For example, for many abuse survivors, interpersonal difficulties contribute to erratic employment patterns such as long periods of unemployment or working at jobs far below their education level or abilities.

Childhood abuse survivors are often driven to seek treatment because of these persistent problems in their relationships and a recognition of its profound effect on their daily lives. The most commonly cited interpersonal issues include difficulties with intimacy and trust, and problems with communication, assertiveness, and self-protection. These problems may manifest themselves in a variety of ways that at times may appear extreme or inconsistent. For example, whereas some women demonstrate excessive self-sufficiency and detachment, others are prone to dependence, overcompliance, and nonassertiveness in their relationships (Courtois, 1993). Whereas some women manage conflict in their relationships by becoming aggressive and controlling, others respond passively by giving up their personal rights and needs for the sake of smoothing things over. The problems in modulating emotions, irritability, sensitivity to rejection, and avoidance, which are characteristic of abuse survivors, can be socially unappealing and often drive others away. In addition, common comorbid psychiatric conditions such as depression, PTSD, anxiety, panic, and phobias further limit social interactions and make the lives of some survivors severely circumscribed. When addiction is a feature of a survivor's life, interpersonal problems can be exacerbated, with increased interpersonal instability, conflict, or isolation.

Many childhood abuse survivors demonstrate extreme shifts between a wish for intense intimacy and rageful, overwhelming withdrawal (Herman & van der Kolk, 1987). Early relationships have taught a survivor that each new relationship carries the risk of exploitation and abandonment. Yet she longs to find someone protective and, as a result, may fail to recognize or heed warning signs. Intense relationships sometimes result from this desire and the tendency to idealize another as having the potential to rescue her, combined with a fragile sense of self and a limited capacity to set appropriate boundaries. Alternatively, some women find isolation preferable to the risks associated with trusting and relying on someone.

In other situations, the survivor may find that she has become the caretaker to everyone around her. Having assumed the role of caregiver and possibly mediator during her abusive upbringing, she is quick to read the desires, moods, and signals of those around her and readily seeks to please them. Although these qualities make her an appealing friend and partner, they often put her in a position to be taken advantage of and overwhelmed by the demands of others. She often ends up feeling resentful and unappreciated. Over time, these feelings may become intense and surface in a way that seems out of proportion to the situation. The woman may end up expressing her anger in a way that feels out of control to her and leaves others feeling confused or blindsided.

Nevertheless, even troublesome or difficult relationships can meet some needs and provide some security for a survivor (Hazan & Shaver, 1994). Women whose past relationships suggest that expectations of others are not likely to be met may settle for friendships and other relationships that are less than ideal. Women may have absorbed through their abuse that to be loved and wanted one has to submit to someone else's demands and sacrifice one's own needs, and they sometimes find themselves in relationships that confirm this. In some cases these relationships become emotionally or physically hurtful, reenacting some of a woman's own traumatic past (van der Kolk, 1989).

Revictimization

One of the most troubling sequelae to childhood abuse is the vulnerability of women to be repeatedly victimized. As Cloitre, Cohen, and Koenan (2006) detailed, this entails relatively high rates of bullying and scapegoating experiences in childhood (e.g., see Shipman, Zeman, Penza, & Champion, 2000), sexual assaults and date rape among adolescent girls and in young adulthood (e.g., see Krahe, Sheinberger-Olwig, Waizenhofer, & Koplin, 1999), domestic violence (Polusny & Follette, 1995), and repeated sexual assaults among women (Cloitre, Tardiff, Marzuk, Leon, & Portera, 1996). Although the occurrence of childhood sexual abuse is the best-documented predictor of revictimization, experiencing multiple traumas, including childhood physical abuse, is associated with higher risk of revictimization (Classen, Palesh, & Aggarwal, 2005). Revictimization in adulthood often takes place in the context of intimate partner relationships. For example, in clinical samples childhood sexual abuse survivors exhibit greater risk of physical maltreatment by male partners than women without a childhood sexual abuse history (Briere & Runtz, 1987, 1988). Perpetrators of sexual assault are often known by the woman. In fact, the majority of adult sexual assaults experienced by revictimized women are at the hands of a male acquaintance (Cloitre, Scarvalone, & Difede, 1997).

There are several ways to understand the phenomena of revictimization in adult women. Women who have been repeatedly exploited or harmed often have not learned to identify signs of danger and may not have a good sense of what constitutes safe and appropriate boundaries in human interactions. Typically they have had poor role models to help them identify and assert self-protective impulses. As a result, they may inadvertently put themselves in high-risk situations or allow their boundaries to be violated without an eye toward negative consequences until it is too late. Use of alcohol and drugs can exacerbate these risks by further impairing judgment and interfering with the ability to solve problems or escape from unsafe circumstances. Studies have indicated, for example, that use of alcohol by the victim as well as by the perpetrator increases the likelihood of rape or sexual assault (Marx, Van Wie, & Gross, 1996). Even after the fact, many clients have difficulty identifying these experiences as abuse or assault. Clients often absorb these incidents as if experiencing this kind of maltreatment, even as adults, is an expectable and unavoidable part of living. Part of working clinically with these women includes helping them to relearn what is safe and unsafe and what is unacceptable and actually avoidable.

Even when women are aware of the potential for victimization, difficulties labeling feeling states and problems with assertiveness may be additional barriers to self-protective behavior. Women may fear retaliation if they do set limits with others and instead may rely on trying to please or placate them. This behavior may be misinterpreted as an admission of guilt or as consent for unwanted sexual activity. Other women with abuse histories may be so used to experiencing fear and discomfort in relation to others that they have learned to ignore self-protective instincts and are unable to rely on internal cues for important information. Women who are prone to dissociation under stress are particularly vulnerable to being taken advantage of by others. Dissociation further impedes women's ability to notice and heed signs of danger. These women can appear confused or preoccupied and seem unaware of their environment, making them easy targets for predators. Finally, some women who have been repeatedly abused understandably come to identify themselves as victims. A stance of powerlessness and feelings of low self-regard can pull for aggressive or domineering behaviors from others.

These observations have led some to characterize revictimized female abuse survivors as having masochistic tendencies or self-defeating personalities (see Cloitre, Cohen, & Scarvalone, 2002), thereby placing further blame on women who have been repeatedly exploited. Cloitre et al. (2006) proposed an alternative and nonpathologizing model for revictimization based on the notion of interpersonal schema theory, an outgrowth of attachment theory. Schemas are models of relationships that guide future expectations and behaviors. The tendency to rely on past experiences to predict the future is not limited to abuse survivors and can in fact be viewed as an adaptive strategy for negotiating one's interpersonal world. Unfortunately for those who were raised in abusive environments, early negative relationship patterns are those that get applied in adulthood. Specifically, children from abusive homes learn that interpersonal connectedness is associated with abuse (Cloitre, 1998). Thus, the aspects of revictimization that come from habitual modes of interpersonal relating are actually based in a healthy impulse to engage. This impulse, however, has been distorted by the abuse and learning that has taken place in the context of abusive relationships. As a result, abuse survivors are often more likely to expect and to accept some degree of victimization in their intimate relationships. These continued experiences serve as self-fulfilling prophecies in adulthood and tragically tend to further confirm the idea that women must be willing to settle for some mistreatment to maintain connections. Survivors may become involved with others who treat them as they expect to be treated without realizing that this type of familiarity, comfort, and attraction should be a warning sign against involvement (Gold, 2000). Many women also identify ways in which their attraction to men who they know are "bad boys" has become so ingrained that they do not find other men attractive. They are caught between entering into relationships that some of them know to be potentially dangerous, and relationships that may be safer, but unappealing and boring.

Aggression and Perpetration of Abuse

Women with abuse histories may become aggressive themselves or take on the role of an abuser in their subsequent relationships with lovers, friends, colleagues, or children. As we discussed, it is not uncommon for those with extensive abuse histories to feel, either consciously or unconsciously, that there are limited interpersonal roles available to them and to continue to operate within a perpetrator–victim relationship dynamic. This is often a part of the presentation of couples in which a woman is battered or abused by a male partner. For some survivors, an alternative to maintaining a role of victim is to dominate or manipulate others, identifying with the role of perpetrator as a way to stay in control and avoid further victimization.

In a small number of cases, it may be the woman who introduces violence into a relationship with a male partner. Women in same-sex relationships may also find themselves as either perpetrator or victim with their partners. The importance of calling attention to the devastation of male aggression toward women in intimate relationships has been a priority among advocates and many researchers for the past several decades; however, researchers have increasingly begun to highlight and explore the capacity for women to initiate and engage in physical aggression toward their partners (Holtzworth-Monroe, 2005) and to tease out some of the contributing factors, including past history of trauma. Not only do many studies of adults with past histories of childhood physical or sexual abuse report higher rates of adulthood revictimization, but these individuals are more likely than individuals without this history to report perpetrating violence against others (see Feerick, Haugaard, & Hien, 2005). This includes evidence that women who witnessed or experienced violence in their families as children (i.e., witnessing physical violence between their parents or being hit by their parents) are more likely to perpetrate violence against their partners as adults (Kalmuss, 1984; Straus & Gelles, 1986). In our own work, women with a history of childhood sexual abuse were also 4 times more likely to perpetrate violence against a partner than women without a history of childhood sexual abuse (Feerick et al., 2005). Although it is recognized that the potential to inflict severe physical harm is typically less than that of a male perpetrator against a female victim, it is important to recognize the capacity for women to harm a partner and to attend to that possibility in treatment.

Sexual Functioning

A number of studies have examined interpersonal sexual functioning among abuse survivors. Most empirical work has focused on subsequent sexual behaviors of women with histories of childhood sexual abuse. Less is known about how other commonly co-occurring types of abuse exposure, including childhood physical abuse, influence adult sexual functioning, although most studies on sexual functioning include participants who have been exposed to other traumas in addition to childhood sexual abuse. On the basis of a review of studies conducted since 1990, Fergusson and Mullen (1999) concluded that there is a significant relationship between childhood sexual abuse and sexual difficulties during adolescence and adulthood. These findings are consistent with those of several other studies illustrating that women with sexual abuse histories often struggle with pervasive and multiple sexual problems (see Leonard & Follette, 2002, for review).

These difficulties can take a number of forms, although the most frequently reported problems are those of sexual desire and arousal, fear of sexual contact, and feelings of repulsion or lack of enjoyment. Women who have been sexually abused report increased risk for dysfunctional sexual behavior ranging from sexual avoidance to compulsive sexual activity. Whereas some women report little sexual desire and a tendency to avoid sexual relationships, other women report a compulsive desire for sexual contact and are likely to engage in multiple, short-term sexual relationships (Briere & Runtz, 1993; Browne & Finkelhor, 1986).

For women in the latter group, sexual activity is often associated with sexual risk taking and use of substances. Increased sexual risk taking, moreover, combined with difficulty in self-protection and asserting themselves interpersonally also make it more difficult for women in these situations to consistently protect themselves against sexually transmitted diseases or unwanted pregnancies, with health consequences to complicate their lives and their recoveries.

The fact that two seemingly divergent outcomes—sexual avoidance and compulsive sexual activity—can both be associated with trauma history has been described by Herman as the "dialectic of trauma" (Herman, 1992b, p. 1). Finkelhor and Browne's (1985) model of traumatogenic dynamics provides a useful framework to conceptualize how childhood sexual abuse may derail the development of a healthy sexual identity and lead to enduring sexual difficulties. Traumatic sexualization can happen in a variety of ways. Outcomes are, in part, related to the specific associations a child makes and contingencies she learns in the context of sexual abuse experiences, which may subsequently be generalized to other sexual relationships. For example, in some cases a child is rewarded and given attention and affection for her sexual "participation." As a result, she may confuse sex with love or attention and may develop the belief that sexual activity is a way to receive or give care. As an adult, she may be more likely to oversexualize relationships or use sex to satisfy nonsexual needs, which may in turn put her at risk for having promiscuous or risky sex. In other cases, a sexually abused child may learn to associate sexual arousal and activity with extreme negative feelings and memories involving fear, disgust, or helplessness. As an adult, she may continue to associate these overwhelming reactions with sexual activity, making it more likely that she will experience difficulty becoming sexually aroused or develop a pattern of avoidance of sexual activity, with clear implications for maintaining a satisfying adult partner relationship.

Many survivors also report that they can only participate in a sexual relationship under the influence of drugs or alcohol. Only by numbing their affective arousal or by blunting their abuse memories with substances are they able to be sexually active. For some survivors, sexual activity is also associated with significant physical pain, which many have also overridden with substance use. This is one more challenge in helping clients like these to abstain from substances; giving up drugs or alcohol also means learning to engage in sexual activity when clean and sober. Depending on the pressures of their current relationships, their own sexual needs, and the intensity of their affective and physical reaction to sexual intimacy, and whether they are reexperiencing symptoms or flashbacks, the need to relearn how to be intimate can be a significant obstacle to recovery. Until PTSD symptoms are resolved, it may in fact be impossible for some sexual abuse survivors to tolerate any sexual activity in early recovery.

Another model for understanding the sexual behavior of survivors of childhood abuse is Polusny and Follette's (1995) *contextual behavioral approach*, which emphasizes the role of experiential avoidance and views behavior in terms of its function as opposed to its manifestation. In this framework, both sexual avoidance and sexual compulsivity are characterized as mechanisms used to avoid, minimize, or manage painful internal experiences including trauma-related flashbacks, intrusive thoughts, memories, or unpleasant physical sensations that survivors often report having during sexual activity (Briere & Runtz, 1987). Although these experiential avoidance strategies may work in the short term to decrease distress, ultimately they exacerbate sexual problems (Merrill, Guimond, Thomsen, & Milner, 2003) and have been linked with poorer individual functioning (Leitenberg, Greenwald, & Cado, 1992).

IMPACT OF INTERPERSONAL PROBLEMS ON THE THERAPEUTIC RELATIONSHIP

The complexity of the interpersonal experience of survivors of trauma poses challenges as well as opportunities for healing in the context of a therapeutic relationship. Issues around building trust, establishing safety, and setting boundaries come up repeatedly throughout treatment.

Trust Versus Mistrust

The client's experiences of trust or mistrust have enormous influence on whether and how therapy unfolds. Although forming a trusting relationship with a clinician is always an important component of treatment, for a trauma survivor, developing trust can be a precarious process. People who she was supposed to trust in the past may have betrayed her, so how should a survivor determine whether a therapist is trustworthy and able to help her on her road to recovery? So many of the difficult moments in treatment can be attributed to the instability of going through this process as therapist and client dance around and with one another in an attempt to establish a reliable and therapeutic alliance. If they are able to negotiate this process successfully, a significant part of the therapeutic course will be underway because the interaction with her therapist can form a new template for negotiating other interpersonal relationships in a survivor's life. Clients who are able to sort through issues of suspicion and distrust with their clinicians can begin to grapple with this process with others in their lives as well.

Safety and Boundaries in the Therapeutic Process

Issues of trust apply to not only telling the "trauma story" in a client's life but, more basically, allowing herself to be open to other people, to reach out for and accept help from others, and to allow others to know what she is like inside. The intensity of the shame and guilt that often pervades much of a survivor's internal experience makes it that much harder to expose herself to others. Clients who can safely engage with a clinician or with a therapy group report profound gratitude and exhibit greater treatment progress. Nevertheless, arriving at this place requires hard work and a willingness to take risks by the client and by the therapist, which may take months or even years. It is reasonable to assume that in a short-term treatment setting, such as detoxification or rehabilitation programs lasting several weeks, many clients will not let their guard down. Ongoing aftercare is almost always an essential part of establishing and maintaining sobriety, but it is especially valuable for trauma survivors who need the extended opportunity to develop a trusting working alliance with a therapist and to work through the impact of their trauma on their addiction and recovery.

As we reviewed earlier, a client's internal working models or schemas of interpersonal relationships, formed in early attachment relationships, color the nature of the client–clinician relationship similar to how these schemas affect other personal connections. Helping clients to recognize and change their characteristic ways of viewing and interacting with others is a central goal of treatment, and the therapeutic relationship often offers clues to these patterns. Expecting others to be unreliable or untrustworthy is only one characteristic pattern common to many survivors.

In fact, for some survivors a reverse dynamic is common. Because the desire to be known, understood, loved, and valued is so strong for some survivors, they dive into relationships head first before they have tested the waters. Opening themselves up too quickly or too broadly can put women at risk of being taken advantage of or hurt. Opening up too quickly in treatment can also be dangerous. Clinicians need to be genuinely respectful of what the journey to recovery represents for these clients and to suppress the impulse to jump into talking about the trauma with a client. Moving ahead before clients are ready often undermines the treatment relationship and may prompt clients to leave treatment or relapse.

Early disclosures in a therapeutic relationship may be enticing to a clinician and may be perceived as evidence of deep work. Many therapists have the humbling experience, however, of seeing those early disclosures send a client out of treatment. An important goal of treatment is to help survivors learn how to better moderate their interpersonal boundaries and to reveal themselves more slowly. Clinicians need to model this process by helping clients slow down at the beginning and to discourage them from exposing potentially dysregulating material too quickly. Sometimes this is necessary even when clients say they are ready and willing to discuss what happened to them. Clinical judgment in determining a client's stability and her ability to safely tolerate what may emerge as a result of talking about her trauma is necessary.

Overcompliance in the Treatment

Clinicians should also be attentive to ways in which clients may seem overly amenable and agreeable in treatment. Another way for some survivors to ensure their likeability may be to acquiesce to whatever the clinician suggests. The clinician may find this gratifying initially, but it is often a hollow therapeutic experience in that the client's needs and wishes are not adequately engaged. When this occurs, initial attempts to please are frequently not accompanied by follow-through, adding to a client's experience of shame and to a clinician's feelings of frustration and disappointment. Addiction clinicians are well acquainted with clients who make promises with what seem to be the best intentions but do not keep them. For clients who are also survivors of trauma, engaging with someone honestly about their recovery, in a way that makes sense to them and without the fear of retaliation that many have come to associate with honesty and self-assertion, is a radical departure from their usual way of relating to others. Providing a client the opportunity to experiment with and learn from this kind of genuine interaction has profound implications for treatment.

Rescuing the Client

Another complicated interpersonal dynamic that arises in the treatment of many survivors of abuse relates to the pull in counseling for the therapist to assume much of the active role in helping a client move toward recovery. A more traditional psychotherapy model might include a caution against clinicians' assuming too much responsibility in a client's recovery—making calls or plans for a client, for example. This perspective assumes that the client is being allowed to remain childlike in her relationship to the therapist, who becomes her champion in a supporting, parent-like role, and prohibits the client from assuming those roles for herself. Most trauma-informed models that account for the developmental deficits that many survivors bring to the table in treatment, however, recognize the value of an active therapeutic stance in these situations. Although the goal is to help clients become active proponents of and participants in their recovery, initially clients may need the therapist to guide them in taking the steps they need to take. Clinicians need to balance the need for assuming some client functions with helping clients take over those roles. Clinicians must hold clients accountable for their recovery while also recognizing ways in which clients continue to need their active help and support.

Nevertheless, when the need to help a client gives way to the feeling of becoming a client's "savior," for example, a clinician may need to reexamine the interpersonal context of her aid to her client. This can be a very seductive role for some therapists, but it is often accompanied by a clinician going beyond what is clinically needed and extending her own boundaries uncharacteristically. Clients who have learned ways in which to get others to take care of them may reenact this dynamic with their clinicians, which, if left unattended, can prevent the client from learning how to care for herself. When this is addressed, a client can learn that she can have a more equitable relationship with someone else that does not require her to be in the position of needing to be "saved."

Attention to Transference and Countertransference Issues

When working with survivors of trauma, clinicians need to be aware of their own clinical intuition and countertransferential experience as they sort through their feelings and involvement in a client's care. Learning to pay attention to and understand these internal and interpersonal experiences can provide a clinician with useful information about the internal and interpersonal life of her client. This knowledge can provide a framework to help the clinician and client to surmount obstacles and conflicts that can derail a therapeutic relationship as well as to highlight areas to work on in treatment.

The capacity for a client's traumatic past to reenter a current therapeutic relationship surfaces most notably through reenactments between client and clinician. Often in these situations clients will "reexperience and reenact their role in previous abusive relationships . . . [and] shift from being the victim to being identified with the aggressor, and, for the client who has experienced intrafamiliar abuse or incest, to being the 'favorite' or 'special' child" (McCann & Coletti, 1994, p. 88) in their therapeutic relationship, drawing a therapist into playing a complementary role in this drama, for example, of victim or abuser or seducer. Issues around trust may lead the client to fear that the clinician will betray, abandon, or neglect her. Past experiences of intrusion and aggression may lead the client to fear that "the therapist will recapitulate experiences of threat, terror, and boundary violations" (McCann & Coletti, 1994, p. 88). Pearlman and Saakvitne (1995) wrote,

> Survivors of childhood interpersonal traumas will bring fear, profound mistrust, and anger, as well as yearning, intense loneliness, and fragile hope to the therapeutic relationship. They will be acutely attuned to the most subtle signs of inattention, abandonment, or betrayal in their therapist's demeanor; they will also be influenced by her communication of compassion and respect. Our client's attunement requires that our self-awareness be as acute. (p. 16)

At any given time over the course of working with a survivor of trauma, a clinician may experience any or all of these different interpersonal paradigms, which reflects the shifting intrapsychic and interpersonal experience of many survivors.

Later in this book (see chaps. 8 and 9), we discuss some of the more potent countertransferential reactions that clinicians may confront when bearing witness to a client's trauma experience. We also focus on the importance of supervision, and at times personal therapy, in helping a clinician to recognize her own negative and overwhelmed responses to working with her clients, to get support to handle frustrations that arise, and to learn new techniques to help her client in her recovery.

ASSESSMENT OF INTERPERSONAL FUNCTIONING

Often it is the difficulties in a relationship or relationships that prompt a client to seek treatment. Others in the client's life may be objecting to her behavior or threatening to leave if she does not get help. Alternatively, the client may be dealing with a painful rupture or loss or trying to extricate herself from a difficult relationship. Equally common is a client coming to treatment because she is struggling with a sense of isolation after years of avoiding intimate relationships and profound feelings of disconnection from others that have become unbearable. Regardless of the presenting problem, the clinician will want to assess a client's interpersonal functioning across multiple relationship domains, including romantic/sexual relationships, friendships, work relationships, and relationships with family members, to get a picture of the types of problems the client typically encounters in her relationships and the level of distress and disruption they cause. It is valuable to identify common patterns across relationships as well as to note any discrepancies. For example, a client may have tremendous difficulty asserting herself with her partner but be quite comfortable taking the lead with friends or delegating tasks at work.

Because a client may cycle between seemingly opposite behaviors in relationships, it is critical for the clinician to go beyond a superficial understanding of overt behavior and be more attuned to underlying causes. For example, a client may be extremely cautious and self-protective, shutting people out in extreme ways. The same client may at other times show poor judgment and appear to be indiscriminate about who she allows to get close to her. Both aspects of the client's pattern need to be identified and the cyclical nature understood if the clinician is to help the client make changes in how she relates to others. Also, although it can be complicated when the client has had exposure to multiple or chronic trauma, it is important to assess how these experiences may have affected her behavior and attitudes in relationships.

The clinician will want to get a good sense of who is in the client's social network as well as any major problems she is having in important relationships. A clear priority is to determine whether there are any immediate safety concerns in relationships. Clients, of course, may not be forthcoming with such information, especially right away, and it is important for the clinician to inquire again at various times over the course of the treatment relationship. The clinician should also be aware of common interpersonal problems survivors of trauma often encounter, as discussed throughout this chapter, so that these areas can be attended to and followed appropriately. See Exhibit 5.3 for a list of domains and questions for assessing interpersonal functioning.

EXHIBIT 5.3
Helpful Questions in Assessing Interpersonal Functioning

Social network
- Who are the important people in the client's life?
- Are there any people the client feels close to?
- Are there individuals the client can rely on for emotional support?
- What about financial support? Logistical support?
- How often does the client interact with others on a weekly basis and in what capacity?

Current relationship problems
- Are there any major current conflicts in the client's important relationships? What is the nature and history? How has the client handled the problem?
- What would the client most like to see change or go differently in her relationships?
- What issues do other people have with the client? Have others raised complaints or given feedback about the client's way of interacting?

Safety/revictimization
- Are there any current safety concerns in any of the client's relationships? Is the client in danger of being harmed or revictimized?
- Is the client mistreating or victimizing others?

Problems with trust and intimacy
- Does the client have difficulty trusting others?
- Does the client often feel threatened or intimidated by other people even in the absence of overt threat or danger?
- Does the client have trouble feeling love for or by others or demonstrating affection?
- Does the client typically have difficulty socializing?
- What types of situations are most difficult?
- Does the client tend to avoid contact with others? If so, why?

Problems with anger or aggression
- Does the client feel easily angered or irritated by others? How does the client typically express this?
- Does the client tend to have difficulty respecting authority or listening to others' points of view or concerns?
- Does the client often get into fights or conflicts? Have many relationships ended because of a fight or conflict?

Problems with assertiveness and dependency
- Does the client struggle with being assertive and making her needs known to others?
- Is the client uncomfortable saying no or setting boundaries?
- Does the client have difficulty expressing anger or taking on a role of authority?
- Is the client easily exploited?
- Does the client have difficulty spending time alone?

Because the interpersonal sequelae of trauma are so significant, many treatments attend to the interpersonal needs of clients. Optimally, clients reflect on how their traumatic experiences and involvement with substances have shaped their abilities to relate to others and to notice areas of strength as well as areas that they would like to change. For many survivors of trauma, enhancing their awareness of the interpersonal impact of their trauma and its relationship to substance use is essential to recovery and treatment and can help clients broaden their choices in their relationships with others. The following are some of the common interpersonal treatment issues for survivors that are often targeted in clinical work.

Improving Interpersonal Relationships

Many treatments help women to develop more adaptive interpersonal behaviors to improve both casual and close relationships. There are many models for doing this kind of work, but more trauma-focused treatments often ask clients to consider ways in which present feelings about others may at times have little to do with current interpersonal situations and more to do with the presence of emotional triggers related to their past abuse. Once abuse-related patterns and the ways in which they may be disrupting current relationships are recognized, clients can begin to find new patterns of relating. Attention to helping clients learn how to resolve conflicts and develop more flexible interpersonal expectations is useful in enabling clients to break out of victim–abuser roles.

Some treatments specifically work with clients on their *interpersonal schemas*. In these approaches (e.g., see Cloitre et al., 2006), the therapist and client work to identify problematic interpersonal schemas, which are often variations of "to be attached means to be abused" and tend to involve themes of fear, despair, shame, and grief. The schemas illustrate negative beliefs about self and expectations of others that limit the range of perceptions the individual can have of herself and her experiences with others. Alternative schemas and associated experiential exercises are proposed. The alternative schemas are the basis for exploring, testing, and practicing alternative ways of relating to others. This contrast helps move the client from a view of herself as a victim with limited options to a sense of herself as an adult with new resources, choices, and new ways to think through and plan for the future.

It is important to remember, though, that many interpersonal schemas are implicit beliefs about oneself that are developed during early preverbal attachment periods (Briere & Scott, 2006). These core experiences are typically out of conscious awareness, or they are not part of explicit memory but are often strong felt experiences. Examples of these beliefs include "The world is a dangerous place" or "Others are powerful, and I am helpless." Inside the survivor, however, these may be wordless experiences that often take much more time to access, if they can be accessed at all, through verbal therapies. In these situations, some of the body-focused interventions (e.g., somatosensory psychotherapy; Ogden, Minton, & Pain, 2006) are a helpful component of treatment at some point in a client's recovery.

Creating Safe Boundaries in Relationships

Many treatments address clients' deficits in establishing safe and appropriate boundaries. Clients benefit from attention to relationship patterns that reflect boundaries that may be too permeable, leaving clients persistently vulnerable to exploitation, or boundaries that are drawn too tightly, leaving clients isolated and alone. Optimally, through treatment women learn how to interact safely with others. Sometimes this process also enables a woman to reevaluate the safety of her close relationships and to consider the possibility of leaving dangerous or abusive partners.

Strengthening Self-Identity

Improving interpersonal relationships and establishing healthy boundaries are further supported as clients develop a greater self-understanding and more stable self-identity. Early in treatment survivors often have a limited awareness of who they are as independent people, with a vague, primitive, fractured, or dissociated experience of their identities. Women often feel invisible or even nonexistent. Over time, treatment can help clients to clarify and support who they are and what is important to them, and these changes have far-reaching implications for the ways in which they relate to people around them. Many treatments support the perspective that it is in part through the therapeutic alliance that clients develop more consistent identities and positive self-worth, as well as an enhanced ability to "recognize, tolerate, modulate and integrate his/her own feelings" (Saakvitne et al., 2000, p. 60).

Improving Interpersonal Communication

Focused work on helping clients to improve communication with others is an important skill covered by many treatments. Clients have often become so fearful about asserting themselves, speaking honestly, or negotiating difficult situations that they often retreat rather than expose themselves to negative consequences. Many women have never had adequate role models or opportunities to learn effective ways to interact verbally. Through treatment, clients can learn how to speak to others effectively and safely. Treatment can also be important in helping survivors to grapple with the idea of honesty and differentiate times in which complete honesty may be unsafe, such as with an abuser who may harm the client if told the truth.

Treatments that emphasize role-playing are particularly useful in promoting interpersonal communication skills. Role-plays are a valuable tool in helping clients learn and integrate new interpersonal skills. Clinicians typically role-play salient current situations facing clients with the clients playing themselves. Clinicians may need to step into the role of the client to model a response if she is struggling with how to reply and then ask the client to step back into playing herself in order to practice what she has just heard demonstrated. Role-plays can be enacted in groups with the same guidelines. Having the clinician role-play with a client in group prevents other members from feeling put on the spot by being asked to participate in another client's role-play. When done well, role-plays help to crystallize an otherwise vaguely presented interpersonal situation, bring out the details of the situation through the role-play setup, and enable a client to conceive of and practice new ways of handling a situation that has been difficult (see Foa & Rothbaum, 1998, and Kipper, 1986, for elaboration on role-play techniques).

Enhancing Social Networks

In recovery from both trauma and addiction, establishing sober and safe networks of people is an important part of healing. For many survivors of maltreatment, however, treatment needs to focus attention on what it means to be able to reach out for help and companionship and how hard it frequently is for survivors to ask others for assistance. Many clients learned long ago that reaching out for help can mean being ignored, ridiculed, or even punished. As a result, these clients learn to be self-sufficient, even later when there are safe people to whom they could turn for help. Treatment can help clients reevaluate their beliefs about others and consider and experiment with allowing others to help them. Often, coming to treatment is a first step in this direction.

Building social support has numerous values for recovery, another of which is to provide the survivor with the sense that she can achieve control over the trauma (Carlson et al., 1989). The ability to disclose the trauma to a nonjudgmental listener, whether clinician or friend, is a critical part of recovery, and having someone who can assume this role is invaluable for the person who has experienced victimization. Someone who offers a compassionate response to her struggle also helps the survivor to mourn what she has lost as a consequence of victimization and to rebuild her sense of who she is.

Reducing Emotional Volatility

For many clients, learning to be less reactive in interpersonal situations is a critical part of changing their relationships. The various skills that clients can learn in order to regulate when they become angered, annoyed, or otherwise overwhelmed naturally enhance the quality of their interpersonal relationships. Clients who are able to achieve greater mood stability have better opportunities to engage in more stable relationships with fewer disruptive outbursts. More general emotion regulation skill building and, in some cases, pharmacotherapy target these processes. Many women may also benefit specifically from anger management training. Interpersonal anger is one of the emotions that are most disruptive to the establishment and maintenance of secure and steady relationships.

Developing emotion regulation skills dovetails well with client experiments in new ways of relating interpersonally. Clients who, through therapy, take risks in reaching out to others or in changing their typical ways of interacting with others need to know how to handle any emotional dysregulation that occurs when those efforts do not go as planned. Treatment that supports active changes in interpersonal relating needs to help clients be prepared for both best and worst case scenarios, including how to manage feeling overwhelmed if others do not respond optimally to new gestures.

Providing Hope

Hopelessness about their ability to change and recover is a common experience among many survivors by the time they reach treatment. Often survivors have struggled for years to manage their problems on their own, and it is only as they have come to feel more desperate, or as their lives or relationships have deteriorated, that they seek help. Offering a sense of hope to these women is a core element of treatment throughout the recovery process.

Along these lines, Risking Connection (Saakvitne et al., 2000), a treatment curriculum for survivors of childhood sexual abuse, advocates general principles for supporting clients' interpersonal growth through the development of RICH. therapeutic relationships. Clients are treated with *respect*; clinicians share useful *information* with clients; client and clinician achieve a healing *connection* based on empathy, sensitive listening, understanding, and responding; and clinicians communicate *hope*.

INDIVIDUAL VERSUS GROUP MODALITIES

Many of the areas of interpersonal difficulty identified are addressed well in individual or group counseling. Clients healing from trauma as well as addiction will most likely experience both modalities over the course of their recovery; clients may be ready for group or individual treatment at different stages of the process. Because of the difficulties in learning to trust someone, it is easier for some individuals to open up in individual treatment. Other clients, however, will find the one-to-one experience too intense and will prefer group. Feelings engendered by authority figures may underscore this, making it easier for some survivors to open up to a group of their peers rather than to a clinician.

Clearly, individual treatment enables clients to work more intensively on their own material, providing more opportunity for in-depth exploration of emotion and cognition than does group therapy. Individual therapy may also provide a safer environment in which to express details of trauma when a client is ready to do so, typically later in a client's recovery. Unless explicitly called for by the group framework (e.g., see Foy, Ruzek, Glynn, Riney, & Gusman, 2002), most therapy groups are not safe venues for clients to reveal the details of their abuse for fear of triggering other members in the group. Individual therapy can provide a better opportunity for clients and clinicians to monitor how emotionally activated clients are becoming and to prevent them from becoming too overwhelmed. Nevertheless, most clients can benefit from individual and group to further their recovery, and in chapter 9 we discuss strategies for safely attending to and managing emotional activation in group.

The salience of interpersonal issues among survivors of abuse supports the value of group psychotherapy as a treatment modality for many women. In particular, the potential for group participation to decrease the secrecy and isolation of survivors who have felt alone in their experience is very powerful. Meeting women who have experienced similar traumatic events and symptoms is often a profound interpersonal encounter. Survivor groups offer support that many have never experienced, and connections that help to alleviate a sense of alienation, hopelessness, and mistrust that many survivors present to treatment. Some clients report that group members sometimes feel like family, or rather. the family they never had.

CONCLUSION

Given that individuals develop in the context of relationships, when abuse occurs both a sense of self and the capacity for relating are disturbed (Cloitre, 1998). The clinical presentation of women with histories of multiple or prolonged interpersonal traumas often reflects the profound impact of trauma on self-definition and interpersonal functioning. Because of the disruptions in interpersonal trust and boundaries, which are key to the establishment of relatedness, friendship, and social supports, treatment should address these issues. Ideally, an understanding of a survivor's interpersonal vulnerabilities and their role in substance use will assist clinicians in their efforts to provide effective treatment.

6
PARENTING

The majority of women entering substance abuse treatment programs are of childbearing age and have lifetime histories of sexual, physical, or both sexual and physical assault. Although there are no comprehensive data on the number of mothers with comorbid substance use and trauma-related disorders, estimates show that of the 3 million American women regularly using illicit drugs, up to 80% are mothers of at least one child (Center on Addiction and Substance Abuse, 1996). Feelings of intense guilt and shame around perceived parenting inadequacies are common among this group and may further contribute to the negative spiral of using substances to manage painful affects (Luthar, Cushing, Merikangas, & Rounsaville, 1998). For many of these women, the motivation to improve relationships with their children or regain custody of them is a strong impetus for seeking treatment (Becker et al., 2005).

Whereas some attention has been given to parenting issues among substance-abusing women, less attention has been paid to ways in which trauma-related difficulties (e.g., disturbed interpersonal functioning, problems managing emotions) can further impair parenting. It has been well documented that an individual's relationship history is an important variable that influences parenting behavior and that a history of abuse can seriously disrupt a parent's caretaking abilities in ways that may have far-reaching consequences. For example, maladaptive parenting, including child abuse and neglect, puts the next generation at high risk for developing psychopathology (Banyard, Williams, & Siegal, 2003). Despite the range of adverse outcomes and the fact that women in this population have expressed a need for trauma-specific parenting services, these issues are often overlooked in both research and clinical settings.

In this chapter, we address ways in which a woman's ability to parent her own child may be affected by her abuse history and explain the concept of *intergenerational transmission of trauma*. Some women with trauma histories may reenact aspects of their traumatic experiences with their offspring, either through direct instances of abuse or through inadequate protection from other traumatic experiences. Early trauma can influence a woman's patterns of attachment, which has further implications for her relationship with her children. Furthermore, we discuss ways in which parenting can act as a trigger for women with trauma histories, how it can be difficult for survivors to set appropriate boundaries with their children, and the impact of dealing with feelings and consequences of child custody and removal. We also discuss appropriate interventions, including assessment and available parenting curricula.

INTERGENERATIONAL TRANSMISSION OF TRAUMA

It is widely accepted that the quality of early relationships with primary caretakers is pivotal in shaping emotional functioning and that many problems of children are known to arise from their early environment (Cicchetti & Toth, 1998) and family interactions (Cowan, Powell, & Cowan, 1998). The majority of women in substance abuse treatment programs who are struggling with trauma-related symptoms were raised in difficult family environments. Most did not have adequate parenting models themselves (Harmer, Sanderson, & Mertin, 1999), leaving them at high risk for problems in parenting across a continuum, which at an extreme may include instances of child abuse and maltreatment. We have seen clinically that despite their best intentions and efforts, many women end up repeating at least some aspects of their own traumatic upbringing. Often these women are not only distressed but also confused as to why they find themselves in the position of perpetuating such dynamics with their own children.

Although the potentially harmful impact of trauma on parents and their capacity to be caretakers for their children is well recognized in the clinical realm, empirical research in this area has been lacking until recently. There is, however, a growing body of research demonstrating that traumatic experiences and their effects can be transmitted within a family across generations. Many mechanisms contribute to the transmission of trauma. Parenting practices have been identified as one channel through which families can become "trauma-organized systems" (Banyard, Englund, & Rozelle, 2001). Studies examining the relationship between childhood physical or sexual abuse and a range of parenting outcomes have found that parents' own abuse histories are risk factors for negative parenting behaviors, including use of more punitive, aggressive, and physical discipline (Banyard, 1997; Gara, Allen, Herzog, & Woolfolk, 2000).

In the field of trauma there has been an increasing focus on the detrimental effects of cumulative experiences and how women who are victims of multiple or prolonged interpersonal traumas beginning in childhood often exhibit a range of serious psychological, emotional, and interpersonal problems across multiple life roles (van der Kolk, 1996). Banyard, Williams, and Siegal (2003) were the first to apply these concepts to the parenting role. They explored the impact of cumulative trauma on parenting in a sample of 152 mothers with different types of interpersonal trauma exposure in both childhood and adulthood. Findings showed that overall, higher levels of trauma exposure were linked with decreased parenting satisfaction, reports of child neglect, use of physical punishment, and a history of protective service reports. Research by Cohen, Hien, and Batchelder (2008) parallels these results with cumulative maternal trauma being a significant predictor of parental abuse potential, punitiveness, physical discipline, and psychological aggression even after accounting for demographic and diagnostic variables.

Cycle of Violence and Maltreatment

One conceptual framework used to understand these findings is the *cycle of violence theory*, derived from the social learning model (Cole, Woolger, Power, & Smith, 1992; Downs, Miller, Testa, & Panek, 1992; Kashani, Daniel, Dandoy, & Holcomb, 1992; B. A. Miller, 1990; O'Keefe, 1994; Truscott, 1992). The cycle of violence theory suggests that children learn to become abusive through socialization experiences in their families, putting survivors of abuse at risk for using greater physical punishment with their own children. Support for the cycle of violence theory has been found in samples of physical abuse survivors (e.g., see Caliso & Milner, 1992; White & Humphrey, 1994) as well as sexual abuse survivors (e.g., see Cole et al., 1992; Cole & Woolger, 1989).

Concerns and criticism, however, have been raised about the adequacy of data and research used to support the cycle of violence hypothesis (Widom, 1989b). For example, there is controversy around the use of retrospective reports of child maltreatment, which may in part account for the wide range of histories of abuse among abusing parents. On the basis of a comprehensive review of the literature, Kaufman and Zigler (1987) suggested that unqualified acceptance of the intergenerational transmission hypothesis is unfounded. It is clear that not all abusive parents have trauma histories and that not all traumatized children become abusive parents. Data indicate that among adults who were abused as children, approximately one third abuse their own children (Belsky, 1993; Kaufman & Zigler, 1987). These findings underscore that although the transmission of violence and trauma is not uncommon, quite often women with trauma histories and substance abuse find ways to interrupt this detrimental cycle.

The social learning model can also be applied more broadly; abusive families tend to exhibit multiple areas of dysfunction in addition to the actual abusive behavior itself. For example, caretakers in these family environments often have significant difficulties managing their emotions in an appropriate or effective manner. Because of inadequate opportunities to observe and learn from healthy parenting models, victims of familial sexual or physical abuse are also at risk for perpetuating unstable emotional environments.

Although there is existing research on childhood physical abuse cycles, less is known about the risk of child sexual abuse being transmitted to the next generation. There are data, however, indicating that a maternal history of sexual abuse significantly increases a daughter's risk of sexual abuse (McCloskey & Bailey, 2000; Oates, Tebbutt, Swanston, Lynch, & O'Toole, 1998) and when occurring in conjunction with maternal drug use this risk is exacerbated. In contrast to physical maltreatment, which may be transmitted through direct perpetration by adult victims against their own children, the relative infrequency with which women perpetuate sexual abuse (D. E. H. Russell, 1983) suggests that intergenerational transmission involves more indirect pathways, and abuse may be perpetrated by someone else besides the adult victim. More research exploring potential mechanisms of intergenerational violence is clearly needed.

Clinically we have seen many ways in which women with sexual abuse histories and substance problems may expose their children to unsafe situations in which the child's risk of sexual victimization is increased at the hands of a partner, stranger, or even by the mother's own perpetrator. Although victimized women often express great concern about their children's safety and do not easily trust others, trauma-related symptoms or substance use may impede judgment or make them less able to attend to potential danger signs. Ironically, for example, some survivors are so averse to the possibility that something abusive could be happening to their children that they are less attentive to or even disregard potentially suspicious indicators of danger. Potential clues can be obvious, for example, seeing inappropriate behavior between a partner, babysitter, or family member and the child, or through less obvious changes in a child's mood or behavior. Other mechanisms seem to be at work in cases in which mothers knowingly expose their daughters to sexual or physical violation, often in exchange for money, favors, or drugs for themselves. A mother's own drug cravings and intoxication as well as her inability to grasp the potential damage she is inflicting on her daughter are often central to this type of maternal abuse.

Application of Attachment Theory

Attachment theory provides another framework to understand how transmission of trauma can occur through parenting attitudes and behaviors (e.g., see Fonagy, Steele, & Steele, 1991). As we discussed in chapter 5 of this volume, this perspective proposes that templates of relationships are set down for organizing the self in relationship to others on the basis of a biological drive to attach to caretakers for survival. These templates or internal working models are brought into adulthood and affect relationships. Thus, how parents are attuned to and respond to their children is believed to be a function of the parents' own internal working models of relationships and attachment style. This in turn affects the attachments their own children form to them (Haft & Slade, 1989). Whereas adults with secure attachments tend to have securely attached children, children who are insecurely attached, because of disruptions in their relationships with primary caregivers, can grow up to become insecurely attached parents with poor internal templates for managing interactions with their children.

In an abusive household, unfortunately, the drive to attach may mean attaching to somebody who is abusive, and survival and interpersonal connection become linked with abuse. When an abused child's internal understanding and expectations of relationships are characterized by insecure attachment, formed through her interactions with neglectful or abusive primary caretakers, there are clear implications for parenting when the child becomes a parent. Themes associated with insecure attachment observed in abusive families include (a) rejection of the child and her needs; (b) parentification of the child, including the expectation that the child should attend to the parent's needs and desires, in some cases even sexually; and (c) fearful, disorganized attachment in the parent, which leads to an environment of chaos in which abuse may literally go unnoticed or unheeded (Alexander, 1992). Mothers of infants with disorganized attachment styles also report significantly greater levels of violence with their current partners than mothers of infants who develop secure attachment styles (Zeanah et al., 1999).

Parental Posttraumatic Stress Disorder as a Pathway to Child Posttraumatic Stress Disorder

Another way in which trauma may be transmitted to the next generation is through symptoms of posttraumatic stress disorder (PTSD). Although there is not much empirical work in this area to date, clinical evidence indicates that behavioral and emotional symptoms characteristic of PTSD (e.g., flashbacks, startle responses) can negatively affect a parent's functioning and ability to parent effectively.

E. Hesse and Main (1999) described how parents still overwhelmed by a past experience of maltreatment may negatively affect their infants by engaging in "frightened and frightening" behavior. These frightened and frightening behaviors (e.g., exaggerated startle, freezing, threatening, or dissociated behavior) are consistent with PTSD symptoms. Lyons-Ruth, Bronfman, and Parsons (1999) expanded on this work by identifying a broader set of maternal behaviors reflecting disrupted affective communication between mother and infant, which are hypothesized to be related to infant fear and disorganization. Support for these models is demonstrated in findings that mothers of infants displaying disorganized and fearful attachment behavior showed elevated rates of frightening behavior, affective communication errors, hostile–intrusive behavior, and role confusion (Lyons-Ruth et al., 1999; Schuengel, Bakermans-Kranenburg, & Van IJzendoorn, 1999).

It also appears that children of parents with PTSD are more likely to develop a specific vulnerability to traumatic stress and other psychiatric symptoms themselves. Much information regarding this pathway has come from literature focused on children of Holocaust and war survivors (e.g., see Bar-On, 1996; Danieli, 1998; Rosenheck & Fontana, 1998). These findings clearly have implications for children of parents with PTSD related to other types of trauma as well.

Early observational studies indicated that children of Holocaust and war survivors appeared to exhibit symptoms of PTSD similar to those of their parents (Barocas & Barocas, 1983; Rosenheck & Nathan, 1985) as well as a host of other psychiatric problems. Recent studies have more carefully examined whether PTSD and other psychopathology in offspring of trauma survivors can be attributed to the effect of parental trauma by ruling out alternative explanations. For example, Yehuda, Schmeidler, Wainberg, Binder-Byrnes, and Duvdevani (1998) compared offspring of trauma survivors with a matched control group and systematically evaluated additional traumatic events other than those related to parental trauma. Their findings demonstrated that although offspring of Holocaust survivors did not directly experience more traumatic events than the comparison group, they had a greater prevalence of current and lifetime PTSD and psychiatric diagnoses. Thus, in addition to being affected by parenting, which may be compromised by parental PTSD symptoms, children of traumatized parents may also be affected by directly experiencing posttraumatic symptoms themselves.

IMPACT OF SUBSTANCE USE DISORDERS AND OTHER COMORBID DIAGNOSES ON PARENTING

Research on the relationship between trauma exposure, PTSD, and parenting is in the initial stages; thus, we devote specific space in this chapter to reviewing the more established literature on the link between maternal substance use, psychiatric disorders, and parenting difficulties. In this way, we alert readers to the potential areas of vulnerability for mothers and children with these co-occurring issues.

Substance Use Disorders and Parenting

A number of studies have indicated that women who are addicted to substances display problems in interaction with their children when compared with other mothers (see Mayes, 1995, for a review). These problems have been observed with women who use different types of drugs and who have children of various ages (Hans, Bernstein, & Henson, 1999). A few studies of maternal–infant interaction among drug users (Burns, Chethik, Burns, & Clark, 1997; Neira, Fineman, Beckwith, Howard, & Espinosa, 1997) confirm that substance-using mothers differ significantly from control participants on bonding, mutual enthusiasm, ego development, and psychiatric symptoms. Other research on parenting with school-age and older children suggests less maternal emotional involvement (Ammerman, Kolko, Kirisci, Blackson, & Dawes, 1999), increased use of problematic parenting behaviors (Harmer et al., 1999), increased maternal failure to set limits (Bernardi, Jones, & Tennant, 1989), parent and child dissatisfaction (Wright, Garrison, Wright, & Stimmel, 1991), and poor parenting attitudes (Kettinger, Nair, & Schuler, 2000) in substance-using families in contrast to non–substance users.

Substance-using mothers are more often punitive toward their children (B. A. Miller, Smyth, & Mudar, 1999) and may be more likely than comparison mothers to use more severe and threatening disciplinary practices (Bauman & Dougherty, 1983; Hien & Honeyman, 2000). Mothers addicted to substances have been found to rate higher on *authoritarian involvement,* indicating a mother who is likely to exclude outside influences in her mothering role and to overly try to control the child and his or her development (Wellisch & Steinberg, 1980).

Furthermore, there is ample evidence for a link between parental substance abuse and increased risk for child maltreatment. Children whose parents abuse substances may be at 2 times the risk of experiencing physical or sexual abuse, compared with children with non-substance-abusing parents (C. Walsh, MacMillan, & Jamieson, 2003). Mothers who use alcohol or drugs are often responsible for such maltreatment (Chaffin, Kelleher, & Hollenberg, 1996). Also important are findings that chemically dependent women often have limited parenting knowledge and hold various misconceptions about parenting practices (Velez, Jansson, Montoya, Schweitzer, Golden, & Svikis, 2004).

Psychiatric Diagnoses and Parenting

Mothers with psychiatric diagnoses are also more likely to show a range of difficulties during interactions with their children. The primary focus of this research has been on maternal depression (see Lovejoy, Graczyk, O'Hare, & Neuman, 2000, and Oyserman, Mowbray, Meares, & Firminger, 2000, for reviews), the most common mental disorder in women of child-bearing age. Observational studies indicate that depressed mothers manifest higher levels of hostility and irritability toward their children, have more negative parent–child interactions, and are more likely to use coercion rather than negotiation in trying to control their child's behavior (Cohn, Campbell, Matias, & Hopkins, 1990; Cohn, Matias, Tronick, Connell, & Lyons-Ruth, 1986). Mothers with depression are often less responsive to their child's communicative behavior and less likely to be in sync with their infants (Field, Healy, Goldstein, & Guthertz, 1990; Goodman & Brumley, 1990). In addition, women with depression report more negativity toward the demands of parenthood and describe feeling less competent and adequate than other parents (Webster-Stratton & Hammond, 1988).

Taken together, most existing studies suggest that mothers who struggle with substance abuse or depression are at higher risk for using harsher, more coercive and punitive parental strategies and for having more negative interactions with children, which at the extreme end of the continuum can perpetuate a cycle of child maltreatment. Recently there has been growing recognition of the need to go beyond a symptom-based approach to understanding parenting difficulties. This includes examining the importance of other psychosocial risk factors, such as a mother's developmental history and her relationship with her partner, that may directly or indirectly contribute to poorer parenting skills (e.g., see Hans et al., 1999) for women with substance use or psychiatric disorders. The movement to broaden the context in which to examine parenting patterns converges with recent research on the effects of maternal trauma history on parenting, discussed earlier.

Also in line with trauma-focused parenting research is consideration of the role of emotion regulation and its effects on parental stress, functioning, and behavior. For example, Lovejoy et al. (2000) proposed a framework in which aggressive and coercive behaviors displayed by mothers might be accounted for by negative affect states rather than by depression or other specific disorders per se. Emotion regulation deficits have been consistently demonstrated in women with chronic trauma histories as well as those struggling with substance use disorders, including mothers (Hien & Honeyman, 2000; Hien & Miele, 2003; van der Kolk, Roth, Pelcovitz, Sunday, & Spinazzola, 2005). Research by Hien et al. provides strong evidence for emotion regulation deficits as strong predictors of adverse outcomes, including aggressive behavior toward children (e.g., see Hien & Honeyman, 2000) and with partners (e.g., see Hien & Miele, 2003), exceeding other variables, including psychiatric and substance use disorders.

VULNERABLE PARENTING AREAS
FOR WOMEN WITH ABUSE HISTORIES

Some specific problematic parenting patterns have been observed in parents with histories of interpersonal trauma. Although some of these vulnerabilities are unique to this population, many of these patterns have also been found in parents with substance use and other comorbid disorders and have been associated with abusive and neglectful parenting (Bavelok, 1984).

Discipline

As discussed earlier, many women with trauma histories, particularly childhood abuse, have difficulty managing discipline with their children. Although finding a healthy and effective balance is challenging for most parents, women with trauma histories often resort to strategies on either end of the continuum from harsh authoritarian parenting to overly permissive parenting, and may be more prone to cycling between these two extremes (DiLillo & Damashek, 2003). For example, many parents who have an abuse history find setting limits particularly uncomfortable and avoid invoking appropriate parental authority for fear of being "mean" or alienating their children. They often have difficulty integrating discipline with affection (Cross, 2001), and find the idea of being firm and kind at the same time quite foreign. These parents may create an excessively permissive environment in which problematic behavior is not met with consequences. As a result, parents often describe feeling taken advantage of or disrespected by their children, heightening their sense of ineffectiveness and enabling the problematic behavior to continue and often snowball into other difficult and disrespectful behavior. Over time frustration and resentment can build up, culminating in the use of the very type of harsh punishment these women set out to avoid.

Other parents find themselves resorting to physical punishment because they know of no other way to handle their child's misbehavior. Although they may feel bad or fearful that they are now abusers of their own children, these parents are often unable to generate alternative strategies. If they are triggered by their children's misbehavior, they may be faced with their own arousal and reactivity, making it even harder to think clearly and construct calmer, less threatening responses. Survivors of their own abuse also may not understand the negative consequences of relying on punishment in which children comply on the basis of fear. Some parents who are prone to harsh or abusive punishment believe that children are trying to get away with bad behavior; they believe that children need to be shown who has authority (Bavelok, 1984). From this perspective physical punishment can seem like an appropriate and valuable form of discipline. If corporal punishment is in line with values or cultural norms of their own family of origin, they feel further entitled to use it. Children who learn that violence is a useful way to solve problems are more likely to punish their children severely when they become parents themselves.

Often corporal punishment methods are not considered abusive. This becomes evident when clients are asked questions regarding past abuse and current behaviors. If a question about abuse is posed generally, such as "Did you ever experience any kind of abuse?", even clients who have experienced severe corporal punishment may say "no," not because they are attempting to hide or deny their experience but because it was considered "acceptable" punishment in her family or community and was not identified or labeled *abuse*. Alternatively, if clients are asked about specific types of punishments or behaviors, they will often acknowledge them.

Parental Knowledge and Expectations

Parents with abuse histories may also have unrealistic expectations of their children's developmental abilities. It is often the case that their caretakers had limited parenting information and unrealistic ideas about how children are supposed to behave. Now as parents they may inaccurately perceive the skills and capabilities of their own children, not understanding the sequential stages of child development and expecting a child to perform tasks he or she is not cognitively or biologically able to accomplish. These parents may have a particularly difficult time understanding or tolerating that a certain amount of testing—such as a 2-year-old who is experimenting with saying "no"—is a normal part of a child's maturation process. When a parent experiences intense grief, distress, or anxiety at a particular stage in her child's development, the picture is further complicated because it triggers painful memories of past trauma. When children cannot meet unrealistic expectations, it often leads to frustration, anger, and disappointment on the part of the parent. Vulnerable parents may manage these emotions with abusive or neglectful behaviors leading their children to experience feelings of shame and worthlessness.

Parents with trauma histories may also have unrealistic expectations about ways in which they should behave as parents, making them especially susceptible to internal and societal pressures to be a "perfect" parent. To break the cycle of problematic parenting, it is important for parents to be able to identify their expectations of themselves and of their children and to understand the strong influence these underlying beliefs have on their own and their children's behaviors. For this reason, it is often clinically relevant to make sure that trauma survivors who are mothers have access to psychoeducational parenting material and interventions. In addition to the supportive nature of these opportunities, many women find it invaluable to learn about what is considered normal development and appropriate ways of responding to their children.

Family Boundaries

Parents with trauma histories may also look to their children to meet their own unmet needs (DiLillo & Damashek, 2003). This often takes the form of a parent acting helpless and dependent and looking to her child for care. It can also become manifest in a parent using a child as a friend or confidant, sharing inappropriate information to which children should not be privy. In these scenarios the child becomes responsible for providing comfort and emotional support for the parent, and the family structure focuses on meeting the parents' needs, often leaving children to take care of themselves. Such reversal of roles makes it less likely that the parent will be effective when they do want or need to take on authority in the relationship. Alternatively, in an effort to belatedly assert her authority, a previously passive parent may resort to authoritarian or abusive behavior to regain control. Children who grow up in an atmosphere of blurred boundaries may be more likely to have subsequent problems in their interpersonal relationships. At the extreme end there may be severe emotional and physical abuse and neglect, or sexual abuse in cases in which parental needs are sexualized. Parent–child role reversal has, in fact, been identified as a common pattern among parents who abuse their children (Bavelok, 1984).

It is important for parents to understand that their desire to be cared for and their hope that the relationship with their children will alleviate or mitigate some of their own childhood pain are not unusual or necessarily problematic. Damage may occur, however, when parents cannot contain or prevent themselves from acting on these desires or identify appropriate sources and outlets for these feelings, allowing instead their children to take responsibility.

Safety and Monitoring

Parents with abuse histories also often struggle with managing their child's safety and determining an appropriate level of involvement in this realm. Their own experiences affect behavior in this area; for example, parents who had overprotective or controlling caretakers may try to give their own children more independence, whereas children who were neglected or ignored may be more likely to closely monitor their children's activities. Some parents may go to extremes ranging from intrusiveness and inability to allow their children age-appropriate autonomy on one end of the spectrum to a lack of involvement and neglectful behavior such as leaving young children to care for themselves before they are capable. In her memoir *The Glass Castle*, Jeannette Walls (2005) detailed how she regularly cooked for herself at age 3, resulting in a fire that left her seriously burned and scarred. These kind of matter-of-fact descriptions of early autonomy, sometimes with dangerous consequences, are not uncommon among survivors of abuse or neglect.

Nevertheless, in an effort to keep their children safe and to deal with their own understandable fears, some traumatized parents may be hypervigilant and teach their children to be afraid and mistrustful of their environments. For example, one mother explained that every time she changed her son's diaper she pointed to his penis and told him, "Nobody is ever to touch this." Unfortunately, this type of behavior often instills high levels of anxiety in children, which can have negative consequences, including the continuation of the cycle of trauma. Many women in treatment are ashamed and horrified that despite their strong desire to protect their children their own issues with substance abuse or involvement in volatile relationships have put their children at risk. Although painful, coming to terms with how such behavior can make children vulnerable to unsafe situations can often be a catalyst for change.

PARENTING ASSESSMENT

Assessments can help focus on individual and interpersonal sequelae from trauma and can provide an understanding of parent–child interactions, discipline, communication, and other areas of family functioning, including the partner relationship. When inquiring about parenting related experiences, it is essential that the clinician assume a nonjudgmental stance and communicate an understanding that the parental role can be complicated and at times overwhelming. The clinician should ask about parenting in a balanced way, posing questions about positive and negative aspects, thereby evaluating parental strengths as well as challenges. This also includes asking about a range of situations—how the parent handles structured and unstructured time, how she manages problem situations as well as ways in which she has fun with or enjoys her children. This type of evaluation highlights parental strengths that can be tapped into as treatment progresses, as well as containing feelings of hopelessness in the parent. It also gives the clinician an opportunity to see how well the parent is able to integrate different aspects of her parenting experiences and a sense of how well she can tolerate a range of feelings. See Exhibit 6.1 for a list of common parenting assessment domains.

There are several ways to inquire about parenting practices. For example, in discerning disciplinary strategies, the parent can be asked how she would typically respond to a number of hypothetical situations in which her child may have misbehaved, or the parent can be asked about specific disciplinary behaviors she has actually used with her children ever or in a specified time frame. Asking about specific disciplinary behaviors may be more likely to result in guarded answers or elicit more socially desirable responses; therefore, a combination of these methods may be preferable to get the most representative picture. In addition to specific behaviors, it is important to get a sense of parenting

EXHIBIT 6.1
Important Parenting Assessment Domains

Household composition
- How many children (i.e., biological and adopted) are there? What are the children's ages?
- How many children live in the home? How many live outside of the home?
- Is there anyone else living in the home besides the parent and children?

Caregiver arrangements
- Who is (are) considered the primary caretaker(s)?
- Are other adults involved in caring for the children (e.g., siblings, babysitters, grandparents, friends)?
- Do older children in the family have responsibility caring for the younger children?
- If the parent works or needs to be out of the home, what are the child care arrangements? Does the parent feel comfortable with those arrangements?

Contextual factors
- What is the parental employment status?
- What is the parental financial status?
- Are there any children in the family with significant medical or psychological problems, developmental issues, or physical disabilities?
- What is the parental support (i.e., emotional and practical) system like?
- Are there any open child protection cases, and, if so, what is the status?
- Have any children been removed from the home?

Relationship status
- Is the parent in a stable partner relationship?
- Is a partner involved in caring for the children?
- If divorced or separated, what are the custody arrangements, and are there any disputes?
- If the partner is not the father to the child(ren), what is the nature of the relationship between the parent and the children's father(s)?
- Is there ever violence between partners? Are children ever witnessing violence?

Parenting attitudes
- How does the parent feel about being a parent? What are some positives and negatives?
- Level of satisfaction: Which areas of parenting are most and least enjoyable?
- Level of parental stress: What areas of parenting are most stressful? Does the parent generally feel in control?
- How does the parent generally feel about her decision to have children?

Parenting practices
Discipline
- What disciplinary strategies does the parent rely on?
- How effective are the parent's disciplinary strategies?
- How does the parent set limits? Do children understand contingencies?
- Are there explicit guidelines children understand?
- Does the parent carry through with discipline consistently?
- Does the parent believe in corporal punishment?
- Does the parent use physical discipline? If so, what kind, and how often?
Anger management
- How does the parent manage when she feels angry at her children?
- How does the parent manage her child's anger or aggression?

(continues)

EXHIBIT 6.1
Important Parenting Assessment Domains   (Continued)

Involvement
- Does the parent promote her children's autonomy in an age-appropriate way?
- How involved is the parent on a daily basis?
- How involved is the parent in the children's school activities?
- How does the parent attend to the children's safety?

Communication
- How well does the parent talk to her children?
- Does the parent discuss the children's needs and feelings with them?
- Does the parent problem solve with the children?
- Does it seem as if the parent is confiding in her children inappropriately?

Free time and leisure activities
- What does the parent do with the children that is fun or rewarding?
- Does the parent ever play with the children?

Parental self-care
- How does the parent take care of herself? If she does not, what are the obstacles?
- Does the parent take time for herself?

attitudes—how the parent generally feels in her role as a parent and her level of parenting satisfaction and stress.

When considering assessment, it is also important to keep in mind that there are multiple risk factors and protective factors whose combination may help foster or interrupt the transmission of trauma across generations. Broader contextual and often multilevel factors, such as family financial status, parental employment, number of dependent children, and availability of social and community support systems, also need to be included in a comprehensive evaluation. Social and community supports can be critical in providing options and ongoing help to parents facing multiple personal challenges.

TREATMENT: INTEGRATING PARENTING INTERVENTIONS

Many women, including those with substance abuse and trauma histories, view parenting as the central purpose in their lives (Substance Abuse and Mental Health Services Administration [SAMHSA], 2000). Nonetheless, the majority of current service models in mental health and substance abuse treatment programs still use an individual-focused rather than a family-focused approach (Child Welfare League, 2001; Finkelstein et al., 2005; Luthar & Walsh, 1995; Nicholson et al., 2006). Incorporating parenting components that address the complex needs and circumstances of this population not only can provide the opportunity for critical early intervention efforts but also can encourage women with these co-occurring problems to draw on a potentially key source of treatment motivation. There is research showing that effective parenting skills can benefit the child and may improve the mother's self-esteem and sense of competence (Bauman & Dougherty, 1983; Zweben, Clark, & Smith, 1994). Improved feelings of self-efficacy in the parenting role are likely to increase hope and positively affect other recovery issues for trauma- and substance abuse–related disorders.

It is important to note that a number of substance abuse treatment programs do offer services for drug-dependent mothers and their children, including parenting interventions. However, issues related to trauma and its relationship to substance abuse have typically not been directly addressed in this context. Given the prevalence of trauma in mothers with substance use disorders, treatments that do not explicitly address the impact of these life events on the parenting role are less likely to be effective.

Another major gap in services for substance-using mothers is that available services usually focus on pregnant women or on women with babies, despite research demonstrating that school-age children are very much at risk for serious psychopathology (G. Chang, Carroll, Behr, & Kosten, 1992; Luthar et al., 1998; Luthar & Walsh, 1995). Also, there is a paucity of manual-driven treatments, making systematic delivery and investigation of these interventions difficult. There are, however, some notable exceptions.

PARENTING INTERVENTIONS FOR SUBSTANCE-ABUSING PARENTS

The *Strengthening Families Program* (SFP; Kumpfer, 1987) is a 12 to 14 session behavioral and cognitive skills training program originally designed to reduce vulnerability to drug abuse in 6- to 12-year-old children of substance-abusing parents. This program has since been modified (SFP 10–14) to meet the needs of 10- to 14-year-olds. Both programs have three components: parent training, children's skills training, and family skills training. Parent training focuses on understanding developmental characteristics of children, setting appropriate limits, providing support and nurturing, managing conflict, and sharing beliefs and expectations about using substances. SFP's effectiveness was first demonstrated in a study sponsored by the National Institute on Drug Abuse and has since been replicated with several at-risk populations, including children of substance users, abused and neglected children, and low-income urban minority families (Kumpfer & Alvarado, 1995; Kumpfer, Molgaard, & Spoth, 1996). Results have shown that parents made gains in specific parenting skills, including setting appropriate limits and building positive relationships with their children. Equivalent positive results were also found for SFP 10–14 in a large-scale randomized, controlled study (Spoth, Redmond, & Chungyeol, 2001). In many ways the empirically validated parenting component of SFP serves as a good model for parent-focused interventions; however, SFP does not specifically focus on women's treatment issues nor is it informed by trauma theory.

The *Nurturing Program for Families in Substance Abuse Treatment and Recovery* (Camp & Finkelstein, 1997) is an example of a parent training program developed for pregnant and parenting women in substance abuse treatment. This program is an outcome of the parenting component of a 5-year demonstration project, the Coalition on Addiction, Pregnancy and Parenting (CAPP). The goal of the demonstration project was to integrate parenting and parent-child services into substance abuse treatment.

In the initial part of this project, women from two urban residential treatment programs for pregnant and parenting chemically dependent women received specialized individual and group services. As part of these services, women participated in a structured parenting skills group based on the curriculum of the Nurturing Program for Parents of Children Birth to Five Years for 2.5-hour weekly sessions over 23 weeks. This curriculum, developed by Bavelok and Bavelok (1989), has been established as an effective intervention for improving parenting skills and reducing the risk of child maltreatment. It focuses on the four identified parenting domains associated with abusive and neglectful parenting (i.e., inappropriate expectations, lack of empathy, corporal punishment, and role reversal) described earlier.

Certain modifications were made to the Nurturing Program in the CAPP project to make it more responsive to the needs of women in substance abuse treatment. Findings showed that women who completed parenting skills training appeared to make significant improvements in parenting attitudes and knowledge as well as on measures of self-esteem (Camp & Finkelstein, 1997). In addition, the women rated their experiences in the group as very positive and valuable. As Camp and Finkelstein (1997) noted, these changes are remarkable given the disadvantages and challenges facing study participants, such as poverty, history of physical and sexual abuse, and chronic history of substance abuse.

Building on these encouraging findings, the modified Nurturing Program became the Nurturing Program for Families in Substance Abuse Treatment and Recovery (Moore & Finkelstein, 2001). The four original core treatment domains were expanded to include information about adult development, the process of recovery, parenting development, as well as intergenerational patterns of substance abuse and child maltreatment. New material exploring participants' cultural heritage was added. The program has been implemented in multiple substance abuse treatment programs including residential treatment centers. Preliminary results are positive in terms of the interventions enhancing parents' satisfaction and competence.

The *Relational Psychotherapy Mother's Group* (RPMG; Luthar & Suchman, 2000) is another intervention for substance-abusing mothers that incorporates attention to interpersonal and developmental issues. RPMG is a 24-week manualized treatment that was developed as a supplement to standard methadone treatment for heroin-addicted mothers and their children up to age 16. It is a semistructured supportive treatment that addresses parenting deficits and draws on gender-sensitive perspectives as well as on interpersonal psychotherapy models. Sessions focus on specific parenting issues such as developing strategies for managing conflict, using alternatives to physical punishment, establishing age-appropriate limits in discipline, and encouraging warm yet effective parenting styles. Therapists also address the mothers' own negative childhood experiences by helping women negotiate their own developmental tasks and modeling effective parenting and communication.

In a randomized treatment trial, the 37 heroin-addicted mothers assigned to RPMG demonstrated lower levels of risk for child maltreatment, greater involvement with their children, and more positive psychosocial adjustment than women who received methadone counseling alone. In addition, women in this group showed greater reductions in opioid use than those receiving drug counseling alone. This finding supports the argument that addressing psychological and interpersonal issues of substance-abusing women can have substantial spillover effects on their capacity to abstain from drug use (Brunswick, Messeri, & Titus, 1992).

RPMG clearly represents an advance in that it addresses interpersonal and parental issues in addition to issues of addiction. However, this treatment may not be generalizable to other settings with other substance-abusing populations. As the RPMG developers Luthar and Suchman (2000) noted, their sample is not necessarily representative given that there were a greater proportion of Caucasian women than women of color among participants. Modifications may be necessary to meet the specific needs of an urban minority population, including culturally informed interventions that address parenting styles that vary cross-culturally. Additionally, a 24-session intervention may not be feasible given the difficulties in treatment compliance and retention in this population.

TRAUMA-SPECIFIC PARENTING INTERVENTIONS

Although the development and incorporation of trauma-specific parenting services are still in the early stages, there have been some encouraging developments.

Women, Co-Occurring Disorders and Violence Study

The Women, Co-Occurring Disorders and Violence Study (WCDVS), which is discussed in chapters 2 and 11 of this volume, was the first large-scale study to address the lack of appropriate services for women with co-occurring substance use, mental health disorders and trauma histories (Becker et al., 2005). The majority (87%) of the 2,729 participants receiving services at various substance abuse treatment sites were parents. More than half of the sample retained custody of at least one child, and most had one child or more under the age of 18. Many of the women had lost custody of at least one child, and women who still had custody expressed concerns over the potential removal of a child. In response to questions about how they viewed themselves as parents, less than half reported feeling that they were good parents, and only about one third felt that their family life was under control. In addition, only 37% felt that their current service providers were helping them in their role as parents. These data underscore the need for parenting services for this population of women and the importance of considering interrelationships between trauma, parenting, and women's roles as mothers.

Sites participating in this study found standard parenting curricula to be in need of modification to address the relationship between trauma and parenting (Huntington, Jahn Moses, & Veysey, 2005). A variety of parenting interventions were used including a version of the Nurturing Program for Families in Substance Abuse Treatment and Recovery, which was further adapted to add a trauma focus. Other parenting interventions implemented in the WCDVS were The Impact of Early Trauma on Parenting Roles, a group exploring the impact of trauma on feelings and expectations of motherhood, and Parenting at a Distance, a group for women who are not primary caregivers to their children (Harris & Parenting Workgroup, 2001). Researchers involved in the project describe challenges to integrating trauma-specific material into parenting groups. The need to develop understanding about how traumatic stress and family experiences may affect parenting was difficult to balance against the need to avoid triggers that could pull women off track and away from more concrete learning objectives (Jahn Moses, Reed, Mazelis, & D'Ambrosio, 2003). Sites handled this in different ways, from decreasing material on family of origin to creating more structured formats.

The WCDVS also included a Children's Subset Study in which 4 of the 9 sites implemented an intervention to address the issues that children of mothers with co-occurring disorders and histories of trauma confront (Finkelstein et al., 2005). This intervention was specifically designed for children between ages 5 and 10 because of the lack of treatment resources typically available for school-age children. Results at 6-months postintervention showed children's improvement was predicted by their mother's improvement and recovery. At 12-months postintervention, regardless of their mother's outcomes, children at intervention sites showed greater positive changes than children at comparison sites (Noether et al., 2007). This study further illustrates the importance of prevention and intervention with children of mothers with co-occurring disorders and histories of trauma as a way of disrupting potential intergenerational cycles of violence, mental illness, or substance abuse.

The Women's Health Project

The Women's Health Project Treatment and Research Center (WHP) is our hospital-based community treatment program for women survivors of trauma, many of whom have substance abuse histories. Much of the experience drawn on for this book is based on our clinical and research experience in this program. We describe our work at the WHP more fully in chapter 11 but highlight here some of our work in developing a trauma-focused parenting intervention.

Many WHP clients have expressed a strong interest in participating in groups that focus on parenting issues. Similar to SAMHSA's WCDVS findings, women at the WHP have voiced serious concerns about their parenting abilities and expressed a desire to increase their level of competency, confidence, and satisfaction in this area of their lives. These include women with children in their custody as well as women seeking to regain custody of children who have been removed from the home. Many are struggling with complicated custody issues, such as fear of losing their children and maintaining relationships with their children who are living with other caretakers. Parenting groups have been attractive to women who are parents of young children, as well as to women who are overwhelmed by the issues presented by their adolescent children. For these women, parenting their children is often identified as a key source of motivation for recovery, but also as a frequent trigger for feelings of emotional distress and shame.

Treatment at the WHP has sought to address some common dilemmas (discussed in the sections that follow) facing the mothers in the program.

Managing Anger Safely and Effectively

Without the ability to effectively modulate their emotion, women report that they easily go from "zero to 100," reflecting the speed with which they can go from seeming calm to being consumed with anger. For women presenting to treatment with few resources on how to handle their surging feelings of anger, parenting and anger management groups are critical in helping them learn how to prevent situations that are likely to trigger their anger and manage anger without hurting or frightening their children if they do become enraged.

Improved Ability to Reflect on Their Children's Experience

Because of their own upbringing, many mothers in our program have tremendous difficulty understanding what their children may be feeling, making it difficult to respond appropriately. Learning to recognize their children's needs in therapy makes it easier for them to respond to their children effectively and with empathy, as well as to set appropriate boundaries. For many of the women at our program, either the mothers are unable to set any limits on their children's behavior, leading to an even more chaotic home environment and problematic relationships with their children, or the limits are too severe, often initiating battles for control. Typically this can lead the children to further challenge limits, with potentially dangerous or abusive consequences. Especially when these conflicts erupt during adolescence, the consequences often include increased truancy and running away. Mothers of these children end up feeling scared and out of control, occasionally leading them to petition the state to assume legal oversight of their children. Treatment aims to help mothers preempt some of these escalated situations. Mothers gradually learn how to consider the emotional experiences of their children and try new ways of responding to their children and reaching out to others for help and support.

Grappling With Issues of Sexuality

Issues around sexuality and sexual relationships in their adolescent children also typically cause extreme stress in mothers who are themselves survivors of abuse. When their daughters start to mature and develop, these mothers often reexperience their own abuse histories with greater intensity. Frequently they overidentify with their daughters and recall their own experiences at that age, possibly experiences of having been molested, as well as experiences around their own sexual experimentation or sexual acting out. Eager for their daughters not to go through some of the same negative experiences, survivor mothers are often at a loss as to how to respond to their daughters, and therapy can be crucial to helping them negotiate this time period.

Reducing Guilt and Shame

For women who have mistreated or neglected their children—because of either their drug or alcohol abuse, their mental or physical illnesses, or their own parenting challenges—helping to manage acute shame and guilt is paramount. Knowing that they may have become abusive or neglectful themselves, or that they may have allowed or overlooked the abuse of their children at someone else's hands, can be devastating to these clients who were themselves once victims. At the WHP we have found that the support and understanding of other mothers in a group setting is often vital to helping a woman process this experience and make changes in her role as a mother.

Parenting Group for Survivors of Trauma

In an effort to respond to the needs of our clients and to honor the fact that parenting is often an essential aspect of their identities, we have been interested in providing parenting interventions, with a focus on trauma-related issues. Given that the empirically based parenting skills curriculums that are available do not address the specific trauma-related difficulties (e.g., problems managing negative affect, interpersonal conflict, trauma-related symptoms) with which many of our clients struggle, we developed our own protocol (Cohen, 2006). The development of our parenting intervention for women with histories of trauma was based directly on the literature described earlier in this chapter as well as on our own clinical experiences with this population. The goal of this intervention is twofold: (a) to increase participants' awareness of how their traumatic experiences and associated difficulties can negatively affect parenting attitudes and behaviors and (b) to develop a repertoire of strategies to interrupt problematic parenting patterns that have the potential to further the cycle of trauma. Additional aims are to decrease social isolation and shame and increase parenting confidence and flexibility.

The Parenting Group for Survivors of Trauma is a time-limited and structured group treatment. Each of the 12 sessions provides psychoeducation on a specific area of parenting vulnerability and incorporates cognitive–behavioral skills such as grounding, self-monitoring, assertiveness, or distress tolerance techniques. Although time is spent raising awareness and making connections between women's trauma histories and current parenting challenges, the treatment is generally oriented toward the present and focused on problem solving. Topics include managing trauma-related triggers and traumatic stress symptoms in the context of parenting, identifying and tolerating strong emotions of their children and toward their children, dealing with anger and negotiating power dynamics in parent–child relationships, generating alternatives to harsh physical punishment, balancing discipline and affection, establishing and maintaining healthy family boundaries, enhancing knowledge of child development, developing realistic expectations, establishing safe and appropriate levels of involvement with and monitoring of children, and increasing self-care.

This treatment has several strengths. It is consumer driven and based on ongoing collaboration with our specific client population and treating clinicians. It also has a strong theoretical foundation and draws on the most current trauma-related research. Recently collected pilot data will be used to inform refinements to the intervention and to further future research efforts.

CONCLUSION

Identifying a client's cycle of trauma and providing hope that it can be disrupted are essential components to recovery. Drawing attention to ways that a client may demonstrate resiliency and strength is also needed. Clinicians should keep in mind that there are multiple pathways and combinations of risk and protective factors that influence whether familial violence and trauma gets transmitted to the next generation. Parenting skills interventions that focus on trauma-related difficulties are an important part of women's substance abuse services. Although studies have documented the necessity and promise of such interventions, there is still a great need for development and empirical study in this area.

7
PHYSICAL HEALTH

Physical health is an integral, although often overlooked, component of women's addiction recovery. Women presenting to substance abuse treatment programs have often neglected their physical health for years, resulting in an increased incidence of chronic diseases and overall poor health due to bodily stress, neglect, and unhealthy behaviors (e.g., obesity, smoking, poor diet; Deykin et al., 2001; Kimerling, Clum, & Wolfe, 2000).

Women with histories of emotional, physical, and sexual trauma also experience a multitude of health problems, both with and without physical origins (e.g., see Felitti et al., 1998). Trauma survivors face unique challenges in self-care and the appropriate use of medical services related to experiences of mistrust, intrusiveness, and vulnerability, low self-worth and inability to assert themselves, tendencies to avoid and deny their physical experiences, fear of being out of control or further traumatized by medical procedures, and limited understanding of their own bodies and the importance of caring for their health. When treating women with trauma-related symptoms and addiction, it is essential to address at least some of these barriers. The failure to deal with health-related issues can often impede other treatment objectives and goals, forcing clinicians to spend significant amounts of time coordinating medical services, and can result in clients missing treatment appointments because of medical service needs.

In this chapter, we address the physical and medical repercussions for women with trauma histories who are in substance abuse treatment. We review the literature on both health problems with clear physical origins as well as the range of relevant somatoform disorders that are associated with past exposure to trauma, particularly as they apply to women with addictive disorders. To our knowledge, there are no current publications reporting physical health outcomes for women with comorbid substance use disorders and posttraumatic stress disorder (PTSD); therefore, our information comes mainly from studies focusing on populations with childhood trauma histories and those experiencing combat trauma with and without PTSD. We present background on stress responses and health and medical treatment seeking, and we examine models for considering physical influences on mental health and addictions treatment. Clinical examples are used to illustrate treatment approaches that can be applied to address mind and body in a holistic fashion.

TRAUMA AND THE BODY

There is evidence showing that individuals with PTSD report worse physical health outcomes than women without PTSD. Common physical and sexual health outcomes include complaints of chronic abdominal or back pain, headaches, loss of appetite, gastrointestinal distress, and gynecological problems including sexually transmitted diseases, vaginal bleeding and infections, chronic pelvic pain, painful intercourse, and urinary tract infections (e.g., see Campbell et al., 2002; Friedman & Schnurr, 1995; E. A. Walker, Gelfand, et al., 1999). Our overall review of the trauma literature examining physical and sexual outcomes, displayed in Table 7.1, documents a clear association between PTSD and poor health outcomes. The majority of these studies focused on self-reported health outcomes and health perceptions or service utilization as proxies for overall health status, with significantly fewer reporting objective outcomes (i.e., physician diagnoses) and mortality. In addition, a review of the literature supports the idea that PTSD is a mediator between traumatic experiences and poor health. That is, traumatic experiences that lead to PTSD influence the severity and intensity of physical health outcomes.

Unfortunately, studies of civilian populations (i.e., nonmilitary samples) have been limited, and studies of women with co-occurring substance use disorders even more so. However, the studies conducted to date have tended to corroborate overall findings. For example, Weissbacker and Clark (2007), reporting on results from the Substance Abuse and Mental Health Service Administration Women, Co-Occurring Disorders and Violence Study, composed of women with substance use and mental health disorders with trauma histories, found that more severe trauma histories were associated with poorer perceived health, more physical illness, and more somatic symptoms.

TABLE 7.1
Summary of Selected Studies of Trauma,
Posttraumatic Stress Disorder, and Physical Health

Studies	Population	Measurement domain	Outcome(s)
Koss, Woodruff, and Koss (1990)	2,291 women, primary care setting (i.e., HMO)	Health perception	Victimization severity was significantly predictive of poorer health perception.
Breslau and Davis (1992)	93 young men and women with PTSD	Self-reported medical problems	Group with chronic PTSD averaged significantly more medical conditions.
Moeller, Bachmann, and Moeller (1993)	668 gynecological patients, abused and nonabused	Objective and subjective measures of medical visits and physical health	The more types of abuse experienced as a child, the poorer the health outcomes reported, including hospitalizations and perception of physical and psychological problems.
McFarlane, Atchison, Rafalowicz, and Papay (1994)	140 Australian firefighters, 40 with PTSD	Self-reported physical problems, physician consult	Group with PTSD had significantly more physical problems and higher number of doctor consults.
Wolfe, Schnurr, Brown, and Furey (1994)	Female Vietnam veterans	Perceived physical health	Trauma exposure and PTSD independently associated with health outcomes; exposure association smaller when combined with PTSD.
Kimerling and Calhoun (1994)	115 women with past rape compared with 87 non-victim control participants	Perceived physical health	Victim group had more somatic complaints, poorer perceived health, more psychological distress, and more medical visits; no differences between groups on mental health service utilization.
Najavits et al., (1998)	122 cocaine-dependent men and women with $(n = 25)$ and without $(n = 97)$ PTSD	Self-reported medical problems (Addiction Severity Index)	Group with PTSD reported higher overall medical problem severity.

(*continues*)

TABLE 7.1
Summary of Selected Studies of Trauma,
Posttraumatic Stress Disorder, and Physical Health   (*Continued*)

Studies	Population	Measurement domain	Outcome(s)
Andreski, Chilcoat, and Breslau (1998)	Male and female HMO patients	Somatization symptoms	Baseline history of PTSD was linked with increased complaints of pain and conversion symptoms.
Felitti, Anda, Nordenberg, Williamson, Spitz, Edwards, Koss, and Marks (1998)	The Adverse Childhood Experiences Study, male and female HMO patients ($n = 8,056$ respondents; 60% of those receiving surveys)	Health-related behaviors and health problems (survey), health appraisal questionnaire (medical clinic)	Graded relationship between number of childhood risk exposures and adult health risk behaviors (e.g., alcoholism, drug abuse, depression, poor self-rated health) and disease (e.g., ischemic heart disease, cancer, chronic lung disease; as number of risk exposures in childhood increased, morbidity and mortality risk in adulthood increased.
Schnurr, Spiro, Aldwin, and Stukel (1998)	Male veterans with and without combat and noncombat trauma	Self-reported physical symptoms	Those with both types of trauma had a 16% increase in symptoms at all age points compared with the group without trauma.
Walker, Gelfand, Katon, Koss, Von Korff, Bernstein, and Russo (1999)	2,291 women from primary care setting (i.e., HMO)	Objective and subjective physical health	Those with childhood maltreatment and sexual maltreatment had higher prevalence of most indices of physician diagnoses, history of physical problems, functional disability, and risk behaviors.
Zoellner, Goodwin, and Foa (2000)	76 women with PTSD	Perceived	Negative life events, anger, depression severity of the re-experiencing PTSD cluster were predictive of perceived health; PTSD severity explained health outcomes above and beyond these other variables.

TABLE 7.1

Summary of Selected Studies of Trauma,
Posttraumatic Stress Disorder, and Physical Health   (*Continued*)

Studies	Population	Measurement domain	Outcome(s)
Kimerling, Clum, and Wolfe (2000)	52 female Vietnam veterans, 24 with PTSD	health Self-reported acute physical symptoms	PTSD-mediated trauma exposure and health outcomes.
Wagner, Wolfe, Rotnitsky, & Proctor (2000)	2,301 male and female Gulf War veterans	Self-reported health problems	PTSD symptoms predicted physical health, controlling for demographics, combat exposure, and initial health problems; gender did not predict health outcomes.
Ouimette et al. (2004)	134 male and female Veterans Administration medical patients	Self-report and physician diagnosed health status	Patients with PTSD more likely to have musculoskeletal and circulatory disorders and poorer health-related quality of life (i.e., functioning and physical role).
van Zelst, de Beurs, Beekman, van Dyck, and Deeg (2006)	Elderly, Dutch sample with PTSD, sub-threshold, and no PTSD	Days in bed, disability days, health care utilization	Group with PTSD or sub-threshold PTSD spent more days in bed, had greater days of disability, used health care primarily for somatic needs, and evaluated the care they received as poor.

Note. HMO = health maintenance organization; PTSD = posttraumatic stress disorder.

Along with health implications, there are significant social and clinical rationales for examining physical health in relation to trauma histories. Research indicates that failing to address physical health and barriers to medical services may (a) increase health care costs over time (E. A. Walker, Unutzer, et al., 1999), (b) increase the overall number of medical visits, especially acute care visits (Arnow et al., 1999; Deykin et al., 2001; Kimerling & Calhoun, 1994), (c) lead to misdiagnosis and subsequent lack of appropriate services (van Zelst et al., 2006), (d) increase PTSD symptoms and risk behaviors (Cloitre, Cohen, Edelman, & Han, 2001), and (e) impede the planning of combined substance use and trauma treatments. The combined experience of substance use and trauma has serious ramifications for the client, treatment program, and medical service setting.

Service Utilization

Examining health outcomes using a service utilization model provides further indication of the social costs and consequences of untreated trauma in women. Many studies indicate that the presence of a trauma history increases service use, especially acute medical care. Arnow et al. (1999) studied a sample of 206 women from an HMO primary care clinic and found that childhood sexual abuse with comorbid psychiatric distress was associated with higher numbers of emergency room visits and pain-related problems compared with groups with only childhood sexual abuse or control participants with no childhood sexual abuse and no psychiatric distress. Similarly, E. A. Walker, Unutzer, et al. (1999), looking at a sample of 1,225 women divided into three maltreatment groups (i.e., no maltreatment, nonsexual maltreatment, and sexual maltreatment), found that those with childhood sexual abuse had significantly higher annual medical care costs and higher numbers of outpatient visits, including emergency department visits. Deykin et al. (2001) found in their study of 156 male veterans that those with current PTSD had a significantly greater number of health care visits, on average, compared with those without PTSD (34.9 vs. 22.6) and averaged more health conditions (7.9 vs. 3.7). Thus, individuals with higher numbers of health care visits were twice as likely to have current PTSD as those with lower levels of health care use. Our research has shown that PTSD reexperiencing and hyperarousal symptom severity are correlated with greater frequency of recent outpatient visits and past year emergency room visits (Litt, Cohen, & Hien, 2001).

Although many trauma survivors may overuse health care resources or present to inappropriate or acute health care services, other trauma survivors consistently underuse and avoid seeking health care. Clearly, this underutilization of care can lead to increased health problems and subsequent medical costs because these women may come to attention of medical professionals only when they are in an emergency or crisis situation and health-related problems are at more severe levels.

The Stress Response

The human body is designed to manage stress through activation of neural, neuroendocrine, and immune mechanisms. This process by which the body's systems cope with challenges and achieve equilibrium has been called *allostasis* or "stability through change" (P. Sterling & Eyer, 1988, p. 631). Allostatic systems may either be overstimulated or not perform normally, a condition referred to as *allostatic load,* in which those very systems that normally function protectively can begin to cause illness or injury (McEwen, 1998). It is not surprising that chronic or acute stress can have a major impact on the body's ability to regulate itself, leading to a state of allostatic load.

Health can also be compromised by lifestyle choices and coping mechanisms, such as smoking, substance use, poor nutrition, and lack of exercise, all of which are common in women with histories of trauma and comorbid substance use disorders. Physical problems associated with PTSD and substance use include cardiovascular problems, high blood pressure, decreased bone density in women, hippocampal damage (i.e., memory impairment), increased susceptibility to insulin resistance (i.e., diabetes), and immune system suppression (see Table 7.1).

There is an emerging body of neuroscience findings that document the relationship between traumatic stress and the brain. Although this field of study is beyond the scope of this chapter, a brief review places the research findings on trauma, substance use disorders, and physical health into a meaningful context. When an individual is exposed to stress, intense fear, or terror, neurotransmitters are released that activate parts of the brain involved in memory, emotion, and self-regulation. What is currently known is that exposure to trauma leads to a cascade of stress responses that have many characteristic neurobiological components and may be unique to trauma. These include neurobiological changes to the volume and activity levels of major structures in the limbic system (e.g., hippocampus, nucleus accumbens), which influence emotional states, memory, reward and pleasure responses, including the fight–flight reaction.

Given these biological responses, it is also likely that early childhood stressors and maltreatment—such as physical or sexual abuse—may affect brain development with direct effects on adulthood vulnerability to developing PTSD and addiction. Exposure to chronic traumatic stress, in particular, has been related to overload in the stress hormone, cortisol, which plays a part in the body's immune functioning. Thus, hypernormal cortisol levels over time have been shown to depress immune functions among individuals with trauma. Yehuda (2006) provided some explanation for research demonstrating the physical consequences of traumatic stress exposure. Yehuda suggested that hormonal differences in individuals, such as lower cortisol levels, may help determine whether PTSD develops through neuroendocrinologic responses to trauma.

In line with the robust relationship between traumatic stress and its impact on the body, Schnurr and Jankowski (1999) posited that if individuals develop more severe psychological consequences of trauma such as PTSD or depressive disorders, their physical health will more likely be compromised. Elements of their model explaining stress and physical health include psychological states, symptom perception (i.e., mislabeling psychological symptoms as physical symptoms; Kimerling et al., 2000), biological function, illness behavior, and health risk behaviors (i.e., smoking, substance abuse, and poor nutrition). Deykin et al. (2001) offered several explanations for why they found increased service use and medical conditions among male veterans with

PTSD, concluding that PTSD is a risk factor for further physical morbidity and requires greater medical care. As others have noted (e.g., see Kimerling et al., 2000; Wolfe, Schnurr, Brown, & Furey, 1994), PTSD-related problems, such as poor self-care, substance use, and lack of key social supports, can also lead to greater physical health problems. Traumatic exposures that lead to other psychiatric consequences appear most likely to adversely affect physical health.

THE IMPACT OF CHILDHOOD SEXUAL ABUSE ON SEXUAL HEALTH

Research on the long-term sequelae of childhood abuse in women, and of childhood sexual abuse in particular, supports an association with subsequent problems in sexual functioning and sexual health. Several theories have been posited to explain why childhood sexual abuse might negatively affect later sexual health and functioning, including developmental intrusions that affect sexual functioning, negative association with sex and sexual intimacy, and the development of negative coping mechanisms (e.g., abusive relationships, substance use) to deal with sexual encounters and painful memories and emotions. For example, a woman may not remember sexual encounters with partners because of dissociation during sexual intimacy. For some survivors, dissociative behavior becomes an automatic response to sexual intimacy, making it difficult to enjoy intimate situations with partners.

The impact of trauma on sexual health and risk is relatively less researched than the general area of physical health, but with increased risk for HIV exposure among women, and addicted women in particular, consideration of trauma consequences on sexual behavior is an imperative issue. Heterosexual transmission of HIV now accounts for an estimated 70% of new transmissions, surpassing injection drug use (Centers for Disease Control and Prevention, 2004). Substance abusing women are at greater risk for engaging in unprotected sexual intercourse (Leigh & Stall, 1993; Rasch et al., 2000; Semple, Grant, & Patterson, 2004); in addition, they tend to report a greater number of sexual partners (Hoffman, Klein, Eber, & Crosby, 2000; Santelli, Robin, Brener, & Lowry, 2001) and are more likely to exchange sex for money or drugs (Edlin et al., 1994; Hoffman et al., 2000; Logan & Leukefeld, 2000). Maladaptive coping mechanisms exhibited by trauma-exposed women, including dissociation, substance use, and impulsivity, tend to exacerbate sexual risk behaviors. Wyatt et al. (2002), in a sample of 490 women, found that those who were HIV seropositive had more severe trauma histories and a higher likelihood of experiencing adult sexual violence than were those who were HIV negative. Findings indicate that cumulative trauma may place women at higher risk for sexually transmitted infection, including HIV.

In contrast with over- or inappropriate use of general medical services described earlier in this chapter, Loeb et al. (2002) summarized some of the sexual health problems associated specifically with childhood sexual abuse, including underutilization or inconsistent use of gynecological services, shame and discomfort during gynecological exams, and an inability to recognize potentially problematic symptoms until they become acute. Women may distance themselves from their bodies as a way of minimizing unpleasant memories and associations. Traumatic memories and experiences may also lead to physical manifestations. For example, chronic pelvic pain is frequently cited by individuals with abuse histories, often with no medical explanation (Loeb et al., 2002). In addition, Schloredt and Heiman (2003) found in a self-selected community sample of 148 women (70 with sexual abuse and 78 without) that those with abuse had more negative affect during sexual arousal, although the groups did not differ on sexual desire, arousal or orgasm, sexual pain, and masturbation.

Sexual risk behaviors, linked to HIV and other sexually transmitted infections, are exacerbated by experiences of intimate partner violence, difficulties in partner negotiation, and dissociative responses during sexual intimacy. Loeb et al. (2002) again provided a summary of research indicating that women with childhood sexual abuse have earlier sexual debuts, more sexual partners, less self-efficacy in regard to condom use, less consistent use of condoms, increased likelihood of intravenous drug use and sexually transmitted infections, and greater likelihood of unintended pregnancies. Combining drugs or alcohol with sexual interactions may make it more difficult to make decisions about condom use and to refuse unwanted sex (Loeb et al., 2002). The finding that women with abuse histories have higher numbers of sexual partners has been corroborated in other studies as well (Schloredt & Heiman, 2003). Schloredt and Heiman found that women with abuse histories experience more negative perceptions of sexuality during their worst psychological states, positing that this may be linked to increased number of sexual partners. They explained that women with ongoing negative perceptions may be looking for different, more positive experiences with sexual partners, leading to increases in the number of partners and sexual encounters.

Adult revictimization and retraumatization occurs frequently among women with childhood trauma histories and PTSD. Moreover, studies show that women with childhood sexual abuse who are also sexually abused as adults have more severe reactions to the adult trauma, engage in riskier sexual behaviors, and experience more negative sexual interactions (e.g., painful intercourse, vaginal infections; for a more extensive review of this literature, see Loeb et al., 2002).

SOMATOFORM DISORDERS

The attention to the mind–body connection has been central to evolving work in the area of trauma treatment. This includes the identification that some traumatic pain appears to be psychological in origin. Somatoform disorders, according to the *Diagnostic and Statistical Manual of Mental Disorders* (4th ed., text rev.; DSM–IV–TR; American Psychiatric Association, 2000), are medical complaints that are, at least partially, unexplained by a medical condition, substance use, or another psychiatric condition. It is important for clinicians to be aware that somatic disorders do not constitute a motive on the part of the client to gain benefits or to "trick" medical personnel. Physical complaints and symptoms are not intentionally fabricated and they cause significant distress or impairment to the client. The following is a list of somatic disorders:

- *Somatization disorder* includes a history of multiple physical complaints (i.e., a combination of pain, gastrointestinal, sexual, and pseudoneurological symptoms) that occur over a period of several years and often result in the individual seeking medical treatment.
- *Conversion disorder* is characterized by unexplained symptoms or deficits affecting voluntary motor (e.g., paralysis, inability to talk) or sensory functioning (e.g., loss of touch, pain, hallucinations) that cannot be fully explained by a medical condition and that are judged to be associated with psychological factors given their initiation or exacerbation is proceeded by one or more stressors.
- *Pain disorder* is defined by the presence of pain in one or more areas of the body, including pelvic, head, and back. Psychological factors are believed to play a significant role in the onset, severity, worsening, or maintenance of the pain.
- *Hypochondriasis* is the preoccupation with the fear of having, or the belief that one has, a serious disease and is based on misinterpretation of bodily symptoms or functions. The preoccupation persists despite medical evaluation and reassurance.

No discussion of traumatic stress and physical response can be complete without reference to a lengthy body of literature first evident in some of Freud's case histories of conversion symptoms (e.g., see Breuer & Freud, 1895/2000). These cases provided documentation of the expression of traumatic stress through nonverbal and physical symptoms that patients, and often their doctors, believed to have a physical origin. Today, there is ample empirical evidence for the ubiquity of psychosomatic complaints in populations exposed to traumatic events. Often, because of the severe psychological sequelae of trauma, physical complaints may mask psychological symptoms. In addition, individuals with trauma histories often lack awareness of the emotional origin of their symptoms because of dissociative mechanisms and thus may feel that it is more appropriate to seek medical services for physical complaints as opposed to psychological services. For example, Golding (1994) examined sexual assault history and physical health in a sample of 1,610 women from the Los Angeles area. Her findings from this nontreatment sample support an increase in both physical and somatic symptoms in women with sexual assault histories. In addition, women with sexual assault histories had more chronic disease (i.e., diabetes, arthritis, and physical disability) and reported poorer overall health.

In support of the notion that those with more severe trauma may seek treatment for physical rather than emotional problems, E. A. Walker et al. (1992) studied 100 women receiving diagnostic surgery for chronic pelvic pain or nonpainful gynecological conditions, categorizing them into severely abused or no abuse–less severe groups (women with no abuse or less severe abuse were clinically similar and, thus, combined). Those with more severe abuse histories had significantly higher risk for lifetime diagnosis of somatization and pain disorders. In addition, the number of medically unexplained symptoms, a history of substance use disorder, and panic disorder were predicted by severe abuse histories. The pathways between childhood abuse and somatization is unclear but may be related to lack of control or powerlessness experienced during the trauma. For some clients, seeking medical care may be a form of coping whereby the client receives social support and attention and can vocalize distress in a way that is less frightening and more acceptable than addressing trauma symptoms directly through mental health channels.

In a unique prospective study by Escobar, Canino, Rubio-Stipec, and Bravo (1992), 375 men and women completed the Diagnostic Interview Schedule before and 1 year after a natural disaster. The investigators looked at the occurrence of somatic symptoms, defined as new (i.e., reported only after the disaster) or persistent (i.e., present before and after the disaster). All somatic symptoms met severity criteria and were unrelated to a medical condition or drug and alcohol use. Overall, participants exposed to the disaster reported significantly more physical symptoms, but only in the gastrointestinal (e.g., abdominal pain, nausea, vomiting) and pseudoneurological (e.g., amnesia, fainting, double vision) categories. As Escobar et al. suggested, and as described within DSM–IV–TR somatoform disorder, gastrointestinal and neurological categories of symptoms can be psychologically based or linked to a specific stress response.

A related phenomenon among those with substance use disorders and PTSD, although not limited to individuals with trauma histories, is the inability to describe emotion. The phenomenon of alexithymia or being "without words" was described by Sifneos (1973) in the early 1970s and related to individuals with psychosomatic or somatoform disorders. Many of the techniques and strategies for coping with addiction and trauma involve increasing awareness of (i.e., cognition) and labeling or differentiating many emotional states. In the absence of language and symbolic abilities, emotional distress is often manifested in the body.

Research findings provide support for this clinical phenomenon. In a study of 205 women in a primary care setting, Spertus, Yehuda, Wong, Halligan, and Seremetis (2003) found that emotional abuse and neglect predicted adult emotional and physical distress (which they determined using the Symptom Checklist–90–R Somatic, Anxiety, and Depression scales [Derogatis, 1992] assessing physical complaints) as well as exposure to additional traumatic events. These findings remained even when accounting for the variance of physical and sexual abuse. This study indicates that emotional abuse may have long-lasting effects or at least contribute to later vulnerability to additional traumas. Spertus et al. suggested mechanisms by which emotional abuse and neglect may lead to increased service utilization: (a) an increase in psychological symptoms that affect physical health, (b) a decrease in self-care or an increase in risk behaviors as a result of the abuse leading to poorer general health, and (c) a decrease in the threshold at which care is sought.

MONITORING AND EVALUATING PHYSICAL HEALTH

Findings such as those previously reviewed support the need for accurate diagnosis of physical and psychological complaints. Accurate diagnosis requires appropriate assessment and treatment planning because psychological responses to trauma appear to result in and be associated with increased physical symptoms that may sometimes be an expression of psychic pain.

There are many methods of defining and describing physical health symptoms. Research studies use different concepts of physical health, including client perception, quality of life and functioning, service utilization and visit counts, medical diagnosis, symptom presence and severity, symptom categories, symptom intensity (including pain levels), and somatization. In addition, data can be collected through self-report, clinician interview, medical chart review, and physician report, among other methods. Each of these definitions and methods contributes different types of information. There is no right or wrong way to report physical health. To a large extent, programs interested in assessing physical well-being base their approach on the particular client and her presenting issues. Some types of health outcomes may not be relevant to certain clients (i.e., somatization), but universal screening of clients is essential to capture problems and avoid biases in assessment. Certain clients may have particular issues about attending medical visits, in which case it might make sense to monitor service utilization (i.e., visit counts and types) as well as determine how to overcome barriers and challenges to making and attending appointments.

There are multiple standardized measures for assessing physical health. Standardized measures can be useful in clinical settings to consistently assess treatment impact and changes over time. Because physical health is often subjectively or inconsistently reported, it can be helpful to use more objective tools to track change. Accessing both subjective and objective measures of health is particularly important for women with PTSD, as physical complaints may mask other types of problems and emotions. A client may find that physical health symptoms are highly distressing, limiting her ability to handle other treatment issues. A service provider may need to address physical issues before moving on to other mental health or substance abuse concerns. In addition, it is often the case that interdisciplinary efforts on the part of mental health and physical health providers are necessary to provide the best mental, physical, and substance abuse treatment care.

Exhibit 7.1 lists assessment domains of different types of health outcomes. This is by no means an exhaustive list but can be used as a starting point and as a way to determine which types of physical health categories make sense to assess in your program and population. Some assessments are copyrighted and require permission from the developer or a small fee per use. Others are public domain. Appendix B at the end of this volume provides a list of specific physical health assessments.

PREVENTION AND INTERVENTION

Given that a range of health problems can be instigated or exacerbated by trauma exposure and subsequent development of PTSD, and further complicated by substance use, prevention and treatment efforts for women in substance abuse treatment should incorporate assessment, referral, and intervention for physical and sexual health issues when possible. A multimodal approach can address some of the negative health consequences of trauma and addictions. Indirectly, treatments that address symptoms related to PTSD may also affect physical symptoms. As Cloitre et al. (2001) noted, even

---

EXHIBIT 7.1
Physical Health Assessment Domains

- Physical health diagnosis (i.e., self-report or medical chart review)
- Physical health symptoms (e.g., count, intensity, severity, onset, duration)
- Level of distress
- Functional impairment
- Perceived health status
- Quality of life
- Medication prescription and use
- Medical service utilization (e.g., visit counts)

---

perceived health improvement could initiate protective mechanisms against medical conditions and illness. Reduction of symptoms can help diminish physical vulnerability and lower stress levels. In addition, ongoing medical problems and visits may act to reinforce feelings of being different, bad, or sick—common thoughts among individuals with childhood abuse histories (Cloitre et al., 2001; E. A. Walker, Gelfand, et al., 1999). We now address some of the main clinical treatment challenges and materials to consider regarding the integration of physical health approaches into substance abuse treatment for women.

Interfacing With Health Professionals

Higher levels of medical service use in women experiencing trauma-related symptoms suggest the need for mental health, health, and substance use treatment providers to collaborate in the care given to this population (Kimerling & Calhoun, 1994). In addition, because trauma victims might be more likely to seek medical treatment as opposed to psychological services, physicians and nurses may have a greater opportunity to intervene (Cloitre et al., 2001; Koss, Woodruff, & Koss, 1990; E. A. Walker, Gelfand, et al., 1999). Therefore, one area of intervention may be in the training of medical providers to assess for trauma exposure and PTSD and to make referrals to appropriate mental health services. In addition, physicians and other medical professionals who are made aware of the long-term medical and physical outcomes of early trauma and PTSD can make informed assessment and treatment decisions (E. A. Walker, Gelfand, et al., 1999). Substance use treatment providers can try to use medical service referrals, whether on or off site, with providers who understand or have training to specifically address the needs of this population. Addiction providers can discuss upcoming medical appointments with clients to help prepare clients for the experience.

Women with PTSD and substance use disorders often experience authority in extremely threatening ways. The patient–doctor relationship is one with a significant power differential, and it can be a strong trigger for these women. Having to relinquish control in a very intimate setting may trigger unwanted memories and emotions, raising issues of mistrust, vulnerability, and an inability to assert themselves. Working with clients on this issue, through either exposure therapy, role-playing, problem solving, or coping skills training, may make seeking services less daunting and frightening and ultimately more productive and effective. For example, in working with a client who has not sought gynecological services for many years, a clinician may spend several weeks or months helping to prepare the woman for what the experience might be like. This might entail acting out questions the provider may ask or questions the client may have in role-playing sessions. A clinician might have the client visualize the experience and then debrief her. In addition, the clinician and client can talk about coping strategies to use before, during, and after the visit. Strategies include going to the appointment with a friend, using relaxation techniques, or meeting the medical provider prior to the actual exam. Finally, if collaboration with medical providers is limited, agencies may want to examine the potential for additional integrated community health services. This is an opportunity to connect with service providers in the area and begin networking with regard to community service provision (see chap. 11 for more discussion on community service integration in case example 1).

Case Management

Treatment programs need to be prepared to address the health problems discussed in this chapter and to be able to direct clients to appropriate and acceptable service referrals. Some have suggested that mental health facilities explore integrated treatment models, including health care within the program, to address the extensive needs of clients (Schnurr & Green, 2004). Integrated services would be a recommended goal for substance abuse treatment programs, given the high association between trauma, PTSD, substance abuse, and physical illness. At minimum, case management practice should include strong relationships with medical providers who can provide services that are accessible and acceptable to clients in substance abuse treatment. As Schnurr and Green (2004) pointed out, medical services that are close by and easily accessible will increase retention and compliance, producing better outcomes in general. In addition, medical professionals can be trained in the specific issues and challenges facing this population, including the necessity of having female physicians on staff.

As we mentioned, clinicians should be comfortable using problem solving skills in working with clients' barriers to seeking medical care along with using different types of therapies to address avoidance of health care services. In cases in which clients are fearful of interactions with medical providers, and in which there are limited or no outside supports, clinicians may want to discuss with clients whether it might be helpful for the clinician to have contact with a health care provider directly. This is often outside the realm of what clinicians are accustomed to, and many clients will not want this type of clinician involvement. Some clients (with express written consent), however, may benefit from the assistance of a clinician speaking to a health care provider. A clinician may be able to alert and prepare the provider regarding some of the client's fears, and may have the opportunity to help clarify communication between the client and the provider. Clients who are distressed during medical appointments find it difficult to retain and process information. During a medical visit, especially a nonroutine visit in which decisions are necessary or instructions are provided, a client may appreciate the help of her clinician if she has no one else to attend the visit with her.

CLINICAL INTERVENTIONS

A number of therapeutic approaches specifically target women's thoughts and feelings about their bodies and physical symptoms they experience. The examples presented in the sections that follow can be used alone or in conjunction with other mental health and addictions interventions.

Empowerment Approaches

Empowerment-based theories, including those that incorporate a feminist perspective, are highly recommended in work with women exposed to trauma and addiction, especially with regard to medical concerns. Empowerment strategies come in a number of different forms. On a systems level, empowerment approaches address oppression and injustice that occur because of membership in a stigmatized group. As one example, a feminist perspective emphasizes female oppression due to multidimensional patriarchal domination and how this oppression has profound effects on women's views of themselves and their capacity for self-determination. Feminist-informed approaches support the identification and naming of systems of oppression and the promotion of individualized self-realization (Robbins, Chatterjee, & Canda, 2006). Consistent with working with trauma survivors, they support meeting the client where she is and acknowledging the client as the expert in her own life. These approaches may entail the identification of consumer leaders who can model advocacy, social action, and use their own voice to attain appropriate and needed services. On an individual practice level, in treating women who have been exposed to exploitive situations, such as childhood abuse or intimate partner violence, empowerment-based therapeutic interventions can address issues related to self-efficacy, the feeling that one has the power to produce and control life events (Robbins et al., 2006). Self-efficacy can be increased through information, knowledge, and normalizing fear and distressing experiences through group work with like individuals.

Lack of empowerment can be detrimental in interactions with health care professionals. Better health outcomes occur with higher levels of communication between the patient and doctor (M. A. Stewart, 1995). Patient self-advocacy and patient–doctor collegiality contribute to successful health care. Steinhart (2002) further pointed out that moving the locus of control to the patient supports a quality-of-life model of recovery, rather than a traditional, paternalistic medical model. Women who have experienced profound losses of control through addiction and trauma histories might understandably have better health outcomes under empowerment-based interactions.

An Intervention Curriculum: Women's Health Education

Developing interventions that empower women—through either psychoeducational models or social support and peer groups—can be beneficial. In the National Institute on Drug Abuse's Clinical Trials Network Women and Trauma Study, we further developed and tested an intervention to address the physical health concerns of women with comorbid PTSD and substance use disorders: women's health education (WHE; Tross, 1998). Providing women with information and practice in discussing health issues promoted confidence that, it is hoped, translated into better interactions with health care providers and motivation to seek appropriate and timely care.

The WHE intervention consisted of twelve 90-minute sessions devoted to a specific area of women's health (see Exhibit 7.2). In addition to providing relevant health information, each WHE session involved specific exercises, which gave women the opportunity to consolidate and personalize the information and to work on specific self-care skills. As we have reviewed, psychological sequelae from abuse and trauma can manifest themselves physically. WHE applies an interactive teaching-style facilitation to increase knowledge about these different health areas, reducing anxiety when discussing these issues and increasing women's self-efficacy to (a) seek medical services, (b) discuss health issues with medical professionals, (c) normalize the experience of talking about potentially uncomfortable issues of the body, (d) use medical or body terminology, and (e) conduct and pursue self-care activities (e.g., breast self-exams, making healthy food choices). The WHE intervention did not focus on trauma specifically and disclosure of abuse or trauma was discouraged. This minimization of trauma-specific discussion allowed the facilitators to stay focused on the health information and main-

EXHIBIT 7.2
Women's Health Education Curriculum Topics

- Basic human biology and body systems
- Anatomy of the female reproductive system
- Breast care
- Infections
- Introduction to HIV/AIDS
- Contraception and safer sex
- Pregnancy and childbirth
- Sexually transmitted infections
- Nutrition
- Blood pressure
- Diabetes
- Menopause

tain a safe learning environment. Materials used during the intervention included workbooks for the clients, resource books, community referrals, videotapes, informational games, charts, and diagrams. See chapter 11 for further discussion of the Women and Trauma Study in Case Example 2. We are currently developing WHE into an Internet-based interactive program for women to use in a self-paced or clinician-assisted modality called BESThealth (Cohen, Miele, Litt, & Hien, 2008).

Body Interventions

A number of therapeutic approaches focus on the body in treating trauma. In her book *The Body Remembers*, Babette Rothschild (2000) addressed the impact of trauma on the body and offered techniques, especially those that increase body awareness, to treat trauma survivors. By focusing on the body and being aware of its tension, pain, and other physical experiences, a trauma survivor can begin to manage some somatic complaints.

Because trauma-related symptoms have a strong somatic component, interventions that focus on relaxing the body can be very effective for women with trauma. A number of therapeutic practices related to breathing, relaxation, and meditation have been used for years to decrease anxiety and relieve psychological and physical symptoms. Some of these were described in chapter 4 for their effectiveness in providing skills to manage emotion dysregulation. In the most general terms, meditation practice focuses on increasing awareness of the present moment. Mindfulness, an aspect of meditation, can be useful in the work of increasing self-awareness, including awareness of the body, physical sensations, and location of discomfort. Meditation has been integrated into many forms of psychotherapies and has been shown to alleviate physical symptoms (see R. Walsh & Shapiro, 2006, for a review). Specific types of mindfulness meditation practice have been examined with substance-using populations, as well, with promising findings (e.g., see Bowen et al., 2006; Marlatt, 2002). Elements of progressive relaxation also continue to be useful in decreasing anxiety and dissolving body tension (see Appendix B of this volume for further resources).

In our practice treating women with addictions and trauma, we frequently integrate breathing, relaxation, and mindfulness training (Kabat-Zinn, 1990) into treatment. As mentioned in the description of the WHE intervention, a breathing exercise concludes most of the sessions. In our Internet-based adaptation of WHE for trauma survivors, BESThealth, breathing exercises also conclude every session. Exhibit 4.2 (see chap. 4, this volume) presented a demonstration script for a basic breathing relaxation exercise that we have used with clients with trauma histories.

Eye movement desensitization and reprocessing (EMDR) is a trauma-focused therapy that integrates an awareness of the body and bodily sensations throughout an intervention (Shapiro & Forrest, 1997). In EMDR, the question "Where do you feel it in your body?" is always evaluated in relation to the target traumatic memory during reprocessing. In this way, EMDR explicitly pairs the physiological with the psychological in addressing the patient's trauma. The body scan, carefully focusing on the sensations of the body from head to toe, draws greater attention to physical sensations. EMDR integrates the focus on the body with frequent evaluations of emotional state and negative thoughts, in conjunction with eye movements or other bilateral stimulation, to relieve traumatic stress.

EMDR provides a number of exercises to relieve the physical manifestations of stress, such as the light stream exercise. The client is guided into a relaxed state and then instructed to identify a source of tension in the body (as in the body scan) and create a concrete visual image of the sensation. The client is asked to imagine a color associated with healing and then imagine a soothing beam of colored light penetrating that area, softening, shrinking, and eliminating the tension or pain. The use of visual imagery, paired with a relaxed state, intensifies the focus on the bodily sensation while affording some control over that sensation. Teaching these types of skills and resources can be very healing for women who struggle with the physical manifestations of trauma and provide additional skills for self-care and soothing of trauma-related symptoms.

CONCLUSION

As we detailed in this chapter, women with trauma histories experience myriad physical health issues. Such problems are augmented by the bodily neglect that often accompanies substance abuse. Treatment plans for women experiencing comorbid trauma and addiction should consider the models presented in this chapter as well as techniques for intervention and treatment. Together, they provide critical components of an integrated and comprehensive clinical approach that will benefit this population of women.

III

STRATEGIES
FOR IMPLEMENTATION

8

PREPARING, TRAINING, AND SUPERVISING STAFF IN PROVIDING INTEGRATED TREATMENT

Significant strides have been made in identifying important pathways to providing integrated substance use, trauma, and mental health services in settings more traditionally oriented to treat addictions. Addictions treatment centers have begun to reconceptualize how to help women who are survivors of abuse or trauma in their programs. In Parts I and II of this book, we discussed the importance of providing a treatment environment that is sensitive to the trauma issues in women's lives, in addition to the specific, multimodal components of treatment to address trauma when possible. The reader should now have the necessary background and understanding to frame considerations for expanding programs or creating new programs that incorporate these therapeutic approaches.

In Part III, we offer clinicians and programs practical guidance in approaching this task. In this chapter we approach the implementation of trauma treatment from the perspective of the clinicians who are trained in treating addiction and are preparing to integrate trauma treatment into their work and from the perspective of the addiction programs, directors, and supervisors who are supporting them. We address the reluctance felt by many clinicians to undertake this work and some of the issues they face in learning to talk about and hear about trauma and emphasize the importance of clinician self-care to protect against becoming overwhelmed by this work.

We also identify some basic approaches to undertaking trauma training for substance abuse clinicians. In particular, we discuss how agencies can use a train-the-trainer model to develop an existing staff member to become a resident trauma expert. In addition, we focus on supervision. Ongoing supervision is intrinsic to integrating trauma services into addiction work. Particularly when clinicians are being introduced to trauma-specific treatment, it is not enough to provide training without providing the opportunity to discuss and give feedback to clinicians about their experience introducing the new curriculum. Frequently it is not until clinicians have had a chance to sit with clients using the new material that their concerns crystallize in a way that can be discussed and addressed.

PREPARING AND SUPPORTING CLINICIANS

For clinicians trained and primarily working in addictions treatment, training in understanding the role of violence in women's lives and working with trauma survivors is a necessary, but not sufficient, first step toward working with women with trauma. Most clinicians have had limited experience with trauma treatment, and providing them with a foundation of knowledge and setting them on the path to continued learning are critical. Nevertheless, even clinicians who have had some exposure to treatment for trauma through existing agency or other learning opportunities may hesitate to embark on a course of treatment that elevates attention to trauma in their addiction work.

Initial Hesitancy

As suggested earlier, many clinicians tend to be wary of undertaking the clinical treatment of trauma for fear of opening Pandora's box. There is the fear that allowing or encouraging clients to talk, or even think, about their abusive backgrounds will set off a series of damaging events: (a) Clients will become overwhelmed and out of control and clinicians will not know how to handle the crisis; (b) clinicians may feel overwhelmed by hearing a client's trauma story and not know how to manage their own distress; or (c) clients will relapse, act out, or drop out of treatment as a result of becoming dysregulated by attending to their traumatic past. Clinicians may worry about their own or others' safety, fearing that a client may become angry or violent as a result of thinking about her trauma. Clinicians also worry about the safety of the client, fearing she may resort to self-destructive or even life-threatening behavior. Clinicians express concern that once that box is opened, it will be difficult to close again and that they will have prevented their clients from doing what they ostensibly came to treatment to do—work on their sobriety.

Underlying these fears may be cautionary tales learned from other clinicians, some based on true experiences, others consisting of more myth than truth. A clinician's own training, clinical experience, and personal history also play an important role in determining her readiness to attend to a client's abusive past.

Many substance abuse clinicians and mental health practitioners come to the field of addiction having survived their own traumatic experiences and involvement with substances or other dangerous behavior. Their own paths to recovery often create an important precedent and standard for recovery, which they apply to their own work with clients. If the recovery of a clinician who is a survivor of trauma did not provide an opportunity to consider the role that abuse may have played in her addiction, then it may not come naturally to see attention to trauma as central in the recovery of her clients. "After all," a clinician may argue, "I got clean, and talking about what happened to me didn't matter. I worked the program [e.g., Alcoholics Anonymous], and that is what mattered most."

Clinicians who are committed to the type of treatment that proved helpful to them in their recovery need to develop the flexibility to consider that there are other ways of achieving sobriety and stability. Not every clinician makes that leap readily. It means acknowledging that perhaps they might have benefited from a different approach, in this case one that considered their trauma history and mental health issues more centrally. At the very least, clinicians need to consider that treatment is not a one-size-fits-all proposition and that what may have worked for them, and maybe for scores of friends and clients, may not work for everyone. Furthermore, some clinicians in recovery have difficulty shifting to new treatment approaches for fear that it will jeopardize their own sobriety by challenging the ideas and beliefs that they have come to rely on. Support and good training are vital in helping clinicians in this regard.

Historically, though, the centrality of the medical model and the strong role of 12-step groups in most addictions treatment practices have at times made it difficult for clinicians to embrace alternative models. The medical model has promoted an understanding of alcoholism and drug addiction as a disease and underlies some of the tenets of Alcoholics Anonymous and other 12-step groups. The neurobiological underpinnings and correlates of addiction are not in dispute, and the strength of the medical model in helping vast numbers of men and women achieve and maintain sobriety is extraordinary. However, it has often been embraced in a way that minimizes some of the environmental factors at play in a client's route to addiction. Many survivors in recovery from addiction have commented on a dismissive stance toward their personal histories and experiences when attending 12-step meetings. So many of the sayings embraced by 12-step adherents lend hope and inspiration to recovery, but some messages, such as "get off your pity potty/party," suggest to survivors little tolerance or compassion for someone in recovery who is immersed in and working through other hardships. For a trauma survivor who cannot easily get beyond the struggles imposed by her traumatic past, this message can lead to feelings of humiliation and failure and can undermine her determination to get clean. For clinicians raised on and trained in these models, it can be a challenge to take a different stance toward trauma, or even the role of other mental health disorders, in a client's recovery.

Even if a clinician is willing to embrace a new way of thinking, her own trauma history may make the idea of trauma work more frightening. In particular, a clinician who has not had a chance to address her own past abuse or exposure to violence may feel emotionally ill prepared to work with someone else's trauma. She may experience a heightened sense of vulnerability in approaching this work, uncertain whether she will be able to contain her own history in the process. In fact, although all clinicians are at risk of developing reactions to working with survivors of trauma, survivor therapists have been shown to be more susceptible to emotional distress and "vicarious traumatization" (McCann & Pearlman, 1990; see also Pearlman & Mac Ian, 1995; Pearlman & Saakvitne, 1995) than nonsurvivor clinicians. Other risks include the potential to overidentify with clients in their recovery, potentially damaging a client's treatment and jeopardizing the mental health of the clinician (A. R. Hesse, 2002; Yassen, 1995). Vicarious traumatization and ways to prevent and manage it are discussed later in this chapter. Other concerns about client and clinician safety are addressed in chapter 9 of this volume.

Talking About Trauma

As substance abuse clinicians come to understand the importance of trauma in the lives of the women they see in addiction programs, they often need guidance and preparation in how to talk about trauma in a way that is safe for them and the women they work with. Training can help prepare clinicians with effective ways of discussing trauma in treatment. For example, in the context of both training and supervision, it is important to address the appropriate degree of discussion of traumatic events. This is often the primary quandary raised by clinicians regarding trauma: "How much should the client talk about her abuse?" "When should she talk about her abuse?" and "Should I encourage her to talk about her abuse?" We cannot emphasize enough that a good rule of thumb for working with trauma survivors is to go slow. Especially at this stage of their recovery and in the context of substance abuse treatment, in which women are just starting to acknowledge and approach trauma work, the therapist must go in with the mind-set of containing affect and symptoms, not engaging in deep exploration and uncovering or exposing traumatic materials, even if the client herself is urging this. As we discussed in chapter 2, some trauma-specific treatments (see Appendix A at the end of this volume) advocate more explicit discussion and reporting of traumatic events. However, most therapies stress that for survivors with deficits in regulating affect or who use substances, counseling should first emphasize that containment and stabilization are key aspects of early trauma work.

The common clinical error of working too quickly to address trauma is often driven by a clinician's enthusiasm. When a client begins to disclose details of trauma, a clinician may become overly eager to pursue and uncover the details of the traumatic experience and the impact on the client. Although the clinician's underlying intentions are to assist the client in working through the effects of victimization, the result may be that the client becomes inadvertently revictimized by the discussion. Clinicians need to be aware of not only issues related to their clients' verbal report but also the nonverbal information communicated by their clients. Attending to the process of disclosure, especially to signs of dissociation or emotional dysregulation, helps clinicians recognize the need to titrate discussion of trauma during a session. Providing specialized trauma training and supervision for clinicians increases their attunement to and awareness of the issue of trauma in the lives of their clients and its place in their recovery and can help clinicians and their clients better learn how to manage the pace of talking—or not talking—about trauma in clinical work.

Specialized training is particularly useful in preparing clinicians who have personally been exposed to traumatic events or violent relationships to address trauma safely. To do this work effectively, clinicians must be able to deal with their own trauma histories, or their responses can become problematic. Training can provide an important opportunity to direct clinicians to consider their readiness for this work and possibly to decide that they need further personal preparation before undertaking trauma treatment. Exhibit 8.1 provides an example of a clinician who was not prepared to facilitate a trauma-related group.

Recovered Memories

As they are learning to be aware of and to address trauma, clinicians should also be attentive to the debate over repressed memories, recovered memories, or false memory syndrome. In the mid-to-late 1980s, there was increasing

EXHIBIT 8.1
Clinical Case Example: Therapist Readiness for Trauma Treatment

---

A clinician unprepared for taking on trauma-related treatment needed to discontinue facilitating a group because she became too emotionally activated and overwhelmed by discussions of trauma. She became unable to participate as a result of her emotional reaction. Although her coleader was able to manage the group, the members were aware of her lack of participation. Her withdrawal inhibited the group process and also triggered group members' memories of nonprotective family members who had likewise shut down and abandoned them. Supervision uncovered that the clinician had witnessed violence in her own family and had underestimated the effect her experience would have when hearing about the traumatic experiences of others.

concern about the number of reports of childhood abuse and the veracity of memories of childhood victimization. Discussions about memory, false memories, and the idea that clinicians suggested to clients that they may have been abused became common. Many professional organizations, such as the American Psychiatric Association (1993), the American Medical Association (1995), and the American Psychological Association (1995), provided statements and guidelines about repressed memory. The conclusions in these reports were consistent. They indicated that memory is a complex phenomenon, including both explicitly and implicitly remembered events. Memory also depends on context and developmental level. In general, instances of child abuse are recalled by survivors, either in whole or in part. However, there are some instances, due to dissociation or age of abuse, in which abuse is not recalled until many years after the fact. This is sometimes referred to as a *recovered memory*.

All of the published guidelines recommend that therapists maintain an empathic, nonjudgmental, and neutral stance toward reported memories of abuse. Clinicians should avoid prejudging the cause of a client's difficulties or the truthfulness of her report. Clinicians who have a strong prior belief that sexual abuse or other factors are or are not the cause of the client's problems are likely to interfere with appropriate assessment and treatment. Furthermore, clinicians should avoid suggesting that a woman has been abused on the basis of her current symptom picture. Many a well-meaning clinician has asked, "Do you think something bad happened to you as a child?" without the client having suggested that this is the case. By focusing on current symptoms and the impact of symptoms on current functioning rather than delving into the past, the clinician can be of most benefit to the client.

Sexuality

Female trauma survivors often have experienced sexual trauma, which affects their sexual functioning, relationships, and many other areas of their lives. These experiences are painful to discuss, and many women are fearful of talking about their sexual history or abuse. Therapists also may not be accustomed to discussing a woman's sexuality or comfortable hearing about it. However, sexuality and sexual abuse often become an important area for clients to address. Therapists may need additional training and preparation to address sexual issues over the course of treatment. Given the social constraints with regard to talking openly about sexuality and personal discomfort, therapists may feel ashamed, embarrassed, shocked, or disapproving when discussing sexual issues.

Some therapists may benefit from desensitization exercises to become more comfortable discussing sex and sexuality with clients. Sexual desensitization training typically includes exercises designed to raise an individual's comfort level in talking about sexual matters and familiarize them with sexual vernacular that clients may use in discussing sexual experiences. Desensitization exercises can also help therapists become more sensitized to difficulties others have when talking about sexual behaviors and recognize and minimize judgmental biases about sexuality.[1]

Vicarious Traumatization and Self-Care

As the field of trauma treatment has grown, clinicians and researchers have been attentive to the impact that working with trauma survivors may have on the clinician. The issues addressed in this chapter so far have touched on the personal ways that working with trauma survivors can influence a clinician. Although training in the use of structured trauma-specific protocols helps to reduce the potential shock of bearing witness to the traumatic experience of clients, many, if not all, clinicians often experience a shift in their own experience as well as a result of this work. This may range from a subtle change in awareness of the potential dangers in the world around them to personal experience of clinical trauma symptoms themselves. Intrusive thoughts and nightmares, hypervigilance, and a heightened sense of personal vulnerability (Herman, 1992b), for example, are not uncommon among clinicians working with trauma survivors.

McCann and Pearlman (1990) identified a process of vicarious traumatization. They described the short-term impact or "long-term alteration in the therapist's own cognitive schemas, or beliefs, expectations, and assumptions about the self and others" (p. 132) that arises in the course of working with survivors of trauma. Some clinicians experience "painful images, thoughts and feelings associated with exposure to their clients' traumatic memories" (p. 132) that without proper attention may be disruptive to their work and personal life. Other terms that have been used are *compassion fatigue*, *secondary traumatization*, *traumatic countertransference*, and more recently, *impact of trauma work* (Arledge & Wolfson, 2001). The last arose out of the belief that prior terminology reflected weakness or insensitivity on the part of the clinician (i.e., burnout or compassion fatigue) or the possibility that the client could be harmful to the therapist; a more neutral term was thought to be useful.

A number of methods have been suggested to help clinicians manage or prevent the symptoms associated with secondary trauma. Supervision is an invaluable support for a clinician who provides trauma treatment. It can

---

[1] It is important to set special ground rules for this type of training, including, of course, confidentiality and full participation of all trainees. It is also useful to prepare trainees for possible reactions to such exercises, such as embarrassment, discomfort, or even having sexual feelings come up while discussing sex. Any desensitization exercise must be followed by full debriefing of the experience so that participants are able to discuss reactions they had to the exercise and how these feelings and attitudes could affect their work on sexual issues with their clients.

help to mitigate the otherwise emotionally draining impact of working with survivors. Speaking with supervisors and colleagues about feelings arising from listening to survivors' experiences is a potent method by which clinicians can handle those emotions (Astin, 1997; Conrad & Perry, 2000). Supervisors may also support clinicians in their interactions with agencies to help moderate case loads and negotiate supportive working conditions (A. R. Hesse, 2002). Approaches to supervising clinicians for this work are discussed later.

Agency support is critical in helping clinicians minimize and repair the experience of vicarious symptoms. In addition to having a safe and confidential place to speak about her experiences, a clinician needs to have the understanding of the agency in which she works. This is a valuable component of placing trauma-specific treatment in the context of a trauma-informed agency. Not all of the trauma care for a client should fall on one clinician, for example. A survivor who may be in crisis should be able to turn to any number of supports within an agency for help and know that they will all have an understanding of her needs from the perspective of understanding trauma and its impact. Agency support may also help to reduce another frequent clinician response to working with trauma survivors: feeling the need to rescue her client in ways that compromise good therapeutic boundaries (Herman, 1992b). Although clients often benefit from a proactive stance of their clinicians, allowing clients to rely too heavily on clinicians may ultimately be disempowering.

Other useful suggestions for preventing and coping with vicarious trauma focus on the clinician's self-care. Balancing a case load and setting appropriate boundaries around work are particularly important. In his spoof *Ten Tried-and-True Methods to Achieve Therapist Burnout*, Richard Belson parodied the poor self-care habits clinicians fall into: "Take on lots of hard cases and see them one after another, preferably three or four in a row. Think about them even when not at work—at dinner and at 3 a.m. are good times" (as cited in Wylie & Markowitz, 1992). For working with trauma survivors, especially, it is important to find ways to establish breaks, to limit exposure to traumatic material (Conrad & Perry, 2000; Pearlman & Saakvitne, 1995; Yassen, 1995), and to separate work life from personal time.

Similarly, clinicians need to be encouraged to follow through on their own self-care at home: getting adequate rest and exercise, carving out time for relaxation or creative expression, and seeking out spiritual activities or other activities that may be a source of renewal (see A. R. Hesse, 2002, for a review). Personal psychotherapy can also be a valuable tool for preventing or coping with vicarious trauma. Experts agree that seeking help in processing the emotions raised in working with survivors benefits the clinician, which may in turn positively affect work with clients and personal relationships outside the work environment (Pearlman & Saakvitne, 1995). Another way in which agencies can provide support for their clinicians is to ensure that medical benefits provide adequate mental health coverage. Encouraging self-care, which may often include personal psychotherapy, is part of creating a supportive work environment. Agencies also provide support by treating supervision as valuable, not as easily expendable when time is short.

We mentioned earlier that many clinicians come to the mental health and addiction fields as survivors in recovery from addiction or trauma themselves. These clinicians may be particularly vulnerable to strong emotional reactions and secondary traumatization. In these cases, personal psychotherapy may be critical. A. R. Hesse (2002) wrote,

> Trauma therapists who are themselves survivors of trauma can benefit tremendously from psychotherapy and support groups for survivors, in which they can safely explore feelings, reactions, and experiences—a necessary part of healing and of continuing to work with clients who have been traumatized. (p. 304)

Without the opportunity to address their own trauma histories, clinicians may find themselves more easily triggered upon hearing about a client's history, which may exacerbate their own trauma-related symptoms and interfere with their ability to work effectively with their client (as in the previous example; see Exhibit 8.1). Clinicians with their own histories of trauma may find themselves vulnerable to dissociative symptoms in response to client references to traumatic events, resulting in withdrawal or detachment. Clinicians may hear about a client's story and relive their own traumatic memories, and they may confuse their client's healing with their own (A. R. Hesse, 2002; Yassen, 1995). They may not be able to be fully present for their clients and may consequently be unable to create a safe therapeutic space.

Because working with trauma survivors has the potential to raise so many feelings, choice for clinicians is essential. A clinician should not be forced to work with trauma survivors or address trauma if she is not comfortable doing so. Because the rates of co-occurring substance use disorders and trauma-related symptoms are so high, clinicians are undoubtedly working with survivors all of the time, whether they are aware of it or not. In addition to recommending that addiction treatments be sensitive to the issues of survivors in general, we recommend that clinicians undertake trauma work voluntarily, when they are willing to do so.

TRAINING

As programs consider integrating new treatment approaches for use with their clients who are trauma survivors, staff training and supervision become important aspects of the planning and implementation of this effort. Given the challenges in working with women with substance use disorders and trauma and in imparting new skills to already busy clinicians, it is important for agencies to invest the necessary time and resources in training and supervising professional staff in the most thorough yet practical way possible. After the adoption of an implementation plan for trauma treatment (ideas and examples for implementation are discussed in chap. 11), training is the next step.

The Train-the-Trainer Model and the Trauma Expert

Substance abuse programs can take several approaches to training staff to provide a clinical environment that is sensitive to trauma issues or to provide specific trauma treatments, with primary decisions often involving who to train or how many staff to train. In our experience, however, a critical part of a trauma implementation plan is to ensure that at least one clinician becomes trained as a resident trauma expert. Instead of relying on external consultants to provide periodic services, an on-site trauma expert ensures the continuity of resources to do the needed work involved in training and providing ongoing supervision for trauma work. Identifying and training the trauma expert is part of a train-the-trainer model that we recommend in starting and continuing to provide trauma treatment.

Many substance abuse treatment programs are staffed by a diverse group of individuals who come together as a treatment team. Each person brings his or her various interests, experiences, formal education, and viewpoints to working with clients, especially clients with comorbid trauma and addiction. Within a treatment program, often a more senior staff member—for example, a supervising psychologist, social worker, or other clinician—has some specialized training and expertise in treating clients with more complex issues. Ideally, an individual with this type of background also has a good understanding of psychopathology, as well as experience and clinical skills in working with clients with a broad range of issues. With such qualifications, this clinician might be an ideal candidate to become the resident trauma expert in the program, although even less-seasoned staff members with interest and good clinical skills could be developed into a trauma expert.

This person would be designated to receive the trainings and certifications required for the treatment approaches being implemented in the program, ultimately becoming the trainer and go-to person for trauma-related issues at the program. Identifying a trauma expert within a train-the-trainer model can provide a cost-effective means of teaching staff to work effectively with trauma survivors. Agencies can invest in formal didactic training for the selected experts, who can then disseminate their learning through on-site training and follow-up for other staff.

Training in trauma-specific interventions is usually intensive in time and effort. Different trauma treatments have different training approaches. For example, some intervention developers recommend having professional staff trained and certified by experts before using the interventions in the field. These trainings can range from several days to more than a week to an extended schedule of regular training meetings. Typically, training models recommend that a trainee also conduct a pilot case or cases to practice the new intervention and that she receive regular supervision after training.

Agencies need to ensure that there is time in an individual's schedule for follow-up clinical and administrative work needed to complete the training. If the trauma expert usually does not provide clinical service, the agency may need to make arrangements for the individual to carve out some clinical practice time in this training capacity, as well as supervisory time going forward if she will be overseeing the work of other clinicians.[2] Unfortunately, staff who are taking on this new role are often expected to do so without eliminating other responsibilities in their schedules, which is typically unsustainable and frustrating.

Once trained and, if necessary, certified in providing a model of treatment, the resident trauma expert can begin the process of training other staff. Some staff in the position of trauma expert may already be familiar with training other staff. For those who can benefit from guidance, Appendix C offers materials that could form the foundation of a training presentation, as well as guidelines for effective training on the topic of trauma. The resident trauma expert or on-site trainer may find these tips helpful in preparing to train clinicians to integrate trauma treatment into their work.

Diagnostic Training

In substance abuse programs, the staff may be well acquainted with the signs and symptoms of substance use disorders but may not be as well versed in the issues surrounding the identification and definitions of trauma and posttraumatic stress disorder (PTSD). Even in substance abuse treatment settings, clinicians may not be familiar with diagnostic issues, such as the difference between substance abuse and substance dependence or the standard definition of a traumatic event. As a result of the different backgrounds of trainees, clinician training might include basic information about substance use disorders, trauma, and PTSD as introductory components of their trainings. Even if they are familiar with many of the concepts, trainees will benefit from a review of diagnostic procedures and symptoms. In Appendix C at the end of this volume, Figure C.3 offers sample training slides that describe diagnostic issues related to

---

[2]More formal trainings may require video- or audiotaping sessions. If clinicians intend to pursue this, administrators should check with local institutional review boards to determine what consent forms must be used. Typically, clear and informed consent outlining the purpose and use of the recordings needs to be obtained in writing. In any case, if participants are taped for any purpose, every effort must be made to protect the confidentiality of those involved.

PTSD. Readers may use and/or modify these materials as relevant to their training needs.

SUPERVISION

Training is the first important component in introducing new therapy skills. Supervision is the next component that will help therapists stay on track and continue to learn and grow over time. A recent review of dissemination techniques of practices for substance abuse indicated that didactic, workshop-type training should be followed by ongoing supervision in order to maintain therapist skills (W. R. Miller, Sorenson, Selzer, & Brigham, 2006), with training conceptualized as an ongoing process to maximize therapist performance.

Part of supervision involves directing, monitoring, and evaluating a clinician's work. The supervision process requires authority, specific knowledge, and good interpersonal skills to help a clinician maintain the quality of her work following training in specific interventions. Supervision specific to a new trauma treatment model offers the invaluable opportunity to help a clinician fully integrate the learning of new techniques.

For many treatment centers, a significant commitment is required to provide the initial training for learning new models of treatment. But, as so many attendees of training will attest, there is often a long and winding road from training to successful and competent implementation. In this way, treatment-specific supervision offers a chance for supervisors trained in the model to provide feedback to supervisees about their use of the new model. Supervisors have a chance to demonstrate effective ways of implementing the new model with practice opportunities for clinicians working on new skills.

Good supervision helps clinicians stay faithful to the intervention, which can be important in increasing the likelihood that clients will benefit from the treatment. Posttraining drift, or moving away from the intentions of the intervention, is common after people receive training, but supervision can help clinicians stay true to the methods and intentions of the material. The process of meeting and providing ongoing feedback, support, and intervention options is the best way to maintain high-quality clinical performance and provide ongoing professional development to clinical staff.

In chapter 9, we elaborate on a number of issues facing substance abuse clinicians as they learn to integrate trauma treatment into their work. Although all of the concerns we discuss are possible, an important role of supervision is to reassure clinicians that careful and sensitive implementation of trauma treatment can minimize these potential problems. For example, supervision is important in helping clinicians feel that even if a client expresses some frightening material or dangerous impulses (managing clients with dysregulated affect is also discussed in chap. 9), the clinician has the skills and the where-withal to address them safely and effectively, as well as a time and place with a supervisor to process these concerns.

The majority of currently available trauma protocols (described in Appendix A) are oriented toward stabilization and helping survivors to improve their abilities to manage overwhelming affect and tolerate distress by introducing them to more adaptive ways of coping than using substances. These are critical skills for survivors, but this approach also helps to ease clinicians into the role of addressing trauma. These treatment models, most of which offer significant psychoeducational and manualized support, provide clinicians with guidance as to how to safely open up a dialogue about trauma without opening Pandora's box (see Exhibit 8.2). Clinicians and clients learn ways to proceed collaboratively, creating safety for both and, in the case of group treatment, other group members.

It is particularly important that supervision be a safe place for clinicians. In the same way that clients need a safe and confidential environment in which to work therapeutically, clinicians need to know that they have a place in which to express the reactions and concerns that arise for them in the context of trauma work, without fear that they will be mocked or undermined for pre-senting their honest experiences. Only in this context can clinicians enhance their clinical skills and confidence in working with a traumatized population. If this need is not met, there is a much greater likelihood that clinicians will experience burnout and potentially some form of vicarious traumatization.

Supervision can take a variety of forms. Although individual supervision offers a level of personal attention to developing a clinician's individual skills, it may not be pragmatic in a setting in which time for both supervisors and clinicians is extremely limited. Group supervision, in which several clinicians meet with a supervisor in a group, can provide a rich and supportive learning opportunity. Peers in group supervision may practice new clinical techniques and skills with one another. Group supervision also enables clinicians to learn from one another's attempts to introduce a new treatment model.

Clinicians working with trauma survivors often appreciate the chance to share their experiences of working with this population with other clinicians

EXHIBIT 8.2
Clinical Case Example: Limiting Trauma Disclosure

In response to participating in a manualized trauma-specific treatment, one of our clients offered that she was comfortable with the treatment because she was not pushed to talk about her trauma. She said, "Most therapists, if you tell them some-thing, they just dig, dig, dig." It is interesting to note that this was a client who, in her first session, was averse to the point of hostility about beginning structured, manual-ized psychotherapy. At the end of 12 sessions of treatment, without ever talking about the details of her trauma, she experienced a significant reduction in her trauma symptoms and cocaine and alcohol consumption.

---

engaged in this type of work. Many trauma survivors have long been captive to their secrets of abuse, and in a parallel way clinicians are often left with their own secrets in response to listening—the client's trauma story and the clinician's feelings engendered by being a witness to it. Sharing in group supervision offers an outlet for these emotions and a chance to receive support and encouragement. It also affords an opportunity to have experience normalized by hearing the experiences of other clinicians. Nevertheless, clinicians should always feel that they know where to turn for individual support, from either a peer or a supervisor, should something powerful and unexpected emerge in their clinical work. Moreover, clinicians need to know that an agency understands their need for support. They should not be made to feel that they need to handle what emerges from this work by themselves.

Enhancing Clinical Skills

Supervisors are often able to identify areas for growth in a clinician's therapeutic style. When clinicians work with trauma survivors, they should become aware of ways in which they interact with clients that may not initially reflect an awareness of a survivor's needs or sensitivities. Clinicians' training and backgrounds vary widely in addictions treatment settings. Most clinicians range from having experience at the CASAC (i.e., credentialed alcohol and substance abuse counselor) level to having more advanced clinical training through master's programs. Clinicians also come with experience in a variety of fields: social work, education, psychology, vocational counseling, art, drama, or recreational counseling. Such diverse formal clinical training means that clinicians will bring different skill sets to their work. In approaching treatment with trauma survivors, clinicians may need help in reorienting or expanding their treatment style.

For example, clinicians may not be aware of ways in which they are particularly directive, domineering, or confrontational—ways of interacting that may disempower a survivor rather than empower her in her recovery. Clinicians may not realize how their efforts to control the treatment may be undermining. We have commented on how a clinician's treatment stance may be influenced by having learned, and perhaps lived, a more traditional addictions treatment approach. Many clinicians report that they are used to taking charge in sessions and to establishing themselves as the authority. It takes some adjustment to learn to establish a collaborative relationship with clients, allowing a client to take the lead in treatment and relinquishing the need to control treatment. Many of the skills taught in connection with motivational interviewing (W. R. Miller & Rollnick, 2002) or motivational enhancement therapy (W. R. Miller, Zweben, DiClemente, & Rychtarik, 1992), methods geared toward developing a collaborative relationship with a client to enhance his or her recovery, are also helpful in working with survivors. Other common challenges include not appreciating that they are interrupting clients repeatedly or cutting them off, not attending to issues of safety in group, and having difficulty keeping a group on task. Clinicians may also not be attentive to important nonverbal signals that are coming from clients or may not be thinking about what these might mean in the context of trauma. Does a clinician recognize, for example, when a client who seems distant or unengaged is dissociating and not just being resistant? Detailed information about sessions allows a supervisor to catch and comment on many of these issues.

Clinicians may also be unaccustomed to providing statements of praise and support and may be unaware of the absence of such validating comments in their interventions. Most treatments geared toward trauma survivors highlight the importance of providing supportive, validating comments to clients. For women whose experiences with others have typically been invalidating, emotional validation is an important component to growth and recovery. Some clinicians who were taught to take either a more confrontational position with their clients or, alternatively, a more neutral or reserved posture, may not be comfortable using more supportive language. Many admit that it does not feel natural. Supervision can help clinicians find language that feels comfortable and authentic. Offering emotional validation does not need to sound like cheerleading. For some people, that is the connotation. Clinicians beginning work with survivors often need guidance in how to offer praise that sounds genuine and in hearing underlying expressions of emotion that need to be validated. Expressions such as "great!" or "fantastic!" can be useful in commending a client's efforts, but other less exclamatory remarks are often as good, if not better, in supporting and validating a client's hard work. For example, "Jane, we have been talking about how hard it is for you to set a limit with your son, and it is great to see you experimenting with some new ways of doing that this week."

Clinicians may also not realize how important it is to be engaging in their work. Clients can be very aware of the clinician's level of interest and, given a history of trauma, may be even more sensitive to interpersonal interactions. A clinician may come across as bored, withdrawn, or disconnected, which in part may be a way of protecting herself from overwhelming thoughts and feelings triggered by the client or from experiencing a client's own numbness and split off emotional life. However, if left unaddressed, this posture can seriously disrupt a therapeutic relationship with a client. Supervision can provide a place to address these feelings and help clinicians understand what is happening for them and how to become more consistently engaged.

It is also important to consider the level of a clinician's training in working with trauma survivors. Learning to integrate a trauma perspective into her work with survivors in recovery from addiction does not immediately make her an expert in addressing trauma. Clinicians in addiction settings should not feel that they are the only ones working on the client's trauma unless they have had specific and substantial training in the area of trauma and have demonstrated strong clinical skills in managing what may emerge in treatment. The resident trauma expert or a trauma consultant may help alleviate this concern. She can support ongoing treatment, oversee issues raised by clinicians working with survivors, and help clients find additional therapy in the community to supplement treatment. As valuable as it may be to have trauma treatment integrated into addictions treatment, a survivor's recovery will most likely be a long process that continues beyond her substance abuse treatment.

Even while working in conjunction with a trauma specialist, clinicians' ongoing education about trauma and trauma treatment should always be encouraged and supported. Although it can be hard to ask clinicians to carve out time in already tight schedules for additional reading, they may find it gratifying to fill in gaps in their own knowledge about trauma. With more knowledge comes more clinical confidence. Supervision can create the structure to ask clinicians to make a commitment to their own learning, perhaps by asking them to identify topics they would like to learn more about and follow through on.

Use of Audio or Video Recordings in Supervision

The use of audio or video session recordings in supervision offers a number of potential learning advantages for both general clinical skill and implementation of new treatments. They provide a gold mine of clinical information, which can be used to give feedback to a clinician learning a new model. Clinicians have the rare opportunity to see or hear themselves in session and to get direct feedback on how to improve their clinical work. Most substance abuse treatment clinicians have never had the opportunity for this level of supervision. Although many clinicians (and supervisors) are initially uncomfortable with the recording process, most find that the benefits outweigh the discomforts.

This is similar to the experience of therapists who learn to conduct therapy with the help of live supervision through a one-way mirror. In addition to helping clients refine their skills, direct observation has the potential to instill a unique sense of confidence. In an article in which clinicians were interviewed about the value of supervision, one therapist said,

> Live supervision is a good antidote to insecurity. It seems very frightening at first—you risk being naked in front of your peers—but, if the people watching you are generous and supportive, it is actually a great relief. You discover that you don't really have to hide anything; your work has been seen and validated, which is something you can carry with you for the rest of your life. (David Treadway, as cited in Wylie & Markowitz, 1992, p. 29)

Supervision of recorded sessions can also help validate skills and provide opportunities for growth. Supervisors who have supervised clinical work with and without audio or video recordings can attest to the wealth of information gleaned from recordings that they would not otherwise hear in more traditional supervision, which is based solely on the report of the clinician (Abass, 2004; Aveline, 1997; Goldberg, 1983).

In this context, supervisors have a chance to comment on a range of the clinician's work. Recorded accounts of what transpires in sessions can highlight a clinician's unawareness of how she may approach her work in ways that are potentially threatening or undermining for trauma survivors. In some cases clinicians' own experiences correspond to the observations of the supervisor, but in other cases supervisors detect important elements of the therapeutic relationship of which a clinician is not aware. Without the opportunity to view or listen to sessions, valuable clinical information remains unknown and inaccessible to supervisory feedback and suggestions.

By reviewing recorded sessions, supervisors also have a chance to identify and commend all of the things that a clinician is doing well. Although some clinicians are able to report confidently the aspects of treatment that are going well, often these experiences remain unspoken in supervision based on self-report. By using recorded sessions, supervisors are able to provide specific and direct positive feedback about clinicians' strengths: how well they may have formed an alliance with a difficult client, how well they may have handled a crisis, or how deftly they may have helped a client address an important issue, for example.

Treatment-specific supervision, in particular, is enriched tremendously by recorded sessions. Supervisors listening to or watching recorded sessions can best monitor how well clinicians learning to integrate trauma-specific treatment are implementing the treatment. Periodic, ongoing review also helps to ensure that clinicians do not deviate dramatically from delivering the treatment in its intended format over time. Many trauma treatment or other manualized treatment trainings include attention to how to monitor treatment fidelity by teaching attendees how to use appropriate treatment-specific rating scales.[3] Treatment programs can decide how important it is for clinicians to conduct treatment that is adherent to the treatment protocol. We offer some suggestions later in our discussion of adapting treatment to the clinical setting. For programs wishing to monitor clinicians' use of new material, however, recorded sessions with supervisor fidelity ratings offer the best opportunity to do so.

---

[3]In studies designed to test the effectiveness of a given treatment model, a great deal of time is devoted to ensuring that clinicians are using the model as it is intended. Researchers carefully examine how clinical sessions are conducted to determine adherence or fidelity to a model. New behavioral treatments designed to treat mental health and addiction issues are carefully operationalized so that researchers can ascertain that a clinician is performing all of the essential components that define a treatment. To determine treatment fidelity, research treatment sessions are typically video- or audiotaped with the informed consent of the participants. These recordings provide the basis for adherence ratings.

Fidelity rating scales typically describe dimensions critical for adequate administration of treatments. Often on a continuous scale ranging from poor to excellent, rating forms offer a systematic method of evaluating the use of the interventions and create a common language for supervision, helping to identify specific skills and areas that need work and to make sure that clinicians are following the essential elements of an intervention. Rating forms also provide a gauge of improving adherence or subtle drift from core intervention components, which may not be caught in more traditional supervisory interactions. Some interventions have standard materials that can facilitate learning the use of rating scales, such as demonstration videotapes accompanied by a coded rating scale or key that indicates what the ratings should be.

Even if strict fidelity to the treatment is not important to the program, use of rating scales can still be useful to the resident trauma expert in training and supervision. One useful training exercise is to have both the supervisor and the clinician co-rate an entire session or portion of a session, then discuss the ratings and reasons why ratings were assigned. This provides the clinician with practice and a greater understanding of the important elements of the treatment modality as well as the thought process involved in using the rating scale. Although a clinician may become proficient at a manualized treatment, having a sense of the desired standards in conducting and implementing the treatment will only enhance and improve her administration of the intervention.

For the use of audio or video recordings to be helpful, it is not necessary to undertake the level of observation used for research purposes. Even periodic use of audio or video recording can enhance supervision. Many clinicians find audio recordings less intrusive, but even video recording can be made less intrusive to clients by focusing the video camera on the clinician alone. Although the clinician may feel as if she is under a microscope, the clients are less easily identified, which may be reassuring. In our experience, clients have been amenable to audio and video recording of sessions once they are briefed on the purpose and benefits as part of the process of obtaining their informed consent.

When time is also a consideration, clinician and supervisor may not need to preview a tape but instead watch or listen to excerpts of a session during the supervisory hour. Another useful model is to watch excerpts from session during group supervision in which each clinician presents a segment of a session or alternates with other clinicians in presenting session material. In this fashion, all group supervision members benefit from seeing or listening to the work of fellow clinicians (Abass, 2004).

CONCLUSION

In this chapter we provided highlights of what it takes to prepare, support, train, and supervise substance abuse clinicians to treat women with trauma. We also advocated the use of a train-the-trainer model in which a program identifies and invests in a resident trauma expert who can support a stance within the agency that is sensitive to trauma-related issues and who can become proficient in the use of trauma-specific treatments that can be integrated into the addiction program. The resident trauma expert becomes the on-site trainer and supervisor of other staff who wish to learn and conduct treatment within the agency. Preparation, support, and supervision to address the concerns clinicians have in approaching this work can enable the substance abuse treatment program to integrate trauma treatment safely and successfully.

9

SPECIAL CONSIDERATIONS IN APPROACHING TRAUMA WORK

Implementing changes to address the clinical needs of trauma survivors in addictions treatment settings raises a number of practical issues that may be new to this kind of clinical environment and to substance abuse clinicians who are less familiar with managing the consequences of trauma.

In this chapter, we focus further on the struggles inherent in integrating trauma treatments into existing addiction settings. In particular, we address the importance of paying attention to safety and some of the more difficult and potentially dangerous aspects of working with women who have been victims of abuse or trauma or who continue to be involved in violent relationships. We present ideas for handling a dysregulated client, for working with women with children, and for working in a group modality.

SAFETY

Safety should always be a priority for clients as well as clinicians. Clients need to feel—emotionally and physically—that nothing in the treatment environment threatens their security. Although this should be relevant to the care of clients in all human services, it is especially critical in helping to provide a therapeutic environment for women whose lives have been repeatedly marred by a lack of safety. Safety is equally important for clinicians, given the hurdles they may face in undertaking the integration of trauma treatment in clinical practice.

A safe environment may start with something as simple as having a therapy room in which client and clinician cannot be overheard by others and that provides a comfortable space in which to begin the work of healing. Attending to the therapeutic space is an important component of recovery (La Torre, 2006). Environmental psychology has demonstrated that the more familiar, comfortable, and in control of the environment a client feels, the more powerful the healing response (Bilchik, 2002). Exhibit 9.1 provides some of the comments our clients offered at The Women's Health Project Treatment and Research Center, our clinical treatment program in New York City, after staff undertook a beautification project to enhance our clinical surroundings.

Safety is also communicated by explicit permission for clients to say as much or as little as they wish in therapy and by the messages conveyed by the program. For many survivors, even the concept of establishing safety for themselves, a concept at the core of many trauma treatments, is vague and new. It is important that the program provide a consistent and supportive message that their clients' safety is vital at the same time that treatment is focusing on how to be safe. To ask a client to travel to work or treatment either at unsafe times or in unsafe neighborhoods, for example, undermines her attempts to recognize and attend to her own safety. Counseling and treatment need to be attentive to and avoid situations that may be retraumatizing for clients.

Maintaining appropriate boundaries with clients is also a critical part of providing a safe treatment environment. Throughout this book we have

EXHIBIT 9.1
Comments From Women's Health Project Clients on Space Improvement

- "The aromatherapy works very well with the scenery. It feels like a home away from home, and when I am anxious and stressed or depressed, I sit here and meditate. Afterwards I feel good. Thank you for thinking of the way we feel and giving us this little space."
- "Thank you very much for thinking about the clients. The space you provided is nice, refreshing. It is relaxing, soothing, and great before starting the session. The reading material is appropriate."
- "Thank you very much for thinking about the client and their needs, as well as the needs of their children. It is very clean, and my daughter likes coming here, which makes it less stressful when I don't have a baby-sitter."
- "Very, very, very nice and pretty. Comfortable. Great improvement!"
- "The new waiting area is great. It feels very homey and comfortable. If someone comes stressed like myself, they will feel so much better sitting in the new waiting area. Thank you for making it better and thinking of us patients."
- "Comfort is very important in a waiting area because most people are stressed while waiting, and the look you have is more like home. Thank you."

identified the pull that clients can exert on clinicians to cross boundaries in treatment, including well-intended efforts to "rescue" clients or befriend them. Intentionally, but more often unintentionally, clients may reach out to clinicians and invite them to participate in some kind of special relationship, and clinicians need to be attentive to the nuances of these situations to avoid breaching a safe boundary and jeopardizing clients' recoveries. Clinicians also need to carefully monitor their own impulses to reach out and potentially take advantage of a client's intense emotional connection to them and her associated vulnerability. When boundaries are violated in this context, and particularly when there is sexual seduction and violation, treatment becomes yet another damaging and devastating traumatic interpersonal relationship rather than an opportunity for healing. Clinicians from all disciplines should be aware of the prohibition against sexual involvement with a client, but given the ongoing presence of this extreme violation among providers (Bouhoutsos, Holroyd, Lerman, Forer, & Greenberg, 1983; Feldman-Summers & Jones, 1984; Kardiner, Fuller, & Mensch, 1973) and its impact on clients, it cannot be underscored enough. Clients are at risk for being taking advantage of in multiple ways, and clinicians are ethically obligated to be cautious not to do so.

We commented in chapter 8 on how some traditional addictions treatment approaches that emphasize confrontation can be disempowering or retraumatizing for survivors of trauma. As such, they have the potential to jeopardize a client's safety. Many clients find attempts to break down their defenses and their "denial" to be not just ineffective but also invasive and damaging. This invasion can lead to reexperiencing of past traumatic or violent intrusions at the hands of perpetrators. Treatment that induces these types of traumatic stress symptoms is unlikely to retain women in the treatment process. Moreover, women who leave treatment under these circumstances may be more likely to relapse to manage their symptoms and distress. Relapsing itself may lead to dangerous situations, as might the consequences of flashbacks and dissociation if they are triggered. In a dissociated state, women are more likely to behave impulsively and without good judgment. Women will also have difficulty returning to a treatment or a treatment provider that felt abusive.

Other procedures and techniques in some addictions treatment settings have presented particular threats to trauma survivors. For example, to increase the veracity of drug tests and ensure accurate readings, some addiction programs, especially those serving clients from criminal justice settings, require that clients are "supervised" or observed by staff when giving a urine sample. Although many good reasons led to the implementation of this procedure, asking a woman to remove her clothing under the watch of a stranger is also likely to be retraumatizing. Because of the intrusive and staff-intensive aspects of this procedure, many addiction programs have adopted an alternative collection method that involves monitoring urine temperature without direct observation. In this method, a heat-sensitive strip attached to the collection container provides the temperature of the urine specimen. When the reading falls within a normative range, the temperature is a reliable indicator that the specimen is from the donor. This method has been demonstrated to be as effective as supervised collection (Moran, Mayberry, Kinniburgh, & James, 1995) and provides a method consistent with trauma-informed treatment and assessment.

ISSUES RELATED TO ONGOING INTIMATE PARTNER VIOLENCE

Preparing staff to handle issues of safety related to possible intimate partner violence (IPV) is an important element in the creation of a safe environment. Unfortunately, the traumatic experiences faced by clients are often not all in the past but also very much a threatening element of their current lives. Women in addiction settings have reported rates of current IPV between 25% and 57% (see El Basel, Gilbert, Wu, Go, & Hill, 2005). In practice, however, women do not always report that they are being abused. The shame and humiliation of being in an abusive relationship, as well as fear of the consequences of reporting the abuse, profoundly influence a woman's decision about whether to reveal this information. A sensitive and thorough initial assessment does not necessarily capture this information. It may be only in the course of treatment that the abuse comes to light.

Jane Seskin (1994), a social worker and counselor to battered women, writes, "One of the most courageous things a battered woman can do is to walk through the door of my office. It is her admission that something terrible and unspeakable is happening in her life" (p. CV11). Of course, this courage is also needed in an addiction setting, in which a woman might not expect to find herself revealing her abuse. Clinicians need to be prepared to respond to a client who shares this information, clinically and from a standpoint of safety. Knowing how difficult it may have been to talk about what is happening to her provides another opportunity to commend clients for their ability to convey the information and to open up an inquiry. Rather than sound the alarm by trying to mobilize a client into immediate action, the clinician needs to offer the client an opportunity to discuss what is happening in safety. The clinician should not assume that discussion means that a client is ready to walk out of an abusive relationship, rather it may be only the beginning of a long process in which the client grapples with her feelings for her abusive partner and the implications of leaving. For many women this process is complex. A clinician may not be able to understand the anxiety of a woman who stays in a violent or destructive relationship. Seskin (1994) wrote,

> Why do they stay in these deadly relationships? Each woman has her own answers. Because she has no money and no way to make money. Because her religion disapproves of separation or divorce. Because she's ashamed to let anyone know she's being beaten. Because she is alone in the world

except for her abuser. Because she is caught in the kissing–kicking cycle, still hoping he will again become the man she fell in love with. (p. CV11)

In a trusting therapeutic relationship, a woman who is being abused may at least begin to consider her options, to think about how she feels and how the abuse is hurting her and possibly her children, and to begin to develop the conviction that she does not deserve or have to tolerate her partner's abuse. Clinicians should have safety planning guidelines accessible to review with clients who are ready: how to plan for possible violence, what to do if abuse occurs, and how to keep as safe as possible (sample domestic violence safety planning guidelines are readily available online; e.g., see http://www.ncadv.org/protectyourself/SafetyPlan_130.html). Guidelines should also cover what the therapist should do if the client is injured. Resources in the community should be readily available for clients who are willing to consider shelter, need advocacy, or require the more specific skills of a battered woman's clinician. Agencies can help by maintaining relationships with these programs to facilitate interaction in times of crisis.

In remaining sensitive to the issues related to trauma, clinicians should address a client's drug and alcohol use in the context of her current abusive relationship, which may be helpful in her recovery. Ultimately, though, clinicians may have to grapple with feelings stemming from the knowledge that a client is walking out of her office and back into a potentially abusive home. Clinicians have reported that knowing a client may be in imminent danger (A. R. Hesse, 2002) and being helpless to prevent it can be traumatizing. Supervision can provide an invaluable opportunity for clinicians to process their own feelings associated with hearing about a client's abuse.

Additional issues of partner violence arise if a client's violent partner does not know that she is in treatment. Clients who are trying to get sober or get therapy without the knowledge of a partner, especially an abusive one, are often frightened to bring anything home that might be a clue to what she is doing. Clinicians and programs need to respect the client's wish that phone calls and correspondence be made only when necessary and that the agency or clinician do not identify themselves so as not to arouse a partner's suspicions.

A clinician may share in the fear that a partner will find out about a woman's treatment. Clinicians sometimes worry about what a partner will do if he discovers that the client is in treatment or perhaps suspects that she has been talking about their relationship. A hallmark of IPV is the perpetrator's need to control his partner. A threat to that control is one factor that may provoke a violent episode, threatening the safety of the client and worrying clinicians and other agency staff that the perpetrator will come after them. Although in practice, clinicians rarely face actual danger, perpetrators do sometimes make frightening threats. These threats need to be taken seriously and need to be responded to by the agency in support of the clinician. If possible, a description or a photo of a partner may need to be circulated and given to security personnel so that agency personnel may watch for him. Precautions may need to be taken to help a clinician feel that she can get home safely. Even if a woman has separated from a partner, or holds an order of protection against him, real safety concerns may still exist within the agency. Remember that although most instances of IPV occur between a male perpetrator and a female victim, many instances in which women are perpetrators of violence against male partners have been observed. Violence also occurs between same-sex couples.

Agencies can also support the clinician's general self-protective strategies. Although the risk of harm or harassment is relatively small, many clinicians feel that it is a useful precaution not to list their home address in public telephone directories, not to disclose personal information to clients, to learn techniques in managing assaultive client behaviors, and to avoid working alone in an office when possible (Guy, Brown, & Poelstra, 1992).

Agencies may face a different problem if, in fact, a client's partner is also in the program. In this situation it is essential that the agency maintain a team approach to ensure that dangerous interactions do not have a chance to develop. Although always a priority, confidentiality assumes greater importance in assuring that information imparted by one partner is not in any way revealed to the other partner. When possible, enabling one partner to receive treatment at another facility may be a safer alternative.

As previously mentioned, although most instances of IPV against women occur at the hands of a male partner, clinicians need to consider the possibility that a female client in a same-sex relationship may also experience abuse by her female partner. Clinicians should not assume that a woman in a relationship with another woman is safe. Similarly, clinicians should also be attentive to clues that a female client is herself perpetrating violence against her partner, either male or female. If this is the case, the clinician needs to take this violence as seriously as if it were coming from a male client and neither minimize nor dismiss it. Although there is a great deal in the literature about survivors of abuse experiencing episodes of revictimization in later life (Rodriguez, Vande Kemp, & Foy, 1998; Schaaf & McCanne, 1998), findings also support that female survivors become violent with others.

In addition to attending to the safety needs of the client and her partner in these situations, a client's treatment plan should clearly address the issues contributing to the violence. This is likely to include the role of substances but is also likely to require skill-building in affect and anger management to better manage distress and impulsivity. Some agencies already have groups dedicated to these skills; if not, they are worth introducing. Anger management groups are relevant not only to this subset of women but also to any client in recovery from addiction or trauma. In some agencies the clinical expertise or training needed to deliver some of these interventions may not be available. Connecting a woman with these services in an alternative setting, such as a mental health program, or enabling the resident trauma expert to become trained in these modalities to disseminate these skills in the agency can be exceptionally valuable. Through specialized treatments oriented toward reducing and redirecting anger and hostile impulses, clients gain better control over their violent or impulsive tendencies, which further enhances their own safety. A list of some suggested protocols for managing anger and distress more effectively are listed in Appendix A at the end of this volume.

Hearing about a client's impulses to harm someone else requires a good clinical appraisal of the situation before taking action. It is important to recognize that a client's discussing her fantasies about harming someone, possibly a past or recent perpetrator, does not necessarily mean that she will act on those fantasies. If therapy offers an environment that is safe enough for a survivor to articulate her thoughts and feelings, it is possible that some of these fantasies will emerge. Clinicians should not assume that hearing a survivor speak about violent or vindictive fantasies will lead to action, although it can be a frightening or unnerving disclosure, particularly when the expressed desires seem to rise to the level of homicidal ideation. Clinicians should take time to assess the likelihood of danger on the basis of a current assessment of the client and a consideration of her past actions. For example, can she identify and articulate the difference between thinking about harming someone and acting to harm someone? Does she seem to have the intent to harm someone and the plan and wherewithal to do so, or does she fully acknowledge that she has no plans to harm anyone and will commit to safety? Does she have sufficient control over her impulses and is her substance use in control so that she will not hurt someone unintentionally? (We should note that although we are using the word *fantasy* here, it is not a word we would necessarily use with clients; some clients do not always understand what is meant by it, and some find it has unpleasant connotations.)

Knowing a client's history is helpful in making a determination about safety. A client who has no history of acting on her violent impulses poses a different level of threat than a woman who has been known to lash out aggressively in the past. Likewise, a client prone to dissociative or psychotic episodes in which she does not have adequate judgment also poses a higher risk. If a clinician concludes that a client may pose a real danger to someone else, she needs to consider how imminent the threat is. Clear intention to imminently harm someone calls for emergency psychiatric evaluation with possible inpatient stabilization. Threats that seem serious but not imminent may also require psychiatric evaluation, especially if a client's ability to control her impulses is questionable and a clinician fears her client could do something dangerous even though she denies any intent to do so. Clinicians should take comfort in knowing that they will rarely face these serious situations. Of course, some women do take action, either in self-defense or premeditated, typically following years of being abused or battered (A. Brown, 1987). In extreme cases these actions can result in fatal consequences (e.g., O'Keefe,

1998). Clinicians should be aware of the possibility of these situations and how to approach them.

If there are concerns about the potential for a client to harm someone else, a pharmacotherapy consultation is advisable to determine whether adding or changing a psychotropic medication can help the client reduce these impulses. Although many of the more sedating benzodiazepine medications are not appropriate for survivors in recovery from addiction because of the pills' addictive potential, several other medications can achieve similar results without the risk of dependence. To be helpful here, a psychopharmacologist or nurse practitioner working at an addictions agency should be familiar with the pharmacotherapy of trauma or posttraumatic stress disorder symptoms.

Risk of imminent danger to someone may also trigger the "duty to protect" that person, depending on the obligations of clinicians in a given state. Most clinicians understand this requirement to protect a potential victim, even though it entails breaching the confidentiality of the client, which emerged through the *Tarasoff* ruling in California (see Weinstock, Vari, Leong, & Silva, 2006, for a discussion of *Tarasoff*). There may be additional implications for clients who are on parole or who are otherwise involved in treatment as an alternative to incarceration. Clinicians need to be clear about what kinds of reporting obligations they have and should inform clients of the specific limits of confidentiality. In addition, clinicians also need to be prepared to report child abuse if they learn in the course of treatment that a woman is perpetrating abuse against a child or is in a household in which a child is being abused. More detail about child abuse reporting issues is provided in a later discussion of issues particular to women with children.

MANAGING A DIFFICULT OR DYSREGULATED CLIENT

Clinicians can be easily daunted by trauma survivors' reputations for being challenging clients: They can be angry, hostile, labile, dissociative, suicidal, and antisocial. Only some trauma survivors demonstrate these characteristics, but clinicians will feel more confident about their work if they are prepared to deal with these issues. In chapter 4, we outlined some of the environmental and neurobiological factors that contribute to these challenging behaviors. An understanding of why clients may behave in certain ways can help clinicians take a more compassionate view of their clients and may help them formulate ways of responding that will help contain, rather than escalate, clients' feelings.

This is particularly important given the knee-jerk reaction clinicians often have in the face of some of these behaviors, especially when managing angry, hostile, and aggressive behavior. Clinicians typically attempt to reestablish authority; clients get angry, clinicians set limits; clients challenge a clinician's expertise, clinicians assert their knowledge and power; clients refuse to follow rules, clinicians and agencies add more structure and reduce privileges. Rather, clinicians need to consider how responding in these ways may intensify conflict and hostility rather than appease it. Exhibit 9.2 provides a scenario in which emotion escalates rather than deescalates.

In this scenario, staff is focused on adhering to agency policy, but the implementation of the policy is handled by exerting authority in a way that feels threatening and frightening to the client, who is already in a fragile, easily dissociated state. Instead of providing a containing and safe therapeutic experience the agency becomes caught up with the client in what may even be a traumatic reenactment of past abuse.

It may be helpful to keep in mind that survivors of trauma are often coming from a place of powerlessness and that setting rules and limits, although necessary, may underscore that feeling of powerlessness. Conflict with authority comes in part from a client's attempt to reestablish her own authority rather than risk the feelings of shame and degradation she experiences by being stripped of control. An empowerment perspective can help clinicians figure out ways of enforcing limits without disempowering clients; clients who are treated respectfully and collaboratively feel as though they are participating in decisions about their care. They are less likely to bristle under the rules if they are given an opportunity to consider how to follow those rules without being shamed or coerced. A great deal of angry and hostile behavior by clients can be avoided by finding ways to reduce power struggles.

Of course, not all angry and aggressive behavior can be attributed to conflicts over authority within the agency. There are many other reasons that a client can become dysregulated related to interactions with other program participants, friends and family outside of the program, or any number of other contributing factors. Again, clinicians should monitor their initial impulses to attempt to rein in a client's behavior by asserting their authority. It is helpful to take time to validate that clients appear to be experiencing some intense emotions and invite them to articulate what they can about their feelings at that moment and what may have been the trigger. Depending on the level of escalation and how out of control a client feels, she may or may not be able to

EXHIBIT 9.2
Clinical Case Example: Emotional Escalation

A client is triggered by something during treatment and is found huddled and dissociating in a corner. Staff work with her to ground her and calm her, but during this process she alludes to having fallen. Staff are concerned that she may have hit her head. On-site medical staff evaluate her and find no signs of neurological impairment but insist that she be evaluated at an emergency room per agency policy. The client is fearful of the emergency room and refuses. As staff continue to insist, the client becomes enraged and retriggered and violent until medical personnel arrive, and the client is so dysregulated that she needs to be physically restrained and pharmacologically sedated.

discuss feelings and emotions. Asking a client to talk about her experience can ease pressure and begin the process of calming down. This can occur in conjunction with other emotion regulation exercises when needed. If clients become more upset by talking about what is triggering them, an approach that is focused on the present may be most valuable. Techniques to manage distress and a wider range of dysregulated affect and dissociation were detailed in the chapter on emotional regulation (see chap. 4).

These active and effective methods provide both the client and the clinician with the means to address a client's distress that is sensitive to how trauma may have played a role in her emotional and behavioral response to the situation. Clinicians report greater confidence in working with clients after they have developed their own "tool box" of techniques to help clients through difficult moments. Just as clients need reassurance that learning and applying these skills take time, clinicians should be mindful that clients may not immediately embrace the skills. Clinicians may need to remind clients about using new skills as well as emphasizing the range of skills from which they can choose.

WORKING WITH WOMEN WHO HAVE CHILDREN

Working with women who have children poses particular challenges for substance abuse clinicians, especially when there is a history of violence for the mothers and any possibility of current violence toward or neglect of their children. Clinicians may have to contend with issues ranging from child care to child custody and the particular ways in which a mother's trauma history influences these situations.

Child Care and Child Services

The majority of substance abuse programs in the United States do not provide child care or children's services. Some evidence shows that when programs include these services for children, women are more likely to enter and attend treatment. For example, Beckman and Amaro (1986) found that alcoholism treatment facilities providing child-care services attracted more women into treatment.

Agencies that provide on-site child care help women with young children to attend treatment at times they might not otherwise be able to. It is important to note that they also provide a close and safe place for children while the mothers receive care. For many women, knowing that their children are nearby and under the supervision of someone they trust provides great relief. In many cases, women are forced to decide between leaving their children in less-than-ideal child-care situations and getting help for themselves. Alternatively, some clients will simply not attend treatment rather than leave their children attended by someone else because of the acute fear of what could happen to them, predicated on their own recollections of abuse as children. Agencies that are unable to provide on-site child care can work with clients to identify safe child-care arrangements and to assist clients in locating child-care resources in their communities. In some communities, women may be able to apply for free child care. To the degree that it is possible, being flexible about appointment times to accommodate a woman's child-care needs is also valuable.

For women with school-age children, many programs recognize the value of conducting treatment during school hours, so that a client can be available to children before and after school. Summers and vacations naturally present a problem to regular treatment attendance. Rather than penalize a woman for attending to her family obligations, programs should think about how to accommodate these time periods (e.g., to think of them as temporary leaves of absence with the intention to begin work with the client once the school year resumes). Preparing for this situation with clients is helpful. Knowing that a clinician and program understand her dilemma makes planning for these absences from treatment an opportunity for problem-solving and empowerment. Otherwise, a woman may feel she has to pretend that she is committed to treatment even when she cannot attend regularly. When she fails to show up as required, she risks early discharge from the program for noncompliance. Leaving on this negative note may make it harder for her to return to treatment than would a planned absence that helps her prepare ways to keep herself safe and sober.

Identifying and Reporting Abuse and Neglect

A particular challenge for clinicians working with mothers, especially women who are using drugs or alcohol, is the need to be vigilant about child abuse and neglect. Although some women who present for treatment may have open cases with child welfare authorities, instances of abuse and neglect may be identified through assessment or in the process of treatment, and clinicians need to be aware of how to respond. Clinicians need to learn how to assess for suspected abuse, how to determine whether a report is necessary, when to report abuse to child welfare authorities, and how to continue to engage a woman in treatment once a report is made.

In their role as *mandated reporters,* clinicians who become aware of or have a reasonable suspicion about abuse or neglect of a child are obligated to report this behavior to the state child welfare office. Clients should be made aware of this obligation on admission to the program or at the beginning of treatment and also be informed of other circumstances under which their confidentiality cannot ethically be maintained (e.g., harm to self or others or to older people). In the event that a clinician does need to make a report, the child welfare office then makes a decision about whether to investigate the allegations. If the child welfare office investigates, it decides whether a case is substantiated and begins assessment of the family and possible referral for services, or in more extreme cases, removal of the child into protective custody.

Taking a trauma-informed approach to reporting child abuse can sometimes help to salvage a woman's treatment, which otherwise can be destroyed by a report to the state agency that oversees child welfare. The initial reaction to learning that what she has revealed in treatment is cause to file a mandatory report is typically one of rage and betrayal. For clients and clinicians alike, having to report a client after she may just have come to feel safe enough to be honest about her behavior is a hugely painful process. Developing trust to open up to a therapist is often the crux of the beginning of treatment for trauma survivors. After working so hard to develop a trusting relationship and finally feeling able to talk about what is really going on, it can feel like a slap in the face when confronted with the knowledge that her clinician has to make a mandated report.

Reflecting with a client about her own history can be helpful at these times. Although clients report feeling angry and betrayed, often they recognize that they have become afraid of their own impulses. They sometimes come to understand that, at some level, telling the clinician was a way to reach out for help, even though the initiation of a report is scary and the outcome potentially terrifying. It is important for clinicians to recognize this, to support the client for taking the incredible risk involved in revealing the abuse, and to commend the courage it took to do so. Clinicians do not always realize that they are being put into multiple roles by the disclosure of abuse. They are witness to their client's painful story and are asked to offer commendation and validation for sharing this information. As mandatory reporters they are obligated to inform someone about what they learn. They also have a chance to model for an abuse survivor what it means to have a report of abuse taken seriously and acted on. The client is giving the clinician the chance to act on behalf of her child in a way that no one may have acted for her. Enabling clients to see this part of the process is sometimes useful and helps clients to maintain ties to their clinicians and to treatments rather than to simply sever the relationship. In the case of a new report, it is helpful to let clients know that making a report may help them to get the services that they need and that their worst fears of having their children removed from the home may not be realized. Clients may end up feeling relieved that there is now additional oversight to help them address their problems with their children. Of course, it is not the role of the clinician to determine the full extent of the abuse, and a clinician is not in a position to promise what may or may not happen as a result of opening a child welfare case.

Clinicians should be prepared, though, that despite their best efforts, the mere mention of filing a report of child abuse or neglect can signal the end of the therapy relationship. Clients may not desire or be able to engage in a dialogue at that moment and may leave the treatment room or treatment. Some survivors who are prone to dissociating under stress may respond to the news of a report in this way. Depending on the degree of dissociation, a clinician may need to assess whether the client is safe to leave, but he or she should probably assume that the client is unable to effectively interact about the issue at that time. If a clinician suspects that this could happen, it may be helpful to highlight some of what he or she wanted to convey to the client in writing. The clinician can either give the client the written response directly or send it to the client if it seems safe to do so, essentially trying to maintain a connection to treatment despite the rupture.

Because the potential to disrupt treatment and the client's life by filing a report is extremely high, it is also imperative that clinicians and agencies be clear about reporting guidelines. Although, as noted earlier, it is not the clinician's responsibility to substantiate the abuse or neglect report, if the possible abuse is not clear and does not require immediate intervention, clinicians and agencies do have the discretion to explore a worrisome situation with a client before filing a report. Rather than raise the alarm as soon as a clinician hears something that is of concern, clinicians should be taught how to gently encourage the client to give more details about the situation. What sounds like a cause for concern and reason to file a report may not be so once a clinician has a chance to learn more information. To do this effectively, clinicians need to know how to elicit information without sounding accusatory or putting clients immediately on the defensive. Telling a client something like, "You know I am a mandated reporter," as soon as she begins to reveal something questionable about her treatment of her child, for example, is more likely to create an atmosphere of fear and antagonism than collaboration.

Rather, clinicians who learn to take a nonjudgmental, exploratory stance stand to learn the specifics of the situation without unnecessarily alarming the client. A client who had indicated that she "hit" her child, for example, may elaborate that she slapped her child on the bottom once. Although this may still be an area to address clinically, it probably does not constitute a reportable event in the way that more substantial physical "discipline" would (e.g., hitting in the face, using an object to hit a child, leaving marks on a child from severe beatings). Similarly, a mother who is using marijuana at night when her children are all asleep presents a different threat than a mother who is using drugs in the bathroom while her children are in the next room and as a result of being intoxicated either neglects their care or puts them in danger through her actions or exposure to her drugs or drug paraphernalia.

By eliciting the information carefully and sensitively, clinicians can make an informed decision about the need to report a client to child welfare. An effective exploration of what is happening with a client's children may also have a valuable motivational component. If a client is able to align with her clinician's concerns, she may become more aware of the need to address potentially dangerous behavior toward her child. Motivational interviewing principles (W. R. Miller & Rollnick, 2002) can help guide clinicians in these types of situations. Clinicians can use nonconfrontational questioning, attempt to roll with a client's resistance to the topic rather than assume a defensive or authoritarian position, and help clients to evaluate their behaviors themselves rather than accept (or reject) the judgment of someone else.

Custody Issues

Child custody issues are also common for many women in substance abuse treatment programs. Because women are typically the primary and often sole caretakers for their children, these issues are more prevalent among female clients than male clients. Unlike facing new reports of abuse, clinicians working with women who are already involved with child welfare agencies often have the benefit of seeing clients who are now motivated for treatment on behalf of their children, either to prevent losing or to regain custody of their children. Women whose parental rights are going to be terminated may hope to mitigate the damage of losing their children by obtaining the right to visit and have a relationship with their children.

Especially in substance abuse settings, in which finding motivation and keeping motivated are so important to success, it is always valuable to help keep a mother's focus on her children at the forefront. Many women will say that first and foremost they want to get better to be a better mother to their children—before they will identify the importance of getting clean for themselves. Some programs that stress the need for recovery for oneself over recovery for anyone else, may struggle with this prioritization. For women whose ability to care for themselves is compromised by their own lack of adequate or appropriate caretaking as children, finding motivation for recovery through their children may, in fact, be a more important and accessible factor. Wanting to get clean on behalf of their children may also be a strong counterbalance to mandated treatment and the resentment that obligatory treatment often elicits.

Because of the involvement of child welfare agencies in women's lives, it is important clinically that women are clear about the clinician's and agency's involvement. The degree to which information about their treatment is confidential, and the exceptions to confidentiality, should be made explicit to clients. To feel safe, women need to understand what may or may not be shared with child welfare agencies or other agencies interested in their treatment (e.g., parole officers, other legal representatives). Specifically, how the results of drug screenings will be used and reported should be discussed. For survivors whose lives were riddled with disingenuous and manipulative behavior by people they were supposed to trust, providing candid and clear information is an important cornerstone in establishing an effective therapeutic relationship.

Naturally, clinicians, like their clients, need to be prepared for the setbacks that their clients may experience with regard to custody issues. Even postponed court dates, agency demands, and missed deadlines are likely to upset a client in her recovery. There is the possibility that more serious situations will arise, in which clients learn in the course of treatment that they will lose their children, either temporarily or permanently. Helping clients prepare for these eventualities should be factored into recovery plans. In the same way that effective substance use treatment addresses triggers and how to anticipate and manage them, child custody issues should be seen as setbacks with severe triggering potential. Many mothers in recovery who face the loss of their children reexperience the pain of this loss repeatedly near anniversary dates such as children's birthdays or dates on which they were removed from the home. It is important for clinicians to understand that these scenarios may be retraumatizing for their clients who are survivors and may cause a resurgence of trauma symptoms. Clients need to learn how to safely manage their reactions to these setbacks without relapsing or resorting to other unsafe behavior.

GROUP WORK

We have highlighted throughout this book the value that group work can have in recovery from trauma and addiction. Although some women immediately welcome the idea of being able to share in group part of themselves that they have long kept secret, many clients are initially fearful of what it means to enter into a group. Specifically, women worry about hearing others' stories, that they will be triggered or further overwhelmed; "I already have enough to deal with" is not an uncommon refrain. Clients worry about the confidentiality of revealing some of their experiences, especially in areas where women come from the same communities. In addition, many clients have difficulty overcoming the prohibitions against "sharing my business" that often they have heard for years. In substance abuse settings in which women may be living together in a residential setting, fears of what other members will do with information revealed in group are heightened. Every effort needs to be made to stress the importance of not sharing member information outside of group.

Women who are initially nervous about the idea of joining a group with other trauma survivors will benefit from discussing these concerns in pregroup meetings. To encourage women to participate in group, clinicians will want to validate a woman's concerns and comment on the value that many women find in group, including feeling less isolated and alone, decreasing secrecy, and finding new connections with women who have had similar experiences and symptoms. Potential new members need to know that they never have to talk about their traumatic experiences unless they want to and are ready and that it is the job of the clinician to make sure that members talk about their experiences only in ways that feel safe for the individual and the group.

Group psychotherapy intrinsically offers opportunities to address problematic interpersonal patterns, especially if they emerge as a within-group experience among members. However, clinicians need to carefully consider the fragility of group members before using the group to process and understand interpersonal conflicts between members. The opportunity to address these situations in group as real-time examples of similar interpersonal conflicts that clients struggle with outside the group should be weighed against a group's ability to handle the discussion without compromising the stability of the group and its members. It may not be until much later in a group's development that members can tolerate the interpersonal stress of facing one another about what they experience as threatening, including feelings of anger, envy, confrontation, exclusion, or even gratitude or affection. Manualized or structured protocol treatments can be helpful in minimizing the potential for interpersonal conflict to disrupt the group. By keeping the attention of clients focused on a given topic, the group has less opportunity to founder because of interpersonal issues that cannot comfortably be resolved without jeopardizing the group in some way.

Intense group connections often extend outside of the boundaries of the group or program as well, with clients forming friendships that go beyond group. More traditional psychotherapy groups often discourage out-of-group contact among members to preserve the safety of the group as a place to work therapeutically and not to dilute the in-group relationships, which can provide important therapeutic material. In groups for survivors, however, the need for safe social contact among members often overrides the need to maintain a traditional group boundary. Clients will often override the boundary anyway, making it difficult to enforce. Working with survivors in group who have out-of-group friendships presents different challenges than groups whose connections with one another are only in group, but by continuing to encourage relationships and stressing the importance of personal and group safety, these situations are usually manageable. Sexual relationships between group members, however, should always be discouraged, and clinicians need to remember to mention this prohibition in women-only groups as well.

Some additional guidelines that we have found helpful include (a) discouraging clients from borrowing or lending money to one another; (b) agreeing that members should not be asked, nor should they agree, to keep secrets that could be potentially dangerous (e.g., information about self-harmful or life-threatening behavior); (c) agreeing to bring into group for discussion any significant interpersonal issues that arise with another member that may jeopardize the ability to use group effectively (e.g., an out-of-group conflict or disagreement); and (d) agreeing that reaching out to another client when in distress means that the client will strongly consider, and not reject, safe suggestions made by that member. The latter suggestion is commonly followed in dialectical behavior therapy programs to prevent members from being put in the frightening position of having a client–friend in serious distress turn to them for help and then dismiss their helping suggestions.

Because of the difficulty maintaining safe boundaries and stable relationships, many of these guidelines will be challenged over the course of group treatment and will often need to be reviewed. Prohibitions against buying or selling drugs or alcohol to one another and using drugs or alcohol when with one another or when in or near the treatment facility are generally program wide. Additional reminders not to share prescription medications or any type of vitamin or supplement are also useful. The importance of discussing medication needs, pharmaceutical or alternative, with a psychopharmacologist cannot be stressed enough. Also, it should be stressed that group members, no matter how concerned they are for another member, should not assume an "MD" role for themselves. Because of their own distrust in the ability of people in authority to help them and because they may be accustomed to taking responsibility themselves, some survivors easily fall into this role of helping their peers, sometimes with dangerous consequences. Whenever possible, having a group cofacilitator is helpful in groups for trauma survivors. Two leaders can better monitor the intensity of the emotional experience of the group members. Because of the potential for clients to be easily triggered, it is helpful for a second leader to survey the group when the other facilitator is interacting with a client or clients and may be unable to attend to what is happening in the group. Two group leaders also present groups with the opportunity to activate different interpersonal schemas or transference dynamics, which can provide useful therapeutic information. In a similar way, a second facilitator is often vital to being able to defuse a heated interpersonal situation that can arise between the other cofacilitator and a client. We recognize that having two facilitators in one group is a luxury in most addictions treatment settings, but where resources make it possible, employing two facilitators in trauma-specific group treatment is useful for this population.

In constructing a group for survivors of abuse or trauma, group facilitators may need to consider whether certain clients will be manageable in group, despite the gains they stand to make from participating. If the interpersonal issues that a survivor brings to treatment are too difficult to contain, individual treatment alone might be a better alternative. Clients whose ability to trust others is so compromised by paranoid or malevolent attributions to others, for example, will defeat efforts by facilitators to promote feelings of safety in the group. Clients with severe dissociative features, including dissociative identity disorder features, may be frightening to other group members if they switch self-states during group or appear to the group as a violent or threatening identity. They may also worry other members if they are easily triggered by the group content and need constant attention in the group. Clients who dominate group and show little awareness of the needs of others or empathy for their situations also tend to undermine the safe progression of a group.

Clinicians also need to be prepared to manage a dysregulated client in group. Unlike individual treatment, in which there may be increased opportunity to notice a client becoming overwhelmed as indicated by shifts in her interpersonal interactions, clinicians may not always notice or immediately be able to attend to a client who is becoming distressed during group. In a group for survivors of trauma, however, it is especially important for clinicians to have their "antennae" up for distress signals. Often with vigilance, clinicians may notice when a client appears overtly upset or tearful, is becoming agitated or irritable, or appears to be losing touch with the group by not paying attention, rocking, or otherwise appearing dissociated.

Depending on the intensity of the group at that moment, clinicians may take note and continue to observe the client without disrupting the group, or they may ask the group to pause in order to check in with the client. Some clinicians are uncomfortable with the idea of taking group time to deal with the needs of one client. Often, though, if clinicians have noticed that a client is upset, other members will also have noticed that the client is upset. Rather than experience the shift of attention to that client as an intrusion, many members will feel relief that a clinician is paying attention to the client's needs. As groups develop and members get to know one another, some members may reach out to check in with other members themselves, but for women who have been accustomed to being silent or ignored or ridiculed for seeking help, they will often feel uncomfortable reaching out themselves and grateful that the clinician has done so. Group members may be particularly grateful to see a clinician come to the aid of a distressed member, as this may be in marked contrast to past experiences in which others stood by in the face of abuse or distress. In this way, clinicians model important caretaking behavior.

This can extend to the need for a clinician to have to leave the group to briefly attend to a client in such distress that she cannot tolerate staying in group. To the degree that it is possible, clinicians should do as much as they can to help a client deescalate in group using the emotion regulation skill exercises we have described. At times, though, a client will not be able to stay despite a clinician's best efforts; her affect at that moment is too intense, and she needs to leave the room. If this is the case, it is generally important to follow a client out of the room to be sure that she is safe. Preferably a client will agree to stay near the group in a safe waiting area or office and speak with the clinician after the group. Many clients are willing to do this. If a client insists on leaving the building, the clinician can assess her safety by asking her about her plans for when she leaves. This may include assessing her urges to pick up drugs or alcohol and any other unsafe impulses and talking through ways in which she will keep herself safe. Occasionally a client will run out of group and refuse to talk to the clinician. At that point the clinician needs to quickly appraise the client's situation, current level of distress, and history to determine whether emergency services may need to be called to pursue a client or check on the client later.

Situations such as this underscore the accepted and recommended practice of conducting trauma groups with cofacilitators whenever possible. It is much easier to follow a client out of group when there are two cofacilitators, enabling one to stay and one to step out if needed. Understandably, it is a potential dilemma for a clinician who is conducting a group on her own. Clients typically report, though, that they are reassured by a clinician who leaves group to check on a client. For members as well as clinicians it can be anxiety provoking and upsetting to see another member in such distress and more upsetting to think that the clinician did nothing about it.

Nevertheless, other members may become less empathic and supportive of this process over time if a client persistently needs this kind of attention. Sometimes clinicians can work with clients who are easily triggered to enable them to better manage their distress without continuing to "hijack" the group. Clients can potentially learn to ground themselves during group or they can come to an agreed-on process for leaving group to safely calm themselves. Some clients find it helpful to leave group to further ground themselves by running cold water over their hands, by taking a drink of water, or by taking a quick walk in the hall for a change of scene. These clients often are able to return to group. Identifying these strategies with clients is probably best handled in individual meetings outside of group time. If a client is able to adopt and implement these plans, they signify to her that her clinician has taken her distress seriously and that she has collaborated with her and respected her ability to take charge of her distress management. This is an empowering position, sending the message that the client does not need to depend on her clinician to help her regulate her feelings. It also frees the clinician and group from having to actively and repeatedly manage her distress. Not all easily distressed clients will readily assume this role, however, and clinicians may need to reevaluate whether a group may be too stimulating for a client.

We want to emphasize that when counseling and therapy are done safely, clients rarely become dysregulated to this extent, but clinicians should feel prepared for the clients for whom this applies. Women participating in groups specifically designed to address recovery and trauma are likely to present with a higher level of emotional lability or intensity than clinicians may have been accustomed to. In our research experience, some community-based addictions treatment programs that actively advertised addictions treatment for survivors of trauma noticed a significant difference in the participants who responded to this outreach compared with standard outreach to women with addiction. Their clinical and case management needs were greater than those of participants who typically attended treatment and required more clinical attention than other clients.

We emphasized earlier that clinicians should deliver trauma treatment voluntarily, and this applies to group as well as to individual treatment. Clinicians who are fearful or apprehensive about working with survivors may have a particularly difficult time with the intensity of group work. Their discomfort may lead to a variety of therapeutic dynamics that, if not noticed and addressed, can negatively affect the group. The inclination to approach psychotherapy groups more didactically or authoritatively, with less opportunity for emotional exploration, is one way that clinicians sometimes manage their own anxiety in these situations. Rather than open up opportunities to explore, these clinicians are likely to be overly directive or talkative, shutting down opportunities for clients to explore their thoughts and feelings. Clinicians also sometimes report the experience of shutting down themselves, unable to remain present and interactive with their groups. This can feel like a traumatic reenactment for clients as members experience the clinician as distant and inattentive. When the leader does not appear present enough to intervene protectively groups can begin to feel out of control and unsafe; the mute leader assumes the familiar status of nonprotective bystander.

CONCLUSION

Working with survivors of trauma raises many personal and clinical concerns for the clinician. Despite worries about conducting treatment with trauma survivors, with appropriate help and support clinicians can navigate the challenges of learning to integrate trauma treatment for women into their methods for helping women recover from addiction. By adopting a stance toward clients that is sensitive to trauma histories and learning about treatment models developed for recovery from trauma, clinicians can overcome anxieties about opening Pandora's box and provide good clinical help to their clients, even in the most challenging clinical situations.

10

ETHNOCULTURAL CONSIDERATIONS IN THE TREATMENT OF TRAUMA AND ADDICTIONS

Ethnocultural differences must be taken into account in integrating trauma treatment. Substance abuse treatment populations come from diverse demographic backgrounds, including ethnic and racial subgroups. Like many of our clients seeking treatment, the majority present with histories of early and ongoing traumatic events. Moreover, ethnic or racial minority women, who might also be from lower income neighborhoods, may experience specific types of trauma from exposure to community violence, challenges of immigration, racism, discrimination, and a host of other stressors, which provide a distinct backdrop for cumulative trauma on a multisystemic level.

We devote this chapter to reviewing some of the most important ways to understand ethnocultural differences in working with traumatized women in addictions treatment. Rates of trauma and psychopathology in ethnically diverse populations are explored through a review of the research literature on this subject, with emphasis on areas that differ with regard to the consequences of trauma. We also discuss the potential barriers in working with ethnically diverse clients that can complicate the fragile process of establishing a therapeutic alliance with trauma survivors.

ETHNICITY AS A RISK FACTOR
FOR TRAUMA EXPOSURE AND ITS CONSEQUENCES

Some basic assumptions about race and class are important to consider in work with trauma survivors. Although this may be a surprising finding for some, research tells us that socioeconomic status predicts trauma exposure better than do race and ethnicity. A high proportion of our female clients come from lower income backgrounds and live in inner-city neighborhoods, yet violent trauma in the lives of inner-city women has been underrecognized and understudied (Fullilove et al., 1993; Fullilove, Lown, & Fullilove, 1992). Nationwide statistics reveal that one in three women report histories of childhood sexual abuse, and one in four have been raped (Russell, 1986). Among women living in the inner cities, however, the prevalence of interpersonal violence appears to be significantly higher. For example, a number of studies (e.g., see Paone, Chavkin, Willets, Friedmann, & des Jarlais, 1992; Russell, 1983; Wyatt, 1992) suggest that a majority (up to 62%) of randomly sampled women living in low-income areas report having been sexually abused at some point in their lives.

Being socioeconomically disadvantaged has been shown to place one at a greater risk of experiencing interpersonal violence (Belle, 1990; Sorenson, Upchurch, & Shen, 1996). Likewise, women from low-income families, often racial/ethnic minorities, are disproportionately represented among those with histories of depression and substance abuse (Bruce, Takeuchi, & Leaf, 1991; Flaskerud & Hu, 1992; Murphy, Olivier, Monson, & Sobol, 1991; Trautman, Rotheram-Borus, Dopkins, & Lewin, 1991). Fullilove (2004) referred to the ongoing context of stress in urban poor communities as *root shock*, a traumatic stress reaction related to the destruction of one's emotional ecosystem (p. 11). Understanding clients through this lens of ongoing trauma and stress is important in developing appropriate and relevant treatment environments and plans.

Are There Ethnocultural Differences in Rates of Trauma Exposure?

Notably, a review of research on ethnocultural differences in violence exposures does not reveal specific ethnic differences in victimization or perpetration rates of either childhood or adulthood violence exposure when income status is controlled. Thus, it appears that with respect to interpersonal violence involvement, the stressors of poverty may exert more influence than ethnocultural differences. We recognize, however, that women from lower income backgrounds who seek substance abuse treatment are an ethnically and racially heterogeneous group. Apart from economic disadvantage, race and ethnicity may contribute to differences, particularly with regard to the longer term impact of abuse.

In the trauma and substance use literature, little is formally known about cultural differences between ethnic groups such as African Americans, Latinas,[1] and Native Americans. Researchers typically report findings on one ethnic group in comparison to Caucasians, often because studies are not able to recruit sufficient numbers of any one minority group. Moreover, in research studies, the definition of an ethnic group can be problematic, because there may be many culturally different dimensions within a single major ethnic category. Among Latinas, there are a multitude of ethnic groups from disparate regions of the globe, including the Caribbean, Mexico, Latin America, and South America, each with its own unique geography, history, culture, and view of mental health. Therefore, what we do know from the research must be viewed from a broad perspective with the recognition that the most meaningful distinctions within a particular ethnic group are probably still unknown.

The National Crime Victims Survey, conducted between 1993 and 1998, identified "being black, young, divorced or separated, earning lower incomes, and living in urban areas" (Rennison & Welchans, 2000, p. 3) as characteristics most closely associated with having been a victim of interpersonal violence. African American women had a 35% higher reported rate of intimate partner violence (IPV) than Caucasian women during this 5-year span and were more than twice as likely to report experiencing severe violence as Caucasian women (Hampton & Gelles, 1994; Rennison & Welchans, 2000; Tjaden & Thoennes, 2000). However, as previously mentioned, when socioeconomic status is controlled, ethnic differences in IPV exposure are significantly reduced or become nonexistent (e.g., see Coley & Beckett, 1988; Straus & Gelles, 1990), underscoring that race/ethnicity often serves as a proxy for socioeconomic disadvantage.

In an overview of studies examining ethnocultural differences in rates of trauma, there have been conflicting findings. Some studies show that ethnic minority groups are more likely than Caucasian counterparts to be exposed to domestic violence (Hampton & Gelles, 1994; Neff, Holamon, & Schluter, 1995; Vasquez, 1998), whereas others reveal no statistical differences across racial/ethnic groups (e.g., see Asbury, 1987; Kanuha, 1994). Or, the differences between minority and Caucasian women, even in a disadvantaged population, reveal greater socioeconomic barriers in African American or Latino women (Amaro et al., 2005). Indeed, in one study that did control for socioeconomic status, lower rates of violence were reported in ethnic minority homes (Coley & Beckett, 1988; Straus & Gelles, 1990). Likewise, the body of research that considers ethnicity in relation to childhood sexual abuse and adult sexual violence reveals mixed findings similar to those previously

---

[1] We denote geographic subgroups of Latinas by name (i.e., Mexican American or Caribbean women) when we can refer to a specific group. We use the term *Latinas* to describe a diverse group of women from Spanish-speaking countries who share cultural and political ties and who are heterogeneous in national and regional origin and in economic and immigration histories with regard to the United States.

described. African American women were equally as likely as Caucasian American women to have been sexually abused before age 18, as well as in adulthood (Urquiza & Goodlin-Jones, 1994; Wyatt, 1992). In one study of a large sample of women in community treatment, contrary to expectations, it was the Caucasian women, not the African American and Latino women, who had significantly higher mental health impairment and mental health disorders, despite the fact that the minority women had lower socioeconomic status and income (Amaro et al., 2005).

A few studies do support the notion that rates of trauma exposure for Latinas are different from those for Caucasians or African Americans, although findings are not consistent. For example, Sorenson and Siegel (1998) found lower lifetime prevalence rates of sexual trauma among Latinas than among Caucasians. Urquiza and Goodlin-Jones (1994) reported lower rates of childhood sexual abuse among Latinas than among either African American or Caucasian women. In a study of 4,132 child abuse cases, however, Latinas had the greatest incidence of sexual abuse in the home compared with other racial groups (Lindholm & Willey, 1986).

The concept of intergenerational trauma derived from experiences of the European holocaust has been applied to understanding trauma in the lives of Native Americans. Braveheart (2003) defined *intergenerational trauma*, also known as *historical trauma*, as "cumulative emotional and psychological wounding over the lifespan and across generations, emanating from massive group trauma experiences" (p. 7). Accordingly, the trauma response among Native Americans may be identified in nonspecific diagnostic symptoms of depression, despair, self-destructive behavior, suicidal thoughts, anxiety, anger, grief, and substance abuse (Braveheart & DeBruyn, 1998). Empirical research into this phenomenon has been slowed by the absence of measures to define historical grief and to tease apart current situational experiences from past, intergenerational trauma. However, new measures have been developed to encourage research on this topic. At present, it remains unknown how the experiences of Native Americans with regard to trauma compare with those of African American, Latina, immigrant, and other minority groups, although the links between substance abuse and trauma among Native Americans have been posited in clinical studies (i.e., Braveheart, 2003).

Ethnocultural Differences in Response to Trauma

Although the prevalence rates of interpersonal violence exposure may not differ by race, the literature clearly suggests that ethnic minority women experience and respond to trauma differently than do Caucasian women in terms of lethality, coping strategies and access to resources, and disclosure. These response differences are important to consider in providing treatment for addictions.

The impact of traumatic exposure with respect to lethality appears to be greater among minority clients than among Caucasians. For example, domestic violence in African American homes was more often lethal than domestic violence in Caucasian Americans' homes, often attributable to a lack of police response (Root, 1996). Wyatt (1990a) reported that African American women with a history of childhood sexual abuse were more likely to evidence significant long-term difficulties in interpersonal functioning and symptoms secondary to their trauma. Likewise, African American incest survivors evidenced more negative life experiences (i.e., revictimization), resulting in more severe and chronic psychological symptoms and more emotional distress than Caucasian American survivors (Russell, Schurman, & Trocki, 1988). Coping strategies may also differ across ethnic groups on the basis of cultural norms and expectations. In one study (Sander-Phillips, Moisan, Wadington, Morton, & English, 1995) of ethnic differences in trauma among adolescents, African American girls were reported to be more likely than Latino girls to display emotional responses (e.g., crying, pouting, sulking) and more likely to use coping strategies such as avoidance, withdrawal, and isolation. Latino girls, however, had significantly higher depression scores than African American girls (Sander-Phillips et al., 1995). In this study, Latino girls' exposure to abuse started when they were younger, with a higher likelihood of being abused by a family member than African American girls. Specific cultural or experiential differences may account for some of these findings.

Often, sexual abuse survivors (i.e., children and adults) may be confused about their own participation in the abuse. In many cases, the perpetrator has told them repeatedly that it is their fault, and victims characteristically blame themselves. As a consequence, they may be reluctant to report the abuse because they feel guilty and fear punishment. Many even have their own self-punishing behaviors that result in repeat victimization, suicidal ideation and attempts, or self-mutilation. These self-punishing behaviors are thought to arise from an originally adaptive psychological attempt to gain control and mastery over what is experienced as uncontrollable. Unfortunately, this normal response to trauma (i.e., blaming the self) becomes highly maladaptive over time.

Among ethnic minorities, findings consistently reveal an even greater reluctance to disclose than among Caucasian abuse survivors. Thus, African American women have been shown to be less likely to disclose their sexual abuse history and are more likely to feel that they are to blame (Wyatt, 1992). Likewise, Sander-Phillips et al. (1995) found that African American girls were more likely to report that they hoped no one found out about their abuse. Stigma and shame influence self-disclosure of mental illness, substance use, and violence among Asian Pacific Islanders, resulting in underreporting of these problems even in large, nationally representative surveys (Wynaden et al.,

2005). Cultural and ethnic differences may influence how one attempts to cope with distressing events, including weighing the costs of disclosing.

One of the most significant reasons for the differential consequences of traumatic exposures for ethnic women may be a reluctance to disclose arising from cultural norms and suspicion of authorities, influenced by racism and discrimination (Wyatt, 1992; Wyatt, Notgrass, & Newcomb, 1990). Years of work in therapy may be required for the victim to understand that she was not to blame for childhood sexual abuse. In families with competing stressors, such as severe financial difficulties, children may feel less able to present distressing information. More generally, as discussed earlier, in families with abuse dynamics, secrecy and fears of retribution result in a decreased likelihood that an abuse survivor will reveal the abuse.

When a cultural group has experienced negative stereotyping and questions about credibility, there is even less likelihood of trauma disclosure for fear of not being believed or not receiving the desired and needed support. There may be further reluctance to report African American perpetrators to the legal system because of the harsh treatment these men typically receive in criminal justice settings (Abney & Priest, 1995). African American women may be faced with additional guilt over protecting themselves versus "betraying" their community (Abney & Priest, 1995), causing even less likelihood of disclosure. Latino women face a similar dilemma when deciding to disclose their experience of trauma to the legal system at the expense of maintaining loyalty to their family (Vasquez, 1998). Also, "the disempowerment that results from gender and ethnicity for women of color . . . muffles the voice of the woman of color and prevents her from being taken seriously" (Root, 1996, p. 371). Problems with immigration status or other concerns about the impact of legal involvement with respect to self and family further reduce the likelihood of formally reporting instances of trauma.

Ethnic minority women in the United States typically have to deal with the overlapping experiences of racism, sexism, discrimination, poverty, and immigration. Wyatt (1990b) argued that racism is a form of victimization that results in stigmatization and feelings of powerlessness. The experiences of other oppression in addition to ongoing violence may have a substantial psychological impact (Walker, 1995). All of these issues may significantly impede ethnic minorities' recovery and responses to trauma and are part of what may be used to inform the discussion of the impact of trauma for women with diverse cultural and ethnic backgrounds.

IMMIGRATION CONSIDERATIONS

Leaving one's country of origin, one's loved ones, and all that is familiar in favor of entering a new country, social system, and culture are all common challenges for the immigrant. Stressors such as social support disruption, language barriers, economic hardships, loss of socioeconomic status, discrimination, and real or perceived pressures from the host society to assimilate are part and parcel of the immigration process. In addition, the individual may be confronted with conflicting worldviews and moral values, particularly as they relate to sex roles, family and community paradigms of independence versus relatedness, and intergenerational family dynamics and challenges (Storer, 1985). Immigration is a time when the demands on coping systems are the highest and stressors are most intense. To meet these challenges, immigrant individuals and families must maintain continuity, identity, and stability at a time when new patterns of behavior, interactions, and beliefs are evolving.

Resilient immigrant families use key processes to reduce stress and risk of dysfunction to enable optimal adaptation (Walsh, 1996). Immigrant families are able to maintain salient aspects of their cultural narratives while modifying others and thus are able to restore a sense of continuity and coherence in their lives. Trauma exposure is a great strain and may ultimately rupture a family's resilience in attempting to adapt to new circumstances. If the trauma comes from outside of the family, it may either threaten coherence or cause further harm, depending on how the community or new culture responds. Latino cultural and ethnic groups present a good example of how immigration may play a role in increased violence within the family. The Latino ethnic population doubled in the United States during the last 2 decades of the 20th century, growing from 6.4% in 1980 to 12.5% in 2000 (Hobbs & Stoops, 2002). Latino immigrants often live in the inner city, below the poverty line, and they are at particular risk for exposure to violence. Few studies have investigated the role of violence in the lives of immigrant Latino women in spite of the fact that they live with great fear of being victimized and that once victimized, they are frequent targets of revictimization (e.g., see Parker, McMorris, Smith, & Murty, 1991). Therefore, further research is needed to clarify the degree to which ethnic differences contribute to the effects and course of trauma exposure, but to date, the bulk of findings point to consequences of immigration and economics as the most significant predictors of interpersonal violence.

The traditional concepts of *machismo*, *marianismo*, and *respeto* in Latino cultures reflect norms of dominant and submissive roles within the family system (e.g., see Amaro & Russo, 1987; Comas-Diaz, 1990). When traditional familial roles are threatened, as when female immigrants are better able to find work than their male partners, an increase in partner violence may occur in response to shifting power dynamics within the family (Gondolf, Fisher, & McFerron, 1988; Torres-Matrullo, 1976). Moreover, despite the fact that partner violence may be increasingly common for low-income first-generation Latino women, women from these families appear to be less likely to seek help for problems associated with violence, even within their own social networks

(Comas-Diaz, 1990; Gondolf et al., 1988; Vazquez-Nutall, Romero-Garcia, & De Leon, 1987). Thus, immigrant women may find themselves more isolated than their American-born counterparts, increasing the likelihood of continuing exposure to family violence.

Domestic violence is also considered a significant public health problem among Asian and South Asian immigrant groups (Bui & Morash, 1999; D. F. Chang, 2002; Yoshihama, 1999). It is unclear whether IPV among Asians is greater in the country of origin or in the United States. This is of considerable interest because the majority of people of Asian ethnicity currently residing in the United States are foreign born (Uba, 1994). Marital violence may be higher among Asian Americans because of stressors attached to the immigration process (Song, 1996). In surveys conducted between 2001 and 2002 by the All-China Women's Federation, an organization raising awareness of violence against women in China, rates of domestic violence were found to be between 23% and 35%. Women were the victims in the vast majority of these cases (i.e., 87%–90%; United Nations Development Fund for Women, n.d.). Lifetime rates of male-to-female domestic violence among Caucasian Americans in the United States are reportedly close to 30%, as well (Straus, Gelles, & Steinmetz, 1980). Given the comparable rates of IPV for Chinese families living in China, additional research is required to understand in what ways Asian immigrants and Asian American women may be at increased risk for IPV while living in the United States.

TREATMENT AND PROGRAM IMPLICATIONS

Clearly, our ethnically diverse clients come to addictions treatment with significant exposures to trauma that either equal or exceed those of other clients, especially when we consider the impact of additional sources of stress and trauma linked to immigration, community violence, racism, and discrimination. Despite the significant need for services among diverse clients, there remain many barriers and hurdles to planning treatment components or programs that can be culturally competent; that is, that can address the unique needs of clients taking into account diverse ethnic minority group experiences, strengths, and vulnerabilities. The need for cultural sensitivity extends from engaging and retaining clients, to understanding barriers that can often lead to early treatment dropout, to creating a treatment environment that allows for the intimate work of trauma disclosure and recovery to occur.

Ethnocultural Differences in Help-Seeking

It appears that even though the need is great, ethnic minority women choose not to seek or to receive the services that they require. Cultural proscriptions against seeking help outside of the family or the immediate cultural milieu, as well as exposure to negative experiences secondary to being an ethnic minority in the United States (Hampton, Oliver, & Magarian, 2003), may make it harder for certain subgroups of women to seek help.

Profound stigma and shame have been identified as key factors for the low use of mental health services among minority ethnic groups in general (Tsang, 2004; Wynaden et al., 2005). Latinos may seek help through more informal social networks, religious organizations, or individuals as opposed to formal social service agencies. Thus, the cases that do find their way into community-based substance abuse treatment may often be the most severe, including minority women who have few community or social resources and are significantly more impaired (e.g., see Hu, Snowden, Jerrell, & Nguyen, 1991; Neighbors, 1988; Sussman, Robins, & Earls, 1987).

For those who do access mental health or addictions treatment systems, the retention rates may also be affected by race/ethnicity status. Sue (1977) conducted a landmark epidemiological survey on treatment outcomes that examined ethnocultural differences. According to this study, African Americans were reported to have received unequal treatment and had significantly greater dropout rates than did Caucasian Americans. Across all types of treatment, 70% of Caucasians returned after the initial session, compared with only 50% of African Americans. In this same study, Latinos, even after receiving treatment equal to that of Caucasians, had higher rates of premature termination (Sue, 1977). Notably, controlling for demographic factors such as socioeconomic status in the analyses did not reduce the significant differences between ethnic minority groups and Caucasians. Over a decade after Sue's 1977 study, O'Sullivan, Peterson, Cox, and Kirkeby (1989) reported the same trends in a replication study, indicating that African Americans continued to have poorer outcomes. In addition, O'Sullivan et al. reported that minorities were less likely to be seen in individual therapy, and when they were in treatment, they were more likely to have been treated for fewer sessions than Caucasian participants.

There are three overarching reasons for minority group underutilization of mental health and addictions services: cultural factors, service access barriers, and economic constraints (Hampton et al., 2003; Mears, Carlson, Holden, & Harris, 2001; Zoellner, Goodwin, & Foa, 2000). *Cultural factors* refer to the stigma associated with seeking outside help for one's personal problems, culturally insensitive treatment, and service provision by therapists from dissimilar cultural backgrounds who have little cross-cultural awareness and competence (Sue, 1998). *Service access barriers* refer to lack of time because of work schedule constraints, limited resources in specific communities, or lack of knowledge of available resources. Finally, ethnic minority groups often have economic constraints, such as limited access to health insurance, that result in a limited ability to utilize private therapeutic services that might be most appropriate to meet their needs. In combination, these factors reduce the likelihood that ethnic minorities will seek out or be retained in treatment.

Being Latino was a significant predictor of premature termination of outpatient and residential substance abuse treatment (Ozer, Best, Lipsey, & Weiss, 2003). In a recent comorbidity trauma study, ethnic differences in relapse rates in patients seeking substance abuse treatment were highest among African American and other non-Caucasian patients (U.S. Department of Health and Human Services, 2001). Finally, even when an ethnic minority woman does begin psychotherapeutic treatment, many of the factors previously mentioned, including time and financial constraints and cultural factors about help-seeking, can significantly affect the development of a solid working alliance and, ultimately, therapeutic outcomes.

Ethnocultural Differences and Therapeutic Alliance

Given that there are often ethnocultural differences between therapists and clients, matching therapists and clients on race or ethnicity has been a large focus of research examining treatment alliance. The basic assumption is that similarities in ethnicity will promote better outcomes because the therapist may be better able to empathize with a client from a shared cultural background (Ridley, 1984; Thompson, Worthington, & Atkinson, 1994). This assumption derives partly from the notion that experiences of racism, discrimination, and oppression in the United States result in client distrust of nonminority therapists (Morris, 2001). It is assumed that a client who sees a therapist of the same ethnic background is more likely to self-disclose about a whole range of topics, including trauma exposure. Conversely, nonminority therapists may unknowingly invalidate a client's feelings of discrimination because of a fundamental lack of awareness and experience.

In actual fact, research that addresses treatment alliance and racial/ethnic matching has not involved real therapist and patient dyads. Rather, there are a host of analogue studies with college students assessing ethnic minority groups' preference for and perception of ethnically similar versus dissimilar therapists (see Coleman, Wampold, & Casali, 1995, for a review). A meta-analysis of these analogue studies indicated that ethnic minorities preferred ethnically similar therapists over Caucasian therapists and that similar therapists were perceived more positively than were ethnically dissimilar therapists (Coleman et al., 1995). Whether these studies generalize to real therapist and client dyads remains in question.

Studies that have examined actual therapist and patient dyads on racial and ethnic differences have yielded mixed results, but few have measured the therapeutic alliance directly. Ethnic match has been found to be a positive predictor of outcome in some studies (e.g., see Russell, Fujino, Sue, Cheung, & Snowden, 1996; Takeuchi, Sue, & Yeh, 1995; Yeh, Eastman, & Cheung,

1994); however, in other studies no such relationship has been found (e.g., see Fiorentine & Hillhouse, 1999; Sterling, Gottheil, Weinstein, & Serota, 1998). Among the few studies examining client-to-therapist ethnic matching among drug treatment populations, no relationship between ethnic matching and outcomes has been found. One study of clients' needs, services received, perceptions of clinician empathy, and outcomes was conducted with 302 clients entering an addictions program in Los Angeles County (Fiorentine & Hillhouse, 1999). The Perceived Empathy Scale was a three-item measure that included the items "My counselor understands me," "My counselor realizes how my experiences feel to me," and "My counselor understands me even when I don't express myself." In this study, although ethnic match was unrelated to treatment retention or treatment outcomes, clients who were ethnically matched perceived their clinicians as having higher levels of empathy than those who were not. Surprisingly, however, there was no relationship between perceived empathy and treatment outcomes. Similarly, in another large study of 967 cocaine-dependent African Americans (Sterling et al., 1998), no relationship between ethnic matching and treatment participation or positive outcomes was identified.

Research specifically exploring ethnic differences in outcomes among individuals in treatment for trauma and posttraumatic stress disorder (PTSD) is limited, although two studies demonstrate little impact of therapist–patient racial or ethnic matching. Zoellner, Feeny, Fitzgibbon, and Foa (1999) failed to find any differences between African American and Caucasian women in pretreatment functioning and outcome using active cognitive–behavioral therapy (CBT) treatments (i.e., prolonged exposure [PE], stress inoculation treatment [SIT], combined PE and SIT). Ethnic matching and treatment alliance were examined specifically in a National Institute on Drug Abuse randomized clinical trial of two CBT treatments in a sample of urban, low-income women with comorbid PTSD and substance use disorders (Hien, Cohen, Miele, Litt, & Capstick, 2004). Once demographic variables were controlled for, ethnic minority and Caucasian women did not differ in terms of pretreatment symptomatology. The ethnic minority and Caucasian women had equally positive outcomes after receiving CBT for their PTSD and substance use symptomatology. These findings did indicate the benefits of treatment regardless of ethnic match. African American women, however, had significantly lower therapeutic alliance ratings than Caucasian women. For the Caucasian women, ratings of the alliance were significantly related to positive outcomes, whereas for the African American women, alliance showed no relationship to outcome. This study highlights the need for more research in this area to understand the conditions under which ethnic minority women can maximize the benefits received from treatment and the overall importance of therapist–patient ethnic matching and alliance in terms of actual treatment outcomes.

Culturally Congruent Treatment and Program Planning With Trauma Survivors

Ethnocultural values and histories should be considered in developing a treatment approach to enhance engagement and validate the experiences of traumatized clients. Such an approach would take into consideration unique racial, ethnic, and cultural values, such as affirming heritage, rights and responsibilities, cultural identity, self-esteem, pride, spiritual awareness, and acceptability of treatment methods. To be culturally sensitive, for example, the aims of treatment might include the promotion of collectivism for individuals from cultures that rely heavily on community and group processes. Thus, additional programming could support relationship-building and peer support development, which are so commonly disrupted among immigrants and minorities who find themselves in substance abuse treatment (Karenga, 1988; Triandis, 1994).

Issues in Assessment and Goal Setting

Clients with trauma histories frequently present to treatment with a pronounced lack of entitlement and low empowerment. Those who have had long histories of childhood trauma and ongoing interpersonal violence and who have turned to drugs and alcohol as a form of coping are typically alienated from their families, are viewed as parental failures, experience major role losses, and are socially isolated from support networks. Thus, identity functioning is impaired, and shame and humiliation are prominent. Working in treatment to help engage and repair these broken relationships when possible is critical for the minority client because a positive, close relationship with family and community—to a greater extent than for nonminorities—may be at the center of normative identity. This should involve some assessment period during which an inventory of social support systems and relationships, even if they are currently ruptured, will be critical in determining a set of treatment goals that can promote recovery in a culturally responsive way.

Of course, this may not be possible if the family itself has been involved in the abusive dynamics. As is the case in many of our clients' backgrounds, avoidance of the topic of intrafamilial abuse by family members (those involved in the abuse and those who were not) can undermine a woman's recovery. Healing through the reestablishment of familial relationships can be conflictual and, in some situations, without resolution. The majority of women in substance abuse treatment come with substantial histories of abuse across the life course. Although they demonstrate substantial resilience, individuals with such histories may also demonstrate low self-esteem. This manifests most clearly in feelings of self-blame. Both of these emotional states, low self-esteem and self-blame, can prevent a woman from taking action against an abuser or exacerbate a family system that is hostile and invalidating of the survivor's experiences. This is one reason why abuse survivors often must receive intensive psychotherapy before deciding to bring a case against their abusers. Although our ethnically diverse clients are not different in this regard, what may be different is the extent to which the individual depends on connections within the family system for a fundamental sense of identity. Failing to fully understand that these important connections need to be supported and upheld can be a basic fault in a treatment that adopts a more Western view of family, one that considers a separated, individuation model as a standard of healthy outcome. Thus, encouraging a Latino adult woman to confront her mother (i.e., the grandmother and main caretaker of her children), who, she believed, knew that her stepfather was abusing her as a child, might not be the best therapeutic direction to take with a client who depends on her mother for help with child rearing and emotional support.

Assessment and discussion of trauma can be a complicated process that takes time to unfold in a safe treatment relationship. Trauma survivors are often confused about what to call a traumatic event. Did they participate? Does that mean that it was not really traumatic? Many trauma survivors fail to view certain events or ongoing patterns of relating as traumatic, because of denial or dissociation. Adding cultural differences to the equation increases the complexity of the situation. For example, African American parents may use parenting styles that are more authoritative, with strong beliefs in obedience, expectations of early responsibility, and encouragement of children's involvement in decision making (Taylor, 1991). These parenting styles can incorporate the use of corporal punishment. These parenting precedents raise the threshold for what one might consider abusive when certain practices are considered part of the normal parenting spectrum and in line with community and social norms.

A primary goal for African American parents is to prepare their children to function in two different societies: the local community culture and the mainstream culture, the latter of which is frequently experienced as hostile (Taylor, 1991; Zayas & Solari, 1994). Disciplinarian parenting practices of African Americans are a result of this dual socialization goal; African American parents use stricter discipline methods than do Caucasians to prepare their children to respond immediately to authority and avoid later problems with individuals and organizations in positions of power, such as the police. If minority parents need to prepare their children for growing up in a society in which they may be discriminated against, a stricter, more authoritarian parenting approach might make sense as a way to provide greater control and decrease the likelihood of getting into trouble. With cultural context in mind, a parenting response that might be interpreted as an act of abusive parenting in a different context would more likely be seen as a legitimate expression of parental authority by a parent of color. In fact, use of corporal punishment itself has not been found to be a negative predictor of outcome among African American families in contrast to its use among Caucasian families (e.g., see Deater-Deckart & Dodge, 1997).

Historically, confusion and disagreement about what constitutes physical abuse have often led minority parents engaging in what was a culturally normative form of discipline within their cultural groups and communities of origin to be accused of abusive behavior by child protection workers (Ahn, 1994; Bluestone & Tamis-Lemonda, 1999). It is therefore important for clinicians to differentiate between physical abuse and the use of corporal punishment consistent with cultural values. In addition, clinicians should conduct a culturally sensitive exploration of the impact of corporal punishment on a client's emotional state and psychological development. This would be true in the case of assessing an African American client for her own history of childhood physical abuse, as it would be for considering whether and how to manage a Latino or Asian mother who uses corporal punishment as a form of discipline with her own children. As we discussed in chapter 9 of this volume, context is critical in understanding whether a report of child abuse needs to be made.

Another feature in the early assessment process that may be particularly relevant for nonminority clients is the exploration of the impact of historical trauma in the individual's life. For example, as a part of her treatment for alcohol abuse and IPV, a Native American client may not directly discuss how her people have been treated over the course of time. Similarly, an African American client living in the inner city may not discuss the impact of urban renewal and the construction of housing projects on her great-grandmother's family, prompting entry into the public welfare system. It is the responsibility of the clinician to recognize that historical and intergenerational factors may be important in understanding her recovery process and the full meaning of her psychological distress.

Engagement and Retention

Once a treatment process has begun and therapeutic goals have been set, development of a trusting working alliance may require more sensitivity and focus for racial/ethnic minority clients with trauma backgrounds. Naturally, some might question how any therapist can truly understand a client if she has not shared similar experiences. This question underlies every new treatment and can encompass age and life experience, substance abuse background and trauma histories, and ethnic differences. If therapist and patient are from different racial/ethnic backgrounds, these questions may remain unspoken in the beginning of a treatment, although they are clearly at the heart of whether a client will feel comfortable and come back for more sessions. Depending on the treatment model, these questions may be taken on and verbalized earlier or later in the process, or not at all. Anyone working with a patient of different racial, ethnic, or cultural background should be listening to the clinical material for issues that suggest concerns about ethnic differences. At the least, the therapist should be aware of fluctuations in session attendance that might be related to cross-cultural unease. Raising the subject of differences in a forth-right manner can often put early client worries to rest and help with treatment engagement by setting a tone of openness about potentially threatening feelings and dynamics.

Similarly, keeping secrets, which is so much a part of an incest survivor's familial makeup, may be linked to specific cultural norms. A clinician should be alert to clues that a client may be uncomfortable about disclosing information, unready to disclose it, or purposely withholding it, especially if previous attempts at telling the truth were met with dismissal or disbelief. Power differentials between clinician and client may also make disclosure of certain information difficult, putting the client in a vulnerable situation. Part of the job of the clinician is to be aware of this and to create an environment that is safe, as well as to acknowledge the role that racial, ethnic, or cultural differences might be playing. There are also norms with regard to disclosure of any personal information; thus another part of therapeutic engagement will involve sensitivity to ways that clients may choose to hold back. As in the principle highlighted in the motivational interviewing style of therapy, denial or defensiveness on the part of the client may result from the clinician moving ahead too quickly. Rather than confronting denial, a sensitive clinician can validate and show understanding of the ways that a client might be afraid to come forward with very personal information. This validation would serve as a model to teach a client that sharing what might be considered a family secret or private family business can actually lead to healing. Again, these are all nuances of trauma and addictions work that may be magnified in clients from diverse backgrounds.

Clinicians are often confronted with the question "How would you understand?" or faced with a client's comment, such as "You've never had to deal with that." It is understandable for clients to wonder how someone might be able to understand or relate to their own overwhelming experiences. It is important to acknowledge that clinicians often do not share the experiences of their clients. Although these types of questions may lead to defensiveness or anxiety on the part of clinicians, especially inexperienced clinicians, such questions can be useful in strengthening the therapeutic alliance and building a trusting relationship. Clinicians should be straightforward and honest in their responses and inquisitive about what the question means to the client. For example, to the question "How would you understand? You're not a woman of color," the clinician might respond, "You're right. I don't have first-hand experience of what it's like to be a woman of color. Can you help me understand what that's like for you?" Some clients will not wish to engage in this dialogue, or they may feel that they are a clinician's instructor, but by acknowledging differences and being genuinely interested in understanding a client's perspective, a deeper relationship can form with clients who are willing. In all matters, the client is the expert in her own experience, and sharing with the clinician can help bring them closer together and increase treatment engagement.

Finally, intimacy in relationships can be threatening, especially for trauma survivors. Often clients will keep things on safe ground in the treatment by limiting contact or maintaining strict authoritative–hierarchical boundaries. In many groups, such as some eastern Asian cultures, authority is respected above all else (e.g., see Amaro & Russo, 1987; Comas-Diaz, 1990; Pye & Pye, 2006). For example, doctors should not be questioned; clients should be quiet and respectful at all times; and parents have the first and final word. Unfortunately, this may be another prohibition against a client feeling safe to speak her mind and say what she really thinks or needs, or even to ask for clarification and information. A clinician sensitive to these vulnerabilities could observe this phenomenon and even bring it to the client's attention as a topic for discussion. Treatment approaches adopting a more nonhierarchical, collaborative approach between client and clinician rather than placing the clinician as the authority and the client as the recipient of this authority also help to promote and set a model for cultural respect and sensitivity to trauma exposure in a collaborative recovery process.

CONCLUSION

In this chapter, we explored the contextual factors surrounding race, ethnicity, and culture that provide insight into working with trauma survivors from diverse backgrounds. Knowing that the research on minority populations' trauma exposures and treatment outcomes is limited, we reviewed the relevant available empirical base, covering what we do know about risk factors for traumatic exposure among women and the ways that ethnic differences in responses to trauma may have a bearing on treatment engagement, retention, and outcomes. Additional assessments for minority individuals with interpersonal violence may address historical, immigration, and discrimination trauma. We presented these topics in the hope that clinicians delivering addictions treatment and substance abuse treatment programs can use their sensitivity to ethnic and cultural differences to inform decisions concerning treatment planning and program development.

11

MOVING RESEARCH TO PRACTICE: THREE COMMUNITY-BASED EXAMPLES OF CONCURRENT TRAUMA AND SUBSTANCE ABUSE TREATMENT

Recognizing that trauma survivors with co-occurring addictions often face the compartmentalization of treatment, in this chapter we present three diverse examples of program implementation of trauma-specific treatments representing effective ways in which to integrate trauma treatment with other substance abuse and mental health treatment. Throughout the existing psychotherapy research studies for this population, a gap exists between known efficacious treatments that have strong internal validity and the needs of the practice world for interventions that have proven external validity and generalizability. Furthermore, trauma-specific treatments and integrated trauma treatments are diffused and disseminated into the community in sporadic fashion with limited information on how to integrate the interventions into existing program activities.

The strategies behind the success of the dissemination and implementation of treatment for women with histories of trauma and addiction are highlighted in this chapter by presenting three community-based examples: the Substance Abuse and Mental Health Services Administration's Women, Co-Occurring Disorders and Violence Study (WCDVS); the National Institute on Drug Abuse's (NIDA's) Clinical Trials Network (CTN) Women and Trauma Study (WTS); and The Women's Health Project Treatment and Research

199

Center (WHP). These examples illuminate different organizational challenges and considerations for trauma-focused programming while highlighting a variety of program options for adapting treatment models in diverse settings.

CASE EXAMPLE 1: WOMEN, CO-OCCURRING DISORDERS AND VIOLENCE STUDY: A MULTISYSTEMIC FRAMEWORK FOR TRAUMA INTEGRATION

The WCDVS was a national multisite service delivery demonstration project that significantly contributed to the identification of pathways for providing integrative substance use, trauma, and mental health services in diverse community settings. The goal of the project was to develop new approaches to service delivery for this population and to determine their effectiveness (Morrissey, Jackson, et al., 2005). The work completed by the WCDVS supports the use of a comprehensive, trauma-informed, integrated approach to assessing, planning, and implementing services for women with comorbid substance use and mental health disorders.

The WCDVS brought researchers and practitioners together to lay the groundwork for addictions treatment centers to reconceptualize how to help women with trauma and abuse histories and to consider the direct clinical needs of women as well as the broad backdrop of factors relevant to a woman's recovery. The WCDVS was a collaborative investigation implemented at nine intervention sites across the country. Each of the sites had been providing substance abuse and mental health services and several targeted issues related to interpersonal violence (Jahn Moses, Reed, Mazelis, & D'Ambrosio, 2003). Each site selected a local program with comparable services as a control. Women were enrolled in the study if they (a) were 18 years or older, (b) met diagnostic criteria for a *Diagnostic and Statistical Manual of Mental Disorders* (DSM–IV; 4th ed.; American Psychiatric Association, 1994) Axis I or Axis II disorder, (c) met diagnostic criteria for a substance disorder with symptoms in the previous 30 days, (d) had a history of physical or sexual abuse, and (e) had two or more prior service episodes (Cocozza et al., 2005).

The sections that follow summarize elements highlighted by the WCDVS that are important when planning and implementing trauma treatment for women with co-occurring disorders and present 6- and 12-month findings that indicate the promise of integrated trauma treatment.

PREIMPLEMENTATION PLANNING

Successful implementation of new services requires careful planning prior to initiating change. Thinking about how the change will affect multiple levels of the organization—consumer, staffing, and administration—as well as the need to increase or shift resources and review current operating procedures and protocols to ensure adequate procedures are in place is essential. The sections that follow detail preimplementation activities used in the WCDVS.

Client Involvement

One of the defining features of the WCDVS was the involvement of consumers, survivors, and recovering (C/S/R) women in all phases of study planning and implementation (Huntington, Jahn Moses, & Veysey, 2005). The WCDVS included C/S/R women as volunteers and paid staff on the study and members of advisory boards and coordinating committees (including mandatory cochairs on all subcommittees; Giard et al., 2005). These C/S/R women received training on trauma, research, and leadership and were provided resources to support involvement (e.g., stipends, child care, transportation; Huntington et al., 2005). Successful use of client involvement and feedback is best achieved with commitment from all levels of program staff, beginning with management.

A number of positive outcomes can be achieved through consumer involvement. First, clients are seen as the experts on their own lives and needs. Engaging in dialogue with and involving clients ensure that services and procedures are provided while keeping the interest of clients first and foremost in mind. As noted in the WCDVS, working alongside researchers and providers, consumers were able to voice opinions and needs in a way that had traditionally been denied to them by the treatment system as well as by perpetrators of violence (Mockus et al., 2005). Second, the inclusion of clients follows the mandates set forth by empowerment models of treatment, allowing clients to retain a level of control over services they will ultimately be using. Similar to the way that researchers collaborate with providers, providers can collaborate with clients to help preserve treatment relevance, retention, and long-term change goals (for more in-depth and descriptive information on the integration of consumers with the WCDVS, see Mockus et al., 2005).

The WCDVS integrated consumers throughout the decision-making processes of the study, beginning with needs assessment. Assessing current client needs is naturally one of the first steps in determining what changes to make within a program. Although it is tempting to assume what clients need on the basis of past experience or the needs of similar clients, more formal or systematic needs assessments are extremely valuable when determining new treatment approaches or adapting treatments to particular settings. Needs assessment can be conducted by using targeted focus groups within the treatment program or brief in-house surveys or through collaboration with other treatment programs to assess community level needs. Preimplementation assessment can aid in the introduction or adaptation of existing treatments to better fit with specific population needs.

Examining Existing Treatment Models

The WCDVS sites each selected an integrated trauma, addiction, and mental health treatment to address the principle of providing comprehensive services. Four sites selected seeking safety (SS; Najavits, 2002); three sites chose the trauma recovery and empowerment model (Harris & Community Connections Trauma Work Group, 1998); one site chose the addictions and trauma recovery integrated model (D. Miller & Guidry, 2001); and one site developed their own treatment focused on survival, recovery, and empowerment (Clark et al., 2004). As Huntington et al. (2005) noted, there was initial resistance on the part of service providers about delving into trauma-related issues with clients; however, training and ongoing support helped to address some of these initial fears.

Stakeholders, including consumers, can use brainstorming to examine the benefits and challenges of implementing a certain treatment approach. Some questions to consider are as follows: (a) How many sessions are included in the intervention? (b) Will we use all of them? (c) Which topics are most relevant for our clients? (d) What are the staff requirements? (e) How many hours per week can we allocate for additional treatment time? (f) Can we handle the needs for ongoing training and supervision? and (g) How important is it that we adhere specifically to the protocol or do we wish to use the model more flexibly? For example, each WCDVS site made modifications to the preexisting treatment models by altering the number of sessions, group size, group format, order and pacing of sessions, and facilitator characteristics to best fit with their program needs and client populations (Jahn Moses et al., 2003).

Substance abuse treatment programs may find the introduction of trauma-informed services a logical first step instead of specializing in trauma-specific treatments right away. Making adjustments within a program to be more mindful of trauma survivors helps to orient staff to this issue. As the WCDVS findings indicate, specific components of service integration were related to improvement, whereas simply receiving more services were not (Morrissey, Jackson, et al., 2005). In fact, the investigators suggested that the cost of placing greater demands on clients in receiving additional services may counteract the benefits. This finding highlights the need to examine in detail the type and range of program-level additions; more is not necessarily better.

Substance abuse and mental health treatment activities need to reflect an understanding that for survivors, trauma is a central organizing experience, not something to be managed peripherally, and that treatments need to be safe and respectful. Addiction and mental health treatments that can be triggering experiences because of their content, challenging nature, or mixed-gender format may need to be modified to promote security and growth for women who are survivors. Organizations considering the integration of trauma treatment into their programs should review current treatment curricula to make sure that they reflect trauma-informed concepts. Treatment formats and content may need to be modified to complement the introduction of new services. Those who are interested in further assessment of program needs and identifying possible trauma-specific treatments can begin by perusing the trauma and addictions treatment models we describe in Appendix A at the end of this volume.

Organizational Elements

Another main principle laid out in the WCDVS was that organizations and services for women with co-occurring disorders needed to be integrated. Survivors of trauma often experience the compartmentalizing of treatment and rarely receive integrated or even coordinated services. Developed without an understanding and appreciation of the role of trauma in the lives of clients, many existing agencies have failed to provide survivors who come for addictions treatment with an environment that is sensitive to their needs or a program comprehensive enough to treat the range of symptoms they experience—substance use related and otherwise.

The WCDVS implemented integration through a number of mechanisms: (a) developing coordinating committees composed of interested organizations; (b) formalizing cross-agency organization through written roles and responsibilities; (c) conducting cross-training with substance abuse and mental health providers, including trauma-related content; and (d) using case managers to integrate services for women involved in the study (Huntington et al., 2005). On the basis of the WCDVS, Huntington et al. (2005) reported several factors important to the success of integrating services across programs and institutions. First, residential facilities were more likely to integrate components within an agency, whereas outpatient sites needed to integrate across organizations. Given the multiple issues facing this population of women, service integration needed to cross diverse systems, including child protection, criminal justice, public assistance, and health services. Finally, although integration activities were found to be time-consuming and at times difficult, in the end they were valuable and essential to the process of providing superior services.

As previous chapters made clear, trauma treatment should be embedded in larger agency modifications and requires backing from all levels of staff and the willingness to consider comprehensive organizational change. The preparation for providing trauma-informed services encompasses all levels of agency personnel, and when possible, other local agencies and providers in the community, the community itself, and county or state agencies that regulate services and provide funding. Appropriate preparation, planning, and support are required at all of these levels to be successful and improve client care. For example, program directors need to allocate staff time and resources to promote adequate assessment, treatment planning, services, and staff training.

Anticipating and Preparing for Referral Needs

The WCDVS sites found that in providing resource coordination and advocacy services to clients, case managers also needed to be attentive to ways in which trauma affected a woman's use of resources outside of treatment. Survivors needed to be offered skills and support to (a) follow up with medical and dental appointments, often experienced as intrusive and threatening; (b) follow through with safe-sex practices, especially in cases in which negotiating condom use could anger a potentially violent partner; and (c) follow through with referrals for other resources or after-care plans, often with more frequent contact from case managers (Jahn Moses et al., 2003). Organizing a thorough list of appropriate referral sources requires time and planning and should be considered an important preimplementation activity.

Working with clients in preparing for potential emergency situations and planning ahead to ward off crises are useful and empowering activities for clinicians and supervisors (Jahn Moses et al., 2003). Common situations that may arise for clients who are also trauma survivors include alcohol or drug relapse, intensification of psychiatric symptoms, medical emergencies, legal issues, and exacerbation of issues related to an abusive partner or to child protective services. Some sites developed advanced directives for emergency planning, collaborating with clients to identify what they would want to happen in the event of relapse, for example, or a need for psychiatric emergency evaluation (Jahn Moses et al., 2003). According to participants, vital emergency information included "who should be called, where children should go, what other arrangements should be made, and what safety precautions are important" (Jahn Moses et al., 2003, p. 25). When possible, sites implemented or incorporated preventive curricula to avoid particular crises, such as financial difficulties, child custody issues, and ill health. All of these activities can lead to feelings of increased safety and support.

Staffing, Supervision, and Training

Administrative commitment to quality supervision and staffing needs is essential to the incorporation of organizational change. Programs should also consider how both the hiring practices and the philosophy and culture of the program affect staffing. The WCDVS encouraged administrators to consider the inclusion of multidisciplinary staff, particularly those that have an understanding of and a commitment to trauma-informed services within substance abuse treatment settings (Jahn Moses et al., 2003). Diversity in staffing also included cross-agency collaborations that served to increase diversity as well as enabled staff to draw on expertise and resources from the larger community. This high level of commitment on the part of administrators promotes cultural change within the program, highlights the importance of addressing trauma directly, and supports safe environments for staff and consumers.

The WCDVS sites reported that training, education, and supervision were important in providing quality, ongoing, and sustainable trauma services (Jahn Moses et al., 2003). Training occurred repeatedly over the course of implementation and at all staff levels. Not only did this help sustain skills and awareness, but repeated training enhanced retention and dealt with staff turnover, allowing new staff to be brought on board with minimal disruption. It has also been our experience that adequate and consistent supervision of clinicians learning new treatment models or instituting new procedures with clients helps to ensure that clinicians are not overwhelmed, that clients are getting what they need, and that treatments are correctly implemented. Administrative support for "sacred" supervision time and resources to allow reasonable caseloads for clinicians can essentially dictate success or failure of a new treatment endeavor.

Pilot Testing

The WCDVS used a pilot phase to modify interventions, alter organizational procedures, and recognize work and progress along the way (Jahn Moses et al., 2003). Pilot testing interventions prior to full-scale implementation highlights aspects of the intervention that require minor adaptations, gauges staff and consumer response, and can incorporate feedback. Pilot testing also monitors organizational procedures that may need to be tweaked for smoother implementation. Moving progressively from pilot testing to full-scale implementation can empower staff to actively "own" new forms of treatment as well as troubleshoot areas that could clash with existing services or interfere with current systems. Pilot testing new treatments or treatment components also allows supervisors to assess the readiness of clinicians to fully implement the intervention. Additional training may be required, or the supervisor may want to sit in on some of the initial groups as a way of providing extra support and oversight.

IMPLEMENTATION

Successful implementation of new services into community-based organizations requires well-developed monitoring of intervention adherence and consumer outcomes. Also, included within the implementation phase is attention to potential adaptations to the intervention and sustainability efforts. The WCDVS focused heavily on consumer input and empowerment. The sections that follow highlight implementation processes and outcomes from the study.

Assessment

Screening and assessment services varied at the WCDVS sites, but program directors at all sites took the stance that universal screening was necessary; any new client could be a survivor of trauma. Sites supported the need for periodic screenings to give women multiple opportunities to report trauma in their lives and not just during the initial assessment when they may not be prepared to disclose painful, personal life events (Jahn Moses et al., 2003). In some cases, only a careful and sensitive inquiry can identify episodes of victimization; nevertheless, as we discussed in previous chapters, even with these opportunities women may not identify past, or even current, abusive behavior as traumatic. If a woman learned to experience abuse as routine or "something to deal with," or even something she deserved, she may not call her experiences "trauma." The WCDVS sites also confirmed the importance of allowing women to decide the pace of what they had to say and whether to reveal any information (Jahn Moses et al., 2003). This control is reassuring for women for whom many past events have been so disempowering. Specific assessments, such as those documenting general posttraumatic stress disorder (PTSD) symptoms, can be helpful as a clinical monitoring tool as well as a treatment plan outcomes measure.

Client Engagement

Outreach and engagement services should consider how trauma affects the process of engagement, paying attention to how issues of trust make it difficult for individuals with trauma histories to commit to treatment. In the WCDVS, early inquiries about and acknowledgment of histories of abuse helped normalize experiences and demonstrated that this part of their history and symptom picture would be taken seriously and treated sensitively (Jahn Moses et al., 2003). C/S/R women in the WCDVS sometimes served as effective first contacts for women entering treatment.

Client Empowerment

A collaborative clinician–client relationship supports an empowerment model, which the WCDVS integrated throughout the study. An empowerment model is strengths based and responds to the dynamics created and perpetuated by oppression and discrimination (Robbins, Chatterjee, & Canda, 2006). This model works well with previous recommendations, highlighting increased knowledge, self-worth, and competence; validating experiences and choices; minimizing power imbalances; and supporting action and goal setting in collaborative helping relationships. Empowerment models are concerned with enhancing the opportunity for clients to instigate change through increased insight into current and past situations of powerlessness, exploitation, and injustice. In this way, similar to relapse prevention models, empowerment models identify some maladaptive behaviors and symptoms as coping mechanisms for extremely difficult and traumatizing situations. We have discussed the value of reframing these behaviors as adaptive, while acknowledging their negative consequences. This new perspective on client behavior offers staff alternative ways of responding. Within this context, the WCDVS encouraged clients to build resources, social supports, and engagement with others, eventually working toward advocacy for themselves and others.

Many women have found existing addiction settings to be "hierarchical, disempowering, or abusive, with few opportunities for women to play active roles in their own treatment" (Jahn Moses et al., 2003, p. 6). Women who experience treatment as dehumanizing, threatening, or disempowering are unlikely to be motivated to remain in treatment or return once they have left. Often attrition is blamed on substance use relapse or denial when in fact it is linked to the way in which services are offered.

Creating Safety

Researchers and practitioners acknowledge the importance of creating a safe environment in which to receive services (e.g., Herman, 1992b). The WCDVS incorporated this concept throughout. During treatment services, clinicians must understand how group discussions that permit or encourage extensive disclosure may act to trigger symptoms in group members, just as extensive discussions about buying, preparing, and using substances might trigger that behavior in someone recovering from drug or alcohol use disorders. In addition to safety, power imbalances should be minimized within the therapeutic relationship. The clinician–client relationship should be based on mutually agreed-on goals and collaboration, maintaining appropriate boundaries, and respecting choices.

WOMEN, CO-OCCURRING DISORDERS AND VIOLENCE STUDY OUTCOMES

Overall, the WCDVS study group found significant improvements at 6-month follow-up on measures of posttraumatic stress symptoms and drug use severity for women in intervention sites compared with those in comparison sites (Cocozza et al., 2005). There was significant diversity in outcomes across the nine sites, indicating additional mechanisms of action that should be studied. At 12-month follow-up, results indicated significant improvement in mental health and trauma symptoms, with no differences in substance use improvement between intervention and comparison sites (Morrissey, Jackson, et al., 2005). Findings at both time points indicate that integrated counseling—

determined by the number of problem areas (mental health, substance abuse, and trauma) discussed in individual and group counseling at each site—was a predictor of larger effect sizes (Cocozza et al., 2005; Morrissey, Jackson, et al., 2005). These combined findings at 6- and 12-month follow-up from trauma-informed and trauma-specific integrated treatments for women with co-occurring disorders are promising. Given the need for a quasi-experimental design in this community collaborative study, however, other sources of variability between the intervention and comparison conditions and sites cannot be ruled out. The flexibility in preexisting program services, treatment modalities, and residential versus outpatient settings creates additional problems in determining sources of variance.

Morrissey, Jackson, et al. (2005) highlighted an interesting finding from the 12-month follow-up data. Sites that incorporated more core services (e.g., mental health services, trauma-specific services, parenting skills, crisis intervention; see McHugo et al., 2005, for more information) found less improvement in intervention than comparison sites. Morrissey, Jackson, et al. suggested that adding more services may require larger changes in organizational elements, such as service networking and coordination, which could end up taxing sites and clients, reducing effectiveness of services. This is indeed a cautionary finding and suggests that sites start by implementing small, incremental changes and evaluate outcomes before implementing major organizational and service change.

CASE EXAMPLE 2: WOMEN AND TRAUMA STUDY: A COMMUNITY-BASED RESEARCH PARTNERSHIP

Since 2000 the NIDA has funded the CTN, a multisite research network charged with the mandate to develop and implement research protocols in collaboration with community-based treatment programs. This collaboration provided an opportunity to delineate further some of the clinical challenges in implementing trauma treatment in community addiction settings across the United States. The CTN's vision promotes a bidirectional approach and culture, such that researchers and community-based clinicians are considered equal collaborators in the clinical research enterprise. Another important part of the vision of the CTN is addressing the critical need to adopt new and effective treatments, using research as a vehicle for conveying knowledge and promoting dissemination. In the early phases of the CTN, clinicians were clear that trauma was a ubiquitous issue in their substance-abusing female clients and asked that a protocol be developed that addressed the needs of women with trauma and addictions. The CTN WTS began as a result of this collaboration.

The WTS, although similar to the WCDVS in philosophy, differed in several ways. First, the WTS used a hybrid model design (Carroll &

Rounsaville, 2003), combining the scientific rigor of efficacy research with elements of community-effectiveness research. To accomplish this, the WTS used a randomized controlled design but implemented the study at community treatment sites, with community clinicians and supervisors, retaining many real-world intervention features (e.g., rolling group admission). This offered the opportunity to identify causal links between intervention and outcome symptoms. Second, participants in the WTS had co-occurring substance use and PTSDs, whereas WCDVS participants included women with all *DSM–IV–TR* (American Psychiatric Association, 2000) Axis I and Axis II mental health disorders. Thus, the WTS involves a more homogeneous sample and participants, in general, have more severe PTSD profile. For example, the mean baseline posttraumatic stress frequency scores (Foa, Cashman, Jaycox, & Perry, 1997) in the WTS sample was 38.7 compared with 23.7 in the WCDVS, with higher scores indicating more severe PTSD symptoms. The WTS only included outpatient sites with minimal preexisting trauma-specific services. Finally, only one site of the seven was a female-specific treatment program.

The WTS operated within a top-down model; sites were selected into the CTN on the basis of their ability to recruit large and diverse samples of substance users and their willingness to participate in a variety of randomized controlled treatment trials. Researchers approached administrators to collaborate in the study, and program management selected staff to participate on the basis of skill level and potential for ongoing involvement. The buy-in from all levels of the organization, however, helped to facilitate successful project outcomes. Although sites were not able to select trauma-specific treatments individually, as in the WCDVS, other aspects of preimplementation planning were essential in the context of this research. For example, programs needed to ensure that staffing and space were adequate, referral networks needed to be updated, extensive training was provided, and additional supervision was provided. A unique aspect of research is that funding is provided for the specific elements of study, which is rarely the case for community-based treatment providers. The provision of these additional resources eliminated one major hurdle for these community-based treatment programs.

Study Structure

The WTS compared an abbreviated SS (Najavits, 2002) treatment conducted in group modality with an active control women's health education group treatment (WHE; Tross, 1998) that did not address either trauma or addiction. Treatment was conducted in seven community-based substance abuse treatment programs across the United States. Eligible and interested women were randomized to SS or WHE in addition to receiving their usual treatment services at each program. In all, the study enrolled 353 women who met current *DSM–IV–TR* criteria for PTSD—either full or subthreshold[1]—based on a targeted traumatic event. Trained clinicians from each program site conducted the group treatments twice weekly over a 6-week period (i.e., 12 sessions total for both treatments). Participants completed assessments after completing the treatment and up to 1 year later. The study examined the following primary outcome variables: substance use abstinence and PTSD symptom severity. Other outcome variables included treatment retention, other psychiatric symptom severity, and HIV-risk sexual behaviors.

Preexisting Trauma Services

As mentioned briefly earlier, there were differences across programs as to the level of awareness and services in place to support women with co-occurring addiction and PTSD. Some clinicians were aware of and trained in trauma-specific services, whereas others had spent little time training in or thinking about how integrated trauma and drug treatment services might be implemented.

Broadening Eligibility Criteria

The WTS used *DSM–IV–TR* diagnostic criteria to categorize study participants, but the inclusion criteria were broadened to allow for maximum participation by program participants. The number and type of substances used or abused were not limited; neither were other existing psychopathologies (other than psychotic disorders). Participants were free to take medications of any kind while participating in the clinical trial. Finally, the diagnostic criteria were expanded to include subthreshold PTSD because many women who do not meet full criteria for the disorder often have functional impairment that is clinically indistinguishable from individuals meeting full-PTSD criteria. As we discussed in chapter 1, the posttraumatic presentation of many women is often accounted for by complex PTSD, a broader constellation of symptoms that is diagnostically often a subthreshold PTSD accompanied by other stress response symptoms. Such flexibility is uncommon in traditional randomized controlled trials but essential when working in collaboration with community-based providers and clients. In addition, allowing participants to attend addiction and trauma-specific or informed-behavioral treatments with multiple diagnoses lends far more potential for generalizability and real-world applicability to study conclusions (Hufford, 2000).

---

[1]Subthreshold posttraumatic stress disorder (PTSD) is defined as fulfilling a subset of the *DSM–IV–TR* (American Psychiatric Association, 2000) criteria for PTSD. Specifically, patients must meet criteria A, B, (either C or D), E, and F.

Program Philosophies

Sites had different philosophies of how individuals cope with addiction issues, from abstinence only to a harm reduction philosophy (the features of which we presented in chap. 2). In general, programs with a rigid abstinence-only focus can have difficulty fitting the more flexible harm reduction trauma services into their curriculum, whereas programs with a holistic approach to treatment for substance abuse issues can more seamlessly integrate trauma services into their curriculum. For example, we have discussed how individuals often develop maladaptive coping mechanisms to manage distressing psychological symptoms related to trauma histories. Given some of these coping methods, moving directly to an abstinence-based program may be difficult for a client. Allowing clients' flexibility in their process of disclosure, coping, and recovery is a key element in combining addiction and trauma practice.

Resources

Some sites, all outpatient substance abuse treatment programs, were not equipped as well as others to handle an influx of women with more severe clinical profiles, a common finding in this population. Many challenges arose at these sites as staff had to quickly adjust to working with a new client population that had different needs and concerns. One challenge included drug treatment compliance and retention. Some women could not cope with the intensive nature of beginning drug treatment and were difficult to engage. Other women exhibited more severe parasuicidal behaviors and emotions, which was different from the way most other clients presented for treatment. In addition, some of these women were in the beginning stages of change in terms of their substance use, and some were not ready to make any changes despite wanting to find relief from trauma symptoms. As a result, staff had to contend with integrating clients who were not primarily focused on substance abuse treatment goals into their existing culture, which was geared toward outpatient clients seeking abstinence from substances. This challenged providers and programs to accommodate diverse levels of readiness and motivation to change.

Therapist Experience

Substance abuse treatment programs usually employ staff with diverse backgrounds, educational levels, and experience. Staff diversity can make trainings more interesting but also raises challenges. In the WTS, 5% of the therapists had less than a bachelor's degree, 40% had a bachelor's degree, and 56% had a master's degree or higher. This educational background may or may not be representative of clinicians in other substance abuse treatment programs. Therapists and supervisors were selected to participate in the study on the basis of interest and probable skill level. Ability to conduct manualized treatment protocols was also assessed before training through a recorded individual session using structured relapse-prevention material, and therapist and supervisors were randomized to the treatment condition they would be trained in and would practice throughout the study. Using treatment manuals in intervention training is a common way to convey information to clinical staff and is usually enhanced through ongoing supervision and a practice certification process. Clinicians with less experience or more limited clinical skills may need additional support and training to conduct trauma-specific treatment.

Training and Supervision

The training and supervision available to and required of this study was extensive and at an increased level from what therapists and supervisors typically received in their programs. This is an important consideration for implementing any new behavioral intervention but especially in subpopulations of women with multiple co-occurring disorders.

The therapists and supervisors completed the following phases of training: (a) pretraining practice and screening, (b) didactic review of manualized intervention, (c) observation and practice with trainer-conducted mock intervention sessions, (d) trainee-conducted mock intervention sessions, and (e) completion of a training case. The training case entailed conducting a minimum of four group sessions with at least three group members. A trainer rated the sessions for adherence to the intervention manual. During the study, therapists received weekly individual supervision that included review and discussion of randomly selected, videotaped sessions. Similar to the training process, supervisors rated the sessions for adherence prior to the individual meeting with the therapist. If a session fell below the designated adherence cut-off, then additional supervision was provided, including an increase in the number of sessions reviewed. If the therapist fell below the adherence criterion for seven consecutive sessions, the supervisor joined the group as the primary therapist for six sessions. After six sessions, the therapist, with the supervisor still present, resumed the primary therapist role in the group. Supervisors also received ongoing consultation with the intervention experts on a weekly basis during the study. This was an opportunity to review difficult supervisory situations and common problems in delivering the intervention.

Manualized Treatments

Similar to other aspects of research, manualized interventions receive positive and negative feedback. Some therapists were apprehensive about using a manualized treatment. Generally, once clinicians were trained adequately in the intervention, they could integrate the material into their practice and could use the manuals comfortably rather than rigidly as a word-for-word lesson to be delivered. The manuals provided a useful tool to handle issues that therapists were not accustomed to dealing with, such as PTSD symptoms. Therapists participating in the study reported that they were happy to receive a new perspective on manualized treatment. Their main source of less positive feedback concerned research elements of the study and, in some cases, not being able to deviate from the protocol when challenges arose. Research protocols required therapists to approach clients in a way that was different from what they were accustomed to. Nevertheless, each protocol provided significant flexibility to address urgent clinical needs in an appropriate way and in the client's best interest.

The CTN WTS research protocol provided community-based programs with an interest in addressing trauma with the specialized training and ongoing supervision to begin to conduct these services within their organizations. A train-the-trainer model ensured that therapists and supervisors on site learned the treatment approaches and, once the study was completed, were positioned to (a) adopt the intervention within their organization through ongoing practice and training and (b) provide resources in expertise and training on new treatment models for addressing trauma and substance abuse treatment for other local agencies. In all participating programs, plans for integrating both interventions into standard treatment services are under way. One of our community treatment sites, Residence XII in Kirkland, Washington, won the James W. West, M.D. Quality Improvement Award from the National Association of Addiction Treatment Providers. The award was presented in recognition of Residence XII's work adapting SS into their treatment curriculum following participation in the WTS. This highlights how research can be integrated into treatment programs, and with planning, support, and staff dedication translated into long-term program enhancement.

Adaptation—Research and Program

Several modifications to the study treatment and research design were implemented on the basis of feedback from the treatment programs. First, the interventions were made shorter (12 twice-weekly sessions) to better fit with the service delivery systems within the programs. In the programs' experience, 24 sessions (standard SS length) was greater than the typical number of sessions that would be provided in a specialized group in a drug treatment program. The interventions were provided in group format and operated on rolling admission rather than as closed groups. These two alterations allowed the programs to serve more clients and kept individuals from waiting for a new group to start. Several research requirements ultimately slowed the groups down, including needing a minimum of three women enrolled and at least two participants present to run a given session.

Although all sites recognized the need for and importance of trauma services for women in substance abuse treatment, most participating sites did not offer trauma services prior to the study. As mentioned previously, sites found they had more women with identified trauma histories than either was typical or they had been aware of. These new clients, who were then enrolled in "treatment as usual" at the program, could be quite challenging for other staff members who did not have trauma training. This change in patient composition underscores the benefit of providing all staff with an introduction to trauma and training on how clients with trauma histories may present to treatment as well as information on their specialized needs.

Sustaining Program Change

Following completion of the study, each site made its own decision about how to incorporate the two interventions using a number of different criteria: (a) study outcomes (i.e., Which interventions worked best and for whom?), (b) ability to train other clinicians at the site (i.e., Who would train, and what additional skills would be needed for training?), (c) acceptability of the intervention for clients (i.e., Was there enough client interest and motivation?), (d) programs resources (i.e., Without outside research money, could the program sustain the extra training and added services?), and (e) time and motivation of study staff (i.e., Did staff see the importance of adding trauma services?).

One of the CTN's aims is to promote and develop the capacity for the sites to sustain programmatic changes. Notably, the programs that participated in the CTN WTS were eager to integrate both interventions into their repertoire of services. Specific challenges for sites on completion of the study include maintaining appropriate levels of supervision, continuing to assess for adherence to the manualized treatments, and providing training on trauma to incoming administrative, support, and clinical staff.

WOMEN AND TRAUMA STUDY OUTCOMES

The WTS was the largest randomized clinical trial of a trauma-specific behavioral therapy in the field, comparing the effects of SS with an attention control group, WHE, among women enrolled in one of seven community-based substance abuse treatment programs across the United States. Both treatments (i.e., SS and WHE) were associated with large and clinically significant reductions in PTSD symptoms, which occurred rapidly during the acute intervention phase and were sustained through the 12-month follow-up. Differences in PTSD outcomes between the treatments were small but with interactive and trend effects favoring SS, particularly in the subsample of participants who had attended at least 6 of the 12 treatment sessions. There were no overall effects of time (across follow-up assessment points) or of treatment group on substance use outcome, but lower PTSD scores during follow-up were associated with lower levels of substance use. One possibility for the lack of differences between the two groups was assessment prior to treatment, which included assessment for PTSD diagnosis and trauma-related symptoms. All of the participating women knew that they were with other women with similar experiences, which may be an active ingredient for creating safety and acknowledging the impact of traumatic events.

Important lessons for community-based treatment programs can be gleaned from these findings. First, in light of the positive findings from both SS and WHE, most participating sites integrated the treatments into ongoing program curricula. At least one half of the sites also offered training to other local area programs on both interventions, thus enhancing community dissemination and implementation efforts. Second, when provided with appropriate levels of training and supervision, community clinicians can adequately learn and provide integrated trauma and substance abuse treatment. On the basis of data from the Seeking Safety Adherence Scale (Najavits & Liese, 2000) that supervisors completed to determine the level of therapist fidelity to the intervention, the mean adherence score for SS was 2.1, representing an acceptable level of adherence (on a 4-point scale). For WHE, the mean adherence score was 4.02, which corresponds to a rating of *good* on the adherence scale, with the majority of all items rated 4.0 or above (on a 5-point scale). Finally, and in line with findings from the WCDVS, integrated treatment for this population can be delivered safely and without increases in substance use. During active study treatment in the WTS, 49 women reported 83 new study-related adverse events,[2] although only one of these adverse events was evaluated as being severe. The percentage of women experiencing study-related adverse events was not statistically different between the two treatment groups (20% for SS vs. 14% for WHE).

CASE EXAMPLE 3: WOMEN'S HEALTH PROJECT: A SPECIALTY TRAUMA AND ADDICTIONS OUTPATIENT PROGRAM IN A HOSPITAL-BASED DEPARTMENT OF PSYCHIATRY

The WHP (http://www.whpnyc.org), part of the Addiction Institute of New York (AI; http://www.addictioninstituteny.org) at St. Luke's–Roosevelt Hospital Center, was founded and developed by us, the authors of this volume, specifically to meet the needs of women survivors of trauma with addictive disorders. The WHP arose out of our research and clinical practice experience indicating that co-occurring disorders, especially PTSD and sub-

---

[2]*Adverse event* is defined as a worsening of symptoms or behaviors that may or may not be related to study participation.

stance abuse disorders, were quite prevalent in the urban population of women, were difficult to address independently, and that there was no treatment service that could address the needs of these women in a comprehensive way. The program had a clear integrative perspective from its inception and was thus specifically designed to address simultaneously the needs of women in recovery from trauma and addiction. The WHP represents a real-world example of the way that a trauma-specific program simultaneously addresses addiction issues, in this case operating successfully in the context of a hospital-based outpatient psychiatry department.

In the late 1990s, several of us (Hien, Litt, and Miele) were conducting a research project focused on women with comorbid substance use disorders and PTSD (Hien, Zimberg, Weissman, First, & Ackerman, 1997). In the course of recruiting for the study, it became clear that many women who did not meet strict eligibility criteria nonetheless had histories of trauma and addiction and could benefit from integrated treatment; however, no appropriate referrals existed. There was clearly a need for expanded services for women with trauma and substance abuse histories, and St. Luke's–Roosevelt Hospital Center in New York City supported a request to start a clinical program for women with these co-occurring conditions within the Department of Psychiatry in 2000. In instituting this unique and essential service, the WHP had the opportunity to respond to consumer need and clinician motivation as an outgrowth of empirically supported treatment development.

Because this was a new program, many of the challenges of introducing trauma services to a preexisting substance abuse program were minimized, including changing the culture and philosophy of staff and administrators; however, the program still needed to gain traction within other existing addiction and mental health programs in the hospital center. WHP staff needed to select appropriate interventions and grapple with the issues presented by the consumer population without the benefit of guidance from programs doing similar work. In this way, the WHP has been a work in progress.

Programmatic Structure

In an effort to efficiently provide effective treatment that is accessible to both mental health and substance abuse treatment programs within an urban hospital center, the WHP has been structured as an outpatient mental health program. Women are referred to the WHP through the Department of Psychiatry outpatient psychotherapy and evaluation programs and through the addictions treatment and evaluation programs. In this way, women survivors of trauma may be identified and referred through both channels. H. Westley Clark and the Center for Substance Abuse Treatment (CSAT) promoted the No Wrong Door Policy (CSAT, 2005), in which clients can be assured that they will get the appropriate care for their addiction and trauma issues regardless of where they present for treatment. The WHP has sought to meet this need while also providing flexibility in treatment to accommodate women at different stages of their recovery from both trauma and substance use. By operating as a mental health program, medical reimbursement policies also allow WHP clients to receive collateral substance abuse treatment (such as an intensive outpatient treatment) should this be required as part of their treatment plan.

The WHP is informed by a stage model of recovery. A significant component of the program is group psychotherapy oriented toward women in the early stages of addressing the impact of the trauma in their lives, which is how most women present to treatment. Even women who have been in other psychotherapies and addiction treatments throughout their lives have often not had their trauma histories addressed. The WHP works from the model that the first stage of working with trauma often requires a period of stabilization and establishing safety, as we discussed in previous chapters. As much as possible, women are encouraged to join a group with other survivors to work on these issues.

Many women are hesitant about the group aspect of treatment. Given feelings of mistrust common to survivors, especially regarding something as sensitive and difficult as their recovery, clients often express reluctance to enter into groups. As we mentioned in chapter 9, common refrains include "I don't want anyone to know my business" and "I can't listen to other people talk about what happened to them. I have enough of my own problems." Part of an extended initial assessment process is geared toward answering women's questions about our treatment recommendations, addressing motivation to enter treatment, and providing support for trying group psychotherapy. Despite their initial hesitation, many women are surprised by the power of finding women with experiences like their own and with whom they can share the struggles they have often kept secret. Many WHP clients form close and valuable relationships with other group members that extend beyond the treatment. As much as possible, women are also given the opportunity to work in individual psychotherapy, and most clients also take advantage of the chance for pharmacotherapy and case management assistance.

Other programmatic challenges relate to ways in which the WHP has assumed certain milieu characteristics, even though it is only an outpatient setting. The milieu model in traditional psychiatry assumes the treatment community is an integral part of treatment, and the interactions between clients in the community are both a source of support and a therapeutic opportunity to learn more about oneself. Because many women attend multiple treatment modalities at the WHP over the course of the week, they are likely to know or know about many women in the program, not just the few women in a given group. In this way, events that occur in one group sometimes have a ricochet effect in other groups in the program. These events have the potential to affect the program as a whole in ways usually associated with more intensive settings in which clients see each other daily, and the WHP has had to be very attentive to these consequences to maintain the safety of the program.

Because women are presenting to treatment from different clinical venues, the WHP also strives to be attentive to the needs inherent in different stages of recovery from substances. Although all of the women who attend the WHP are survivors of trauma, they present a wide range of recovery from addiction, ranging from long-term recovery to early recovery or, from a stage of change perspective, may be active users in precontemplation or contemplation. In addition, there are women in the program who are there to work primarily on recovery from trauma and have never been involved in substance use. Part of the WHP juggling act involves finding ways to work with each woman at her particular point of recovery while not jeopardizing the recovery of others. For example, clients who are abstinent and whose recovery may be tenuous are not grouped with clients who may still be using and contemplating the next steps in their recovery.

Using and Adapting Manualized Treatments

The empirically supported treatments described throughout this book have mainly been tested in research applications, although many are starting to become more widely disseminated and implemented in community treatment programs, particularly through the help of the large-scale studies previously described. When using these protocols, often with accompanying manuals and workbooks, in standard clinical practice, modifications are often necessary to make them applicable in clinical settings. As touched on in describing the WCDVS, if staff and administration are not sure about the effects that an intervention would have in their program, there is always the possibility of pilot testing the intervention before decisions are made. An individual who is most familiar with an intervention can run a few groups or try a few sessions and then, on the basis of that experience, make recommendations to the implementation team. If pilot testing is done in a group, it is useful to have co-leaders who can debrief others after the group about their experiences and observations and bring that information back for consideration by involved staff. Also highlighted in the experiences of the WCDVS, consumer input is an essential component in programmatic decision making. Hearing from an affected woman about her treatment needs can be very poignant and informative for staff trying to make programmatic decisions in the best interest of the agency and its clients.

WHP groups are generally structured using empirically supported material, such as SS (Najavits, 2002), and operate as open groups with rolling admissions to allow clients to join at any time. Furthermore, women are often encouraged to join additional groups that provide coping skills specific to particular problem areas, such as anger management, stress management, parenting, or dialectical behavior therapy skills groups (Linehan, 1993a). Each of these groups aims to contextualize the need for skills development according to the client's traumatic past and associated deficits in affect regulation, self-care, and caretaking. As clients proceed through the program, they also have the opportunity to participate in groups that are more "advanced stage" in orientation; these groups are less structured and might more directly address traumatic experience either verbally or through the creative arts. Because of their occasional explicit content, these groups have the potential to trigger women and are often not appropriate until the later stages of treatment.

Working Within a Larger Organizational Context

Being located within a large hospital system provides a number of advantages for the WHP. With a rich network of behavioral health, addiction, and medical services, the WHP can be a resource to as well as benefit from other hospital services. Particularly as a behavioral health program, the WHP has an advantage in providing supplementary trauma and addiction services to women who are in addiction programs elsewhere in the hospital center. The WHP is affiliated with AI, formerly the Smithers Alcoholism Treatment and Training Center, a well-known, established full-service addictions treatment center. Women who are in more intensive AI treatment programs, for example, including outpatient rehabilitation programs or methadone maintenance programs or intensive outpatient treatment, may also attend the WHP. This is particularly useful in providing a continuum of care because WHP women may require an episode of more intensive addictions treatment or as AI women are ready to step down into a less intensive program and to continue to address their trauma histories.

Similar opportunities exist within behavioral health for women whose need for a continuum of care may be for more intensive psychiatric inpatient or intensive outpatient treatment. As we discussed in chapter 4, the inability to modulate intense affect is a hallmark experience of many survivors of trauma. When this dysregulation leads to episodes of suicidal or parasuicidal self-injurious behavior, clients are often better served by more intensive dialectical behavior therapy treatment or a short inpatient stay before coming to or continuing at the WHP. As we have pointed out throughout this book, recovery from trauma and addiction is rarely a linear and clear-cut process, and being able to connect with additional or alternative treatments throughout a client's recovery is beneficial in meeting her changing needs.

The spectrum of services available at St. Luke's–Roosevelt Hospital Center has made it possible to define the niche population we serve. More intensive services elsewhere in the hospital enable us to focus on outpatient care, seeing clients anywhere from once per week to three or four times per week depending on their needs. Clients with more intensive addiction or psychiatric needs may need to be referred elsewhere, or as noted, seen adjunctively for substance abuse treatment while continuing at the WHP. Clients with more severe psychotic profiles are also referred to programs within the hospital that are geared toward populations with serious and persistent mental illness.

Medical issues are also a major concern for women within trauma and addiction services. The proximity and connection to medical services at the hospital center also enables the WHP to offer a more holistic approach to women receiving services. We can facilitate medical referrals and encourage compliance for preventive care as well as urgent care visits. WHP clients routinely need follow-up for medical issues related to hypertension, obesity, diabetes, gastroenterological distress, gynecological-related problems, HIV, and asthma among other issues. Affiliation with AI, whose nursing and medical staff are able to provide routine medical care for its clients, has also been helpful in encouraging clients to seek out care, who otherwise would not. The more personalized attention women receive in this smaller, more intimate setting, which also accommodates substance dependent behavior, is less daunting than larger medical clinics and can help smooth the way for participation in other programs.

Training and Education

Multidisciplinary training has been an integral part of the development of the WHP since its inception. The integrative nature of the WHP created a unique training opportunity in trauma psychiatry and addiction medicine and, as such, the WHP has become the primary training program within the New York City area for clinicians focusing on individuals with co-occurring trauma and addiction disorders. Predoctoral clinical psychology externs, social work interns, postdoctoral psychology fellows, and psychiatry residents (i.e., PGY-3s) participate in year-long training rotations, learning and implementing trauma-specific treatments. The WHP has long been dedicated to training both clinicians and researchers. In addition to clinical training, many psychology doctoral candidates have participated in WHP research, and some are continuing their professional research development by furthering WHP research initiatives.

Supervision

We have discussed the importance of supervision for staff when working with trauma survivors. Although time is at a premium in our program, like many others, the professional staff has the opportunity to meet regularly as a group with a supervisor to discuss group and individual cases, general systems issues at the program, and issues related to supervision of trainees. These meetings enable staff to receive both supervisor and peer feedback. Clinical staff come to the WHP with experience in both addiction and trauma treatment but continue to fine tune their skills in supervision and to use supervision to help process the strong emotions elicited by their work with clients. We also attempt to provide clinical staff with a balanced caseload and the opportunity to have some control over their case assignments. The more challenging cases typically go to members of the permanent staff rather than training staff, but the program makes an effort to see that a given clinician is not overloaded with too many high intensity cases. Occasionally this will also affect our intake process if we feel that we cannot take on a client whose clinical needs may stretch our clinicians too far. Administrative and case management staff is also provided with supervision to help them better accommodate clients and be prepared for potentially difficult interactions. The training programs offer individual and group supervision opportunities for all aspects of trainee–client involvement.

Growth

The WHP continues to provide an important niche program that has grown slowly but steadily since its inception. Continuing to engage women in treatment is an ongoing challenge because this population, with the double obstacles of a traumatic past and recovery from substances, is notorious for having trouble attending treatment regularly. Tremendous outreach efforts are required to structure clients' participation, and treatment contracts are used when necessary. Balancing the desire to keep clients who attend sporadically enrolled in treatment with the need to administratively fulfill clinical hours is an ongoing challenge. Part of providing compassionate care is understanding the myriad concrete issues that interfere with clients' attendance and working with clients to address them but recognizing when clients may just not be able to attend treatment. Many of these cases are labor intensive as a result of the need to help clients with entitlements and other case management needs and to help clients navigate crises that arise between sessions. Providing these services is sometimes difficult in a health care climate in which clinicians have less and less time to devote to individual clients. However, these types of ancillary services are essential when working with survivors of trauma.

In summary, the WHP presents an example of an outpatient program that was established within a larger organization in response to a service need. The WHP developed out of an integrated trauma and addiction perspective. Because it is in a psychiatry department in a major hospital center, adjunctive treatments, including higher levels of substance abuse care, medical treatments, and other psychiatric services are available to program participants. The treatment and staffing challenges facing stand-alone treatment programs without a hospital setting infrastructure may be different from a program like that of the WHP.

CONCLUSION

In this final chapter of the volume, multisystemic examples of integrated trauma and addictions programs were presented for recommended organizational and service-level changes in the planning and implementation of trauma treatment into substance abuse treatment programs. Many elements of implementation were similar across settings, with each prioritizing and focusing on components particularly relevant for their client population and purpose. These examples from different settings were derived from the rich experience of the WCDVS as well as our, the volume editors', combined years of clinical and research experience. Even with structural and contextual differences, the case examples highlight the groundswell of interest and enthusiasm from the treatment community in providing services for this population as well as underscoring the population's dramatic need for and positive reception of these treatment approaches.

APPENDIX A: TREATMENTS FOR POSTTRAUMATIC STRESS DISORDER AND SUBSTANCE USE DISORDERS

The sections that follow describe treatment models specifically designed to address both trauma-related symptoms and substance abuse, as well as older models that traditionally have been used with this population. We have chosen to include models that have some evidence base or empirical support. There are numerous additional models that address trauma-related symptoms, but are not included here.

ADDICTIONS AND TRAUMA RECOVERY INTEGRATED MODEL (ATRIUM)

The addictions and trauma recovery integrated model is a 12-session manualized treatment focusing on the effects of trauma on the mind, body, and spirit. The assessment and intervention was developed to educate women on how symptoms of trauma relate to mental health conditions, bodily stress, and spiritual well-being, through didactic and experiential skills training, processing, and outside group homework.

Relevant Reading

Miller, D. (2002). Addictions and trauma recovery: An integrated approach. *Psychiatric Quarterly, 73*, 157–170.

Miller, D., & Guidry, L. (2001). *Addictions and trauma recovery: Healing the body, mind, and spirit*. New York: Norton.

Web site: http://www.dustymiller.org

ANGER MANAGEMENT FOR SUBSTANCE ABUSE AND MENTAL HEALTH CLIENTS

Given the connection between anger management, substance abuse, and trauma, anger management for substance abuse and mental health clients treatment is designed to work with clients in a variety of clinical settings to specifically address these co-occurring disorders. The treatment consists of 12 weekly 90-minute group sessions focusing on cognitive–behavioral interventions, relaxation techniques, and communication skills. There is also an accompanying participant workbook. Both the therapist and participant workbooks are available online.

Relevant Reading

Reilly, P. M., & Shopshire, M. S. (2002). *Anger Management for Substance Abuse and Mental Health Clients: A cognitive behavioral therapy manual* (DHHS Pub. No. SMA 02-3661). Rockville, MD: Centers for Substance Abuse Treatment, Substance Abuse and Mental Health Services Administration.

Therapist Manual: http://kap.samhsa.gov/products/manuals/pdfs/anger1.pdf

Participant Workbook: http://kap.samhsa.gov/products/manuals/pdfs/anger2.pdf

CONCURRENT TREATMENT OF POSTTRAUMATIC STRESS DISORDER AND COCAINE DEPENDENCE

Concurrent treatment of posttraumatic stress disorder (PTSD) and cocaine dependence is a phase-based application of exposure therapy for the treatment of cocaine-dependent individuals with PTSD. The treatment protocol combined Foa and Rothbaum's (1998) empirically supported exposure therapy techniques for PTSD (in vivo and imaginal) with empirically supported cognitive–behavioral therapy techniques for substance dependence. The treatment protocol includes 16 individual 90-minute psychotherapy sessions, 6 to 9 of which included imaginal exposure.

Relevant Reading

Back, S. E., Dansky, B. S., Carroll, K. M., Foa, E. B., & Brady, K. T. (2001). Exposure therapy in the treatment of PTSD among cocaine-dependent individuals: Description of procedures. *Journal of Substance Abuse Treatment, 21*, 35–45.

Brady, K. T., Dansky, B. S., Back, S. E., Foa, E. B., & Carroll, K. M. (2001). Exposure therapy in the treatment of PTSD among cocaine-dependent individuals: Preliminary findings. *Journal of Substance Abuse Treatment, 21*, 47–54.

Foa, E. B., & Rothbaum, B. O. (1998). *Treating the trauma of rape*. New York: Guilford Press.

DIALECTICAL BEHAVIORAL THERAPY (DBT)

Dialectical behavioral therapy (DBT) was initially developed for work with individuals living with borderline personality disorder. Treatment involves 24 sessions addressing distress tolerance, affect regulation, interpersonal effectiveness, and mindfulness.

Relevant Reading

Koons, C. R., Robins, C. J., Tweed, J. L., Lynch, T. R., Gonzalez, A. M., Morse, J. Q., et al. (2001). Efficacy of dialectical behavior therapy in women veterans with borderline personality disorder. *Behavior Therapy, 32,* 371–390.

Linehan, M. M. (1993). *Cognitive behavioral treatment of borderline personality disorder.* New York: Guilford Press.

Linehan, M. M., Tutek, D., Heard, H., & Armstrong, H. (1994). Interpersonal outcomes of cognitive behavioral treatment for chronically suicidal borderline patients. *American Journal of Psychiatry, 151,* 1771–1776.

Web site: http://www.behavioraltech.com

EYE MOVEMENT DESENSITIZATION AND REPROCESSING (EMDR)

Eye movement desensitization and reprocessing (EMDR) is a trauma processing therapy that seeks to decrease distress associated with dysfunctionally stored traumatic memories. A disturbing memory is paired with bilateral stimulation, such as eye movements, hand taps, or sounds. The individual is instructed to think of the disturbing event and the feelings and thoughts that accompany it. The therapist leads the client through the bilateral stimulation, then has the client rate her level of distress associated with the memory and the degree to which she believes a positive cognition associated with the memory. This process continues until the level of distress decreases. EMDR is an integrative treatment that combines elements of cognitive–behavioral, experiential, psychodynamic, physiological, and interpersonal therapies.

Relevant Reading

Foa, E. B., & Meadows, E. A. (1997). Psychosocial treatment for posttraumatic stress disorder: A critical review. *Annual Review of Psychology, 48,* 449–480.

Shapiro, F. (1995). *Eye movement desensitization and reprocessing: Basic principles, protocols, and procedures.* New York: Guilford Press.

Web sites: http://www.emdr.com; http://www.emdria.org

PROLONGED EXPOSURE

Prolonged exposure consists of 10 weekly or twice weekly treatment sessions that are 90 to 120 minutes each. The main two procedures of this treatment designed to reduce PTSD symptoms are prolonged imaginal exposure and in vivo exposure. The goal of imaginal exposure (which usually lasts 30–60 minutes) is to help the client increase her ability to process the traumatic memory by having her relive the memory repeatedly during the sessions. The goal of in vivo exposure is to reduce fears and avoidance that develop after traumatic experiences by having the client approach specific situations she has been avoiding because they remind her of the trauma.

Relevant Reading

Foa, E. B., & Rothbaum, B. O. (1998). *Treating the trauma of rape*. New York: Guilford Press.

RISKING CONNECTION

Risking Connection is a training curriculum for treatment providers who deliver services to populations with trauma histories, especially child abuse survivors. It focuses on teaching clinicians how to deliver treatments in a trauma-informed manner, with emphasis on relationships, empowerment, and transformation. It also addresses vicarious traumatization, dissociation, and suicidal gesturing and ideation.

Relevant Reading

Saakvitne, K. W., Gamble, S., Pearlman, L. A., & Tabor Lev, B. (2000). *Risking Connection: A training curriculum for working with survivors of childhood abuse*. Lutherville, MD: Sidran Press.

Saakvitne, K. W., Pearlman, L. A., & the Staff of Traumatic Stress Institute. (1996). *Transforming the pain: A workbook on vicarious traumatization for helping professionals who work with traumatized clients*. New York: Norton.

Web site: http://www.riskingconnection.com

SEEKING SAFETY

Seeking safety is a 25-session treatment for individuals with substance use disorders and PTSD that focuses on the cognitive, behavioral, and interpersonal aspects of treating both disorders. With an emphasis on safety and coping skills, the seeking safety model provides an integrated treatment that simultaneously addresses the symptoms of PTSD and substance use. It was designed for group or individual format, females and males, all settings, all clinicians, and all trauma and substance types.

Relevant Reading

Najavits, L. (2002). *Seeking safety*. New York: Guilford Press.

Najavits, L. M. (2007). Seeking safety: An evidence-based model for substance abuse and trauma/PTSD. In K. A. Witkiewitz & G. A. Marlatt (Eds.), *Therapist's guide to evidence-based relapse prevention: Practical resources for the mental health professional* (pp. 141–167). San Diego, CA: Elsevier.

Web site: http://www.seekingsafety.org

SKILLS TRAINING IN AFFECTIVE AND INTERPERSONAL REGULATION (STAIR)

Skills training in affective and interpersonal regulation is the first module of a 16-session phase-based treatment focusing on three core disturbances associated with childhood abuse: (a) problems in emotion management, (b) interpersonal functioning, and (c) PTSD symptoms. During the second phase of this treatment, prolonged exposure therapy techniques are used to process traumatic experiences related to PTSD symptoms.

Relevant Reading

Cloitre, M., Cohen, L. R., & Koenen, K. C. (2006). *Treating survivors of childhood abuse: Psychotherapy for the interrupted life*. New York: Guilford Press.

Cloitre, M., Koenen, K., Cohen, L., & Han, H. (2002). Skills training in affective and interpersonal regulation followed by exposure. *Journal of Consulting and Clinical Psychology, 70*, 1067–1074.

STRESS INOCULATION TRAINING

Stress inoculation training (SIT) focuses on both cognitive and affective coping to aid individuals after a traumatic experience as well as boost their ability to deal with future stressors (i.e., inoculate). SIT consists of three phases: (a) the conceptualization phase, which focuses on breaking stressors into smaller problems with short-term coping goals; (b) the skills acquisition and rehearsal phase, which incorporates skill training and practice in vivo; and (c) the application and follow through phase, which makes use of increasing levels of stressful situations, relapse prevention techniques, peer support, and possible booster sessions (Meichenbaum, 1996). SIT utilizes variable treatment lengths depending on the specific needs of the client and her distress level.

Relevant Reading

Foa, E. B., Rothbaum, B. O., & Riggs, D. (1991). Treatment of post-traumatic stress disorder in rape victims: A comparison between cognitive behavioral procedures and counseling. *Journal of Consulting and Clinical Psychology, 59*, 715–723.

Meichenbaum, D. (1985). *Stress inoculation training.* New York: Pergamon Press.

Meichenbaum, D. (1996). Stress inoculation training for coping with stressors. *The Clinical Psychologist, 49*, 4–7.

ASSISTED RECOVERY FROM TRAUMA AND SUBSTANCES (ARTS)

Assisted recovery from trauma and substances was developed from an earlier version of the intervention, substance dependence–posttraumatic stress disorder therapy. It is a 20-week, twice weekly, two-phase, individual cognitive–behavioral therapy using coping skills, stress inoculation, and in vivo exposure. Phase I, occurring over 12 weeks, focuses on developing and maintaining abstinence from substance use through trauma-informed cognitive–behavioral therapy and psychoeducation; Phase II, occurring over 8 weeks, addresses PTSD symptoms through stress inoculation, prolonged exposure, and in vivo "homework."

Relevant Reading

Triffleman, E. (2003). Issues in implementing posttraumatic stress disorder treatment outcome research in community-based treatment programs. In J. L. Sorensen, R. A. Rawson, J. Guydish, & J. E. Zweben (Eds.), *Drug abuse treatment through collaboration: Practice and research partnerships that work* (pp. 227–247). Washington, DC: American Psychological Association.

Triffleman, E., Carroll, K., & Kellogg, S. (1999). Substance dependence–posttraumatic stress disorder treatment: An integrated cognitive–behavioral approach. *Journal of Substance Abuse Treatment, 17*, 3–14.

TRANSCEND

Transcend is a comprehensive treatment program tested in a single study with veterans who had comorbid PTSD and substance abuse. The first 6 weeks consisted of skill development (e.g., problem solving, anger management, emotional awareness) and the second 6 weeks were devoted to trauma processing (i.e., presentations of traumatic events with group feedback and nightmare resolution techniques). Substance abuse education, relapse prevention, peer support, and 12-step attendance were encouraged throughout.

Relevant Reading

Donovan, B., Padin-Rivera, E., & Kowaliw, S. (2001). "Transcend": Initial outcomes from a posttraumatic stress disorder/substance abuse treatment program. *Journal of Traumatic Stress, 14,* 757–772.

TRAUMA AFFECT REGULATION:
GUIDELINES FOR EDUCATION AND THERAPY (TARGET)

Trauma affect regulation: Guidelines for education and therapy (TARGET) is a trauma-focused, present-centered emotion self-regulation model for concurrent treatment for substance use disorders and PTSD. TARGET educates clients about how trauma exposure may affect the body's stress response and ultimately helps to develop ways to alter this maladaptive response. Clinicians teach clients seven core skills, in group or individual settings, to better manage distressing symptoms. The skills include recognizing triggers, checking emotional responses, evaluating thoughts, defining goals, evaluating options, and deciding on a positive course of action.

Relevant Reading

Ford, J. D., & Russo, E. (2006). A trauma-focused, present-centered, emotional self-regulation approach to integrated treatment for post-traumatic stress and addiction: Trauma Adaptive Recovery Group Education and Therapy (TARGET). *American Journal of Psychotherapy, 60,* 335.

Web site: http://www.ptsdfreedom.org

TRAUMA RECOVERY AND EMPOWERMENT (TREM)

Trauma recovery and empowerment (TREM), a 29-session weekly treatment, combines social skills training, psychoeducation, psychodynamic techniques, and peer support in a group modality for women with PTSD and other mental health disorders, later adapted for substance use disorders. Fallot and Harris (2002) focused on women's empowerment, maladaptive coping mechanisms originating as reactions to traumatic events, and education regarding trauma-related symptoms and challenges.

Relevant Reading

Fallot, R., & Harris, M. (2002). The trauma recovery and empowerment model (TREM). *Community Mental Health Journal, 38*, 475–485.

Harris, M., & Community Connections Trauma Work Group. (1998). *Trauma recovery and empowerment: A clinician's guide for working with women in groups.* New York: Free Press.

Web site: http://nrepp.samhsa.gov/programfulldetails.asp?PROGRAM_ID=87

TRIAD WOMEN'S GROUP MODEL (TRIAD)

The triad women's group model (TRIAD) was developed at the Triad Women's Project in Florida as part of the Substance Abuse and Mental Health Services Administration's Women, Co-Occurring Disorders and Violence Study. TRIAD draws upon multiple models of treatment for co-occurring disorders (e.g., TREM, DBT) and was developed through the collaboration of a diverse group of providers, consumers, and researchers. The main goals of the treatment model are to reduce psychiatric or trauma-related symptoms and increase abstinence. TRIAD consists of 16 group sessions, 2 hours each, delivered over 16 weeks by two cofacilitators. The model has four phases: (a) mindfulness, (b) interpersonal effectiveness and skills, (c) emotional regulation, and (d) distress tolerance. This model is based on principles of safety and empowerment and promotes skills building in the domains of emotional awareness; self-soothing and coping; and management of cravings, triggers, and crisis situations.

Relevant Reading

Clark, C., Giard, J., Fleisher-Bond, M., Slavin, S., Becker, M., & Cox, A. (2004). Creating alcohol and other drug, trauma, and mental health services for women in rural Florida: The Triad Women's Project. *Alcoholism Treatment Quarterly, 22*(3/4), 41–61.

Web site: http://mhlp.fmhi.usf.edu/web/mhlp/triad.cfm

APPENDIX B: ASSESSMENT TOOLS

The following is a list of assessment instruments relevant for women with trauma histories, covering the main areas discussed in this book. These measures are ones that we have used and found helpful in our clinical and research work. This list is not exhaustive. There are many other valuable assessment tools available that can also be used by clinicians working with this population.

The first set of measures includes interviewer-administered assessments that require various amounts of training to become proficient in their use. Although the training commitment for some of these measures may be beyond the scope or necessity of some addiction treatment programs, others may consider using them, especially if there are psychologists or social workers who have been trained in these procedures. These measures are also useful when collecting research data or conducting program evaluation, given the reliability and validity of data available.

CLINICIAN ADMINISTERED PTSD SCALE

The Clinician Administered PTSD Scale (CAPS) is a structured, clinical interview for assessing the frequency and intensity of posttraumatic stress disorder (PTSD) symptoms. The CAPS measures associated symptoms of PTSD (e.g., survivor guilt), validity of responses, impairments in social and occupational functioning, and overall symptom severity. The assessment provides a *Diagnostic and Statistical Manual of Mental Disorders* (*DSM–IV*; 4th ed.; American Psychiatric Association, 1994) diagnosis of PTSD.

Relevant Reading

Blake, D. D., Weathers, F. W., Nagy, L. M., Kaloupek, D. G., Gusman, F. D., Charney, D. S., & Keane, T. M. (1995). The development of a clinician-administered PTSD scale. *Journal of Traumatic Stress, 8*, 75–90.

Weathers, F. W., Keane, T. M., & Davidson, J. R. (2001). Clinician-Administered PTSD Scale: A review of the first ten years of research. *Depression and Anxiety, 13*, 132–156.

COMPOSITE INTERNATIONAL DIAGNOSTIC INTERVIEW

The Composite International Diagnostic Interview (CIDI) is a fully structured, interviewer-administered assessment that evaluates nearly all of the *DSM–IV* and the *International Classification of Diseases* (10th edition; World Health Organization, 1994) mental disorders. As a fully structured interview, it does not require clinical expertise for its reliable and valid use; however, standard training procedures by certified trainers are recommended. Various diagnostic modules can be used as stand-alone assessments. A computer-administered version is also available. See http://www.hcp.med.harvard.edu/wmhcidi/index.php for more information about the CIDI, its use, and training recommendations.

Relevant Reading

Cottler, L. B., & Compton, W. M. (1993). Advantages of the CIDI family of instruments in epidemiological research of substance use disorders. *International Journal of Methods in Psychiatric Research, 3,* 109–119.

World Health Organization. (1997). *Composite International Diagnostic Interview* (Core Version 2.1.). Geneva, Switzerland: Author.

DIAGNOSTIC INTERVIEW SCHEDULE

The Diagnostic Interview Schedule assesses all major diagnostic disorders (including somatization).

Relevant Reading

Robins, L. N., Helzer, J. E., Croughan, J., & Ratcliff, K. (1981). National Institutes of Health Diagnostic Interview Schedule. *Archives of General Psychology, 38,* 381–389.

PSYCHIATRIC RESEARCH INTERVIEW
FOR SUBSTANCE AND MENTAL DISORDERS

The Psychiatric Research Interview for Substance and Mental Disorders, often referred to as PRISM, is a semistructured clinical interview specifically developed to assess mental disorders in substance-using populations. The interview includes sections for alcohol and drug disorders and most major mental disorders (e.g., anxiety, mood, psychotic, eating). It also provides procedures to determine whether diagnoses are "primary" or "substance-induced," as defined by the *DSM–IV*.

Relevant Reading

Hasin, D., Samet, S., Nunes, E., Meydan, J., Matseoane, K., & Waxman, R. (2006). Diagnosis of comorbid psychiatric disorders in substance users assessed with the Psychiatric Research Interview for Substance and Mental Disorders for *DSM–IV*. *American Journal of Psychiatry, 163*, 689–696.

Hasin, D. S., Trautman, K. D., Miele, G. M., Samet, S., Smith, M., & Endicott, J. (1996). Psychiatric Research Interview for Substance and Mental Disorders (PRISM): Reliability in substance abusers. *American Journal of Psychiatry, 159*, 1195–1201.

STRUCTURED CLINICAL INTERVIEWS FOR DSM–IV AXIS I AND AXIS II DISORDERS

The Structured Clinical Interview for *DSM–IV* Axis I Disorders is a semi-structured interview to determine *DSM–IV* Axis I diagnoses. The Structured Clinical Interview for *DSM–IV* Axis II Disorders is used to make *DSM–IV* Axis II (personality disorder) diagnoses. These instruments should be administered by a trained clinician, ideally with advanced clinical knowledge and experience. See http://www.appi.org for more information and ordering information.

Relevant Reading

First, M. B., Spitzer, R. L., Gibbon, M., & Williams, J. B. (1995). The Structured Clinical Interview for *DSM–III–R* Personality Disorders (SCID-II): Part I. Description. *Journal of Personality Disorders, 9*(2), 83–91.

Spitzer, R. L., Williams, J. B., Gibbon, M., & First, M. B. (1992). The Structured Clinical Interview for *DSM–III–R* (SCID): Part I. History, rationale, and description. *Archives of General Psychiatry, 49*, 624–629.

The remaining measures are relatively brief, self-report-style assessments that can be easily added to preexisting intake or ongoing assessment procedures. They can also be administered by an interviewer, especially if client reading comprehension or literacy level is an issue. The measures are organized by assessment area.

POSTTRAUMATIC STRESS DISORDER

Impact of Events Scale

The Impact of Events Scale is a 15-item self-report questionnaire assessing both intrusion and avoidance symptoms on a 4-point scale of 0 (*not at all*) to 5 (*often*). The scale inquires about the most stressful life event the person has experienced and the frequency of statements that pertain to those events.

Relevant Reading

Horowitz, M., Wilner, N., & Alvarez, W. (1979). Impact of Event Scale: A measure of subjective stress. *Psychosomatic Medicine, 41*, 209–218.

Posttraumatic Stress Disorder Symptom Scale—Self-Report

The Posttraumatic Stress Disorder Symptom Scale—Self-Report is a 17-item self-report inventory assessing the frequency and severity of PTSD symptoms corresponding to the diagnostic criteria listed in the *DSM–III–R* (American Psychiatric Association, 1987), modified for the *DSM–IV*.

Relevant Reading

Foa, E. B., Riggs, D. S., Dancu, C. V., & Rothbaum, B. O. (1993). Reliability and validity of a brief instrument for assessing posttraumatic stress disorder. *Journal of Traumatic Stress, 6*, 459.

Trauma Symptom Inventory

The Trauma Symptom Inventory is a 100-item measure assessing severe PTSD symptoms. Symptoms are assessed for frequency and severity for the previous 6 months.

Relevant Reading

Briere, J., Elliott, D. M., Harris, K., & Cotman, A. (1995). The trauma symptom inventory: Reliability and validity in a clinical sample. *Journal of Interpersonal Violence, 10*, 387–401.

COMORBIDITY

Beck Depression Inventories I and II

The Beck Depression Inventory is a 21-question multiple choice inventory that is one of the most widely used instruments for measuring the severity of depression. The current version of the questionnaire is designed for individuals ages 13 and older and is composed of items relating to depression symptoms such as hopelessness and irritability; cognitions such as guilt or feelings of being punished; as well as physical symptoms such as fatigue, weight loss, and lack of interest in sex.

Relevant Reading

Beck, A. T., Steer, R. A., & Brown, G. K. (1996). *Manual for the Beck Depression Inventory—II*. San Antonio, TX: Psychological Corporation.

Brief Symptom Inventory

The Brief Symptom Inventory is a standardized measure consisting of ratings of severity of 53 symptoms. It yields nine subscales (i.e., Somatization, Obsessive-Compulsiveness, Interpersonal Sensitivity, Depression, Anxiety, Hostility, Phobic Anxiety, Paranoid Ideation, and Psychotocism). An overall measure of symptoms, the Global Severity Index is also calculated.

Relevant Reading

Derogatis, L. R. (1993). *Brief Symptom Inventory (BSI): Administration, scoring, and procedures manual* (3rd ed.). Minneapolis, MN: National Computer Systems.

Dissociative Experiences Scale

The Dissociative Experiences Scale is a 28-item scale that measures dissociation. It is a brief self-report measure that conceptualizes dissociation as a trait and inquires about the frequency of dissociative experiences in the daily lives of clients.

Relevant Reading

Bernstein, E., & Putnam, F. W. (1986). Development, reliability, and validity of a dissociation scale. *Journal of Nervous and Mental Disease, 174*, 727–735.

Emotional Avoidance Questionnaire

The Emotional Avoidance Questionnaire is a 20-item measure reflecting cognitive and behavioral expressions of emotional avoidance.

Relevant Reading

Taylor, C. T., Laposa, J. M., & Alden, L. E. (2004). Is emotional personality disorder more than just social avoidance? *Journal of Personality Disorders, 18*, 571–594.

Difficulties in Emotion Regulation Scale

The Difficulties in Emotion Regulation Scale is a 41-item measure assessing clinically significant difficulties in emotion regulation. Items reflect difficulties in the following dimensions of emotion regulation: (a) awareness and understanding; (b) acceptance; (c) ability to engage in goal-directed behavior, and refrain from impulsive behavior, when experiencing negative emotions; and (d) access to emotion regulation strategies. Higher scores indicate greater difficulties.

Relevant Reading

Gratz, K. L., & Roemer, L. (2004). Multidimensional assessment of emotion regulation and dysregulation: Development, factor structure, and initial validation of the Difficulties in Emotion Regulation Scale. *Journal of Psychopathology and Behavioral Assessment, 26,* 41–54.

Negative Mood Regulation

Negative Mood Regulation is a 30-item scale measuring generalized expectancies to alleviate negative moods. It asks individuals to indicate the degree to which they believe their use of various coping strategies can counteract a negative mood state. Each item is scored on a 5-point Likert scale with a statement completing the stem, "When I'm upset I believe that. . . ." Higher scores indicate better mood regulation.

Relevant Reading

Catanzaro, S. J., & Mearns, J. (1990). Measuring generalized expectancies of negative mood regulation: Initial scale development and implications. *Journal of Personality Assessment, 54,* 546–563.

Novaco Anger Inventory

The Novaco Anger Inventory assesses cognitive arousal and behavioral reactions to anger. Part A of the inventory requires that subjects rate on a 3-point Likert scale how true each of 48 descriptions are to their typical emotional states and reactions to provocation.

Relevant Reading

Novaco, R. W. (1994). Anger as a risk factor for violence among the mentally disordered. In J. Monahan & H. J. Steadman (Eds.), *Violence and mental disorder: Development in risk assessment* (pp. 21–59). Chicago: University of Chicago Press.

Toronto Alexithymia Scale

The Toronto Alexithymia Scale is a 20-item assessment used to measure differentiation and awareness of affective states. It yields three subscales: Difficulty Identifying Feelings, Difficulty Describing Feelings, and Externally Oriented Thinking.

Relevant Reading

Bagby, R. M., Parker, J. D. A., & Taylor, G. J. (1994). The 20-item Toronto Alexithymia Scale—I: Item selection and cross-validation of the factor structure. *Journal of Psychosomatic Research, 38,* 23–32.

INTERPERSONAL FUNCTIONING

Inventory of Interpersonal Problems

The Inventory of Interpersonal Problems is a 127-item questionnaire assessing degree and type of interpersonal problems. It is used as a measure of general interpersonal distress as well as a way to categorize an individual's general interpersonal style. It uses a 5-point Likert-type scale and organizes interpersonal problems along two axes: affiliation (behaviors range from *friendly* to *hostile*) and control (behaviors range from *dominant* to *submissive*).

Relevant Reading

Horowitz, L. M., Rosenberg, S. E., Baer, B. A., Ureno, G., & Villasenor, V. S. (1988). Inventory of Interpersonal Problems: Psychometric properties and clinical applications. *Journal of Consulting and Clinical Psychology, 56,* 885–892.

Social Adjustment Scale—Self-Report

The Social Adjustment Scale—Self-Report is a 42-item measure of social behavior. It is a general measure of social adjustment asking about the "number of friends seen or spoken to in the past 2 weeks" and the "level of satisfaction with relationships." Items are rated on a 5-point Likert scale, with higher scores indicating greater impairment. Mean scores are calculated for seven role areas (e.g., work, family, friends), and an overall adjustment score is derived.

Relevant Reading

Weissman, E., & Bothell, S. (1976). Assessment of patient social adjustment by patient self-report. *Archives of General Psychiatry, 33,* 1111–1115.

UCLA Loneliness Scale—Revised

UCLA Loneliness Scale—Revised is a 20-item measure assessing social isolation, loneliness, and perceived inadequacy in current social relationships. Items are summed to a total loneliness scale score, with higher scores corresponding to limited social activity and fewer relationships.

Relevant Reading

Russell, D. E. H., Peplau, L., & Cutrona, C. (1980). The revised UCLA Loneliness Scale: Concurrent and discriminant validity evidence. *Journal of Personality and Social Psychology, 39,* 472–480.

PARENTING

Child Abuse Potential Inventory

The Child Abuse Potential Inventory is a 160-item self-report questionnaire that assesses risk for child maltreatment. Subscales include Distress, Rigidity, Unhappiness, Problems With Child and Self, Problems With Family, Problems From Others, Ego Strength, and Loneliness. There are also three validity scales: Faking-Good, Faking-Bad, and Random Response Profiles.

Relevant Reading

Milner, J. S. (1994). Assessing physical child abuse risk: The Child Abuse Potential Inventory. *Clinical Psychology Review, 14,* 547–583.

Conflict Tactics Scales (Parent–Child)

The Conflict Tactics Scales (Parent–Child) measures specific parental disciplinary practices and contains five subscales: Psychological Aggression,

Physical Assault, Nonviolent Discipline, Sexual Coercion, and Injury. Prevalence scores measure whether a disciplinary tactic was ever used by the parent. Chronicity scores provide a rank measure of how often in the past year a tactic was used.

Relevant Reading

Straus, M. A., Hamby, S. L., Finkelhor, D., Moore, D. W., & Runyan, D. (1998). Identification of child maltreatment with the Parent–Child Conflict Tactics Scales (CTSPC): Development and psychometric data for a national sample of American parents. *Child Abuse and Neglect, 22,* 249–270.

Parent–Child Relationship Inventory

The Parent–Child Relationship Inventory is a 78-item measure used to assess mothers' reports of positive maternal behaviors. It consists of six subscales: Communication, Involvement, Limit-Setting, Autonomy, Satisfaction, and Support.

Relevant Reading

Gerard, A. B. (1994). *The Parent–Child Relationship Inventory (PCRI) manual.* Los Angeles: Western Psychological Services.

Parental Punitiveness Scale

The Parental Punitiveness Scale is a 21-item measure designed to assess the potential for parental violence. Respondents rate hypothetical situations for degree of punitiveness from no response to severe physical punishment. The scale is coded by a summed total severity score.

Relevant Reading

Epstein, R., & Komorita, S. S. (1965). The development of a scale of parental punitiveness toward aggression. *Child Development, 36,* 129–142.

PHYSICAL HEALTH

Health and Daily Living Form

The Health and Daily Living Form is a 105-item measure assessing health and social factors, including physical symptoms, medical conditions, substance use, smoking, medication, relationships, network contacts, social activities, and life change events. See http://mindgarden.com for more information.

Relevant Reading

Moos, R. H., Cronkite, R. C., Finney, J. W., & Billings, A. G. (1986). *Health and daily living manual*. Palo Alto, CA: Veterans Administration and Stanford University Medical Center.

Health Symptom Checklist

The Health Symptom Checklist is a 20-item scale assessing the presence and frequency of physical and psychosomatic health complaints.

Relevant Reading

Bartone, P. T., Ursano, R. J., Wright, K. M., & Ingraham, L. H. (1989). The impact of a military air disaster on the health of assistance workers: A prospective study. *Journal of Nervous and Mental Disease, 177*, 317–328.

Multidimensional Pain Inventory

The Multidimensional Pain Inventory assesses multiple facets of chronic pain experiences, including functioning, response from others, and ability to participate in daily activities.

Relevant Reading

Kerns, R. D., Turk, D. C., & Rudy, T. E. (1985). The West Haven-Yale Multidimensional Pain Inventory (WHYMPI). *Pain, 23*, 345–356.

SF-36 Health Survey Questionnaire

The SF-36 Health Survey Questionnaire is a 36-item questionnaire with eight functional health and well-being profile scales, including perceived health status and role limitations due to poor health/pain. It takes approximately 10 to 12 minutes to administer. See http://www.sf-36.org for more information. There is also a shorter version, the SF-12, which takes approximately 1 to 2 minutes to complete.

Relevant Reading

Ware, J. E., Snow, K. K., Kosinski, M., & Gandek, B. (1993). *SF-36 Health Survey: Manual and interpretation guide*. Boston: Health Institute, New England Medical Center.

Women's Medical History Questionnaire

The Women's Medical History Questionnaire is a 43-item questionnaire assessing 43 different health problems (e.g., dermatological, cardiovascular, gynecological, gastrointestinal) with regard to diagnosis, onset, and past 12-month experiences.

Relevant Reading

Wolfe, J., Schnurr, P. P., Brown, P. J., & Furey, J. (1994). Posttraumatic stress disorder and war-zone exposure as correlates of perceived health in female Vietnam War veterans. *Journal of Consulting and Clinical Psychology, 62*, 1235–1240.

APPENDIX C: TRAINING CONSIDERATIONS AND MATERIALS

Although many agencies will be readily able to identify a trauma expert to provide support and supervision, there may not be someone on site who is experienced or comfortable with providing training. The following is a brief introduction to good training practices to help potential trainers identify content and process areas to consider when thinking about conducting training. Exhibit C.1 identifies some of the basic components of a good training.

LEARNING MODALITIES

Although seemingly obvious, the primary goal of training is to successfully transfer knowledge to others. To do so, trainers need to be sensitive to the different ways that people learn. Many people are aware of being either visual learners ("I need to see it to remember it") or auditory learners ("If I don't hear it, I have a hard time recalling"). Trainings must incorporate multiple learning modalities to maximize effectiveness. Adult learners do best when they use and practice the skills they are learning. Therefore, training should be an active endeavor, and participants should get hands-on experience with the materials and concepts they are learning. Each training should incorporate aspects of the learning modalities outlined in the sections that follow.

Hearing

All trainings include some didactic presentation of information. In practical terms, ensure that the participants can hear the trainer. If necessary, arrange for a sound system for proper amplification. Information should be clear and well-organized. Trainers should be aware of tone of voice and speak in a dynamic, varied style, avoiding the monotone. Consider varying the voice by including guest speakers or co-trainers. For example, individuals with special

---

This appendix offers useful recommendations for trainers as well as sample training materials. Figure C.1 is a sample training agenda for a full-day training, Figure C.2 is a sample training evaluation form, and Figure C.3 is a slide set to introduce trainees to the diagnosis of PTSD. Readers may use and/or modify these materials as needed.

EXHIBIT C.1
Elements of Good Training

- Content is clear, accurate, and relevant.
- Presenter is engaging, interested, knowledgeable, and has a sense of humor.
- Format is interactive.
- Materials are varied and organized.
- Time for questions is built in.
- Adequate breaks are incorporated.
- Facilities (e.g., chairs, room temperature, size of room) are comfortable.

---

expertise in trauma treatment could present a case during the training. This also brings new ideas into the training. Using audio- or videotaped demonstrations can be particularly useful when training on different psychotherapy techniques or approaches. Many manualized treatments include videotapes that can be used as supplemental resources for trainers.

Seeing

Trainings, conferences, classes, and presentations are often accompanied by visual aids. Whereas transparencies and film slides are familiar from the past, current technology provides ready access to software for slide presentations (i.e., Microsoft PowerPoint). Presentation software is useful in organizing information and providing an excellent structure, especially for new trainers. Other visual aids that are useful include either a whiteboard or newsprint, specifically somewhere to write down concepts, lists, and questions as they come up during the training. If videotaped demonstrations are available, they can also be quite useful in engaging people's attention.

Discussing

As previously mentioned, adult learners especially derive great benefit from an active learning environment. Group discussion is an excellent way to promote active learning. Whether engaging the entire training group in discussion or breaking into small discussion groups, talking about the issues being taught reinforces the concepts. If using small group discussion, it is best to return to the large group and have a representative from each small group share its ideas so that the entire group can benefit from all discussions. Small group discussion can also increase sharing from those who are reluctant to speak in the larger group.

Experiencing

A deeper level of active learning, experiencing entails the hands-on practice of skills that are disseminated within a training. Experiencing often includes role-playing. The trainer might ask the group to come together and role-play a scenario, such as a client dissociating during group. The trainer would role-play how to deal with the situation, most likely demonstrating a grounding exercise, then leading a discussion of the process, engaging trainees in feedback and questions.

Teaching

The final active learning tool is to teach the material to someone else. If time and format allow, it is useful for each trainee to prepare "teach-backs" of the material being learned in the training. In the previous example, the trainer would ask one of the trainees to prepare a presentation on grounding and present it to the group. The trainee would use the information learned in the training, along with other materials and possible role-plays, to teach others the grounding skill. The trainer then gives feedback on the teach-back exercise, focusing on what was done well and what could be improved. Other trainees learn a great deal by seeing other training styles, listening to the information presented in a different way and gaining from the feedback provided to peers. Trainers may also incorporate the feedback of the trainees by first asking the individual conducting the exercise to note what he or she did well and what might need improvement, then having other trainees give similar feedback, with the trainer concluding the feedback round. If other trainees are enlisted to give feedback, the trainer should precede the exercise with instructions on giving constructive feedback, focusing on specific behaviors and keeping feedback positive and constructive.

PLANNING AND CONDUCTING TRAINING

When conducting a training, a number of practical considerations must be taken into account. The sections that follow provide information that may be useful in preparing for and conducting trainings, especially those related to trauma and posttraumatic stress disorder (PTSD).

Registration

Logistically, to ensure adequate space and materials, it is important to collect registration information so the trainer will know the number of training participants. Using a registration form makes for the easy collection of standard information that will be useful in training planning. At minimum, a person's contact information should be included on the form. Also useful are a person's degree and role on a project. A trainer can always request additional information about previous trainings and so forth to prepare for the audience who will be attending. If appropriate, more specific questions about trauma background and training can be included on the registration form.

Physical Training Environment

Once the trainer knows how many trainees will attend, more of the practical issues can be addressed. Deciding on space is a first step. Where will the training be held? Are the facilities large enough to accommodate the number of trainees? Although it is always helpful to have a large, impressive room for training, some spaces can be too large if the number of trainees is small. The space should be large enough that the trainees are not crowded with their materials but not so large that the room seems empty or the trainer has to rein in those people who have scattered themselves around the room. The layout of the tables, chairs, and audiovisual equipment should be planned ahead. For example, it is helpful for trainees to have a table to place materials on and be seated in a way that enhances interaction among the group while allowing good visibility of slides or videos.

Deciding whether to hold a training on or off site is another consideration in planning. Training off-site of the regular work environment sends a message about the importance of training by removing the trainees from their typical work environment and the responsibilities and distractions that are in the workplace. However, off-site locations can be costly and remove the trainer and staff from the resources that may be available at a local site. These considerations must be accounted for when deciding where the training will be held. Training on-site can be more convenient for trainees. There may be more flexibility in scheduling, such as opportunities to offer the training in shorter time frames (e.g., 4 half-day sessions compared with 2 full days) if training occurs on-site. The trainer may also benefit from not having to transport materials to other sites. On-site training may also allow for upper management to come in at the beginning of training to discuss the importance of the training and demonstrate their commitment to the program. This demonstrates to trainees the commitment of multiple levels of staff and emphasizes the importance of their participation.

Materials

Most training involves preparing and distributing materials to trainees. These mainly include written materials, either collected in a binder or notebook or perhaps presented in a published book for some empirically based treatments. Additional handouts, pads of paper, pens, and other supporting materials may be needed. Sign-in sheets serve as a way to record participant attendance, and name tags are useful for the trainers and participants to learn one another's names. All materials should be checked in advance and organized so that they correspond with the order of presentations (or the agenda) in the training. If the trainer is using a slide presentation, it is always useful to include a copy of the presentation in a format on which trainees can write notes while the presenter speaks. Having participants register in advance helps in determining how many copies and binders will be needed. It is always a good idea to have a few extra copies on hand if nonregistered people attend.

It is essential to be prepared for not only the practicalities of training but also the content. The trainer should be very familiar with the materials to minimize any surprises. If this is the first time a trainer has conducted the training, it might be useful to practice in front of a small group of colleagues to gain greater familiarity and comfort with the materials. If possible, cotraining with someone who has conducted the training in the past is an excellent approach. When training on familiar material or repeating a training, the trainer can review his or her notes beforehand and copy them into a new version of the training materials. This active step not only provides a necessary review of the materials but also helps the trainer remember important points or issues that arose in prior trainings that need to be addressed. An important way to stay on track is to develop and provide an agenda (see Figure C.1). The agenda should be detailed and clear, including the start and stop times of the training and different components of the training. The agenda serves as a guideline, and flexibility is required. Still, the trainer should follow the agenda as much as possible because trainees appreciate knowing what to expect and trainers can facilitate the learning process by adhering to the structure of an agenda.

As mentioned earlier, many trainers use slides to provide visual cues to training and video- or audiotapes to demonstrate important components of a treatment or skill that is being discussed (see Figure C.3 at the end of the appendix). These materials require technology to support them. A PowerPoint presentation requires a computer and a computer-based projector; audio- and videotapes need a VCR, TV, or audiotape player; digital media, such as DVDs or digital audio recordings require appropriate equipment. Sometimes a training is recorded on video so that others can watch it on separate occasions. All equipment needs to be tested before the training session. Many trainers have anxiety-provoking (and humorous, after the fact) stories about equipment malfunctions 5 minutes before the start of a training session. It is essential that the trainer be familiar with the equipment, that he or she has tested it fully before training begins, or that support staff are available to assist when necessary. If technicalities prevent the use of audiovisual materials, a trainer should be ready to present the material using paper handouts, role-plays, and so forth. Flexibility and quick thinking are essential when embarking on any training.

Other practical considerations include whether refreshments, lunch, or both will be provided. This is always a nice gesture if it is possible. Sites sometimes have funds set aside for providing food at different events. However, many times this is a luxury that trainers or sites are not able to provide. A more substantive issue is whether a trainer can provide continuing education (CE) credits, units, or hours. Depending on state education department requirements, many treatment providers need to complete a certain number of CE hours to maintain their licenses or certifications.

Trainer's Name
Training Date and Time
Training Location

Day 1

9:00–9:30	Welcome, introductions, Trainer's Name and ice breaker
9:30–10:30	Introduction to training topic Trainer's Name *(if different from above)*
10:30–10:45	Break
10:45–11:30	Brainstorming Exercise/Group Discussion
11:30–12:15	More presentation of topic
12:15–12:30	Q&A on material from morning session
12:30–1:30	Lunch
1:30–3:00	Continued didactic presentation (*if necessary*) Skill building–guided practice or role-plays
3:00–3:15	Break
3:15–4:30	Small group practice
4:30–4:55	Large group discussion of small group experience
4:55–5:00	Questions and wrap-up

Figure C.1. Sample training agenda.

Therefore, CE credits can be valuable for and appreciated by trainees. Trainers can work with local universities, professional organizations, or other entities that conduct trainings to see whether they can apply for CE credits for training. These types of ongoing relationships can be worthwhile for everyone involved.

Training and supervision require evaluation of the trainee, but it is also useful for the trainer to be evaluated. Training evaluations can provide feedback about how well the trainer presented the material, whether the concepts were understood, and how the participants felt about the training. A sample training evaluation form is included for your convenience (see Figure C.2) and can be modified for use in a variety of trainings. A good evaluation form can also include specific questions that determine whether the goals and objectives of the training were met. For example, in trauma assessment, one of the goals may be for participants to name the three symptom clusters of PTSD. Therefore, a question on the evaluation form could be, "On the basis of the content of this training, I am able to name and describe the three symptom clusters of PTSD." This question can be rated on a 5-point scale, ranging from strongly disagree to strongly agree. By including more specific, content-oriented questions on the evaluation form, the trainer can get a sense of whether the goals of the training have been accomplished. Trainers should also leave space at the end of the evaluation form for participant comments. To obtain the most candid feedback, evaluations should be anonymous and completed at the end of the training without the trainer in the room.

Psychological Training Environment

The training environment should maximize learning. The trainer should be professional, yet relaxed, striking a balance between the role of expert and being approachable and accessible. The trainer needs to create a safe environment that facilitates connecting with others. One way to set the tone is to explain the benefits of training. The clearer the potential benefits, the better trainees will feel about the time and effort they put into the process. The training will be more relevant and in a context that is useful and applicable. In the case of treating women with addictions and trauma, providers are eager to learn more specific skills to provide the best treatment possible for the problems that these clients present, which are often difficult to treat yet ubiquitous in their programs.

Safety is a key concern in every aspect of trauma work, including training. Trainers must be sensitive to the fact that clinicians may be trauma survivors themselves, and information discussed in training might be triggering for some trainees. Even for those without a history of trauma, exposure to stories of traumatic events may result in vicarious traumatization. Trainers should set

Title of Training
Trainer(s') Name(s)
Date and Location

Please rate the following:	Poor	Fair	Good	Excellent
❑ The clarity of the concepts, techniques, and procedures explained	1	2	3	4
❑ The training skills of the instructor/facilitator	1	2	3	4
❑ The training materials provided	1	2	3	4
❑ The methods used in this training	1	2	3	4
❑ The training facilities	1	2	3	4
❑ The relevance of this training to your work	1	2	3	4
❑ The training prepared you to conduct your duties related to this topic	1	2	3	4
❑ The overall quality of this training	1	2	3	4

Please use the space below to provide additional comments:

_____

_____

_____

_____

Figure C.2. Sample training evaluation form.

appropriate ground rules for training. Trainees should be encouraged to keep disclosure of graphic trauma details to a minimum, respect others, and maintain confidentiality, just as they would when running a group or individual treatment session. Setting these types of limits also models how ground rules and boundaries are set when conducting trauma treatment. Trainers should also allow for trainees to debrief from their experience of participating in the training, which can help normalize the response to dealing with trauma. Trainers can check in during the training by making statements such as "I know this can be difficult to discuss" or asking questions such as, "How are people feeling about the material?" or "What reactions are people having right now?"

Know Your Audience

Although trainers may conduct trainings for staff they know from their agencies, many times trainings occur among a group in which not everyone is acquainted. As a trainer, it is important to know your audience. You will have preliminary information from the registration forms, but that is typically limited. Starting the training with introductions of the trainer and the participants serves multiple functions. It models the active, participatory style you want to foster, encouraging others to share about themselves and their experiences. Introductions should include the person's name, the role they have at their agency, or the role they will have when using the new skills they are there to learn. Trainers can include additional components to the introduction as desired. A trainer might want to know about individuals' experience as supervisors or whether they have had trauma training in the past and, if so, what type. You can also keep it light by asking questions such as, "What is one thing about you that would surprise other people?" or "What cartoon character are you most like and why?" Introductions make people feel more comfortable and may start to establish group cohesion. This is particularly relevant in trainings about trauma, as people may have various personal responses to dealing with this material, and the more comfortable they feel the better they will be able to express themselves. As a trainer, it is always good to know the participants and their background. The level of expertise of the trainees informs how much background information may need to be covered. Even though the novice trainer may be intimidated by trainees with a great deal of knowledge on a topic, trainee diversity is good. Each trainee has a different perspective to offer—from the clinician who has been working in the trenches for 30 years to the physician who is interested in trauma because of all the cases she has seen in practice—all have insights and perspectives that can be used to increase interest. A trainer who respects the expertise of trainees and encourages their participation also models the collaborative stance that the trainer hopes clinicians will also use in their work with survivors.

Optimize the Use of Questions

When trainees ask a lot of questions, trainers should be grateful. Questions provide an excellent learning opportunity for all involved. For trainers, questions provide good feedback as to what areas may need increased attention or when something is unclear. It is another active learning tool that trainers can use to their advantage. When a trainee asks a question, it is important that the trainer makes sure he or she understands that question. By repeating the question, you can make sure you understand what is being asked while also ensuring that other participants have heard the question. Trainers can reverse a question from a participant, asking it back to the group at large to get them involved in thinking through the answer. Sometimes questions come at the wrong time, either addressing an issue that will be taken up later in the training or during a section in which the trainer does not want to interrupt the continuity of the training. Trainers can always note the question and come back to it later. It is best to write it down; but even if you forget, the trainees most likely will not. No matter how prepared you are as a trainer, there will always be questions you cannot answer. This also provides a learning opportunity for all involved by modeling how to get an answer (e.g., check with someone, look it up in the manual). Make sure to follow through on any issues that need to be resolved, either later in the day if possible, at a later training, or through written or verbal correspondence. Again, this provides an excellent modeling opportunity to acknowledge that you do not necessarily have all the answers but will be responsive to all questions, including seeking the answer outside training time and getting back to trainees.

Even if an answer is wrong, give positive feedback. Trainers can always shape an answer that is close to being correct by elaborating or rephrasing. Trainers can also use one question to trigger other questions. Trainers can use questions as additional opportunities for learning, helping to maintain attention of the trainees. The most effective questions are open-ended, starting with words such as *what, how,* and *why*. Open-ended questions elicit information and discussion. Closed-ended questions—those that can be answered with a yes or no response—should be used sparingly. Questions can address facts such as, "What are the symptom clusters of PTSD?" Questions can also initiate problem solving such as, "What would you do if a client began to dissociate during a group?"

Trainer Style

A trainer's attitude and style set the tone of a training. It is important to try to stay positive and flexible and exhibit a good sense of humor. Trainers should be involved and enthusiastic because trainees will often mirror trainers' attitudes. Trainers should also remain positive about the material, never saying, "This next part is boring," or other devaluing comments. You can make a training your own by generating your own examples, anecdotes, and exercises to use during a standard training. Using your own experience will increase your sense of ownership and involvement, which will come across to the trainees. Trainers should be animated, using voice and body for emphasis, moving around the room, or at least changing from sitting to standing. If you have handed out nametags or know individuals in the room, always try to refer to trainees by name, which increases their involvement and engagement. This will also help you to involve everyone, but remember not to pick on any one person excessively.

Understanding Post-Traumatic Stress
Disorder

Trainer's Name
Trainer's Affiliation
Location of Training
Date of Training

Diagnostic Criteria for PTSD

- Criterion A: Exposure to Traumatic Stressor

- Criterion B: Re-experiencing Symptoms

- Criterion C: Avoidance, Numbing Symptoms

- Criterion D: Symptoms of Increased Arousal

- Criterion E: Duration of at least 1 month

- Criterion F: Significant distress or impairment

Figure C.3. Training slides: Introduction to posttraumatic stress disorder. PTSD = posttraumatic stress disorder; sxs = symptoms.

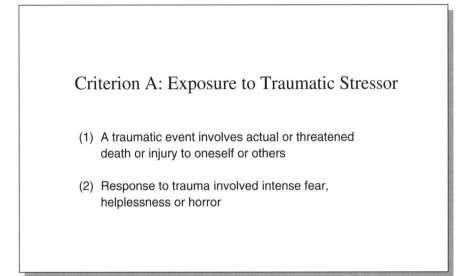

Criterion A: Exposure to Traumatic Stressor

(1) A traumatic event involves actual or threatened death or injury to oneself or others

(2) Response to trauma involved intense fear, helplessness or horror

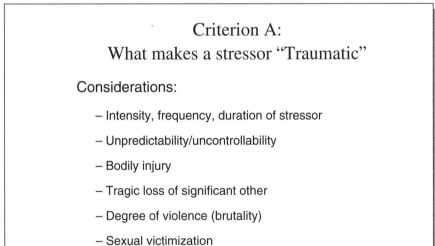

Criterion A:
What makes a stressor "Traumatic"

Considerations:

– Intensity, frequency, duration of stressor

– Unpredictability/uncontrollability

– Bodily injury

– Tragic loss of significant other

– Degree of violence (brutality)

– Sexual victimization

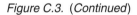

Figure C.3. (Continued)

Examples of Events Likely to Meet Criterion A

Direct:

- Violent physical assault
- Sexual assault or abuse
- Serious accidents
- Natural or man-made disasters
- Being kidnapped, taken hostage

Witnessed:

- Seeing death or injury to another person

Confronted:

- Learning about death or threatened death of close family member

Criterion B: Re-Experiencing

Persistent and distressing re-experiencing of traumatic event in one or more of following ways:

- Intrusive thoughts
- Unpleasant dreams
- Flashbacks
- Psychological distress from triggers
- Physiological reactivity to triggers

Figure C.3. (Continued)

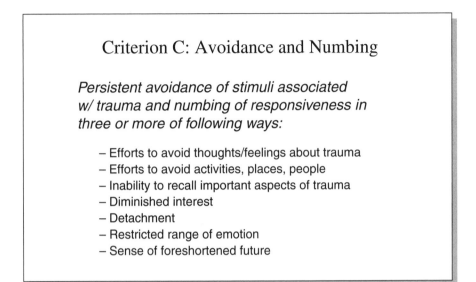

Criterion C: Avoidance and Numbing

*Persistent avoidance of stimuli associated
w/ trauma and numbing of responsiveness in
three or more of following ways:*

- Efforts to avoid thoughts/feelings about trauma
- Efforts to avoid activities, places, people
- Inability to recall important aspects of trauma
- Diminished interest
- Detachment
- Restricted range of emotion
- Sense of foreshortened future

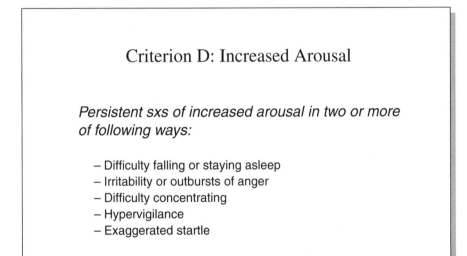

Criterion D: Increased Arousal

*Persistent sxs of increased arousal in two or more
of following ways:*

- Difficulty falling or staying asleep
- Irritability or outbursts of anger
- Difficulty concentrating
- Hypervigilance
- Exaggerated startle

Figure C.3. (Continued)

Criterion E & F

Criterion E:
For diagnosis of PTSD symptom duration must be
at least 1 month

Criterion F:
PTSD sxs must cause clinically significant
distress or impairment

Summary of PTSD Basics

• **Prerequisite is exposure to traumatic stress**

• **Symptoms present for at least one month**

• **3 Symptom Clusters:**

      (1) Re-experiencing of traumatic event
      (2) Avoidance of trauma-related stimuli and
           numbing of general responsiveness
      (3) Heightened physiological arousal

• **PTSD symptoms vs. "normal" remembering:**
      Persistence, emotional distress level,
      disruption to daily functioning (impairment or distress)

Figure C.3. (Continued)

REFERENCES

Abass, A. (2004). Small group videotape training for psychotherapy skills development. *Academic Psychiatry, 28,* 151–155.

Abney, V. D., & Priest, R. (1995). African Americans and sexual child abuse. In L. A. Fontes (Ed.), *Sexual abuse in nine North American cultures: Treatment and prevention* (pp. 11–30). London: Sage.

Ahn, H. N. (1994). Cultural diversity and the definition of child abuse. In R. Barth, J. Berrick, & N. Gilbert (Eds.), *Child welfare research review* (Vol. 1, pp. 28–55). New York: Columbia University Press.

Ainsworth, M. D. S. (1982). Attachment: Retrospect and prospect. In C. M. Parkes & J. Stevenson-Hinde (Eds.), *The place of attachment in human behavior* (pp. 3–30). New York: Basic Books.

Ainsworth, M. D. S., Blehar, M., Waters, E., & Wall, S. (1978). *Patterns of attachment: Observations in the strange situation at home.* Hillsdale, NJ: Erlbaum.

Alexander, P. C. (1992). Application of attachment theory to the study of sexual abuse. *Journal of Consulting and Clinical Psychology, 60,* 185–195.

Amaro, H., Larson, M. J., Gampel, J., Richardsen, E., Savage, A., & Wagler, D. (2005). Racial/ethnic differences in social vulnerability among women with co-occurring mental health and substance use disorders: Implications for treatment services. *Journal of Community Psychology, 33,* 495–511.

Amaro, H., & Russo, N. F. (1987). Hispanic women and mental health: An overview of contemporary issues in research and practice. *Psychology of Women Quarterly, 11,* 393–407.

Amdur, R. L., Larsen, R., & Liberzon, I. (2000). Emotional processing in combat-related posttraumatic stress disorder: A comparison with traumatized and normal controls. *Journal of Anxiety Disorders, 14,* 219–238.

American Medical Association. (1995). Report on memories of childhood abuse. *International Journal of Clinical and Experimental Hypnosis, 43,* 114–117.

American Psychiatric Association. (1987). *Diagnostic and statistical manual of mental disorders* (3rd ed., rev.). Washington, DC: Author.

American Psychiatric Association. (1993). *Memories of sexual abuse: APA position statement.* Washington, DC: Author.

American Psychiatric Association. (1994). *Diagnostic and statistical manual of mental disorders* (4th ed.). Washington, DC: Author.

American Psychiatric Association. (2000). *Diagnostic and statistical manual of mental disorders* (4th ed., text rev.). Washington, DC: Author.

American Psychological Association. (1995). *Questions and answers about memories of childhood sexual abuse*. Washington, DC: Author.

Ammerman, R. T., Kolko, D. J., Kirisci, L., Blackson, T. C., & Dawes, M. A. (1999). Child abuse potential in parents with histories of substance use disorder. *Child Abuse & Neglect, 23,* 1225–1238.

Andreski, P., Chilcoat, H., & Breslau, N. (1998). Post-traumatic stress disorder and somatization symptoms: A prospective study. *Psychiatry Research, 79,* 131–138.

Arledge, E., & Wolfson, R. (2001, Spring). Care of the clinician. *New Directions for Mental Health Services, 89,* 91–98.

Arnow, B. A., Hart, S., Scott, C., Dea, R., O'Connell, L., & Taylor, C. B. (1999). Childhood sexual abuse, psychological distress, and medical use among women. *Psychosomatic Medicine, 61,* 762–770.

Asbury, J. (1987). African American women in violent relationships: An exploration of cultural differences. In R. L. Hampton (Ed.), *Violence in the Black family* (pp. 89–105). Lexington, MA: Heath.

Astin, M. (1997). Traumatic therapy: How helping rape victims affects me as a therapist. *Women and Therapy, 20,* 101–109.

Aveline, M. (1997). The use of audiotapes in supervision of psychotherapy. In G. Shipton (Ed.), *Supervision of psychotherapy and counseling: Making a place to think* (pp. 80–92). Buckingham, England: Open University Press.

Back, S. E., Brady, K. T., Sonne, S., & Verduin, M. L. (2006). Symptom improvement in co-occurring PTSD and alcohol dependence. *The Journal of Nervous and Mental Disease, 194,* 690–696.

Back, S. E., Dansky, B. S., Carroll, K. M., Foa, E. B., & Brady, K. T. (2001). Exposure therapy in the treatment of PTSD among cocaine-dependent individuals: Description of procedures. *Journal of Substance Abuse Treatment, 21,* 35–45.

Banyard, V. L. (1997). The impact of child sexual abuse and family functioning on four dimensions of women's later parenting. *Child Abuse & Neglect, 21,* 1095–1107.

Banyard, V. L., Englund, D. W., & Rozelle, D. (2001). Parenting the traumatized child: Attending to the needs of nonoffending caregivers of traumatized children. *Psychotherapy: Theory, Research, Practice, Training, 38,* 74–87.

Banyard, V. L., Williams, L. M., & Siegal, J. A. (2003). The impact of complex trauma and depression on parenting: An exploration of mediating risk and protective factors. *Child Maltreatment, 8,* 334–349.

Barocas, H., & Barocas, C. (1983). Wounds of the fathers: The next generation of Holocaust victims. *International Journal of Psycho-Analysis, 5,* 331–341.

Bar-On, D. (1996). Attempting to overcome the intergenerational transmission of trauma. Dialogue between descendants of victims and of perpetrators. In R. Apfel & B. Simon (Eds.), *Minefields of their hearts: The mental health of children in war and communal violence* (pp. 165–188). New Haven, CT: Yale University Press.

Bartholomew, K. (1993). From childhood to adult relationships: Attachment theory and research. In S. Duck (Ed.), *Understanding relationship processes series: Vol. 2. Learning about relationships* (pp. 30–62). Newbury Park, CA: Sage.

Bartholomew, K., & Horowitz, J. (1991). Attachment styles among young adults: A test of a four category model. *Journal of Personality and Social Psychology, 61*, 226–244.

Bauman, P. S., & Dougherty, F. E. (1983). Drug addicted mothers' parenting and their children's development. *International Journal of the Addictions, 18*, 291–302.

Bavelok, S. (1984). *Handbook for the AAPI: Adult–Adolescent Parenting Inventory.* Park City, UT: Family Development Resources.

Bavelok, S., & Bavelok, J. D. (1989). *Nurturing Program for Parents and Children Birth to Five Years: Activities manual.* Park City, UT: Family Development Resources.

Beck, A. T. (1964). Thinking and depression: Theory and therapy. *Archives of General Psychiatry, 10*, 561–571.

Beck, A. T. (1967). *Depression: Causes and treatment.* Philadelphia: University of Pennsylvania Press.

Becker, M. A., Noether, C. D., Larson, M. J., Gatz, M., Brown, V., Heckman, J. P., & Giard, J. (2005). Characteristics of women engaged in treatment for trauma and co-occurring disorders: Findings from a national multisite study. *Journal of Community Psychology, 33*, 429–443.

Beckman, L., & Amaro, H. (1986). Personal and social difficulties faced by females and males entering alcoholism treatment. *Journal of Studies on Alcohol, 45*, 135–145.

Belle, D. (1990). Poverty and women's mental health. *American Psychologist, 45*, 385–389.

Belsky, J. (1993). Etiology of child maltreatment: A developmental–ecological analysis. *Psychological Bulletin, 114*, 413–434.

Bernardi, E., Jones, M., & Tennant, C. (1989). Quality of parenting in alcoholics and narcotics addicts. *British Journal of Psychiatry, 154*, 677–682.

Bernstein, E., & Putnam, F. W. (1986). Development, reliability and validity of a dissociation scale. *The Journal of Nervous and Mental Disease, 174*, 727–735.

Bilchik, G. (2002). A better place to heal. *Health Forum Journal, 45*(4), 10–15.

Bion, W. R. (1962). *Learning from experience.* London: Karnac Books.

Bleiberg, K. L., & Markowitz, J. C. (2005). A pilot study of interpersonal psychotherapy for posttraumatic stress disorder. *The American Journal of Psychiatry, 162*, 181–183.

Bluestone, C., & Tamis-Lemonda, C. (1999). Correlates of parenting styles in predominantly working and middle-class African American mothers. *Journal of Marriage and the Family, 61*, 881–893.

Boudewyns, P. A., Albrecht, J. W., Talbert, F. S., & Hyer, L. A. (1991). Comorbidity and treatment outcome of inpatients with chronic combat-related PTSD. *Hospital and Community Psychiatry, 42*, 847–849.

Bouhoutsos, J. C., Holroyd, J., Lerman, H., Forer, B., & Greenberg, M. (1983). Sexual intimacy between psychotherapists and patients. *Professional Psychology: Research and Practice, 14*, 185–196.

Bowen, S., Witkiewitz, K., Dillworth, T. M., Chawla, N., Simpson, T. L., Ostafin, B. D., et al. (2006). Mindfulness meditation and substance use in an incarcerated population. *Psychology of Addictive Behaviors, 20*, 343–347.

Bowlby, J. (1973). *Attachment and loss: Vol. 2. Separation: Anxiety and anger*. New York: Basic Books.

Brady, K. T. (1997). Posttraumatic stress disorder and comorbidity: Recognizing the many faces of PTSD. *Journal of Clinical Psychiatry, 58*(Suppl. 9), 12–15.

Brady, K. T., Dansky, B. S., Back, S. E., Foa, E. B., & Carroll, K. M. (2001). Exposure therapy in the treatment of PTSD among cocaine-dependent individuals: Preliminary findings. *Journal of Substance Abuse Treatment, 21*, 47–54.

Brady, K. T., Dansky, B. S., Sonne, S., & Saladin, M. E. (1998). Posttraumatic stress disorder and cocaine dependence. *The American Journal on Addictions, 7*, 128–135.

Brady, K. T., Killeen, T., Saladin, M. E., Dansky, B., & Becker, S. (1994). Comorbid substance abuse and posttraumatic stress disorder: Characteristics of women in treatment. *The American Journal on Addictions, 3*, 160–164.

Braveheart, M. Y. (2003). The historical trauma response among natives and its relationship with substance abuse: A Lakota illustration. *Journal of Psychoactive Drugs, 35*, 7–13.

Braveheart, M. Y., & DeBruyn, L. M. (1998). The American Indian Holocaust: Healing historical unresolved grief. *American Indian and Alaska Native Mental Health Research, 8*(2), 56–78.

Breslau, N., & Davis, G. C. (1992). Posttraumatic stress disorder in an urban population of young adults: Risk factors for chronicity. *The American Journal of Psychiatry, 149*, 671–675.

Breslau, N., Davis, G., Andreski, P., Peterson, E., & Schultz, L. (1997). Sex differences in posttraumatic stress disorder. *Archives of General Psychiatry, 54*, 1044–1048.

Breuer, J., & Freud, S. (2000). *Studies on hysteria*. New York: Basic Books. (Original work published 1895)

Briere, J. (1992). *Child abuse trauma: Theory and treatment of the lasting effects*. Newbury Park, CA: Sage.

Briere, J., & Runtz, M. (1987). Post-sexual abuse trauma: Data and implications for clinical practice. *Journal of Interpersonal Violence, 2*, 367–379.

Briere, J., & Runtz, M. (1988). Symptomatology associated with childhood sexual victimization in a nonclinical adult sample. *Child Abuse & Neglect, 12*, 51–59.

Briere, J., & Runtz, M. (1993). Childhood sexual abuse: Long-term sequelae and implications for psychological assessment. *Journal of Interpersonal Violence, 8*, 312–330.

Briere, J., & Scott, C. (2006). *Principles of trauma therapy: A guide to symptoms, evaluation, and treatment*. Thousand Oaks, CA: Sage.

Bromberg, P. (1993). Shadow and substance: A relational perspective on clinical process. In P. M. Bromberg (Ed.), *Standing in the spaces: Essays on clinical process, trauma and dissociation* (pp. 165–187). Hillsdale, NJ: Analytic Press.

Brown, A. (1987). *When battered women kill*. New York: Macmillan.

Brown, P. J., & Wolfe, J. (1994). Substance abuse and post-traumatic stress disorder comorbidity. *Drug and Alcohol Dependence, 35*, 51–59.

Browne, A., & Finkelhor, D. (1986). Impact of child abuse: A review of the research. *Psychological Bulletin, 99*, 66–77.

Bruce, M. L., Takeuchi, D. T., & Leaf, P. J. (1991). Poverty and psychiatric status: Longitudinal evidence from the New Haven Catchment Area Study. *Archives of General Psychiatry, 48,* 470–474.

Brunswick, A., Messeri, P., & Titus, S. P. (1992). *Predictive factors in adult substance abuse: A prospective study of African American adults.* Washington, DC: American Psychological Association.

Bui, H. N., & Morash, M. (1999). Domestic violence in the Vietnamese immigrant community. *Violence Against Women, 5,* 769–795.

Burns, K. A., Chethik, L., Burns, W. J., & Clark, R. (1997). The early relationship of drug abusing mothers and their infants: An assessment at eight to twelve months of age. *Journal of Clinical Psychology, 53,* 279–287.

Caliso, J., & Milner, J. (1992). Childhood history of abuse and child abuse screening. *Child Abuse & Neglect, 16,* 647–659.

Calkins, S. D. (1994). Origins and outcomes of individual differences in emotion regulation. In N. A. Fox (Ed.), The development of emotion regulation. *Monographs of the Society for Research in Child Development, 59*(2–3, Serial. No. 240), 53–72.

Camp, J. M., & Finkelstein, N. (1997). Parenting training for women in residential substance abuse treatment: Result of a demonstration project. *Journal of Substance Abuse Treatment, 14,* 411–422.

Campbell, J., Snow Jones, A., Dienemann, J., Kub, J., Schollenberger, J., O'Campo, P., et al. (2002). Intimate partner violence and physical health consequences. *Archives of Internal Medicine, 162,* 1157–1163.

Carlson, V., Cicchetti, D., Barnett, D., & Braunwald, K. G. (1989). Finding disorder in disorganization: Lessons from research on maltreated infants' attachments to their caregivers. In D. Cicchetti & V. Carlson (Eds.), *Child maltreatment: Theory and research on the causes and consequences of child abuse and neglect* (pp. 494–528). Cambridge, MA: Cambridge University Press.

Carroll, K. M. (1996). Relapse prevention as a psychosocial treatment: A review of controlled clinical trials. *Experimental and Clinical Psychopharmacology, 4,* 46–54.

Carroll, K. M. (1998). *A cognitive–behavioral approach: Treating cocaine addiction* (NIH Publication No. 98-4308). Rockville, MD: National Institute on Drug Abuse.

Carroll, K. M., & Rounsaville, B. J. (2003). Bridging the gap: A hybrid model to link efficacy and effectiveness research in substance abuse treatment. *Psychiatric Services, 54,* 333–339.

Center for Substance Abuse Treatment. (2005). *Substance abuse treatment for persons with co-occurring disorders* (TIP Series 42, DHHS Publication No. [SMA] 05-3992). Rockville, MD: Substance Abuse and Mental Health Services Administration.

Center on Addiction and Substance Abuse. (1996). *Substance abuse and the American woman.* New York: The National Center on Addiction and Substance Abuse at Columbia University.

Centers for Disease Control and Prevention. (2004). *HIV/AIDS surveillance report* (Vol. 16). Atlanta, GA: U.S. Department of Health and Human Services.

Chaffin M., Kelleher, K., & Hollenberg, J. (1996). Onset of physical abuse and neglect: Psychiatric, substance abuse, and social risk factors from prospective community data. *Child Abuse & Neglect, 20,* 191–203.

Chang, D. F. (2002, August). *Family violence in Asian immigrant communities: Ethnographic perspectives on the development of culturally responsive services.* Paper presented at the Domestic Violence and the Asian American Family symposium at the 30th annual meeting of the Asian American Psychological Association, Chicago, IL.

Chang, G., Carroll, K. M., Behr, H. M., & Kosten, T. R. (1992). Improving outcome in pregnant opiate-dependent women. *Journal of Substance Abuse Treatment, 9,* 327–330.

Chilcoat, H. D., & Breslau N. (1998a). Investigations of causal pathways between PTSD and drug use disorders. *Addictive Behaviors, 23,* 827–840.

Chilcoat, H. D., & Breslau N. (1998b). Posttraumatic stress disorder and drug disorders: Testing causal pathways. *Archives of General Psychiatry, 55,* 913–917.

Child Welfare League of America. (2001). *Alcohol, other drugs, & child welfare* (Publication No. 0-87868-839-0). Washington, DC: Author.

Cicchetti, D., Ganiban, J., & Barnett, D. (1991). Contributions from the study of high-risk populations to understanding the development of emotion regulation. In J. Garber & K. Dodge (Eds.), *The development of emotion regulation and dysregulation* (pp. 15–49). New York: Cambridge University Press.

Cicchetti, D., & Toth, S. L. (1998). Perspectives on research and practice in developmental psychopathology. In W. Damon, I. E. Sigel, & K. A. Renninger (Eds.), *Handbook of child psychology: Vol. 4. Child psychology in practice* (pp. 479–583). New York: Wiley.

Clark, C., Giard, J., Fleisher-Bond, M., Slavin, S., Becker, M., & Cox, A. (2004). Creating alcohol and other drug, trauma, and mental health services for women in rural Florida: The Triad Women's Project. *Alcoholism Treatment Quarterly, 22*(3/4), 41–61

Classen, C. C., Palesh, O. G., & Aggarwal, R. (2005). Sexual revictimization: A review of the empirical literature. *Trauma, Violence, & Abuse, 6,* 103–129.

Cloitre, M. (1997). Comorbidity of DSM–IV disorders among women experiencing traumatic events. *NC-PTSD Clinical Quarterly, 7,* 52–53.

Cloitre, M. (1998). Sexual revictimization: Risk factors and prevention. In V. M. Follette, J. I. Ruzek, & F. R. Abueg (Eds.), *Cognitive–behavioral therapies for trauma* (pp. 278–304). New York: Guilford Press.

Cloitre, M., Cohen, L. R., Edelman, R. E., & Han, H. (2001). Posttraumatic stress disorder and extent of trauma exposure as correlates of medical problems and perceived health among women with childhood abuse. *Women & Health, 34*(3), 1–17.

Cloitre, M., Cohen, L. R., & Koenan, K. (2006). *Treating survivors of childhood abuse: Psychotherapy for the interrupted life.* New York: Guilford Press.

Cloitre, M., Cohen, L. R., & Scarvalone, P. (2002). Understanding revictimization among childhood sexual abuse survivors: An interpersonal schema approach. *Journal of Cognitive Psychotherapy: An International Quarterly, 16,* 91–111.

Cloitre, M., Koenan, K. C., Cohen, L. R., & Han, H. (2002). Skills training in affective and interpersonal regulation followed by exposure: A phase-based treatment for PTSD related to childhood abuse. *Journal of Consulting and Clinical Psychology, 70*, 1067–1074.

Cloitre, M., Scarvalone, P., & Difede, J. (1997). Posttraumatic stress disorder, self- and interpersonal dysfunction among sexually retraumatized women. *Journal of Traumatic Stress, 10*, 435–450.

Cloitre, M., Tardiff, K., Marzuk, P. M., Leon, A. C., & Portera, L. (1996). Childhood abuse and subsequent sexual assault among female inpatients. *Journal of Traumatic Stress, 9*, 473–482.

Cocozza, J. J., Jackson, E. W., Hennigan, K., Morrissey, J. P., Reed, B. G., Fallot, R., & Banks, S. (2005). Outcomes for women with co-occurring disorders and trauma: Program-level effects. *Journal of Substance Abuse Treatment, 28*, 109–119.

Cohen, L. R. (2006). *Trauma-informed parenting group for women with complex trauma and substance use disorders.* Grant award, Columbia University School of Social Work, Center of Intervention and Prevention Research on HIV and Drug Abuse.

Cohen, L. R., Hien, A., & Batchelder, S. (2008). The impact of cumulative maternal trauma and diagnosis on parenting behavior. *Child Maltreatment, 13*, 27–38.

Cohen, L. R., Miele, G. M., Litt, L. C., & Hien, D. A. (2008). *Body Education for Survivors of Trauma (BESTHealth): A web-based health intervention for women.* Unpublished manualized intervention, Columbia University, New York.

Cohn, J. F., Campbell, S. B., Matias, R., & Hopkins, J. (1990). Face-to-face interactions of postpartum depressed and non-depressed mother–infant pairs at 2 months. *Developmental Psychology, 26*, 15–23.

Cohn, J. F., Matias, R., Tronick, E. Z., Connell, D., & Lyons-Ruth, K. (1986). Face-to-face interactions of depressed mothers and their infants. In E. Z. Tronick & T. Field (Eds.), *Maternal depression and infant disturbance* (pp. 31–45). San Francisco: Jossey-Bass.

Cole, P., Michel, P., & Teti, L. O. (1994). The development of emotion regulation and dysregulation: A clinical perspective. In N. A. Fox (Ed.), The development of emotion regulation. *Monographs of the Society for Research in Child Development, 59*(2–3, Serial. No. 240), 73–100.

Cole, P., & Putnam, F. W. (1992). Effects of incest on self and social functioning: A developmental psychopathology perspective. *Journal of Consulting and Clinical Psychology, 60*, 174–184.

Cole, P., & Woolger, C. (1989). Incest survivors: The relation of their perceptions of their parents and their own parenting attitudes. *Child Abuse & Neglect, 13*, 409–416.

Cole, P., Woolger, C., Power, T., & Smith, K. (1992). Parenting difficulties among adult survivors of father–daughter incest. *Child Abuse & Neglect, 16*, 239–249.

Coleman, H. L. K., Wampold, B. E., & Casali, S. L. (1995). Ethnic minorities' ratings of ethnically similar and European American counselors: A meta-analysis. *Journal of Counseling Psychology, 42*, 55–64.

Coley, S. M., & Beckett, J. O. (1988). Black battered women: A review of the empirical literature. *Journal of Counseling and Development, 66*, 266–270.

Comas-Diaz, L. (1990). Hispanic/Latino communities: Psychological implications. *The Journal of Training and Practice in Professional Psychology, 4*(1), 14–35.

Conrad, D. J., & Perry, B. D. (2000). *The cost of caring: Understanding and preventing secondary traumatic stress when working with traumatized and maltreated children.* Houston, TX: The Child Trauma Academy.

Cottler, L. B., Nishith, P., & Compton, W., III. (2001). Gender differences in risk factors for trauma exposure and post-traumatic stress disorder among inner-city drug abusers in and out of treatment. *Comprehensive Psychiatry, 42,* 111–117.

Courtois, C. A. (1979). The incest experience and its aftermath. *Victimology: An International Journal, 4,* 337–347.

Courtois, C. A. (1993). Vicarious traumatization of the therapist. *NC-PTSD Clinical Newsletter, 3,* 8–9.

Courtois, C. A. (2004). Complex trauma, complex reactions assessment and treatment. *Psychotherapy: Theory, Research, Practice, Training, 41,* 412–425.

Cowan, P. A., Powell, D., & Cowan, C. P. (1998). Parenting interventions: A family systems perspective. In W. Damon, I. E. Sigel, & K. A. Renninger (Eds.), *Handbook of child psychology: Vol. 4. Child psychology in practice* (pp. 3–72). New York: Wiley.

Craske, M. G., & Barlow, D. H. (2007a). *Mastery of your anxiety and panic: Therapist guide.* New York: Oxford University Press.

Craske, M. G., & Barlow, D. H. (2007b). *Mastery of your anxiety and panic: Workbook.* New York: Oxford University Press.

Crick, N. R., & Dodge, K. A. (1994). A review and reformulation of social information-processing mechanisms in children's social adjustment. *Psychological Bulletin, 115,* 74–101.

Crits-Christoph, P., Siqueland, L., Blaine, J., Frank, A., Luborsky, L., Onken, L. S., et al. (1999). Psychosocial treatments for cocaine dependence: Results of the National Institute on Drug Abuse Collaborative Cocaine Treatment Study. *Archives of General Psychiatry, 56,* 493–502.

Cross, C. (2001). A personal history of childhood sexual abuse: Parenting patterns and problems. *Clinical Child Psychology and Psychiatry, 6,* 563–574.

Danieli, Y. (Ed.). (1998). *International handbook of multigenerational legacies of trauma.* New York: Plenum Press.

Dansky, B. S., Saladin, M. E., Brady, K. T., Kilpatrick, D. G., & Resnick, H. S. (1995). Prevalence of victimization and posttraumatic stress disorder among women with substance use disorders: Comparison of telephone and in-person assessment samples. *The International Journal of the Addictions, 30,* 1079–1099.

Davidson, J. R. (2001). The recognition and treatment of posttraumatic stress disorder. *The Journal of the American Medical Association, 286,* 584–588.

Davies, J. M., & Frawley, M. G. (1994). *Treating the adult survivor of childhood sexual abuse: A psychoanalytic perspective.* New York: Basic Books.

Dayton, G., & Rogers, F. (2002). The value of cognitive–behavioral strategies. In A. Tatarsky (Ed.), *Harm reduction psychotherapy: A new treatment for drug and alcohol problems* (pp. 72–105). Lanham, MD: Jason Aronson.

De Bellis, M. D. (2002). Developmental traumatology: A contributory mechanism for alcohol and substance use disorders. *Psychoneuroendocrinology, 27*, 155–170.

de Mello, M. F., Mari, J. J., Bacatchuk, J., Verdeli, H., & Neugebauer, R. (2005). A systematic review of research findings on the efficacy of IPT for depressive disorders. *European Archives of Psychiatry and Clinical Neuroscience, 255*, 75–82.

Deater-Deckard, K., & Dodge, K. (1997). Externalizing behavior problems and discipline revisited: Nonlinear effects and variation by culture, context, and gender. *Psychological Inquiry, 8*, 161–175.

Denning, P. (2000). *Practicing harm reduction psychotherapy: An alternative approach to addictions.* New York: Guilford Press.

Derogatis, L. R. (1992). *Administration, scoring, and procedures: Manual II.* Baltimore, MD: Clinical Psychometric Research.

Deykin, E. Y., Keane, T. M., Kaloupek, D., Fincke, G., Rothendler, J., Siegfried, M., & Creamer, K. (2001). Posttraumatic stress disorder and the use of health services. *Psychosomatic Medicine, 63*, 835–841.

DiLillo, D., & Damashek, A. (2003). Parenting characteristics of women reporting a history of childhood sexual abuse. *Child Maltreatment, 8*, 319–333.

DiLillo, D., & Long, P. J. (1999). Perceptions of couple functioning among female survivors of child sexual abuse. *Journal of Child Sexual Abuse, 7*, 59–75.

Dodge, K. A. (1989). Coordinating responses to aversive stimuli: Introduction to a special section on the development of emotion regulation. *Developmental Psychology, 25*, 339–342.

Donovan, B., Padin-Rivera, E., & Kowaliw, S. (2001). "Transcend": Initial outcomes from a posttraumatic stress disorder/substance abuse treatment program. *Journal of Traumatic Stress, 14*, 757–772.

Downs, W. R., Miller, B. A., Testa, M., & Panek, D. (1992). Long-term effects of parent-to-child violence for women. *Journal of Interpersonal Violence, 7*, 365–382.

Dutton, D. G., Saunders, K., Starzomski, A., & Bartholomew, K. (1994). Intimacy-anger and insecure attachments as precursors of abuse in intimate relationships. *Journal of Applied Social Psychology, 24*, 1367–1386.

Edlin, B., Irwin, K., Faruque, S., McCoy, C. B., Word, C., Serrano, Y., et al. (1994). Intersecting epidemics—Crack cocaine use and HIV infection among inner-city young adults. *The New England Journal of Medicine, 331*, 1422–1427.

Eisenberg, N. (1998). Introduction. In W. Damon & N. Eisenberg (Eds.), *Handbook of child psychology: Vol. 3. Social, emotional and personality development* (5th ed., pp. 1–24). New York: Wiley.

Eisenberg, N., Cumberland, A., & Spinrad, T. L. (1998). Parental socialization of emotion. *Psychological Inquiry, 9*, 241–273.

Eisenberg, N., Fabes, R. A., Guthrie, I. K., & Reiser, M. (2000). Dispositional emotionality and regulation: Their role in predicting quality of social functioning. *Journal of Personality and Social Psychology, 78*, 136–157.

Eisenberg, N., & Morris, A. S. (2002). Children's emotion-related regulation. In R. Kail (Ed.), *Advances in child development and behavior* (Vol. 30, pp. 190–229). Amsterdam: Academic Press.

El-Bassel, N., Gilbert, L., Wu, E., Go, H., & Hill, J. (2005). Relationship between drug abuse and intimate partner violence: A longitudinal study among women receiving methadone. *American Journal of Public Health, 95,* 465–470.

Escobar, J. I., Canino, G., Rubio-Stipec, M., & Bravo, M. (1992). Somatic symptoms after a natural disaster: A prospective study. *The American Journal of Psychiatry, 149,* 965–967.

Fallot, R., & Harris, M. (2002). The trauma recovery and empowerment model (TREM). *Community Mental Health Journal, 38,* 475–485.

Feerick, M. M. (1999). Child maltreatment and adulthood violence: The role of attachment and drug abuse. *Dissertation Abstracts International, 5907B.* (UMI No. AAT 9900081)

Feerick, M. M., Haugaard, J. J., & Hien, D. A. (2005). Child maltreatment and adulthood violence: The contribution of attachment and drug abuse. *Child Maltreatment, 7,* 226–240.

Feldman-Summers, S., & Jones, G. (1984). Psychological impacts of sexual contact between therapists or other health care practitioners and their clients. *Journal of Counseling and Clinical Psychology, 52,* 1054–1061.

Felitti, V. J., Anda, R. F., Nordenberg, D., Williamson, D. F., Spitz, A. M., Edwards, V., et al. (1998). Relationship of childhood abuse and household dysfunction to many of the leading causes of death in adults: The Adverse Childhood Experiences (ACE) Study. *American Journal of Preventive Medicine, 14,* 245–258.

Fergusson, D. M., & Mullen, P. E. (1999). *Childhood sexual abuse: An evidence-based perspective.* Thousand Oaks, CA: Sage.

Ferrada-Noli, M., Asberg, M., Ormstad, K., Lundin, T., & Sundbom, E. (1998). Suicidal behavior after severe trauma: Part I. PTSD diagnoses, psychiatric comorbidity, and assessments of suicidal behavior. *Journal of Traumatic Stress, 11,* 103–112.

Field, T., Healy, B., Goldstein, S., & Guthertz, M. (1990). Behavior-state matching and synchronicity in mother–infant interactions of nondepressed versus depressed dyads. *Developmental Psychology, 26,* 7–14.

Finkelhor, D. (1990). Early and long-term effects of child sexual abuse: An update. *Professional Psychology: Research and Practice, 21,* 325–330.

Finkelhor, D., & Browne, A. (1985). The traumatic impact of child sexual abuse: A conceptualization. *American Journal of Orthopsychiatry, 55,* 530–541.

Finkelstein, N., Rechberger, E., Russell, L., VanDeMark, N., Noether, C., O'Keefe, M., et al. (2005). Building resilience in children of women with co-occurring disorders and histories of violence: Intervention model and implementation issues. *Journal of Behavioral Health Services & Research, 32,* 141–154.

Fiorentine, R., & Hillhouse, M. P. (1999). Drug treatment effectiveness and client–counselor empathy: Exploring the effects of gender and ethnic congruency. *Journal of Drug Issues, 29,* 59–74.

Flannery, R. B. (1990). Social support and psychological trauma: A methodological review. *Journal of Traumatic Stress, 3,* 593–611.

Flaskerud, J. H., & Hu, T. (1992). Racial/ethnic identity and amount and type of psychiatric treatment. *The American Journal of Psychiatry, 149,* 379–384.

Foa, E. B., Cashman, B., Jaycox, L., & Perry, K. (1997). The validation of a self-report measure of posttraumatic stress disorder: The Posttraumatic Diagnostic Scale. *Psychological Assessment, 9,* 445–451.

Foa, E. B., & Meadows, E. A. (1997). Psychosocial treatments for posttraumatic stress disorder: A critical review. *Annual Review of Psychology, 48,* 449–480.

Foa, E. B., Riggs, D. S., Dancu, C. V., Constance, V., & Rothbaum, B. O. (1993). Reliability and validity of a brief instrument for assessing post-traumatic stress disorder. *Journal of Traumatic Stress, 6,* 459–473.

Foa, E. B., & Rothbaum, B. O. (1998). *Treating the trauma of rape: Cognitive–behavioral therapy for PTSD.* New York: Guilford Press.

Foa, E. B., Rothbaum, B. O., & Furr, J. M. (2003). Augmenting exposure therapy with other CBT procedures. *Psychiatric Annals, 33,* 47–53.

Foa, E. B., Rothbaum, B. O., Riggs, D. S., & Murdock, T. B. (1991). Treatment of PTSD in rape victims: A comparison between cognitive-behavioral procedures and counseling. *Journal of Consulting and Clinical Psychology, 59,* 715–723.

Fonagy, P. (1998). An attachment theory approach to the treatment of the difficult patient. *Bulletin of the Menninger Clinic, 62,* 147–169.

Fonagy, P., Steele, H., & Steele, M. (1991). Maternal representations of attachment during pregnancy predict the organization of infant–mother attachment at one year of age. *Child Development, 62,* 891–905.

Foy, D. W., Resnick, H. S., Sipprelle, R. C., & Carroll, K. M. (1987). Premilitary, military, and postmilitary factors in the development of combat-related posttraumatic stress disorder. *Behavior Therapist, 10,* 3–9.

Foy, D. W., Ruzek, J., Glynn, S., Riney, S., & Gusman, F. (2002). Trauma focus group therapy for combat-related PTSD. *Journal of Clinical Psychology, 58,* 907–918.

Friedman, M. J. (1993). Psychobiological and pharmacological approaches to treatment. In J. P. Wilson & B. Raphael (Eds.), *International handbook of traumatic stress syndromes* (pp. 785–794). New York: Plenum Press.

Friedman, M. J., & Schnurr, P. P. (1995). The relationship between trauma, posttraumatic stress disorder, and physical health. In M. J. Friedman, D. S. Charney, & A. Y. Deutch (Eds.), *Neurobiological and clinical consequences of stress: From normal adaptation to PTSD* (pp. 507–524). New York: Lippincott-Raven.

Fullilove, M. T. (2004). *Root shock: How tearing up city neighborhoods hurts America, and what we can do about it.* New York: One World/Ballantine.

Fullilove, M. T., Fullilove, R. E., Smith, M., Winkler, K., Michael, C., Panzer, P. G., & Wallace, R. (1993). Violence, trauma and post-traumatic stress disorder among women drug users. *Journal of Traumatic Stress, 6,* 533–543.

Fullilove, M. T., Lown, A., & Fullilove, R. E. (1992). Crack 'hos and skeezers: Traumatic experiences of women crack users. *Journal of Sex Research, 29,* 275–287.

Gara, M. A., Allen, L. A., Herzog, E. P., & Woolfolk, R. L. (2000). The abused child as parent: The structure and content of physically abused mothers' perceptions of their babies. *Child Abuse & Neglect, 24,* 627–639.

Giard, J., Hennigan, K., Huntington, H., Vogel, W., Rinehart, D., Mazelis, R., et al. (2005). Development and implementation of a multisite evaluation for the Women, Co-Occurring Disorders and Violence Study. *Journal of Community Psychology, 33*, 411–427.

Gold, J. H. (2000). Psychotherapy with women survivors of sexual abuse. *Journal of Psychiatric Practice, 6*, 27–32.

Goldberg, D. A. (1983). Resistance to the use of video in individual psychotherapy training. *The American Journal of Psychiatry, 140*, 1172–1176.

Golding, J. M. (1994). Sexual assault history and physical health in randomly selected Los Angeles women. *Health Psychology, 13*, 130–138.

Gondolf, E. W., Fisher, E., & McFerron, J. R. (1988). Racial differences among shelter residents: A comparison of Anglo, Black, and Hispanic battered women. *Journal of Family Violence, 3*, 39–51.

Goodman, S. H., & Brumley, H. E. (1990). Schizophrenic and depressed mothers: Relational deficits in parenting. *Developmental Psychology, 26*, 31–39.

Gross, J. J. (1999). Emotion regulation: Past, present, future. *Cognition & Emotion, 13*, 551–573.

Grotstein, J. S. (1987). The borderline as a disorder of self-regulation. In J. S. Grotstein, M. F. Solomon, & J. A. Lang (Eds.), *The borderline patient: Emerging concepts in diagnosis, psychodynamics, and treatment* (pp. 347–384). Hillsdale, NJ: Analytic Press.

Guy, J. D., Brown, C. K., & Poelstra, P. L. (1992). Safety concerns and protective measures used by psychotherapists. *Professional Psychology: Research and Practice, 23*, 421–423.

Haft, W. L., & Slade, A. (1989). Affect attunement and maternal attachment: A pilot study. *Infant Mental Health Journal, 10*, 157–172.

Hampton, R. L., & Gelles, R. J. (1994). Violence toward Black women in a nationally representative sample of Black families. *Journal of Comparative Family Studies, 25*, 105–119.

Hampton, R. L., Oliver, W., & Magarian, L. (2003). Domestic violence in the African American community: An analysis of social and structural factors. *Violence Against Women, 9*, 533–557.

Hans, S. L., Bernstein, V. J., & Henson, L. G. (1999). The role of psychopathology in parenting of drug-dependent women. *Development and Psychopathology, 11*, 957–977.

Harmer, A., Sanderson, J., & Mertin, P. (1999). Influence of negative childhood experiences on psychological functioning, social support, and parenting for mothers recovering from addiction. *Child Abuse & Neglect, 23*, 421–433.

Harris, M., & Community Connections Trauma Work Group. (1998). *Trauma recovery and empowerment: A clinician's guide for working with women in groups.* New York: Free Press.

Harris, M., & Fallot, R. (Eds.). (2001). *Using trauma theory to design service systems.* San Francisco: Jossey-Bass.

Harris, M., Fallot, R. D., & Berley, R. W. (2005). Qualitative interviews on substance abuse relapse and prevention among female trauma survivors. *Psychiatric Services, 56*, 1292–1296.

Harris, M., & Parenting Workgroup (2001). *Non-traditional parenting interventions, community connections.* Unpublished manual, Community Connection, Washington, DC.

Hazan, C., & Shaver, P. R. (1994). Attachment as an organizational framework for research on close relationships. *Psychological Inquiry, 5*, 1–22.

Herman, J. L. (1992a). Complex PTSD: A syndrome in survivors of prolonged and repeated trauma. *Journal of Traumatic Stress, 5*, 377–391.

Herman, J. L. (1992b). *Trauma and recovery: The aftermath of violence—From domestic abuse to political terror.* New York: Basic Books.

Herman, J. L., & van der Kolk, B. A. (1987). Traumatic antecedents of borderline personality disorder. In B. van der Kolk (Ed.), *Psychological trauma* (pp. 111–126). Washington, DC: American Psychiatric Press.

Hesse, A. R. (2002). Secondary trauma: How working with trauma survivors affects therapists. *Clinical Social Work Journal, 30*, 293–311.

Hesse, E., & Main, M. (1999). Second-generation effects of unresolved trauma in nonmaltreating parents: Dissociated, frightening, and threatening parental behavior. *Psychoanalytic Inquiry, 19*, 481–540.

Hien, D. A., Cohen, L. R., Caldeira, N. A., Batchelder, S., & Wasserman, G. (2008). *The role of emotion regulation deficits in child abuse potential among mothers with histories of substance use and psychiatric disorders.* Manuscript submitted for publication.

Hien, D. A., Cohen, L. R., & Campbell, A. (2005). Is traumatic stress a vulnerability factor for development of substance use disorders in women? *Clinical Psychology Review, 25*, 813–823.

Hien, D. A., Cohen, L. R., Litt, L. C., & Miele, G. M. (2001, December). Attachment as a predictor of trauma treatment outcome. In C. Stalker (Chair), *Adult attachment and child abuse: Implications for treatment process and outcome.* Paper presented at the 10th Annual Meeting of the International Society for Traumatic Stress Studies, New Orleans, Louisiana.

Hien, D. A., Cohen, L. R., Miele, G. M., Litt, L. C., & Capstick, C. (2004). Promising treatments for women with comorbid PTSD and substance use disorders. *The American Journal of Psychiatry, 161*, 1426–1432.

Hien, D. A., & Honeyman, T. (2000). A closer look at the maternal substance abuse–violence link. *Journal of Interpersonal Violence, 15*, 503–522.

Hien, D. A., & Miele, G. M. (2003). Emotion-focused coping as a mediator of maternal cocaine abuse and antisocial behavior. *Psychology of Addictive Behaviors, 17*, 49–55.

Hien, D. A., Zimberg, S., Weissman, S., First, M. B., & Ackerman, S. (1997). Dual diagnosis in urban substance abuse and mental health clinics. *Psychiatric Services, 48*, 1058–1064.

Higley, J. L., Hasert, M. F., Suomi, S. J., & Linnoila, M. (1991). A nonhuman primate model of alcohol abuse: Effects of early experience, personality, and stress on alcohol consumption. *Proceedings of the National Academy of Sciences of the United States of America, 88,* 7261–7265.

Hobbs, F., & Stoops, N. (2002). *Demographic trends in the 20th century: Census 2000 special reports* (U.S. Census Bureau Series CENSR-4). Washington, DC: U.S. Government Printing Office.

Hoffman, J. A., Klein, H., Eber, M., & Crosby, H. (2000). Frequency and intensity of crack use as predictors of women's involvement in HIV-related sexual risk behaviors. *Drug and Alcohol Dependence, 58,* 227–236.

Holtzworth-Munroe, A. (2005). Male versus female intimate partner violence: Putting controversial findings into context. *Journal of Marriage and Family, 67,* 1120–1125.

Horowitz, H. A., Overton, W. F., Rosenstein, D., & Steidl, J. H. (1992). Comorbid adolescent substance abuse: A maladaptive pattern of self-regulation. *Adolescent Psychiatry: Development and Clinical Studies, 18,* 465–483.

Howell, E. (2005). *The dissociative mind.* Hillsdale, NJ: Analytic Press.

Hu, T., Snowden, L. R., Jerrell, J. M., & Nguyen, T. D. (1991). Ethnic populations in public mental health: Services choice and level of use. *American Journal of Public Health, 81,* 1429–1434.

Hufford, M. R. (2000). Empirically supported treatments and comorbid psychopathology: Spelunking Plato's cave. *Professional Psychology: Research and Practice, 31,* 96–99.

Huntington, N., Jahn Moses, D., & Veysey, B. M. (2005). Developing and implementing a comprehensive approach to serving women with co-occurring disorders and histories of trauma. *Journal of Community Psychology, 33,* 395–410.

Hyler, L., Fallon, J., Harrison W., & Boudewyns, P. A. (1987). MMPI overreporting by Vietnam combat veterans. *Journal of Clinical Psychology, 43,* 79–83.

Institute of Medicine. (1998). *Bridging the gap between practice and research: Forging new partnerships with community-based drug and alcohol treatment.* Washington, DC: National Academies Press.

Jacobsen, E. (1938). *Progressive relaxation.* University of Chicago Press.

Jahn Moses, D., Reed, B. G., Mazelis, R., & D'Ambrosio, B. (2003). *Creating trauma services for women with co-occurring disorders.* Delmar, NY: Policy Research Associates.

Jehu, D. (1988). *Beyond sexual abuse: Therapy with women who were childhood victims.* New York: Wiley.

Jellinek, E. M. (1962). *Encyclopedia of problems of alcohol: Plan of the project.* Stanford, CA: Cooperative Commission on the Study of Alcoholism.

Kabat-Zinn, J. (1990). *Full catastrophe living.* New York: Bantam.

Kabat-Zinn, J. (1994). *Wherever you go, there you are: Mindfulness meditation in everyday life.* New York: Hyperion.

Kalmuss, D. (1984). The intergenerational transmission of marital aggression. *Journal of Marriage and the Family, 46,* 11–19.

Kanuha, V. (1994). Women of color in battering relationships. In L. Comas-Diaz & B. Greene (Eds.), *Women of color: Integrating ethnic and gender identities in psychotherapy* (pp. 428–454). New York: Guilford Press.

Kardiner, S. H., Fuller, M., & Mensch, I. N. (1973). A survey of physicians' attitudes and practices regarding erotic and non-erotic contact with patients. *The American Journal of Psychiatry, 133,* 1324–1325.

Karenga, M. (1988). Black studies and the problematic of paradigm: The philosophical dimension. *Journal of Black Studies, 18,* 395–414.

Kashani, J., Daniel, A., Dandoy, A. C., & Holcomb, W. (1992). Family violence: Impact on children. *Journal of the American Academy of Child & Adolescent Psychiatry, 31,* 181–189.

Kaufman, J., & Zigler, E. (1987). Do abused children become abusive parents? *American Journal of Orthopsychiatry, 57,* 186–192.

Kessler, R., Sonnega, A., Bromet, E., Hughes, M., & Nelson, C. (1995). Post-traumatic stress disorder in the National Comorbidity Survey. *Archives of General Psychiatry, 52,* 1048–1060.

Kettinger, L. A., Nair, P., & Schuler, M. E. (2000). Exposure to environmental risk factors and parenting attitudes among substance-abusing women. *American Journal of Drug and Alcohol Abuse, 26,* 1–11.

Khantzian, E. J. (1985). The self-medication hypothesis of addictive disorders. *The American Journal of Psychiatry, 142,* 1259–1264.

Khantzian, E. J. (1997). The self-medication hypothesis of substance use disorders: A reconsideration and recent applications. *Harvard Review of Psychiatry, 4,* 231–244.

Khantzian, E. J., & Schneider, R. J. (1986). Treatment implications of a psychodynamic understanding of opioid addicts. In R. E. Meyer (Ed.), *Psychopathology and addictive disorders* (pp. 323–333). New York: Guilford Press.

Kimerling, R., & Calhoun, K. S. (1994). Somatic symptoms, social support, and treatment seeking among sexual assault victims. *Journal of Consulting and Clinical Psychology, 62,* 333–340.

Kimerling, R., Clum, G. A., & Wolfe, J. (2000). Relationships among trauma exposure, chronic posttraumatic stress disorder symptoms, and self-reported health in women: Replication and extension. *Journal of Traumatic Stress, 13,* 115–128.

Kipper, D. (1986). *Psychotherapy through clinical role playing.* Philadelphia: Brunner/Mazel.

Klerman, G., & Weissman, M. M. (1993). *New applications in interpersonal psychotherapy.* Washington, DC: American Psychiatric Press.

Klerman, G., Weissman, M. M., Rounsaville, B., & Chevron, E. (1984). *Interpersonal psychotherapy of depression.* New York: Basic Books.

Kling, H. (2000). Antisocial personality disorder in inner-city female drug users. *Dissertation Abstracts International, 60* (10-B), 5227. (UMI No. AAT 9948036)

Koss, M. P., Woodruff, W. J., & Koss, P. G. (1990). Relation of criminal victimization to health perceptions among women medical patients. *Journal of Consulting and Clinical Psychology, 58,* 147–152.

Krahe, B., Sheinberger-Olwig, R., Waizenhofer, E., & Koplin, S. (1999). Childhood sexual abuse revictimization in adolescence. *Child Abuse & Neglect, 4,* 383–394.

Krystal, H. D. (1997). Self representation and the capacity for self-care. In D. L. Yasilove (Ed.), *Essential papers on addiction* (pp. 109–146). New York: New York University Press.

Kulka, R. A., Schkenger, W. E., Fairbank, J. A., Hough, R. L., Jordon, B. K., Marmer, C. R., & Weiss, D. S. (1990). *Trauma and the Vietnam War generation: Report of findings from the National Vietnam Veterans Readjustment Study.* New York: Brunner/Mazel.

Kumpfer, K. L. (1987). Special populations: Etiology and prevention of vulnerability to chemical dependency in children of substance abusers. In B. S. Brown & A. R. Mills (Eds.), *Youth at high risk for substance abuse* (DHHS Publication ADM 90-1537, pp. 1–71). Washington, DC: National Institute on Drug Abuse.

Kumpfer, K. L., & Alvarado, R. (1995). Strengthening families to prevent drug use in multiethnic youth. In G. Botvin, S. Schinke, & M. Orlandi (Eds.), *Drug abuse prevention with multiethnic youth* (pp. 253–292). Newbury Park, CA: Sage.

Kumpfer, K. L., Molgaard, V., & Spoth, R. (1996). The Strengthening Families Program for the prevention of delinquency and drug use. In R. D. Peters & R. J. McMahon (Eds.), *Preventing childhood disorders, substance abuse, and delinquency* (Vol. 3, pp. 241–267). Thousand Oaks, CA: Sage.

La Torre, M. A. (2006). Creating a healing environment. *Perspectives in Psychiatric Care, 42,* 263–265.

Leigh, B. C., & Stall, R. (1993). Substance use and risky sexual behavior for exposure to HIV: Issues in methodology, interpretation, and prevention. *American Psychologist, 48,* 1035–1045.

Leitenberg, H., Greenwald, E., & Cado, S. (1992). A retrospective study of long-term methods of coping with having been sexually abused during childhood. *Child Abuse & Neglect, 16,* 399–407.

Leonard, L. M., & Follette, V. M. (2002). Sexual functioning in women reporting a history of child sexual abuse: Review of the empirical literature and clinical implications. *Annual Review of Sex Research, 13,* 346–388.

Lindholm, K., & Willey, R. (1986). Ethnic differences in child abuse and sexual abuse. *Hispanic Journal of Behavioral Sciences, 8,* 111–125.

Linehan, M. M. (1993a). *Cognitive–behavioral treatment of borderline personality disorder.* New York: Guilford Press.

Linehan, M. M. (1993b). *Skills training manual for treating borderline personality disorder.* New York: Guilford Press.

Linehan, M. M., Dimeff, L. A., Reynolds, S. K., Comtois, K. A., Welch, S. S., Heagerty, P., & Kivlahan, D. R. (2002). Dialectical behavior therapy versus comprehensive validation therapy plus 12-step for the treatment of opioid-dependent women meeting criteria for borderline personality disorder. *Drug and Alcohol Dependence, 67,* 13–26.

Litt, L. C., Cohen, L. R., & Hien, D. A. (2001). Does treatment beget treatment? Treatment use after CBT for PTSD and substance use. In M. McFall (Chair), *New considerations in the treatment of comorbid substance use and PTSD.* Paper presented at the 10th annual meeting of the International Society for Traumatic Stress Studies, New Orleans, LA.

Liu, D., Diorio, J., Day, J. C., Francis, D. D., & Meaney, M. J. (2000). Maternal care, hippocampal synaptogenesis and cognitive development in rats. *Nature Neuroscience, 3,* 799–806.

Loeb, T. B., Williams, J. K., Vargas Carmona, J., Rivkin, I., Wyatt, G., Chin, D., & Asuan-O'Brien, A. (2002). Child sexual abuse: Associations with the sexual functioning of adolescents and adults. *Annual Review of Sex Research, 13,* 307–345.

Logan, T. K., & Leukefeld, C. (2000). Sexual and drug use behaviors among female crack users: A multisite sample. *Drug and Alcohol Dependence, 58,* 237–245.

Lovejoy, M. C., Graczyk, P. A., O'Hare, E., & Neuman, G. (2000) Maternal depression and parenting behavior: A meta-analytic review. *Clinical Psychology Review, 20,* 561–592.

Luthar, S. S., Cushing, G., Merikangas, K., & Rounsaville, B. J. (1998). Multiple jeopardy: Risk/protective factors among addicted mothers' offspring. *Development and Psychopathology, 10,* 117–136.

Luthar, S. S., & Suchman, N. (2000). Relational psychotherapy mother's group: A developmentally informed intervention for at-risk mothers. *Development and Psychopathology, 12,* 235–253.

Luthar, S. S., & Walsh, K. (1995) Treatment needs of drug-addicted mothers: Integrated parenting psychotherapy interventions. *Journal of Substance Abuse Treatment, 12,* 341–348.

Lyons-Ruth, K., Bronfman, E., & Parsons, E. (1999). Maternal frightened, frightening, or atypical behavior and disorganized infant attachment patterns. In J. I. Vondra & D. Barnett (Ed.), *Atypical attachment in infancy and early childhood among children at developmental risk. Monographs of the Society for Research in Child Development, 64*(3, Serial No. 258), 67–96.

Main, M., Kaplan, N., & Cassidy, J. (1985). Security in infancy, childhood, and adulthood: A move to the level of representation. In I. Bretherton & E. Waters (Eds.), Growing points of attachment theory and research. *Monographs of the Society for Research in Child Development, 50*(1–2, Serial No. 209), 66–104.

Main, M., & Solomon, J. (1990). Procedures for identifying infants as disorganized–disoriented during the Ainsworth Strange Situation. In M. Greenberg, D. Cicchetti, & E. M. Cummings (Eds.), *Attachment in the preschool years: Theory, research, and intervention* (pp. 121–161). Chicago: University of Chicago Press.

Marlatt, G. A. (Ed.). (1998). *Harm reduction: Pragmatic strategies for managing high-risk behaviors.* New York: Guilford Press.

Marlatt, G. A. (2002). Buddhist psychology and the treatment of addictive behavior. *Cognitive and Behavioral Practice, 9,* 44–49.

Marlatt, G. A., & Gordon, J. R. (Eds.). (1985). *Relapse prevention: Maintenance strategies in the treatment of addictive behaviors*. New York: Guilford Press.

Marx, B. P., Van Wie, V., & Gross, A. M. (1996). Date rape risk factors: A review and methodological critique of the literature. *Aggression and Violent Behavior, 1*, 27–45.

Mayes, L. C. (1995). Substance abuse and parenting. In M. H. Bornstein (Ed.), *Handbook of parenting: Vol. 4. Applied and practical parenting* (pp. 101–125). Mahwah, NJ: Erlbaum.

McCann, I. L., & Colletti, J. (1994). The dance of empathy: A hermeneutic formulation of countertransference, empathy, and understanding in the treatment of individuals who have experienced early childhood trauma. In J. P. Wilson & J. D. Lindy (Eds.), *Countertransference in the treatment of PTSD* (pp. 87–121). New York: Guilford Press.

McCann, I. L., & Pearlman, L. A. (1990). Vicarious traumatization: A framework for understanding the psychological effects of working with victims. *Journal of Traumatic Stress, 3*, 131–149.

McCann, I. L., Sakheim, D. K., & Abrahamson, D. J. (1988). Trauma and victimization: A model of psychological adaptation. *The Counseling Psychologist, 16*, 531–594.

McCauley, J., Kern, D. E., Kolodner, K., Dill, L., Schroeder, F., DeChant, H. K., et al. (1997). Clinical characteristics of women with a history of childhood violence: Unhealed wounds. *The Journal of the American Medical Association, 277*, 1362–1368.

McCloskey, L. A., & Bailey, J. A. (2000). The intergenerational transmission of risk for child sexual abuse. *Journal of Interpersonal Violence, 15*, 1019–1035.

McEwen, B. S. (1998). Protective and damaging effects of stress mediators. *The New England Journal of Medicine, 338*, 171–179.

McFall, M. E., Veith, R. C., & Murburg, M. M. (1992). Basal sympathoadrenal function in PTSD. *Biological Psychiatry, 31*, 1050–1056.

McFarlane, A. C., Atchison, M., Rafalowicz, E., & Papay, P. (1994). Physical symptoms in post-traumatic stress disorder. *Journal of Psychosomatic Research, 38*, 715–726.

McHugo, G. J., Caspi, Y., Kammerer, N., Mazelis, R., Jackson, E. W., Russell, L., et al. (2005). The assessment of trauma history in women with co-occurring substance abuse and mental disorders and a history of interpersonal violence. *Journal of Behavioral Health Services & Research, 32*, 113–127.

Mears, D. P., Carlson, M. J., Holden, G. W., & Harris, S. D. (2001). Reducing domestic violence revictimization: The effects of individual and contextual factors and type of legal intervention. *Journal of Interpersonal Violence, 16*, 1260–1283.

Meichenbaum, D. (1996). Stress inoculation training for coping with stressors. *The Clinical Psychologist, 49*, 4–7.

Merrill, L. L., Guimond, J. M., Thomsen, C. J., & Milner, J. S. (2003). Child sexual abuse and number of sexual partners in young women: The role of abuse severity, coping style, and sexual functioning. *Journal of Consulting and Clinical Psychology, 71*, 987–996.

Miller, B. A. (1990). The interrelationships between alcohol and drugs and family violence. *NIDA Research Monograph, 103,* 177–207.

Miller, B. A., Smyth, N. J., & Mudar, P. J. (1999). Mothers' alcohol and other drug problems and their punitiveness toward their children. *Journal of Studies on Alcohol, 60,* 632–656.

Miller, D., & Guidry, L. (2001). *Addictions and trauma recovery: Healing the mind, body, and spirit.* New York: Norton.

Miller, W. R., & Rollnick, S. (2002). *Motivational interviewing: Preparing people for change* (2nd ed.). New York: Guilford Press.

Miller, W. R., Sorenson, J. L., Selzer, J. A., & Brigham, G. S. (2006). Disseminating practices in substance abuse treatment: A review with suggestions. *Journal of Substance Abuse Treatment, 31,* 25–39.

Miller, W. R., Zweben, A., DiClemente, C. C., & Rychtarik, R. G. (1992). *Motivational enhancement therapy manual: A clinical research guide for therapists treating individuals with alcohol abuse and dependence.* Rockville, MD: National Institute on Alcohol Abuse and Alcoholism.

Mockus, S., Mars, L. C., Ovard, D. G., Mazelis, R., Bjelajac, P., Grady, J., et al. (2005). Developing consumer/survivor/recovering voice and its impact on services and research: Our experience with the SAMHSA Women, Co-Occurring Disorders and Violence Study. *Journal of Community Psychology, 33,* 513–525.

Moeller, T., Bachmann, G., & Moeller, J. (1993). The combined effects of physical, sexual, and emotional abuse during childhood: Long-term health consequences for women. *Child Abuse & Neglect, 17,* 623–640.

Molnar, B. E., Buka, S. L., & Kessler, R. C. (2001). Child sexual abuse and subsequent psychopathology: Results from the National Comorbidity Survey. *American Journal of Public Health, 91,* 753–760.

Moore, J., & Finkelstein, N. (2001). Parenting services for families affected by substance abuse. *Child Welfare, 80,* 221–238.

Moran, J., Mayberry, C., Kinniburgh, D., & James, D. (1995). Program monitoring for clinical practice: Specimen positivity across urine collection methods. *Journal of Substance Abuse Treatment, 12,* 223–226.

Morris, E. F. (2001). Clinical practices with African Americans: Juxtaposition of standard clinical practices and Africentrism. *Professional Psychology: Research and Practice, 32,* 563–572.

Morrissey, J. P., Ellis, A. R., Gatz, M., Amaro, H., Reed, B. G., Savage, A., et al. (2005). Outcomes for women with co-occurring disorders and trauma: Program and person-level effects. *Journal of Substance Abuse Treatment, 28,* 121–133.

Morrissey, J. P., Jackson, E. W., Ellis, A. R., Amaro, H., Brown, V. B., & Najavits, L. M. (2005). Twelve-month outcomes of trauma-informed interventions for women with co-occurring disorders. *Psychiatric Services, 56,* 1213–1222.

Mullen, P. E., Martin, J., Anderson, J., Romans, S., & Herbison, G. (1994). The effect of child sexual abuse on social, interpersonal and sexual function in adult life. *British Journal of Psychiatry, 165,* 35–47.

Murphy, J. M., Olivier, D. C., Monson, R. R., & Sobol, A. M. (1991). Depression and anxiety in relation to social status: A prospective epidemiologic study. *Archives of General Psychiatry, 48*, 223–229.

Najavits, L. M. (2002). *Seeking safety: A treatment manual for PTSD and substance abuse*. New York: Guilford Press.

Najavits, L. M. (2007). Seeking Safety: An evidence-based model for substance abuse and trauma/PTSD. In K. A. Witkiewitz & G. A. Marlatt (Eds.), *Therapist's guide to evidence-based relapse prevention: Practical resources for the mental health professional* (pp. 141–167). San Diego, CA: Elsevier.

Najavits, L. M., Gastfriend, D. R., Barber, J. P., Reif, S., Muenz, L. R., Blaine, J., et al. (1998). Cocaine dependence with and without PTSD among subjects in the National Institute on Drug Abuse Collaborative Cocaine Treatment Study. *American Journal of Psychiatry, 155*, 214–219.

Najavits, L. M., & Liese, B. S. (2000). *Seeking Safety Adherence Scale (revised)*. Unpublished measure, Harvard Medical School/McLean Hospital, Boston, MA.

Najavits, L. M., Schmitz, M., Gotthardt, S., & Weiss, R. D. (2005). Seeking safety plus exposure therapy: An outcome study on dual diagnosis men. *Journal of Psychoactive Drugs, 37*, 425–435.

Najavits, L. M., Weiss, R. D., & Shaw, S. R. (1997). The link between substance abuse and posttraumatic stress disorder in women: A research review. *The American Journal on Addictions, 6*, 237–283.

Najavits, L. M., Weiss, R. D., Shaw, S. R., & Muenz, L. (1998). "Seeking safety": Outcome of a new cognitive–behavioral psychotherapy for women with posttraumatic stress disorder and substance dependence. *Journal of Traumatic Stress, 11*, 437–456.

Naugle, A. E., & Follette, W. C. (1998). A functional analysis of trauma symptoms. In V. Follette, J. Ruzek, & F. Abueg (Eds.), *Cognitive–behavioral therapies for trauma* (pp. 48–73). New York: Guilford Press.

Neira R., Fineman, N. R., Beckwith, L., Howard, J., & Espinosa, M. (1997). Maternal ego development and mother–infant interaction in drug-abusing women. *Journal of Substance Abuse Treatment, 14*, 307–317.

Neff, J. A., Holaman, B., & Schluter, T. D. (1995). Spousal violence among Anglos, Blacks, and Mexican Americans: The role of demographic variables, psychosocial predictors and alcohol consumption. *Journal of Family Violence, 10*, 1–21.

Neighbors, H. W. (1988). The help-seeking behavior of Black Americans. *Journal of the National Medical Association, 80*, 1009–1012.

Nicholson, J., Finkelstein, N., Williams, V., Thom, J., Noether, C., & DeVibliss, M. (2006). A comparison of mothers with co-occurring disorders and histories of violence living with or separated from minor children. *Journal of Behavioral Health Services & Research, 33*, 225–243.

Noether, C. D., Brown, V., Finkelstein, N., Russell, L. A., VanDeMark, N. R., Morris, L. S., & Graeber, C. (2007). Promoting resiliency in children of mothers with co-occurring disorders and histories of trauma: Impact of a skills-based intervention program on child outcomes. *Journal of Community Psychology, 35*, 823–843.

Nowinski, J., Baker, S., & Carroll, K. (1995). *Twelve-step facilitation therapy manual: A clinical research guide for therapists treating individuals with alcohol abuse and dependence*. Bethesda, MD: National Institute on Alcohol Abuse and Alcoholism.

Nunes, E. V., & Levin, F. R. (2004). Treatment of depression in patients with alcohol or other drug dependence: A meta-analysis. *The Journal of the American Medical Association, 291*, 1887–1896.

Oates, R. K., Tebbutt, J., Swanston, H., Lynch, D. L., & O'Toole, B. I. (1998). Prior childhood sexual abuse in mothers of sexually abused children. *Child Abuse & Neglect, 22*, 1113–1118.

Ogden, P., Minton, K., & Pain, C. (2006). *Trauma and the body: A sensorimotor approach to psychotherapy*. New York: Norton.

O'Keefe, M. (1994). Linking maternal violence, mother–child/father–child aggression, and child behavior problems. *Journal of Family Violence, 9*, 63–78.

O'Keefe, M. (1998). Posttraumatic stress disorder among incarcerated battered women: A comparison of battered women who killed their abusers and those incarcerated for other offenses. *Journal of Traumatic Stress, 11*, 71–85.

O'Sullivan, M. J., Peterson, P. D., Cox, G. B., & Kirkeby, J. (1989). Ethnic populations: Community mental health services ten years later. *American Journal of Community Psychiatry, 17*, 17–30.

Ouimette, P. C., Ahrens, C., Moss, R. H., & Finney, J. W. (1997). Posttraumatic stress disorder in substance abuse patients: Relationship to one-year posttreatment outcomes. *Psychology of Addictive Behaviors, 11*, 34–47.

Ouimette, P. C., Cronkite, R., Henson, B. R., Prins, A., Gima, K., & Moos, R. H. (2004). Posttraumatic stress disorder and health status among female and male medical patients. *Journal of Traumatic Stress, 17*, 1–9.

Oyserman, D., Mowbray, C. T., Meares, P. A., & Firminger, K. B. (2000). Parenting among mothers with a serious mental illness. *American Journal of Orthopsychiatry, 70*, 296–315.

Ozer, E. J., Best, S. R., Lipsey, T. L., & Weiss, D. S. (2003). Predictors of posttraumatic stress disorder: A meta-analysis. *Psychological Bulletin, 129*, 52–73.

Paone, D., Chavkin, W., Willets, I., Friedmann, P., & des Jarlais, D. (1992). The impact of sexual abuse: Implications for drug treatment. *Journal of Women's Health, 1*, 149–153.

Parens, H. (1991). A view of the development of hostility in early life. *Journal of the American Psychoanalytic Association, 39*, 75–108.

Parker, K. D., McMorris, B., Smith, E., & Murty, K. S. (1991). Fear of crime and the likelihood of victimization: A bi-ethnic comparison. *Journal of Social Psychology, 133*, 723–732.

Patrick, M., Hobson, P., Castle, P., Howard, R., & Maughan, B. (1994). Personality disorder and the mental representation of early social experience. *Development and Psychopathology, 94*, 375–388.

Pattison, E. M., & Kahan, J. (1983). The deliberate self-harm syndrome. *The American Journal of Psychiatry, 140*, 867–872.

Pearlman, L. A., & Mac Ian, P. S. (1995). Vicarious trauma: An empirical study of the effects of trauma work on trauma therapists. *Professional Psychology: Research and Practice, 26,* 558–565.

Pearlman, L. A., & Saakvitne, K. W. (1995). *Trauma and the therapist: Countertransference and vicarious traumatization in psychotherapy with incest survivors.* New York: Norton.

Pelcovitz, D., van der Kolk, B. A., Roth, S, Mandel, F., Kaplan, S., & Resnick, P. (1997). Development and validation of the structured interview for disorders of extreme stress. *Journal of Traumatic Stress, 10,* 3–16.

Pitman, R. K., van der Kolk, B. A., Orr, S. P., & Greenberg, M. S. (1990). Naloxone-reversible analgesic response to combat-related stimuli in posttraumatic stress disorder: A pilot study. *Archives of General Psychiatry, 47,* 541–544.

Polusny, M. A., & Follette, V. M. (1995). Long-term correlates of childhood sexual abuse: Theory and review of the empirical literature. *Applied and Preventive Psychology, 4,* 143–166.

Prochaska, J. O., & DiClemente, C. C. (1992). Stages of change in the modification of problem behaviors. In L. M. Vernon, R. M. Eiesler, & P. M. Miller (Eds.), *Progress in behavioral modification* (pp. 184–214). Sycamore, IL: Sycamore Press.

Putnam, F. W. (1989). *Diagnosis and treatment of multiple personality disorder.* New York: Guilford Press.

Pye, L. M., & Pye, M. W. (2006). *Asian power and politics: The cultural dimensions of authority.* Cambridge, MA: Harvard University Press.

Pynoos, R. S., Steinberg, A. M., & Goenjian, A. (1996). Traumatic stress in childhood and adolescence: Recent developments and current controversies. In B. A. van der Kolk, A. C. McFarlane, & L. Weisaeth (Eds.), *Traumatic stress: The effects of overwhelming experience on mind, body, and society* (pp. 331–358). New York: Guilford Press.

Rasch, R., Weisen, C., MacDonald, B., Wechsberg, W., Perritt, R., & Dennis, M. (2000). Patterns of HIV risk and alcohol use among African-American crack abusers. *Drug and Alcohol Dependence, 58,* 259–266.

Regier, D. A., Farmer, M. E., Rae, D. S., Locke, B. Z., Keith, S. J., Judd, L. L., & Goodwin, F. K. (1990). Comorbidity of mental disorders with alcohol and other drug abuse. Results from the Epidemiologic Catchment Area (ECA) Study. *The Journal of the American Medical Association, 264,* 2511–2518.

Reider, C., & Cicchetti, D. (1989). An organizational perspective on cognitive control functioning and cognitive–affective balance in maltreated children. *Developmental Psychology, 25,* 382–393.

Rennison, C. M., & Welchans, S. (2000). *Intimate partner violence* (NCJ No. 178247). Washington, DC: U.S. Department of Justice.

Richards, D. A., Lovell, K., & Marks, I. M. (1994). Post-traumatic stress disorder: Evaluation of a behavioral treatment program. *Journal of Traumatic Stress, 7,* 669–680.

Ridley, C. R. (1984). Clinical treatment of the nondisclosing Black client: A therapeutic paradox. *American Psychologist, 39,* 1234–1244.

Robbins, S. P., Chatterjee, P., & Canda, E. R. (Eds.). (2006). *Contemporary human behavior theory: A critical perspective for social work.* Boston: Pearson.

Rodriguez, N., Vande Kemp, H., & Foy, D. W. (1998). Post-traumatic stress disorder in survivors of childhood sexual abuse and physical abuse: A critical review of the empirical research. *Journal of Child Sexual Abuse, 7,* 17–45.

Rollnick, S., & Miller, W. R. (1995). What is motivational interviewing? *Behavioral and Cognitive Psychotherapy, 23,* 325–334.

Root, M. P. (1996). Women of color and traumatic stress in "domestic captivity": Gender and race as disempowering statuses. In A. J. Marsella, M. J. Friedman, E. T. Gerrity, & R. M. Scurfield (Eds.), *Ethnocultural aspects of posttraumatic stress disorder: Issues, research, and clinical applications* (pp. 363–387). Washington, DC: American Psychological Association.

Rosenheck, R., & Fontana, A. (1998). Warrior fathers and warrior sons: Intergenerational aspects of trauma. In Y. Danieli (Ed.), *International handbook of multigenerational legacies of trauma* (pp. 225–242). New York: Plenum Press.

Rosenheck, R., & Nathan, P. (1985). Secondary traumatization in the children of Vietnam veterans with posttraumatic stress disorder. *Hospital and Community Psychiatry, 36,* 538–539.

Roth, S., Newman, E., Pelcovitz, D., van der Kolk, B., & Mandel, F. S. (1997). Complex PTSD in victims exposed to sexual and physical abuse: Results from the *DSM–IV* field trial for posttraumatic stress disorder. *Journal of Traumatic Stress, 10,* 539–555.

Rothschild, B. (2000). *The body remembers: The psychophysiology of trauma and trauma treatment.* New York: Norton.

Russell, D. E. H. (1983). The incidence and prevalence of intrafamilial and extra-familial sexual abuse of female children. *Child Abuse & Neglect, 7,* 133–146.

Russell, D. E. H. (1986). *The secret trauma.* New York: Basic Books.

Russell, D. E. H., Schurman, R., & Trocki, K. (1988). The long-term effects of incestuous abuse: A comparison of Afro-American and White American victims. In G. Wyatt & G. Powell (Eds.), *Lasting effects of child sexual abuse* (pp. 119–134). Newbury Park, CA: Sage.

Russell, G. L., Fujino, D. C., Sue, S., Cheung, M., & Snowden, L. R. (1996). The effects of therapist–client ethnic match in the assessment of mental health functioning. *Journal of Cross-Cultural Psychology, 27,* 598–615.

Saakvitne, K., Gamble, S., Pearlman, L., & Lev, B. (2000). *Risking Connection: A training curriculum for working with survivors of childhood abuse.* Baltimore: Sidran Press.

Sander-Phillips, K., Moisan, P. A., Wadington, S., Morgan, S., & English, K. (1995). Ethnic differences in psychological functioning among Black and Latino sexually abused girls. *Child Abuse & Neglect, 19,* 691–706.

Santelli, J. S., Robins, L. N., Brener, N. D., & Lowry, R. (2001). Timing of alcohol and other drug use and sexual risk behaviors among unmarried adolescents and young adults. *Family Planning Perspectives, 33,* 200–205.

Sapolsky, R. M. (2000). Glucocorticoids and hippocampal atrophy in neuropsychiatric disorders. *Archives of General Psychiatry, 57,* 925–935.

Schaaf, K. K., & McCanne, T. R. (1998). Relationship of childhood sexual, physical, and combined sexual and physical abuse to adult victimization and post-traumatic stress disorder. *Child Abuse & Neglect, 22*, 1119–1133.

Schiraldi, G. (2000). *The post-traumatic stress disorder sourcebook: A guide to healing, recovery and growth*. Lincolnwood, IL: Lowel House.

Schloredt, K. A., & Heiman, J. R. (2003). Perceptions of sexuality as related to sexual functioning and sexual risk in women with different types of childhood abuse histories. *Journal of Traumatic Stress, 16*, 275–284.

Schnurr, P. P., & Green, B. L. (2004). Understanding relationships among trauma, posttraumatic stress disorder, and health outcomes. In P. P. Schnurr & B. L. Green (Eds.), *Trauma and health: Physical health consequences of exposure to extreme stress* (pp. 247–275). Washington, DC: American Psychological Association.

Schnurr, P. P., & Jankowski, M. K. (1999). Physical health and post-traumatic stress disorder: Review and synthesis. *Seminars in Clinical Neuropsychiatry, 4*, 295–304.

Schnurr, P. P., Spiro, A., III, Aldwin, C. M., & Stukel, T. (1998). Physical symptom trajectories following trauma exposure: Longitudinal findings from the Normative Aging Study. *The Journal of Nervous and Mental Disease, 186*, 522–528.

Schore, A. N. (1997). Early organization of the nonlinear right brain and development of a predisposition to psychiatric disorders. *Development and Psychopathology, 9*, 595–631.

Schuengel, C., Bakermans-Kranenburg, M. J., & Van IJzendoorn, M. H. (1999). Frightening maternal behavior linking unresolved loss and disorganized infant attachment. *Journal of Consulting and Clinical Psychology, 67*, 54–63.

Semple, S., Grant, I., & Patterson, T. L. (2004). Female methamphetamine users: Social characteristics and sexual risk behavior. *Women & Health, 40*(3), 35–50.

Seskin, J. (1994, July 3). Battered woman, tormented counselor. *The New York Times*, p. CV11.

Shapiro, F. (1989). Efficacy of the eye movement desensitization procedure in the treatment of traumatic memories. *Journal of Traumatic Stress Studies, 2*, 199–223.

Shapiro, F., & Forrest, M. S. (1997). *EMDR: The breakthrough therapy*. New York: Basic Books.

Shields, A. M., & Cicchetti, D. (1998). Reactive aggression among maltreated children: The contributions of attention and emotion dysregulation. *Journal of Clinical Child Psychology, 27*, 381–395.

Shields, A. M., Ryan, R. M., & Cicchetti, D. (1994). The development of emotional and behavioral self-regulation and social competence among maltreated school-age children. *Developmental Psychology, 6*, 57–75.

Shipman, K., Zeman, J., Penza, S., & Champion, K. (2000). Emotion management skills in sexually maltreated and nonmaltreated girls: A developmental psychopathology perspective. *Development and Psychopathology, 12*, 47–62.

Siegel, D. J. (1999). *The developing mind: Toward a neurobiology of interpersonal experience*. New York: Guilford Press.

Sifneos, P. E. (1973). The prevalence of "alexithymic" characteristics in psychosomatic patients. *Psychotherapy and Psychosomatics, 22,* 255–266.

Snyder, J., Schrepferman, L., & St. Peter, C. (1997). Origins of antisocial behavior: Negative reinforcement and affect dysregulation of behavior as socialization mechanisms in family interaction. *Behavior Modification, 21,* 187–215.

Solomon, J., George, C., & DeJong, A. (1995). Children classified as controlling at age six: Evidence of disorganized representational strategies and aggression at home and at school. *Developmental Psychopathology, 73,* 447–463.

Song, Y. I. (1996). *Battered women in Korean immigrant families.* New York: Garland Publishing.

Sorenson, S. B., & Siegel, J. M. (1998). Gender, ethnicity and sexual assault: Findings from a Los Angeles study. *Journal of Social Issues, 48,* 93–104.

Sorenson, S. B., Upchurch, D. M., & Shen, H. (1996). Violence and injury in marital arguments: Risk patterns and gender differences. *American Journal of Public Health, 86,* 35–40.

Southwick, S. M., Bremner, J. D., Rasmusson, A., Morgan, C. A., Arnsten, A., & Charney, D. S. (1999). Role of norepinephrine in the pathophysiology and treatment of posttraumatic stress disorder. *Biological Psychiatry, 46,* 1192–1204.

Spertus, I. L., Yehuda, R., Wong, C. M., Halligan, S., & Seremetis, S. V. (2003). Childhood emotional abuse and neglect as predictors of psychological and physical symptoms in women presenting to a primary care practice. *Child Abuse & Neglect, 27,* 1247–1258.

Spoth, R. L., Redmond, C., & Chungyeol, S. (2001). Randomized trial of brief family interventions for general populations: Adolescent substance use outcomes 4 years following baseline. *Journal of Consulting and Clinical Psychology, 69,* 627–642.

Sroufe, L. A. (1988). The role of infant–caregiver attachment in development. In J. Belsky & T. Nexworski (Eds.), *Clinical implications of attachment* (pp. 18–38). Hillsdale, NJ: Erlbaum.

Sroufe, L. A., & Waters, E. (1977). Attachment as an organizational construct. *Child Development, 48,* 1184–1199.

Steinhart, B. (2002). Patient autonomy: Evolution of the doctor–patient relationship. *Haemophilia, 8,* 441–446.

Sterling, P., & Eyer, J. (1988). Allostasis: A new paradigm to explain arousal pathology. In S. Fisher & J. Reason (Eds.), *Handbook of life stress, cognition and health* (pp. 629–640). Hoboken, NJ: Wiley.

Sterling, R. C., Gottheil, E., Weinstein, S. P., & Serota, R. (1998). Therapist/patient race and sex matching: Treatment retention and 9-month follow-up outcome. *Addiction, 93,* 1043–1050.

Stewart, M. A. (1995). Effective physician–patient communication and health outcomes: A review. *Canadian Medical Association Journal, 152,* 1423–1433.

Stewart, S. H., Ouimette, P., & Brown, P. J. (2002). Gender and the comorbidity of PTSD with substance use disorders. In R. Kimerling & P. Ouimette (Eds.), *Gender and PTSD* (pp. 232–270). New York: Guilford Press.

Storer, D. (1985). *Ethnic family values in Australia.* Sydney, Australia: Prentice-Hall.

Straus, M. A., & Gelles, R. J. (1986). Societal change and change in family violence from 1975 to 1985 as revealed by two national surveys. *Journal of Marriage and the Family, 48,* 465–479.

Straus, M. A., & Gelles, R. J. (1990). *Physical violence in American families.* New Brunswick, NJ: Transaction.

Straus, M. A., Gelles, R. J., & Steinmetz, S. K. (1980). *Behind closed doors: Violence in the American family.* Garden City, NY: Anchor.

Substance Abuse and Mental Health Services Administration. (2000). *Cooperative agreement to study children of women with alcohol, drug abuse and mental health (ADM) disorders who have histories of violence* (Publication No. TI 00-006). Rockville, MD: US. Department of Health and Human Services.

Sue, S. (1977). Community mental health services to minority groups: Some optimism, some pessimism. *American Psychologist, 32,* 616–624.

Sue, S. (1998). In search of cultural competence in psychotherapy and counseling. *American Psychologist, 53,* 440–448.

Sussman, L. K., Robins, L. N., & Earls, F. (1987). Treatment-seeking for depression by Black and White Americans. *Social Science & Medicine, 24,* 187–196.

Takeuchi, D. T., Sue, S., & Yeh, M. (1995). Return rates and outcomes from ethnicity-specific mental health programs in Los Angeles. *American Journal of Public Health, 85,* 638–643.

Tatarsky, A. (Ed.). (2002). *Harm reduction psychotherapy: A new treatment for drug and alcohol problems.* Northvale, NJ: Jason Aronson.

Taylor, R. (1991). Child rearing in African American families. In J. Everett & S. Chipungu (Eds.), *Child welfare: An Africentric perspective* (pp. 119–155). New Brunswick, NJ: Rutgers University Press.

Teicher, M. H. (2002). Scars that won't heal: The neurobiology of child abuse. *Scientific American, 286,* 68–75.

Testa, M., VanZile-Tamsen, C., & Livingston, J. A. (2005). Childhood sexual abuse, relationship satisfaction and sexual risk taking in a community sample of women. *Journal of Consulting and Clinical Psychology, 73,* 1116–1124.

Thompson, C. E., Worthington, R., & Atkinson, D. R. (1994). Counselor content orientation, counselor race, and Black women's cultural mistrust and self-disclosures. *Journal of Counseling Psychology, 41,* 155–161.

Thompson, R. A. (1994). Emotion regulation: A theme in search of definition. In N. A. Fox (Ed.), The development of emotion regulation. *Monographs of the Society for Research in Child Development, 59*(2–3, Serial. No. 240), 25–52.

Tjaden, P., & Thoennes, N. (2000). Prevalence and consequences of male-to-female and female-to-male intimate partner violence as measured by the National Violence Against Women Survey. *Violence Against Women, 6,* 142–161.

Torres-Matrullo, C. (1976). Acculturation and psychopathology among Puerto-Rican women in mainland United States. *American Journal of Orthopsychiatry, 46,* 710–719.

Trautman, P. D., Rotheram-Borus, M. J., Dopkins, S., & Lewin, N. (1991). Psychiatric diagnoses in minority female adolescent suicide attempters. *Journal of the American Academy of Child & Adolescent Psychiatry, 30,* 617–622.

Triandis, H. C. (1994). *Culture and social behavior.* New York: McGraw-Hill.

Trickett, P. K., & Putnam, F. W. (1993). Impact of child sexual abuse on females: Toward a developmental, psychobiological integration. *Psychological Science, 4,* 81–87.

Triffleman, E. (2003). Issues in implementing posttraumatic stress disorder treatment outcome research in community-based treatment programs. In J. L. Sorensen, R. A. Rawson, J. Guydish, & J. E. Zweben (Eds.), *Drug abuse treatment through collaboration: Practice and research partnerships that work* (pp. 227–247). Washington, DC: American Psychological Association.

Triffleman, E., Carroll, K., & Kellogg, S. (1999). Substance dependence posttraumatic stress disorder therapy: An integrated cognitive–behavioral approach. *Journal of Substance Abuse Treatment, 17*(1/2), 3–14.

Tross, S. (1998). *Peer activism for female partners of injection drug users.* Unpublished manuscript, HIV Center for Clinical Behavioral Studies, Columbia University, New York.

Troy, M., & Sroufe, L. A. (1987). Victimization among preschoolers: Role of attachment relationship history. *Journal of the American Academy of Child Psychiatry, 26,* 166–172.

Truscott, D. (1992). Intergenerational transmission of violent behavior in adolescent males. *Aggressive Behavior, 18,* 327–335.

Tsang, H. W. H. (2004). Bridging psychiatric services between Asia and America. *Psychiatric Services, 55,* 104.

Uba, L. (1994). *Asian Americans: Personality patterns, identity, and mental health.* New York: Guilford Press.

United Nations Development Fund for Women. (n.d.). *Domestic violence in the People's Republic of China.* Retrieved July 30, 2008, from http://unifem-eseasia.org/resources/others/domesticviolence/PDF/China.pdf

Urquiza, A. J., & Goodlin-Jones, B. L. (1994). Child sexual abuse and adult revictimization with women of color. *Violence and Victims, 9,* 223–232.

U.S. Department of Health and Human Services. (2001). *Mental health: Culture, race, and ethnicity—A supplement to mental health: A report of the surgeon general.* Rockville, MD: Author.

van der Kolk, B. A. (1988). The trauma spectrum: The interaction of biological and social events in the genesis of the trauma response. *Journal of Traumatic Stress, 1,* 273–290.

van der Kolk, B. A. (1989). The compulsion to repeat the trauma: Re-enactment, revictimization, and masochism. *Psychiatric Clinics of North America, 12,* 389–411.

van der Kolk, B. A. (1996). The complexity of adaptation to trauma: Self-regulation, stimulus discrimination, and characterological development. In B. A. van der Kolk, A. C. McFarlane, & L. Weisaeth (Eds.), *Traumatic stress: The effects of overwhelming experience on mind, body, and society* (pp. 182–213). New York: Guilford Press.

van der Kolk, B. A., McFarlane, A. C., & Weisaeth, L. (Eds.). (1996). *Traumatic stress: The effects of overwhelming experience on mind, body, and society.* New York: Guilford Press.

van der Kolk, B. A., Pelcovitz, D., Roth, S., Mandel, F. S., McFarlane, A., & Herman, J. L. (1996). Dissociation, affect dysregulation & somatization: The complex nature of adaptation to trauma. *The American Journal of Psychiatry, 153,* 83–93.

van der Kolk, B. A., Perry, J. C., & Herman, J. L. (1991). Childhood origins of self-destructive behavior. *The American Journal of Psychiatry, 148,* 1665–1671.

van der Kolk, B. A., Roth, S., Pelcovitz, D., & Mandel, F. S. (1993). *Complex PTSD: Results of the PTSD field trials for DSM–IV.* Washington, DC: American Psychiatric Association.

van der Kolk, B. A., Roth, S., Pelcovitz, D., Sunday, S., & Spinazzola, J. (2005). Disorders of extreme stress: The empirical foundation of a complex adaptation to trauma. *Journal of Traumatic Stress, 18,* 389–399.

van Zelst, W. H., de Beurs, E., Beekman, A. T. F., van Dyck, R., & Deeg, D. D. H. (2006). Well-being, physical functioning, and use of health services in the elderly with PTSD and subthreshold PTSD. *International Journal of Geriatric Psychiatry, 21,* 180–188.

Vasquez, M. J. T. (1998). Latinos and violence: Mental health implications and strategies for clinicians. *Cultural Diversity and Mental Health, 4,* 319–334.

Vazquez-Nutall, E., Romero-Garcia, I., & De Leon, B. (1987). Sex roles and perceptions of femininity and masculinity of Hispanic women. *Psychology of Women Quarterly, 11,* 409–425.

Velez, M. L., Jansson, L. M., Montoya, I. D., Schweitzer, W., Golden, A., & Svikis, D. (2004). Parenting knowledge among substance abusing women in treatment. *Journal of Substance Abuse Treatment, 26,* 215–222.

Wagner, A. W., Wolfe, J., Rotnitsky, A., & Proctor, S. P. (2000). An investigation of the impact of posttraumatic stress disorder on physical health. *Journal of Traumatic Stress, 13,* 41–55.

Walker, E. A., Gelfand, A., Katon, W. J., Koss, M. P., Von Korff, M., Bernstein, D., & Russo, J. (1999). Adult health status of women with histories of childhood abuse and neglect. *The American Journal of Medicine, 107,* 332–339.

Walker, E. A., Katon, W. J., Hansom, J., Harrop-Griffiths, J., Holm, L., Jones, M. L., et al. (1992). Medical and psychiatric symptoms in women with childhood sexual abuse. *Psychosomatic Medicine, 54,* 658–664.

Walker, E. A., Unutzer, J., Rutter, C., Gelfand, A., Saunders, K., VonKorff, M., et al. (1999). Costs of health care use by women HMO members with a history of childhood abuse and neglect. *Archives of General Psychiatry, 56,* 609–613.

Walker, L. E. (1995). Racism and violence against women. In J. Adelman & G. Enguidanos (Eds.), *Racism in the lives of women: Testimony, theory, and guides to antiracist practices* (pp. 239–250). New York: Haworth Press.

Walls, J. (2005). *The glass castle*. New York: Scribner.

Walsh, C., MacMillan, H. L., & Jamieson, E. (2003). The relationship between parental substance abuse and child maltreatment: Findings from the Ontario Health Supplement. *Child Abuse & Neglect, 27*, 1409–1425.

Walsh, J. (1996). *Stories of renewal: Community building and the future of urban America: A report*. New York: Rockefeller Foundation.

Walsh, R., & Shapiro, S. L. (2006). The meeting of meditative disciplines and western psychology. *American Psychologist, 61*, 227–239.

Webster-Stratton, C., & Hammond, M. (1988). Maternal depression and its relationship to life stress, perceptions of child behavior problems, parenting behaviors, and child conduct problems. *Journal of Abnormal Child Psychology, 16*, 299–315.

Weinstock, R., Vari, G., Leong, G., & Silva, J. (2006). Back to the past in California: A temporary retreat to a *Tarasoff* duty to warn. *Journal of American Academy of Psychiatry and Law, 34*, 523–528.

Weissbacker, I., & Clark, C. (2007). The impact of violence and abuse on women's physical health: Can trauma-informed treatment make a difference? *Journal of Community Psychology, 35*, 909–923.

Wellisch, D., & Steinberg, M. (1980). Parenting attitudes of addict mothers. *The International Journal of the Addictions, 15*, 809–819.

Westen, D., Lohr, N., Silk, K. R., Gold, L., & Kerber, K. (1990). Object relations and social cognition in borderlines, major depressives, and normals: A thematic apperception test analysis. *Psychological Assessment, 2*, 355–364.

White, J. W., & Humphrey, J. A. (1994). Women's aggression in heterosexual conflicts. *Aggressive Behavior, 20*, 195–202.

Widom, C. S. (1989a). Child abuse, neglect, and violent criminal behavior. *Criminology, 27*, 251–271.

Widom, C. S. (1989b, April 14). The cycle of violence. *Science, 244*, 160–166.

Wolfe, J., Schnurr, P. P., Brown, P. J., & Furey, J. (1994). Posttraumatic stress disorder and war-zone exposure as correlates of perceived health in female Vietnam war veterans. *Journal of Consulting and Clinical Psychology, 62*, 1235–1240.

World Health Organization. (1994). *International classification of diseases* (10th ed.). Geneva: Author.

Wright, L. S., Garrison, J., Wright, N. B., & Stimmel, D. T. (1991). Childhood unhappiness and family stressors recalled by adult children of substance abusers. *Alcoholism Treatment Quarterly, 8*(4), 67–80.

Wyatt, G. E. (1990a). The aftermath of child sexual abuse of African American and White American women: The victims' experience. *Journal of Family Violence, 5*, 61–81.

Wyatt, G. E. (1990b). Sexual abuse of ethnic minority children: Identifying dimensions of victimization. *Professional Psychology: Research and Practice, 21*, 338–343.

Wyatt, G. E. (1992). The sociocultural context of African American and White American women's rape. *Journal of Social Issues, 48*, 77–91.

Wyatt, G. E., Myers, H. F., Williams, J. K., Ramirez Kitchen, C., Loeb, T., Vargas Carmona, J., et al. (2002). Does a history of trauma contribute to HIV risk for women of color? Implications for prevention and policy. *American Journal of Public Health, 92,* 660–665.

Wyatt, G. E., Notgrass, C. M., & Newcomb, M. (1990). Internal and external mediators of women's rape experiences. *Psychology of Women Quarterly, 14,* 153–176.

Wylie, M. S., & Markowitz, L. M. (1992, September/October). Walking the wire. *The Psychotherapy Networker,* pp. 19–30.

Wynaden, D., Chapman, R., Orb, A., McGowan, S., Zeeman, Z., & Yeak, S. H. (2005). Factors that influence Asian communities' access to mental health care. *International Journal of Mental Health Nursing, 14,* 88–95.

Yassen, J. (1995). Preventing secondary traumatic stress disorder. In C. R. Figley (Ed.), *Compassion fatigue: Coping with secondary traumatic stress disorder in those who treat the traumatized* (pp. 178–208). Philadelphia: Brunner/Mazel.

Yeh, M., Eastman, K., & Cheung, M. K. (1994). Children and adolescents in community mental health centers: Does the ethnicity or the language of the therapist matter? *Journal of Community Psychology, 22,* 153–163.

Yehuda, R. (2000). Cortisol alterations in PTSD. In R. Shalev, R. Yehuda, & A. C. McFarlane (Eds.), *International handbook of human response to trauma* (pp. 265–284). New York: Plenum Press.

Yehuda, R. (2006). Advances in understanding neuroendocrine alterations in PTSD and their therapeutic implications. In R. Yehuda (Ed.) *Psychobiology of posttraumatic stress disorders: A decade of progress* (pp. 137–166). Malden, MA: Blackwell Publishing.

Yehuda, R., Schmeidler, K., Wainberg, M., Binder-Brynes, K., & Duvdevani, T. (1998). Vulnerability to posttraumatic stress disorder in adult offspring of Holocaust survivors. *The American Journal of Psychiatry, 155,* 1163–1171.

Yoshihama, M. (1999). Domestic violence against women of Japanese descent in Los Angeles: Two methods of estimating prevalence. *Violence Against Women, 5,* 869–897.

Zanarini, M. C. (2000). Childhood experiences associated with the development of borderline personality disorder. *Psychiatric Clinics of North America, 23,* 89–101.

Zayas, L., & Solari, F. (1994). Early childhood socialization in Hispanic families: Context, culture, and practice implications. *Professional Psychology: Research and Practice, 25,* 200–206.

Zayfert, C., & Black, C. (2000). Implementation of empirically supported treatment for PTSD: Obstacles and innovations. *Behavioral Therapist, 23,* 161–168.

Zeanah, C., Danis, B., Hirsheberg, L., Benoit, D., Miller, D., & Heller, S. (1999). Disorganized attachment associated with partner violence: A research note. *Infant Mental Health Journal, 20,* 77–86.

Zlotnick, C., Zakriski, A. L., Shea, M. T., Costello, E. A. Begin, A., Pearlstein, T., & Simpson, E. (1996). The long-term sequelae of sexual abuse: Support for a complex posttraumatic stress disorder. *Journal of Traumatic Stress, 9,* 195–205.

Zoellner, L. A., Feeny, N. C., Alvarez, J., Watlington, C., O'Neill, M. L., Zager, R., & Foa, E. B. (2000). Factors associated with completion of the restraining order process in female victims of partner violence. *Journal of Interpersonal Violence*, *15*, 1081–1099.

Zoellner, L. A., Feeny, N. C., Fitzgibbons, L. A., & Foa, E. B. (1999). Response of African American and Caucasian women to cognitive behavioral therapy for PTSD. *Behavior Therapy*, *30*, 581–596.

Zoellner, L. A., Goodwin, M. L., & Foa, E. B. (2000). PTSD severity and health perceptions in female victims of sexual assault. *Journal of Traumatic Stress*, *13*, 635–649.

Zweben, J. E., Clark, W. H., & Smith, D. E. (1994). Traumatic experiences and substance abuse: Mapping the territory. *Journal of Psychoactive Drugs*, *26*, 327–344.

AUTHOR INDEX

Coley, S. M., 185
Colletti, J., 91
Comas-Diaz, L., 189, 190, 198
Community Connections Trauma Work
       Group, 22, 34, 202, 230
Compton, W., III, 10, 232
Connell, D., 106
Conrad, D. J., 150
Cotman, A., 234
Cottler, L. B., 10, 232
Courtois, C. A., 13, 15, 82
Cowan, C. P., 100
Cowan, P. A., 100
Cox, A., 230
Cox, G. B., 191
Craske, M. G., 71
Crick, N. R., 60
Crits-Christoph, P., 29
Cronkite, R. C., 240
Crosby, H., 128
Cross, C., 107
Croughan, J., 232
Cumberland, A., 56
Cushing, G., 99
Cutrona, C., 238

Damashek, A., 107, 109
D'Ambrosio, B., 5, 33, 116, 200
Dancu, C. V., 234
Dandoy, A. C., 101
Daniel, A., 101
Danieli, Y., 104
Dansky, B., 10, 15, 20, 21, 26, 29, 31, 224
Davidson, J. R., 12, 231
Davies, J. M., 58, 62
Davis, G., 10, 123
Dawes, M. A., 105
Day, J. C., 59
Dayton, G., 24
Deater-Deckard, K., 195
De Bellis, M. D., 59
de Beurs, E., 125
DeBruyn, L. M., 186
Deeg, D. D. H., 125
DeJong, A., 78
De Leon, B., 190
de Mello, M. F., 48

Denning, P., 25
Derogatis, L. R., 132, 235
des Jarlais, D., 184
Deykin, E. Y., 121, 125–127
DiClemente, C. C., 24, 156
Difede, J., 62, 84
DiLillo, D., 82, 107, 109
Diorio, J., 59
Dodge, K., 60, 195
Donovan, B., 10, 15, 29–31, 229
Dopkins, S., 184
Dougherty, F. E., 105, 113
Downs, W. R., 101
Dutton, D. G., 80
Duvdevani, T., 104

Earls, F., 191
Eastman, K., 192
Eber, M., 128
Edelman, R. E., 125
Edlin, B., 128
Edwards, V., 124
Eisenberg, N., 56, 57
El-Bassel, N., 166
Elliott, D. M., 234
Ellis, A. R., 34
Endicott, J., 233
English, K., 187
Englund, D. W., 101
Epstein, R., 239
Escobar, J. I., 131
Espinosa, M., 105
Eyer, J., 126

Fabes, R. A., 56
Fallon, J., 40
Fallot, R., 5, 230
Fallot, R. D., 34
Feeny, N. C., 193
Feerick, M. M., 78, 86
Feldman-Summers, S., 165
Felitti, V. J., 121, 124
Fergusson, D. M., 86
Ferrada-Noli, M., 41
Field, T., 106
Fineman, N. R., 105
Finkelhor, D., 82, 86, 87, 239

Finkelstein, N., 112, 114, 116
Finney, J. W., 20, 240
Fiorentine, R., 193
Firminger, K. B., 106
First, M. B., 216, 233
Fisher, E., 189
Fitzgibbons, L. A., 193
Flannery, R. B., 59
Flaskerud, J. H., 184
Fleisher-Bond, M., 230
Foa, E. B., 10, 15, 21–23, 29, 31, 96,
        124, 191, 193, 209, 224–226,
        228, 234
Follette, V. M., 10, 14, 83, 86, 87
Follette, W. C., 62
Fonagy, P., 78, 103
Fontana, A., 104
Ford, J. D., 229
Forer, B., 165
Forrest, M. S., 139
Foy, D. W., 12, 98, 168
Francis, D. D., 59
Frawley, M. G., 58, 62
Freud, S., 130
Friedman, M. J., 60, 122
Friedmann, P., 184
Fujino, D. C., 192
Fuller, M., 165
Fullilove, M. T., 10, 184
Fullilove, R. E., 184
Furey, J., 123, 128, 241
Furr, J. M., 23

Gamble, S., 226
Gandek, B., 241
Ganiban, J., 56
Gara, M. A., 101
Garrison, J., 105
Gelfand, A., 122, 124, 134
Gelles, R. J., 86, 185, 190
George, C., 78
Gerard, A. B., 239
Giard, J., 201, 230
Gibbon, M., 233
Gilbert, L., 166
Glynn, S., 98
Go, H., 166

Goenjian, A., 58, 80
Gold, J. H., 85
Gold, L., 80
Goldberg, D. A., 159
Golden, A., 105
Golding, J. M., 131
Goldstein, S., 106
Gondolf, E. W., 189, 190
Gonzalez, A. M., 225
Goodlin-Jones, B. L., 186
Goodman, S. H., 106
Goodwin, M. L., 124, 191
Gordon, J. R., 24, 27, 47
Gotthardt, S., 30
Gottheil, E., 193
Graczyk, P. A., 106
Grant, I., 128
Gratz, K. L., 236
Green, B. L., 135
Greenberg, M., 60, 165
Greenwald, E., 88
Gross, A. M., 84
Gross, J. J., 56
Grotstein, J. S., 32, 63
Guidry, L., 34, 202, 223
Guimond, J. M., 88
Gusman, F., 98, 231
Guthertz, M., 106
Guthrie, I. K., 56
Guy, J. D., 168

Haft, W. L., 103
Halligan, S., 132
Hamby, S. L., 239
Hammond, M., 106
Hampton, R. L., 185, 191
Han, H., 22, 67, 125, 227
Hans, S. L., 105, 106
Harmer, A., 100, 105
Harris, K., 234
Harris, M., 5, 22, 34, 116, 202, 230
Harris, S. D., 191
Harrison, W., 40
Hasert, M. F., 60
Hasin, D., 232, 233
Haugaard, J. J., 86
Hazan, C., 83

Healy, B., 106
Heard, H., 225
Heiman, J. R., 129
Helzer, J. E., 232
Henson, L. G., 105
Herbison, G., 82
Herman, J. L., 27, 45, 62, 63, 76, 80–82, 87, 149, 150, 207
Herzog, E. P., 101
Hesse, A. R., 146, 150, 151, 167
Hesse, E., 103
Hien, A., 28, 31, 59, 60, 79, 86, 101, 105, 106, 126, 138, 193, 216
Higley, J. L., 60
Hill, J., 166
Hillhouse, M. P., 193
Hobbs, F., 189
Hobson, P., 80
Hodroyd, J., 165
Hoffman, J. A., 128
Holaman, B., 185
Holcomb, W., 101
Holden, G. W., 191
Hollenberg, J., 105
Holtzworth-Munroe, A., 86
Honeyman, T., 105, 106
Hopkins, J., 106
Horowitz, H. A., 16
Horowitz, J., 79
Horowitz, L. M., 237
Horowitz, M., 234
Howard, J., 105
Howard, R., 80
Howell, E., 43
Hu, T., 184, 191
Hufford, M. R., 210
Hughes, M., 10, 38, 39
Humphrey, J. A., 101
Huntington, N., 34, 116, 201–203
Hyer, L. A., 20
Hyler, L., 40

Ingraham, L. H., 240
Institute of Medicine, x

Jackson, E. W., 200, 202, 207, 208
Jacobsen, E., 71

Jahn Moses, D., 5, 33, 34, 116, 200–202, 204–206
Jamieson, E., 105
Jankowski, M. K., 127
Jansson, L. M., 105
Jaycox, L., 209
Jehu, D., 82
Jellinek, E. M., 23
Jerell, J. M., 191
Jones, G., 165
Jones, M., 105

Kabat-Zinn, J., 70, 138
Kahan, J., 62
Kalmuss, D., 86
Kaloupek, D. G., 231
Kanuha, V., 185
Kaplan, N., 78
Kardiner, S. H., 165
Karenga, M., 194
Kashani, J., 101
Katon, W. J., 124
Kaufman, J., 101, 102
Keane, T. M., 231
Kelleher, K., 105
Kellogg, S., 20, 31, 228
Kerber, K., 80
Kerns, R. D., 240
Kessler, R., 10, 12, 38–40, 45, 58
Kettinger, L. A., 105
Khantzian, E. J., 15, 16, 20, 24, 56
Killeen, T., 26
Kilpatrick, D. G., 10, 20
Kimerling, R., 121, 123, 125, 127, 128
Kipper, D., 96
Kirisci, L., 105
Kirkeby, J., 191
Klein, H., 128
Klerman, G., 48
Kling, H., 45
Koenan, K., 22, 32, 33, 67, 83, 227
Kolko, D. J., 105
Komorita, S. S., 239
Koons, C. R., 225
Koplin, S., 83
Kosinski, M., 241
Koss, M. P., 123, 124, 134

Koss, P. G., 123, 134
Kosten, T. R., 113
Kowaliw, S., 10, 29–31, 229
Krahe, B., 83
Krystal, H. D., 16, 56
Kulka, R. A., 45
Kumpfer, K. L., 113

Laposa, J. M., 235
Larsen, R., 10
La Torre, M. A., 164
Leaf, P. J., 184
Leigh, B. C., 128
Leitenberg, H., 88
Leon, A. C., 83
Leonard, L. M., 86
Leong, G., 170
Lerman, H., 165
Leukefeld, C., 128
Levin, F. R., 46
Lewin, N., 184
Liberzon, I., 10
Liese, B. S., 215
Lindholm, K., 186
Linehan, M. M., 32, 50, 67, 70, 218, 225
Linnoila, M., 60
Lipsey, T. L., 192
Litt, L. C., 28, 31, 79, 126, 138, 193
Liu, D., 59
Livingston, J. A., 14
Loeb, T. B., 129
Logan, T. K., 128
Lohr, N., 80
Long, P. J., 82
Lovejoy, M. C., 106
Lovell, K., 23
Lown, A., 184
Lowry, R., 128
Lundin, T., 41
Luthar, S. S., 99, 112–115
Lynch, D. L., 102
Lynch, T. R., 225
Lyons-Ruth, K., 104, 106

Mac Ian, P. S., 146
MacMillan, H. L., 105
Main, M., 78, 79, 103

Mandel, F. S., 13, 14, 42, 61, 62
Mari, J. J., 48
Markowitz, J. C., 48
Markowitz, L. M., 150, 158
Marks, I. M., 23
Marlatt, G. A., 24, 25, 27, 47, 138
Martin, J., 82
Marx, B. P., 84
Marzuk, P. M., 83
Matias, R., 106
Matseoane, K., 232
Maughan, B., 80
Mayes, L. C., 105
Mazelis, R., 5, 33, 116, 200
McCann, I. L., 81, 91, 146, 149
McCanne, T. R., 168
McCauley, J., 14
McCloskey, L. A., 102
McEwen, B. S., 126
McFall, M. E., 20
McFarlane, A. C., 79, 123
McFerron, J. R., 189
McHugo, G. J., 208
McMorris, B., 189
Meadows, E. A., 22, 23, 225
Meaney, M. J., 59
Meares, P. A., 106
Mearns, J., 236
Mears, D. P., 191
Meichenbaum, D., 228
Mensch, I. N., 165
Merikangas, K., 99
Merrill, L. L., 88
Mertin, P., 100
Messeri, P., 115
Meydan, J., 232
Michel, P., 57
Miele, G. M., 28, 31, 60, 79, 106, 138,
    193, 233
Miller, B. A., 101, 105
Miller, D., 34, 202, 223
Miller, W. R., 24, 154, 156, 176
Milner, J., 101
Milner, J. S., 88, 238
Minton, K., 22, 66, 95
Mockus, S., 201
Moeller, J., 123

Moeller, T., 123
Moisan, P. A., 187
Molgaard, V., 113
Molnar, B. E., 58
Monson, R. R., 184
Montoya, I. D., 105
Moore, D. W., 239
Moore, J., 114
Moos, R. H., 240
Morash, M., 190
Morgan, S., 187
Morris, A. S., 57
Morris, E. F., 192
Morrissey, J. P., 34, 200, 202, 207, 208
Morse, J. Q., 225
Moss, R. H., 20
Mowbray, C. T., 106
Mudar, P. J., 105
Muenz, L., 31
Mullen, P. E., 82, 86
Murburg, M. M., 20
Murdock, T. B., 21
Murphy, J. M., 184
Murty, K. S., 189

Nagy, L. M., 231
Nair, P., 105
Najavits, L. M., 10, 11, 12, 15, 20, 21,
    27, 30, 31, 34, 47, 71, 123, 202,
    215, 218, 227
Nathan, P., 104
Naugle, A. E., 62
Neff, J. A., 185
Neighbors, H. W., 191
Neira, R., 105
Nelson, C., 10, 38, 39
Neuman, G., 106
Neugebauer, R., 48
Newcomb, M., 188
Newman, E., 13, 61
Nguyen, T. D., 191
Nicholson, J., 112
Nishith, P., 10
Noether, C. D., 116
Nordenberg, D., 124
Notgrass, C. M., 188
Novaco, R. W., 237

Nowinski, J., 29
Nunes, E., 46, 232

Oates, R. K., 102
Ogden, P., 22, 66, 95
O'Hare, E., 275
O'Keefe, M., 101, 169
Olivier, D. C., 184
Ormstad, K., 41
Orr, S. P., 60
O'Sullivan, M. J., 191
O'Toole, B. I., 102
Ouimette, P., 10, 20, 125
Overton, W. F., 16
Oyserman, D., 106
Ozer, E. J., 192

Padin-Rivera, E., 10, 29–31, 229
Pain, C., 22, 66, 95
Palesh, O. G., 83
Panek, D., 101
Paone, D., 184
Papay, P., 123
Parens, H., 61
Parenting Workgroup, 116
Parker, J. D. A., 237
Parker, K. D., 189
Parsons, E., 104
Patrick, M., 80
Patterson, T. L., 128
Pattison, E. M., 62
Pearlman, L. A., 91, 146, 149, 150, 226
Pelcovitz, D., 13, 14, 40, 42, 61, 62, 64,
    106
Penza, S., 61, 83
Peplau, L., 238
Perry, B. D., 150
Perry, J. C., 80
Perry, K., 209
Peterson, E., 10
Peterson, P. D., 191
Pitman, R. K., 60
Poelstra, P. L., 168
Polusny, M. A., 10, 14, 83, 87
Portera, L., 83
Powell, D., 100
Power, T., 101

Priest, R., 188
Prochaska, J. O., 24
Proctor, S. P., 125
Putnam, F. W., 56, 62, 63, 76, 235
Pye, L. M., 198
Pye, M. W., 198
Pynoos, R. S., 58, 80

Rafalowicz, E., 123
Rasch, R., 128
Ratcliff, K., 232
Redmond, C., 113
Reed, B. G., 5, 33, 116, 200
Regier, D. A., 41
Reider, C., 20, 60
Reilly, P. M., 224
Reiser, M., 56
Rennison, C. M., 185
Resnick, H. S., 12, 20
Richards, D. A., 23
Ridley, C., 192
Riggs, D., 21, 228, 234
Riney, S., 98
Robbins, S. P., 136, 206, 207
Robins, C. J., 225
Robins, L. N., 128, 191, 232
Rodriguez, N., 168
Roemer, L., 236
Rogers, F., 24
Rollnick, S., 24, 156, 176
Romans, S., 82
Romero-Garcia, I., 190
Root, M. P., 187, 188
Rosenberg, S. E., 237
Rosenheck, R., 104
Rosenstein, D., 16
Roth, S., 13, 14, 42, 61, 62, 106
Rothbaum, B. O., 21–23, 29, 96, 224,
    226, 228, 234
Rotheram-Borus, M. J., 184
Rothschild, B., 62, 138
Rotnitsky, A., 125
Rounsaville, B., 48, 99, 209
Rozelle, D., 101
Rubio-Stipec, M., 131
Rudy, T. E., 240
Runtz, M., 80, 84, 86, 88

Runyan, D., 239
Russell, D. E. H., 102, 184, 238
Russell, G. L., 192
Russo, E., 229
Russo, J., 124
Russo, N. F., 189, 198
Ruzek, J., 98
Ryan, R. M., 60
Rychtarik, R. G., 156

Saakvitne, K., 91, 95, 97, 146, 150, 226
Sakheim, D. K., 81
Saladin, M. E., 10, 20, 21, 26
Samet, S., 233
Samit, S., 232
Sander-Phillips, K., 187
Sanderson, J., 100
Santelli, J. S., 128
Sapolsky, R. M., 60
Saunders, K., 80
Scarvalone, P., 62, 84
Schaaf, K. K., 168
Schiraldi, G., 71, 73
Schloredt, K. A., 129
Schluter, T. D., 185
Schmeidler, K., 104
Schmitz, M., 30
Schneider, R. J., 16
Schnurr, P. P., 122–124, 127, 128, 135,
    241
Schore, A. N., 63
Schrepferman, L., 56
Schuengel, C., 104
Schuler, M. E., 105
Schultz, L., 10
Schweitzer, W., 105
Scott, C., 66
Selzer, J. A., 154
Semple, S., 128
Seremetis, S. V., 132
Serota, R., 193
Seskin, J., 166
Shapiro, F., 22, 139, 225
Shapiro, S. L., 138
Shaver, P. R., 83
Shaw, S. R., 10, 31
Sheinberger-Olwig, R., 83

Trautman, P. D., 184
Triandis, H. C., 194
Trickett, P. K., 76
Triffleman, E., 10, 12, 15, 20, 29, 31,
  228
Tronick, E. Z., 106
Tross, S., 137, 209
Troy, M., 79
Truscott, D., 101
Tsang, H. W. H., 191
Turk, D. C., 240
Tutek, D., 225
Tween, J. L., 225

Uba, L., 190
Unutzer, J., 125, 126
Upchurch, D. M., 184
Ureno, G., 237
Urquiza, A. J., 186
Ursano, R. J., 240
U.S. Department of Health and Human
  Services, 192

Vande Kemp, H., 168
van der Kolk, B., 13, 14, 40, 42, 58, 60,
  61, 62–64, 79, 80, 82, 83, 101,
  106
van Dyck, R., 125
Van Ijzendoorn, M. H., 104
Van Wie, V., 84
van Zelst, W. H., 125
VanZile-Tamsen, C., 14
Vari, G., 170
Vasquez, M. J. T., 185, 188
Vasquez-Nutall, E., 190
Veith, R. C., 20
Velez, M. L., 105
Verdeli, H., 48
Verduin, M. L., 16
Veysey, B. M., 34, 116, 201
Villasenor, V. S., 237
Von Korff, M., 124

Wadington, S., 187
Wagner, A. W., 125
Wainberg, M., 104

Waizenhofer, E., 83
Walker, E. A., 122, 124–126, 131, 134
Walker, L. E., 188
Wall, S., 78
Walls, J., 109
Walsh, C., 105
Walsh, J., 189
Walsh, K., 112, 113
Walsh, R., 138
Wampold, B. E., 192
Ware, J. E., 241
Wasserman, G., 59
Waters, E., 77, 78
Waxman, R., 232
Weathers, F. W., 231
Webster-Stratton, C., 106
Weinstein, S. P., 193
Weinstock, R., 170
Weisaeth, L., 79
Weiss, D. S., 192
Weiss, R. D., 10, 30, 31
Weissbacker, I., 122
Weissman, E., 238
Weissman, M. M., 48
Weissman, S., 216
Welchans, S., 185
Wellisch, D., 105
Westen, D., 80
White, J. W., 101
Widom, C. S., 101
Willets, I., 184
Willey, R., 186
Williams, J. B., 233
Williams, L. M., 100, 101
Williamson, D. F., 124
Wilner, N., 234
Wolfe, J., 10, 121, 123, 125, 128, 241
Wolfson, R., 149
Wong, C. M., 132
Woodruff, W. J., 123, 134
Woogler, C., 101
Woolfolk, R. L., 101
World Health Organization, 232
Worthington, R., 192
Wright, K. M., 240
Wright, L. S., 105

SUBJECT INDEX

Abilify, 49

Abstinence, 11, 211

Abstinence-based models, 23, 25–26

Abuse. *See also specific abuse, e.g.,*
    Childhood abuse
  history of, 100–101
  identifying/reporting, 173–176
  perpetration of, 85–86

Acceptance, emotional, 69

Acute PTSD, 13

Adaptation, of treatment and research,
    213–214

Addiction, pathways to. *See* Pathways to
    addiction

Addiction Institute of New York, 215

Addictions and trauma recovery inte-
    grated model (ATRIUM), 223

Adults, with PTSD, 13

Adult survivors
  aggression/perpetration of abuse by,
    85–86
  attachment difficulties in, 79–80
  interpersonal functioning of, 82–88
  revictimization of, 83–85
  sexual functioning of, 86–88

Adverse Childhood Experiences Survey,
    124

Adverse events, 215

Affective disorders, 39

Affiliation, with aggressive and sexually
    risky partners, 14

African American women
  abuse disclosure by, 188
  childhood sexual abuse of, 186
  intimate partner violence rates for,
    185
  parenting styles of, 195

trauma responses of, 187
treatment outcomes for, 191, 193

Agency support, for clinicians, 150–151

Agendas, training, 247, 248

Aggression
  in adult survivors, 85–86
  assessing problems with, 93
  in children, 81
  emotion regulation affected by, 59

Agoraphobia, 39, 42

AI (treatment center), 219, 220

Alcohol abuse, 14, 39

Alcoholics Anonymous, 145

Alcoholism treatment facilities, 172

Alcohol use
  biological effects of, on stress
    response, 60
  and group therapy, 179
  as risk factor for victimization, 84
  and sexual relationships, 87

Alexithymia, 131–132, 237

All-China Women's Federation, 190

Allostasis, 126

Allostatic load, 126

Alprazolam, 49

Ambivalent attachment, 78, 79

Ambivalent/preoccupied attachment, 80

American Medical Association, 148

American Psychiatric Association, 148

American Psychological Association, 148

Amnesia, 12

Amygdala, 59, 60

Anger
  assessing, 93
  intimacy anger, 79, 80
  social learning of, 59

Anger inventory tool, 236–237

Attendance, session
    and cultural issues, 196–197
    and emotion regulation, 66, 67
Audience, knowing your, 251
Audio recordings, 153n2, 158–160
Audiotapes, training, 244
Australian firefighters, 123
Authoritarian parenting, 105, 107, 195
Authorities
    African Americans' responses to, 195
    in Asian cultures, 198
    conflict with, 171
    experience with, 134–135
Avoidance
    assessment tool for, 235
    as PTSD symptom, 12
    sexual, 86–88
    in vivo exposure to reduce, 226
Avoidance maneuvers, 66
Avoidant attachment, 78, 79
Avoidant/dismissing attachment, 80
Awareness
    decreased, 12
    increasing emotional, 68–69
Axis I disorders, 233
Axis II disorders, 233

Beck, Aaron T., 47
Beck Depression Inventories I/II,
    234–235
Behavioral coping strategies, 73
Belson, Richard, 150
Benzodiazepine, 49, 170
BESThealth, 138
Binge eating, 44
Bipolar disorder, 41, 48–49
Blame, 76
Body interventions, 138–139
The Body Remembers (Rothschild), 138
Body scan, 139
Borderline personality disorder (BPD)
    and attachment difficulties, 80
    description of, 44–46
    dialectical behavioral therapy for,
        32, 225
    as emotion regulation disorder, 63
    treatment for, 50

Borrowing money, 178
Boundaries
    creating safe, 95
    family, 109
    lack of safe, 84
    in therapeutic relationship, 88–89,
        164, 165
    for training sessions, 251
BPD. See Borderline personality disorder
Brain development, 127
Brain structure, 59–60
Breathing relaxation, 71, 72, 138
Brief Symptom Inventory, 235
Bulimia, 44
Bullying, 79, 83

CAPP (Coalition on Addiction, Preg-
    nancy and Parenting), 114
CAPS (Clinician Administered PTSD
    Scale), 231
Caregivers
    attachment to, 77–79
    and child development, 76
    emotion regulation affected by,
        56–57
Caretaker role, 83
CASAC (credentialed alcohol and sub-
    stance abuse counselor), 156
Case management, 135–136
Caucasian women, 186
Causal pathways to addiction, 15–17,
    20–21
CBT. See Cognitive–behavioral therapy
CE credits. See Continuing education
    credits
Center for Substance Abuse Treatment
    (CSAT), 216
Child abuse
    assessment tool for potential, 238
    factors contributing to, 77
    identifying, 173–176
    and parental substance use, 105
    reporting, 170, 173–176
Child Abuse Potential Inventory, 238
Child care, 172–173
Child custody. See Custody issues

Diagnostic Interview Schedule, 232
Diagnostic training, 153–154
Dialectical behavior therapy (DBT), 32, 50, 70, 225, 230
"Dialectic of trauma," 87
Diazepam, 49
DID. *See* Dissociated identity disorder
Difficult clients, 170–172
Difficulties in Emotion Regulation Scale, 236
Disciplinary practices
    assessing parental, 110–112, 238–239
    and substance use, 105
    types of, 107–108
Disclosure, of abuse
    early, 89
    ethnocultural considerations with, 187–188, 197
    and interpersonal functioning, 81
Discussion (learning modality), 244
Disease model, 23
Disempowerment, 188
Dismissing attachment, 80
Disorders of extreme stress not otherwise specified (DESNOS), 14, 15, 64. *See also* Complex posttraumatic stress disorder
Disorganized/disoriented attachment, 78–79, 103, 104. *See also* Fearful/disorganized attachment
Dissociated identity disorder (DID), 43–44, 77, 179
Dissociation, 62–64, 66, 130
Dissociative disorders
    assessment tool for, 235
    PTSD co-occurring with, 42–44
    treatment for, 49
Dissociative Experiences Scale, 235
Distress management techniques, 69–73
    breathing relaxation, 71, 72
    developing distress tolerance, 72–73
    grounding, 71
    meditation/mindfulness, 70
    progressive muscle relaxation, 71
    safe place exercises, 71, 72
    self-hypnosis, 70

Distress tolerance, developing, 72–73
Disturbing memories, 225
"Doublethink," 76
Drift, posttraining, 154
Drug abuse, 14, 39
Drug-free programs, 23
Drug screenings, 165–166, 176
Drug use
    biological effects of, on stress response, 60
    and group therapy, 179
    by mothers, 99
    as risk factor for victimization, 84
    and sexual relationships, 87
DSM–III–R. *See Diagnostic and Statistical Manual of Mental Disorders—3rd ed., rev.*
DSM–IV. *See Diagnostic and Statistical Manual of Mental Disorders—4th ed.*
DSM–IV–TR. *See Diagnostic and Statistical Manual of Mental Disorders—4th ed., text rev.*
Dual socialization, 195
Dutch sample, elderly, 125
"Duty to protect," 170
Dysthymia, 39

Eating disorders, 44
Economic constraints, 191–192
Education. *See also* Psychoeducation
    health, 137–138
    in transcend, 30
    in WHP, 220
Elderly Dutch sample, 125
EMDR. *See* Eye movement desensitization and reprocessing
Emergency situations, planning for, 204
Emotion(s)
    acceptance of, 69
    awareness of, 68–69
    communication about level of, 66–67
    volatility of, 96–97
Emotional Avoidance Questionnaire, 235
Emotional experiences
    increasing positive, 73
    labeling/naming, 68

Emotion regulation, 55–74
    assessment of capacities for, 64, 65
    assessment tools for, 236–237
    and childhood victimization, 57–59
    complexity of, 56
    defined, 56
    developmental influences on, 56–57
    in difficult clients, 171, 172
    and parenting, 106
    and psychiatric diagnosis, 63–64
    therapeutic management of, 64,
        66–67
Emotion regulation deficits
    and complex PTSD, 15
    defined, 56
    developmental consequences of,
        60–61
    and interpersonal functioning, 80–81
    interventions for, 67–73
    long-term consequences of, 61–63
    neurobiological correlates of, 59–60
    and self-medication model, 16
    STAIR therapy for, 227
Empathy, 118, 193
Employment, 82
Empowerment
    client, 201
    and difficult clients, 171
    dis-, 188
    and physical health, 136–137
    in TREM, 229
    in WCDVS, 206–207
Engagement
    clinician's, 157
    ethnocultural considerations in,
        196–198
    in WCDVS, 206
Environment
    invalidating, 32
    supervision, 155
    supportive work, 151
    training, 246, 249, 251
Epidemiologic Catchment Area study, 20
Equipment, training, 247
Ethnocultural considerations, 183–198
    help-seeking behaviors, 190–192
    immigration as, 188–190

therapeutic alliance, 192–193
    trauma risk factors, 184–188
    treatment/program planning, 194–198
Evaluation form, training, 249, 250
Evidence-based integrated models,
    27–28
Evidence-based sequential models,
    28–30
Expectations
    of abuse, 85
    parental, 108
Experience
    therapist's, 211–212
    trainer's, 253
Experiencing (learning modality),
    244–245
Exposure therapy
    in combined treatments, 28
    in CTPCD, 29, 224
    description of, 22–23
    prolonged. See Prolonged exposure
Eye movement desensitization and
        reprocessing (EMDR), 138–139,
        225

"Fake it till you make it," 70
False memory syndrome, 147, 148
"False self," 81
Family
    and identity, 195
    as trauma-organized system, 100–101
Family boundaries, 109
Fantasies, 169
Fearful/disorganized attachment, 80,
        103, 104
Fears
    of clinicians, 144–146
    in vivo exposure to reduce, 226
Feedback
    audio/video recordings for, 158–159
    questions as, 252
    from supervisor, 154
    for trainer, 249
    in training, 245
    in WTS, 212–213
"Felt security," 77
Feminist approaches, 136

Fidelity ratings, 159–160
Firefighters, 123
Flexibility, 145
Fluoxetine, 48
Foa, Edna, 21
Forgetfulness, 12
Freud, Sigmund, 130
Frightened and frightening behavior, 104

Gastrointestinal symptoms, 131
Gender differences
    with self-medication, 16
    with trauma, 9–13
Generalized anxiety disorder, 39, 42
The Glass Castle (Walls), 109
Global Severity Index, 235
Goal setting, ethnocultural considera-
        tions in, 194–196
Grounding, 71, 181
Group psychotherapy, 177–182
    client concerns about, 177
    clinicians' attitudes in, 182
    cofacilitators for, 179, 181
    guidelines for, 178–179
    identifying clients for, 179–180
    individual vs., 97–98
    managing dysregulated clients in,
            180–181
    for offenders, 50
    and out-of-group contact, 178
    parenting, 119
    pregroup meeting for, 177–178
    role-playing in, 96
    in TREM, 229
    in WHP, 217
    within-group experiences in, 178
Group supervision, 155, 156, 160
Guest speakers, 243, 244
Guilt
    about parenting inadequacies, 99
    about surviving, 12
    reducing, 118–119
Gulf War veterans, 125
Gynecological services, 129, 134–135

Harm-reduction models, 24–25
Health. See Physical health; Sexual health

Health and Daily Living Form, 239–240
Health professionals, interfacing with,
        134–135
Health Symptom Checklist, 240
Hearing (learning modality), 243–244
Help-seeking behaviors, 190–192
Herman, Judith, 27
Heroin-addicted mothers, 115
Hesitancy, clinicians', 144–146
Hesse, A. R., 151
High-risk model, 16
Hippocampus, 59, 60
Historical trauma, 186, 196
HIV, 128, 129
Holocaust survivors, children of, 104
Honesty, 95–96
Hope, sense of, 97
Hormones, 59, 60, 127
Hypochondriasis, 130
Hypomania, 41
Hypothalamic–pituitary–adrenal axis,
        60
Hypothalamus, 59, 60

ICD. See International Classification of
        Diseases
Identity functioning, 194
Imaginal exposure therapy
    in combined treatments, 28
    in CTPCD, 29, 224
    defined, 22
    described, 32–33
    in prolonged exposure, 226
Immigration, 188–190
Immune functioning, 127
Impact of Early Trauma on Parenting
        Roles, 116
Impact of Events Scale, 233–234
"Impact of trauma work," 149
Impulsive behaviors, 62
Impulsivity, 44
Inadequacy, 238
Individual therapy, group vs., 97–98
Informed consent, 153n2
Integrated models, evidence-based,
        27–28
Integrated treatment, 25–26, 203

Intentional human causes (of trauma), 10–12
Intergenerational transmission of trauma, 100–104
  and attachment theory, 103
  and cycle of violence/maltreatment, 101–102
  and parental PTSD as pathway to child's PTSD, 103–104
Intergenerational trauma, 186
Internal working models, 77, 103
International Classification of Diseases (ICD), 232
Interpersonal functioning, 75–98
  of abused children, 80–81
  of adult survivors, 82–88
  assessment of, 92–93
  assessment tools for, 237–238
  attachment difficulties in adulthood, 79–80
  childhood maltreatment and development of, 76–77
  communication as, 95–96
  and disrupted attachment in infants/children, 77–79
  individual vs. group counseling for, 97–98
  interventions for problems with, 94–97
  STAIR therapy for, 227
  and therapeutic relationship, 88–92
Interpersonal psychotherapy (IPT), 48
Interpersonal schemas, 94–95
Interpersonal violence, 3, 10
Intimacy, 81, 82, 93, 198
Intimacy anger, 79, 80
Intimate partner violence (IPV)
  against African American women, 185
  among immigrants, 189–190
  ongoing, 166–170
  as revictimization, 83–84
Intrafamilial abuse, 194
Invalidating environments, 32
Inventory of Interpersonal Problems, 237
In vivo exposure therapy
  in ARTS, 228
  in CTPCD, 224
  defined, 22
  in prolonged exposure, 226
  in SDPT, 29
IPT (interpersonal psychotherapy), 48
IPV. *See* Intimate partner violence

James W. West, M.D. Quality Improvement Award, 213

Klonopin, 49
Knowledge, parental, 108

Latinas
  abuse disclosure by, 188
  childhood sexual abuse of, 186
  help-seeking by, 191, 192
  immigration of, 189
  subgroups of, 185
  trauma responses of, 187
Learning modalities, 243–245
  discussing, 244
  experiencing, 244–245
  hearing, 243–244
  seeing, 244
  teaching, 245
Lending money, 178
Lethality, trauma response in terms of, 186–187
Life events, 233–234
Lifestyle choices, 127
Light stream exercise, 139
Limbic system, 59–60, 127
Limit setting, 107, 118
Lithium, 49
Live supervision, 158
Loneliness, 238
Lorazepam, 49

Major depressive disorder (MDD), 39–41
Male victims, 85, 168
Mandated reporters/reporting, 173–175
Mania, 39, 41
Manualized treatments
  in WHP, 218–219
  in WTS, 212–213
Materials, training, 246–250, 254–258
Maternal behaviors, 239

MDD. *See* Major depressive disorder
Medical history, 241
Medical model, 136, 145
Medical services, 220
Meditation, 70, 138
Memories
    disturbing, 225
    imaginal exposure to, 226
    recovered, 147, 148
    and therapeutic window, 66
Mental health coverage, 151
Methadone treatment, 115
Milieu model, 217
Mindfulness, 70, 138
Money, borrowing or lending, 178
Monitoring
    parental, 109–110
    of physical health, 132–133
Mood disorders
    as emotion regulation disorders, 63
    PTSD co-occurring with, 40–47
Mood stabilizers, 49
Mothers. *See also* Women with children,
        working with
    sexual abuse history of, 102
    substance-using, 99, 105
Motivation, for recovery, 176
Motivational enhancement therapy, 156
Motivational interviewing, 24–25, 156
Multidimensional Pain Inventory, 240
Muscle relaxation, progressive, 71, 138

National Association of Addiction
        Treatment Providers, 213
National Comorbidity Survey, 38–40
National Crime Victims Survey, 185
National Institute on Alcohol Abuse
        and Alcoholism, x
National Institute on Drug Abuse
        (NIDA), x, 113, 137, 193, 208
Native Americans, 186
Natural disaster, 131
Needle exchange programs, 25
Negative Mood Regulation, 236
Neglect, 173–176
Neurobiology
    and emotion regulation deficits, 59–60
    and physical health, 127

Neurological symptoms, 131
NIDA. *See* National Institute on Drug
        Abuse
Nonhuman causes (of trauma), 11
Notes, reminder, 70
Novaco Anger Inventory, 236–237
No Wrong Door Policy, 216
Numbing, 12, 16
Nurturing Program for Families in Sub-
        stance Abuse Treatment and
        Recovery, 114, 116

Offender groups, 50
Off-site training, 246
Olanzapine, 49
On-site training, 246
Open-ended questions, 252
Opioid use, 11, 50, 115
Out-of-group contact, 178
Outpatient facilities, 203
Overcompliance, 90

Pain, 87, 240
Pain disorder, 130
Pandora's box, v
Panic disorder, 39, 41, 131
Paranoia, 179
Parental knowledge and expectations,
        108
Parental Punitiveness Scale, 239
Parent–Child Relationship Inventory, 239
Parent–child role reversal, 109
Parentification, of child, 103
Parenting, 99–112
    assessment of, 110–112
    assessment tools for, 238–239
    and comorbid diagnoses, 104–106
    and intergenerational transmission
        of trauma, 100–104
    vulnerable areas of, 107–110
Parenting at a Distance, 116
Parenting Group for Survivors of
        Trauma, 119
Parenting interventions, 112–119
    integrating treatment with, 112–113
    for substance-abusing parents, 113–115
    trauma-specific, 115–119

Parenting issues, 107–110
    discipline, 107–108
    family boundaries, 109
    parental knowledge/expectations,
        108
    safety/monitoring, 109–110
Parenting styles, 195
Parents, 103–104. *See also* Mothers
Parent training, 113, 114
Paroxetine, 48, 49
Paternalistic medical model of recovery,
    136
Pathways to addiction, 15–17
Patient–doctor relationship, 134–135
Paxil, 48
Pearlman, L. A., 89
Peers, 81
Peer support, 30
Pelvic pain, 129, 131
Perceived Empathy Scale, 193
Permissive parenting, overly, 107
Personality disorders
    PTSD co-occurring with, 44–47
    treatments for, 50
Personal psychotherapy, 150–151
Pharmacotherapy, 48–49
Pharmacotherapy consultation, 170
Phobias, 39, 41, 42
Physical environment, for training, 246
Physical health, 121–139
    assessment domains for, 133
    assessment tools for, 239–241
    and childhood sexual abuse, 128–129
    clinical interventions for, 136–139
    importance of, 121
    monitoring/evaluating, 132–133
    preventions/interventions for,
        133–136
    somatoform disorders, 129–132
    studies of trauma/PTSD and,
        123–125
    and trauma, 122–128
Physiological coping strategies, 73
Pilot testing, 153, 205, 218
Positive emotional experiences, increas-
    ing, 73
Posttraining drift, 154

Posttraumatic stress disorder (PTSD),
    10–17. *See also* Complex post-
    traumatic stress disorder; Concur-
    rent treatment of PTSD and
    cocaine dependence
    acute vs. chronic, 13
    age differences with, 13
    assessment tools for, 231, 233–234
    epidemiology of psychiatric disorders
        co-occurring with, 38–40
    facts about, 11
    gender differences with, 10–13
    high-risk model of addiction and, 16
    onset sequence of disorders with, 20,
        39–40
    parental PTSD as pathway to child's
        PTSD, 103–104
    pathways to addiction with, 15–17
    and physical health, 126–128
    prevalence of, 12
    primary, 16
    profile severity of, 11
    risk of continued cycle of violence
        with, 11
    self-medication model of addiction
        and, 15–17
    susceptibility model of addiction
        and, 16
    symptoms of, 10, 12
    treatment complications with, 11
    treatments for, 21–23
Posttraumatic Stress Disorder Symptom
    Scale—Self-Report, 234
Powerlessness, 171
Praise, 157
Precocious sexualized behavior, 81
Pregnancies
    unintended, 129
    unwanted, 87
Pregroup meetings, 177–178
Preoccupied attachment, 80
Presentation software, 244, 247
Primary care settings, 123, 126
Primary diagnoses, 232
Primary PTSD, 16
PRISM. *See* Psychiatric Research Inter-
    view for Substance and Mental
    Disorders

Social phobia, 39, 41, 42
Socioeconomic status, 184–186
Somatization disorder, 130
Somatoform disorders, 129–132
Sorenson, S. B., 186
Sound systems, 243
South Asian immigrants, 190
SS model. *See* Seeking safety model
SSRI. *See* Selective serotonin reuptake
    inhibitor
St. Luke's–Roosevelt Hospital Center,
    215, 216, 219
Staffing, 204–205. *See also* Clinicians
Stage model of recovery, 217
Stages of change model, 24–25
Stereotyping, 188
Stigma, 191
Strengthening Families Program (SFP),
    113–114
Stressful life events, 233–234
Stress hormones, 59
Stress inoculation training (SIT), 29,
    227–228
Stress response, 126–128
Structured Clinical Interviews for
    DSM–IV Axis I/II Disorders, 233
Style, of trainer, 252–253
Substance Abuse and Mental Health
    Services Administration
    (SAMHSA), 33, 230
Substance-abusing parents, 113–115
Substance dependence–PTSD therapy
    (SDPT), 29, 31, 228
Substance-induced diagnoses, 232
Substance use disorders, 3
    and childhood abuse, 14
    factors affecting recovery from, 34
    onset sequence of PTSD and, 20
    and parenting, 105
    PTSD co-occurring with, 39
    treatments for, 23–26
Subthreshold PTSD, 210
Suicidal ideation, 43
Suicidality, 41
Suicide, attempted, 14
Supervision
    audio/video utilization in, 158–160
    of clinicians, 154–160

and enhancing clinical skills, 156–158
of fidelity to treatment, 159–160
and vicarious traumatization, 149–150
in WCDVS, 204–205
in WHP, 220–221
in WTS, 212
Supportive work environment, 151
Survivor therapists, 146
Susceptibility model, 16
Symptom-based approach, 106

Talking, about trauma, 146–149
Tarasoff ruling, 170
TARGET (trauma affect regulation:
    guidelines for education and ther-
    apy), 229
"Teach-backs," 245
Teaching (learning modality), 245
*Ten Tried-and-True Methods to Achieve
    Therapist Burnout* (Belson), 150
Therapeutic alliance, 192–193, 196–198
Therapeutic context, emotion regula-
    tion in, 64, 66–67
Therapeutic relationship
    and interpersonal problems, 88–92
    and mandatory reporting of abuse,
        174–175
    minimizing imbalances in, 207
    and personality disorders, 50
    RICH, 97
Therapeutic space, 164
Therapeutic window, 66, 67
Therapists. *See also* Clinicians
    experience of, 211–212
    survivor, 146
Threats, 167–170
Tolerance, distress, 72–73
Tone, of voice, 243
Toronto Alexithymia Scale, 237
Training, 243–258
    agenda (sample) for, 247, 248
    and audience, 251
    diagnostic, 153–154
    elements of good, 244
    evaluation form (sample) for, 249, 250
    and learning modalities, 243–245
    materials for, 246–250, 254–258

physical environment for, 246
planning/conducting, 245–258
primary goal of, 243
psychological environment for, 249, 251
and questions as feedback, 252
registration of participants in, 245
slides (samples) for, 247, 254–258
and style of trainer, 252–253
train-the-trainer model and trauma expert, 152–153
in WCDVS, 204–205
in WHP, 220
in WTS, 212
Train-the-trainer model, 152–153, 213
Transcend, 29–31, 228–229
Transference, 91–92
Trauma, 9–13. *See also* Posttraumatic stress disorder; Risk factor(s) for trauma
causes of, 10, 11
field of, 9
gender differences with, 9–13
intentional human causes of, 10–12
nonhuman causes of, 11
and physical health, 122–128
prevalence of, 12
repeated, 11, 13
and service utilization, 126
stage of recovery from, 27
and stress response, 126–128
talking about, 146–149
and therapist training, 146–149
unintentional human causes of, 11
Trauma affect regulation: guidelines for education and therapy (TARGET), 229
Trauma and Recovery (Herman), 27
Trauma experts, 152–153, 158
Trauma exposures, 5, 184–186
Trauma-informed approach, 5, 33, 34, 174
Trauma-organized systems, 100–101
Trauma processing, 228
Trauma recovery and empowerment (TREM), 229–230
Trauma-related services, 3
Trauma response, 186–188

Trauma-specific parenting interventions, 115–119
Parenting Group for Survivors of Trauma, 119
WCDVS, 115–117
WHP, 117–119
Trauma-specific treatments, 33, 34
Trauma Symptom Inventory, 234
Traumatic countertransference, 149
Traumatic events
DSM–IV–TR on, 10
problems in defining, 195–196
types of, 10, 11
Traumatization, secondary/vicarious, 149–151
Traumatogenic dynamics model, 87
Traumatology, 9
Treadway, David, 158
Treatment(s), 19–35
body interventions, 138–139
combined, 26–31
for comorbid psychiatric disorders, 46–50
comparison of, 31
complications of PTSD/substance-use, 11
DBT, 32
for depression/anxiety with PTSD, 46–49
for dissociative disorders with PTSD, 49
for emotion regulation deficits, 67–73
empowerment, 136–137
ethnocultural considerations in planning, 194–198
imaginal exposure therapy, 32–33
manualized, 212–213, 218–219
for personality disorders with PTSD, 50
for physical problems, 136–139
psychoeducation, 67–68
for PTSD, 21–23
sequencing of, 21
STAIR, 32
for substance use disorders, 23–26
WCDVS, 33–34
Women's Health Education, 137–138

Treatment models, 223–230
    anger management, 223–224
    ARTS, 228
    ATRIUM, 223
    concurrent, 224
    DBT, 225
    EMDR, 225
    prolonged exposure, 226
    Risking Connection, 226
    seeking safety, 226–227
    selecting, 202–203
    SIT, 227–228
    STAIR, 227
    TARGET, 229
    transcend, 228–229
    TREM, 229–230
    TRIAD, 230
TREM. *See* Trauma recovery and
        empowerment
Triad women's group model (TRIAD),
        230
Triad Women's Project, 230
Trust
    assessing problems with, 93
    and attachment, 79
    as interpersonal-functioning issue,
        75, 82
    and mandatory reporting of abuse,
        174
    in therapeutic relationship, 88
12-step model, 23, 30, 145

UCLA Loneliness Scale—Revised, 238
Unintentional human causes (of
        trauma), 11
Unwanted pregnancies, 87
Urine samples, 165–166

Validation
    lack of, 58–59
    statements of, 157
Valium, 49
Valproic acid, 49
Veterans, 20, 21, 45, 123–128
Veterans Administration, 125
Vicarious traumatization, 149–151

Victimization, 3. *See also* Childhood
        abuse
    adulthood re-, 4
    conditioned responses to, 82
Video recordings, 153n2, 158–160
Videotapes, training, 244
Vietnam veterans, 123, 125
Violence
    cycle of. *See* Cycle of violence
    witnessing, 86
Violence, parental, 239
Visual aids, 244
Vocal quality, 243
Vulnerability, to trauma, 11

Walls, Jeannette, 109
War survivors, children of, 104
WCDVS. *See* Women, Co-Occurring
        Disorders and Violence Study
WHE. *See* Women's Health Education
WHP. *See* Women's Health Project
        Treatment and Research Center,
        The
"Window of tolerance," 66
Within-group experiences, 178
Witnessing violence, 86
Women, Co-Occurring Disorders and
        Violence Study (WCDVS), 19,
        33–34, 200–208
    assessment in, 206
    client empowerment in, 206–207
    client engagement in, 206
    client involvement in, 201
    and existing treatment models,
        202–203
    health reports from, 122
    implementation of, 205–207
    organizational elements of, 203
    outcomes of, 207–208
    as parenting intervention, 115–117
    pilot testing of, 205
    preimplementation planning for,
        200–205
    referral needs in, 204
    safe environment in, 207
    staffing/supervision/training for,
        204–205
    TRIAD model from, 230

ABOUT THE AUTHORS

Denise Hien, PhD, is a clinical psychologist and professor in clinical psychology at City University of New York. She is also a senior research scientist at Columbia University College of Physicians and Surgeons, and she has been a principal investigator on numerous grants from the National Institute on Drug Abuse, the National Institute on Alcohol Abuse and Alcoholism, and the Office of Research on Women's Health. Dr. Hien also maintains a private practice in New York City and was the founding executive director of The Women's Health Project Treatment and Research Center.

Lisa Caren Litt, PhD, is a clinical psychologist and clinical director of The Women's Health Project Treatment and Research Center. She is an assistant clinical professor of medical psychology in psychiatry at Columbia University College of Physicians and Surgeons. Her private practice is in New York City.

Lisa R. Cohen, PhD, is a clinical psychologist and research scientist at the New York State Psychiatric Institute, Columbia University Medical Center. She is also the trauma research program director in the clinical psychology department at the City University of New York. Her private practice is in New York City.

Gloria M. Miele, PhD, is an instructor of clinical psychology in psychiatry at Columbia University College of Physicians and Surgeons, training director for the Long Island Node of the National Institute on Drug Abuse's Clinical Trials Network, and former program director of The Women's Health Project Treatment and Research Center. She is a personal and executive coach, trainer, and consultant in Southern California.

Aimee Campbell, MSW, is a social worker and project director at The Women's Health Project Treatment and Research Center. She is also a senior research associate at the Social Intervention Group, Columbia University School of Social Work. She is completing her doctorate in social work.